FINLAND

LAND, REAL PROPERTY OWNERSHIP AND AGRICULTURAL LAWS HANDBOOK

VOLUME 1

STRATEGIC INFORMATION AND BASIC LAWS

International Business Publications, USA
Washington DC, USA - Finland

FINLAND

LAND, REAL PROPERTY OWNERSHIP AND AGRICULTURAL LAWS HANDBOOK

VOLUME 1 STRATEGIC INFORMATION AND BASIC LAWS

UPDATED ANNUALLY

We express our sincere appreciation to all government agencies and international organizations which provided information and other materials for this handbook

Cover Design: **International Business Publications, USA**

2018 Edition Updated Reprint International Business Publications, USA
ISBN 1-4387-5901-0

For additional analytical, business and investment opportunities information, please contact Global Investment & Business Center, USA at (703) 370-8082. Fax: (703) 370-8083. E-mail: ibpusa3@gmail.com
Global Business and Investment Info Databank - www.ibpus.com

Printed in the USA

For additional analytical, business and investment opportunities information, please contact Global Investment & Business Center, USA at (703) 370-8082. Fax: (703) 370-8083. E-mail: ibpusa3@gmail.com
Global Business and Investment Info Databank - www.ibpus.com

FINLAND
LAND, REAL PROPERTY OWNERSHIP AND AGRICULTURAL LAWS HANDBOOK
VOLUME 1
STRATEGIC INFORMATION AND BASIC LAWS

TABLE OF CONTENTS

STRATEGIC PROFILE

Capital and largest city	Helsinki 60°10′N 024°56′E60.167°N 24.933°E
Official languages	• Finnish (89.33%) • Swedish (5.34%)
Recognised regional languages	Sami (0.03%)
Religion	• Lutheranism, • Eastern Orthodoxy
Demonym	• Finnish • Finn
Government	Unitary parliamentary constitutional republic
- President	Sauli Niinistö
- Prime Minister	Juha Sipilä
Legislature	Eduskunta
	Independence
- Autonomy within Russia	29 March 1809
- Independence from the Russian SFSR	6 December 1917
- First recognized by the Russian SFSR	4 January 1918
	Area
- Total	338,424 km^2 (64th) 130,596 sq mi
- Water (%)	10
	Population
- 2015 estimate	5,486,101 (113th)
- 2000 census	5,180,000
- Density	18/km^2 (201st) 46/sq mi
GDP (PPP)	2015 estimate
- Total	$224.846 billion
- Per capita	$40,838
GDP (nominal)	2015 estimate
- Total	$235.276 billion
- Per capita	$42,732
Gini	▲25.9 low
HDI (2013)	▬0.879[6] very high · 24th
Currency	Euro (€) (EUR)
Time zone	EET (UTC+2)
- Summer (DST)	EEST (UTC+3)
Date format	d.m.yyyy
Drives on the	right
Calling code	+358
Patron saint	St Henry of Uppsala
ISO 3166 code	FI

Internet TLD	.fi[a]

Finland officially the **Republic of Finland**, is a Nordic country situated in the Fennoscandian region of Northern Europe. It is bordered by Sweden to the west, Norway to the north, Russia to the east, and Estonia to the south across the Gulf of Finland.

As of 2013, Finland's population was around 5.5 million, with the majority concentrated in its southern regions. In terms of area, it is the eighth largest country in Europe and the most sparsely populated country in the European Union. Finland is a parliamentary republic with a central government based in the capital of Helsinki, local governments in 336 municipalities and an autonomous region, the Åland Islands. About one million residents live in the Greater Helsinki area (consisting of Helsinki, Espoo, Vantaa and Kauniainen), which also produces a third of the country's GDP. Other large cities include Tampere, Turku, Oulu, Jyväskylä, Lahti, and Kuopio.

From the late 12th century until 1809, Finland was part of Sweden, a legacy reflected in the prevalence of the Swedish language and its official status. It then became an autonomous Grand Duchy within the Russian Empire until the Russian Revolution, which prompted the Finnish Declaration of Independence. This was followed by a civil war where the pro-Bolshevik "Reds" were defeated by the pro-conservative "Whites" with support from the German Empire. After a brief attempt to establish a monarchy, Finland became a republic. Finland's experience of World War II involved three separate conflicts: the Winter War (1939–1940) and Continuation War (1941–1944) against the Soviet Union and the Lapland War (1944–1945) against Nazi Germany. Following the end of the war, Finland joined the United Nations in 1955 and established an official policy of neutrality. Nevertheless, it remained fairly active on the world stage, joining the Organisation for Economic Co-operation and Development (OECD) in 1969, the European Union in 1995, and the eurozone at its inception in 1999.

Finland was a relative latecomer to industrialisation, remaining a largely agrarian country until the 1950s. Thereafter, it rapidly developed an advanced economy while building an extensive Nordic-style welfare state, resulting in widespread prosperity and one of the highest per capita incomes in the world. Subsequently, Finland is a top performer in numerous metrics of national performance, including education, economic competitiveness, civil liberties, quality of life, and human development. For instance, in 2010 Newsweek chose Finland the best country in the world. Finland is also a member of the United Nations, the Council of Europe and the World Trade Organization.

Background: Ruled by Sweden from the 12th to the 19th centuries and by Russia from 1809, Finland finally won its independence in 1917. During World War II, it was able to successfully defend its freedom and fend off invasions by the Soviet Union and Germany. In the subsequent half century, the Finns have made a remarkable transformation from a farm/forest economy to a diversified modern industrial economy; per capita income is now on par with Western Europe. As a member of the European Union, Finland was the only Nordic state to join the euro system at its initiation in January 1999.

GEOGRAPHY

Location: Northern Europe, bordering the Baltic Sea, Gulf of Bothnia, and Gulf of Finland, between Sweden and Russia

Base 802432 (B00083) 2-96

Geographic coordinates: 64 00 N, 26 00 E
Map references: Europe
Area:
total: 337,030 sq km

land: 305,470 sq km
water: 31,560 sq km

Area - comparative: slightly smaller than Montana

Land boundaries:
total: 2,628 km
border countries: Norway 729 km, Sweden 586 km, Russia 1,313 km

Coastline: 1,126 km (excludes islands and coastal indentations)

Maritime claims:
contiguous zone: 6 nm
continental shelf: 200-m depth or to the depth of exploitation
exclusive fishing zone: 12 nm
territorial sea: 12 nm (in the Gulf of Finland - 3 nm)

Climate: cold temperate; potentially subarctic, but comparatively mild because of moderating influence of the North Atlantic Current, Baltic Sea, and more than 60,000 lakes

Terrain: mostly low, flat to rolling plains interspersed with lakes and low hills

Elevation extremes:
lowest point: Baltic Sea 0 m
highest point: Haltiatunturi 1,328 m

Natural resources: timber, copper, zinc, iron ore, silver

Land use:
arable land: 8%
permanent crops: 0%
permanent pastures: 0%
forests and woodland: 76%
other: 16%

Irrigated land: 640 sq km
Natural hazards: NA
Environment - current issues: air pollution from manufacturing and power plants contributing to acid rain; water pollution from industrial wastes, agricultural chemicals; habitat loss threatens wildlife populations

Environment - international agreements:
party to: Air Pollution, Air Pollution-Nitrogen Oxides, Air Pollution-Sulphur 85, Air Pollution-Sulphur 94, Air Pollution-Volatile Organic Compounds, Antarctic-Environmental Protocol, Antarctic Treaty, Biodiversity, Climate Change, Desertification, Endangered Species, Environmental Modification, Hazardous Wastes, Law of the Sea, Marine Dumping, Marine Life Conservation, Nuclear Test Ban, Ozone Layer Protection, Ship Pollution, Tropical Timber 83, Tropical Timber 94, Wetlands, Whaling
signed, but not ratified: Air Pollution-Persistent Organic Pollutants, Climate Change-Kyoto Protocol

Geography - note: long boundary with Russia; Helsinki is northernmost national capital on European continent; population concentrated on small southwestern coastal plain

PEOPLE

Population: 5,167,486

Age structure:
0-14 years: 18% (male 478,497; female 459,646)
15-64 years: 67% (male 1,747,738; female 1,712,058)
65 years and over: 15% (male 295,177; female 474,370)

Population growth rate: 0.17%
Birth rate: 10.8 births/1,000 population
Death rate: 9.73 deaths/1,000 population
Net migration rate: 0.58 migrant(s)/1,000 population

Sex ratio:
at birth: 1.04 male(s)/female
under 15 years: 1.04 male(s)/female
15-64 years: 1.02 male(s)/female
65 years and over: 0.62 male(s)/female
total population: 0.95 male(s)/female

Infant mortality rate: 3.82 deaths/1,000 live births

Life expectancy at birth:
total population: 77.41 years
male: 73.74 years
female: 81.2 years

Total fertility rate: 1.7 children born/woman

Nationality:
noun: Finn(s)
adjective: Finnish

Ethnic groups: Finn 93%, Swede 6%, Lapp 0.11%, Roma 0.12%, Tatar 0.02%

Religions: Evangelical Lutheran 89%, Greek Orthodox 1%, none 9%, other 1%

Languages: Finnish 93.4% (official), Swedish 5.9% (official), small Lapp- and Russian-speaking minorities

Literacy:
definition: age 15 and over can read and write
total population: 100% (1980 est.)
male: NA%
female: NA%

GOVERNMENT

Country name:
conventional long form: Republic of Finland
conventional short form: Finland
local long form: Suomen Tasavalta
local short form: Suomi

Data code: FI
Government type: republic
Capital: Helsinki

Administrative divisions: 6 provinces (laanit, singular - laani); Aland, Etela-Suomen Laani, Ita-Suomen Laani, Lansi-Suomen Laani, Lappi, Oulun Laani

Independence: 6 December 1917 (from Russia)
National holiday: Independence Day, 6 December (1917)
Constitution: 17 July 1919

Legal system: civil law system based on Swedish law; Supreme Court may request legislation interpreting or modifying laws; accepts compulsory ICJ jurisdiction, with reservations

Suffrage: 18 years of age; universal

Executive branch:
chief of state: President Sauli NIINISTO (since 1 March 2012)
head of government: Prime Minister Juha SIPILA (since 28 May 2015)
cabinet: Council of State or Valtioneuvosto appointed by the president, responsible to Parliament

elections/appointments: president directly elected by absolute majority popular vote in 2 rounds if needed for a 6-year term (eligible for a second term); election last held on 22 January 2012 with a runoff on 5 February 2012 (next to be held on 28 January (first round)and 11 February (second round) 2018); prime minister appointed by Parliament in 2015

election results: Sauli NIINISTO elected president in second round; percent of vote in first round - Sauli NIINISTO (Kok) 37%, Pekka HAAVISTO (Vihr) 18.8%, Paavo VAYRYNEN (Kesk) 17.5%, Timo SOINI (TF) 9.4%, Paavo LIPPONEN (SDP) 6.7%, Paavo ARHINMAKI (Vas) 5.5%, Eva BIAUDET (SFP) 2.7%, Sari ESSAYAH (KD) 2.5%; percent of vote in second round - NIINISTO 62.6%, HAAVISTO 37.4%; Juha SIPILA appointed prime minister

Legislative branch:
description: unicameral Parliament or Eduskunta (200 seats; 199 members directly elected in single- and multi-seat constituencies by proportional representation vote and 1 member in the province of Aland directly elected by simple majority vote; members serve 4-year terms)

elections: last held on 19 April 2015 (next to be held by April 2019)
election results: percent of vote by party/coalition - Kesk 21.1%, PS 17.6%, Kok 18.2%, SDP 16.5%, Vihr 8.5%, Vas 7.1%, SFP 4.9%, KD 3.5%, other 2.6%; seats by party/coalition - Kesk 49, PS 38, Kok 37, SDP 34, Vihr 15, Vas 12, SFP 9, KD 5, Aland Coalition 1

Judicial branch:
highest court(s): Supreme Court or Korkein Oikeus (consists of the court president and 18 judges); Supreme Administrative Court (consists of 21 judges including the court president and organized into 3 chambers); note - Finland has a dual judicial system - courts with civil and criminal jurisdiction and administrative courts with jurisdiction for litigation between individuals and administrative organs of the state and communities
judge selection and term of office: Supreme Court and Supreme Administrative Court judges appointed by the president of the republic; judges serve until mandatory retirement at age 65

subordinate courts: 6 Courts of Appeal; 8 regional administrative courts; 27 district courts; special courts for issues relating to markets, labor, insurance, impeachment, land, tenancy, and water rights

Political parties and leaders:
Aland Coalition (a coalition of several political parties on the Aland Islands)
Center Party or Kesk [Juha SIPILA]
Christian Democrats or KD [Sari ESSAYAH]
Finns Party or PS [Jussi HALLA-AHO]
Green League or Vihr [Ville NIINISTO]
Left Alliance or Vas [Li ANDERSSON]]
National Coalition Party or Kok [Petteri ORPO]
Social Democratic Party or SDP [Antti RINNE]
Swedish People's Party or SFP [Anna-Maja HENRIKSSON]

International organization participation:
ADB (nonregional member), AfDB (nonregional member), Arctic Council, Australia Group, BIS, CBSS, CD, CE, CERN, EAPC, EBRD, ECB, EIB, EITI (implementing country), EMU, ESA, EU, FAO, FATF, G-9, IADB, IAEA, IBRD, ICAO, ICC (national committees), ICCt, ICRM, IDA, IEA, IFAD, IFC, IFRCS, IHO, ILO, IMF, IMO, IMSO, Interpol, IOC, IOM, IPU, ISO, ITSO, ITU, ITUC (NGOs), MIGA, MINUSMA, NC, NEA, NIB, NSG, OAS (observer), OECD, OPCW, OSCE, Pacific Alliance (observer), Paris Club, PCA, PFP, Schengen Convention, UN, UNCTAD, UNESCO, UNHCR, UNIDO, UNIFIL, UNMIL, UNMOGIP, UNRWA, UNTSO, UPU, WCO, WFTU (NGOs), WHO, WIPO, WMO, WTO, ZC

Diplomatic representation in the US:
chief of mission: Ambassador Kirsti KAUPPI (since 17 September 2015)
chancery: 3301 Massachusetts Avenue NW, Washington, DC 20008
telephone: [1] (202) 298-5800
FAX: [1] (202) 298-6030
consulate(s) general: Los Angeles, New York

Diplomatic representation from the US:
chief of mission: Ambassador (vacant); Charge d'Affaires Donna Ann WELTON (since 20 January 2017)
embassy: Itainen Puistotie 14B, 00140 Helsinki
mailing address: APO AE 09723
telephone: [358] (9) 616250
FAX: [358] (9) 6162 5800

Flag description: white with a blue cross that extends to the edges of the flag; the vertical part of the cross is shifted to the hoist side in the style of the Dannebrog (Danish flag)

ECONOMY

Finland has a highly industrialized, largely free-market economy with per capita GDP almost as high as that of Austria and the Netherlands and slightly above that of Germany and Belgium. Trade is important, with exports accounting for over one-third of GDP in recent years. The government is open to, and actively takes steps to attract, foreign direct investment.

Finland is historically competitive in manufacturing - principally the wood, metals, engineering, telecommunications, and electronics industries. Finland excels in export of technology as well as promotion of startups in the information and communications technology, gaming, cleantech, and biotechnology sectors. Except for timber and several minerals, Finland depends on imports of raw materials, energy, and some components for manufactured goods. Because of the cold climate, agricultural development is limited to maintaining self-sufficiency in basic products. Forestry, an important export industry, provides a secondary occupation for the rural population.

Finland had been one of the best performing economies within the EU before 2009 and its banks and financial markets avoided the worst of global financial crisis. However, the world slowdown hit exports and domestic demand hard in that year, causing Finland's economy to contract from 2012 to 2014. The recession affected general government finances and the debt ratio. The economy returned to growth in 2015, posting a 0.3% GDP increase before growing 1.4% in 2016.

Finland's main challenges will be reducing high labor costs and boosting demand for its exports. In June 2016, the government enacted a Competitiveness Pact aimed at reducing labor costs, increasing hours worked, and introducing more flexibility into the wage bargaining system. The Government was also seeking to reform the health care system and social services. In the long term, Finland must address a rapidly aging population and decreasing productivity in traditional industries that threaten competitiveness, fiscal sustainability, and economic growth.

GDP (purchasing power parity):

$231.4 billion (2016 est.)
$228.2 billion (2015 est.)
$227.6 billion (2014 est.)
note: data are in 2016 dollars
country comparison to the world: 63

GDP (official exchange rate):
$236.9 billion (2016 est.)

GDP - real growth rate:
1.4% (2016 est.)
0.3% (2015 est.)
-0.6% (2014 est.)
country comparison to the world: 167

GDP - per capita (PPP):

$42,200 (2015 est.)
$41,700 (2014 est.)
$41,800 (2013 est.)
note: data are in 2016 dollars
country comparison to the world: 41

Gross national saving:
20.9% of GDP (2016 est.)
20.7% of GDP (2015 est.)
19.8% of GDP (2014 est.)
country comparison to the world: 88

GDP - composition, by end use:
household consumption: 55.1%
government consumption: 24.2%
investment in fixed capital: 20.2%
investment in inventories: -0.1%
exports of goods and services: 35.4%
imports of goods and services: -34.8% (2016 est.)

GDP - composition, by sector of origin:
agriculture: 2.5%
industry: 26.9%
services: 70.6% (2016 est.)

Agriculture - products:
barley, wheat, sugar beets, potatoes; dairy cattle; fish
Industries:
metals and metal products, electronics, machinery and scientific instruments, shipbuilding, pulp and paper, foodstuffs, chemicals, textiles, clothing

Industrial production growth rate:
0.8% (2016 est.)
country comparison to the world: 152

Labor force:
2.675 million (2016 est.)
country comparison to the world: 112

Labor force - by occupation:
agriculture: 4.5%
industry: 24%
services: 71.5% (2014)

Unemployment rate:
8.8% (2016 est.)
9.4% (2015 est.)
country comparison to the world: 109

Population below poverty line:
NA%
Household income or consumption by percentage share:
lowest 10%: 4.2%
highest 10%: 21.5% (2015)

Distribution of family income - Gini index:
21.5 (2015)
26.8 (2008)
country comparison to the world: 149

Budget:
revenues: $128.5 billion
expenditures: $132.7 billion
note: Central Government Budget (2016 est.)

Taxes and other revenues:
53.7% of GDP (2016 est.)
country comparison to the world: 9

Budget surplus (+) or deficit (-):
-1.8% of GDP (2016 est.)
country comparison to the world: 71

Public debt:
63.6% of GDP (2016 est.)
63.7% of GDP (2015 est.)
note: data cover general government debt, and includes debt instruments issued (or owned) by government entities other than the treasury; the data include treasury debt held by foreign entities; the data include debt issued by subnational entities, as well as intra-governmental debt; intra-governmental debt consists of treasury borrowings from surpluses in the social funds, such as for retirement, medical care, and unemployment; debt instruments for the social funds are not sold at public auctions
country comparison to the world: 58

Fiscal year:
calendar year

Inflation rate (consumer prices):
0.4% (2016 est.)
-0.2% (2015 est.)
country comparison to the world: 49

Central bank discount rate:
0.25% (31 December 2016)
0.3% (31 December 2010)
note: this is the European Central Bank's rate on the marginal lending facility, which offers overnight credit to banks in the euro area
country comparison to the world: 134

Commercial bank prime lending rate:
1.46% (31 December 2016 est.)
2% (31 December 2015 est.)
country comparison to the world: 182

Stock of narrow money:
$130.2 billion (31 December 2016 est.)
$123.7 billion (31 December 2015 est.)

note: see entry for the European Union for money supply for the entire euro area; the European Central Bank (ECB) controls monetary policy for the 18 members of the Economic and Monetary Union (EMU); individual members of the EMU do not control the quantity of money circulating within their own borders
country comparison to the world: 30

Stock of broad money:
$177.3 billion (31 December 2016 est.)
$174.1 billion (31 December 2015 est.)
country comparison to the world: 44

Stock of domestic credit:
$355.3 billion (31 December 2016 est.)
$357.9 billion (31 December 2015 est.)
country comparison to the world: 32

Market value of publicly traded shares:
$133.7 billion (31 December 2016 est.)
$NA (31 December 2015 est.)
$154.4 billion (31 December 2014 est.)
country comparison to the world: 38

Current account balance:
$-2.511 billion (2016 est.)
$-968 million (2015 est.)
country comparison to the world: 155

Exports:
$59.6 billion (2016 est.)
$57.45 billion (2015 est.)
country comparison to the world: 42

Exports - commodities:
electrical and optical equipment, machinery, transport equipment, paper and pulp, chemicals, basic metals; timber

Exports - partners:
Germany 13.9%, Sweden 10.1%, US 7%, Netherlands 6.6%, Russia 5.9%, UK 5.2%, China 4.7% (2015)

Imports:
$60.51 billion (2016 est.)
$60.46 billion (2015 est.)
country comparison to the world: 43

Imports - commodities:
foodstuffs, petroleum and petroleum products, chemicals, transport equipment, iron and steel, machinery, computers, electronic industry products, textile yarn and fabrics, grains

Imports - partners:
Germany 17%, Sweden 16.1%, Russia 10.9%, Netherlands 9%, Denmark 4.1% (2015)

Reserves of foreign exchange and gold:
$10.6 billion (31 December 2016 est.)

$10 billion (31 December 2015 est.)
country comparison to the world: 73

Debt - external:
$544.7 billion (31 March 2016 est.)
$524.7 billion (31 March 2015 est.)
country comparison to the world: 20

Stock of direct foreign investment - at home:
$153.5 billion (31 December 2016 est.)
$135.9 billion (31 December 2015 est.)
country comparison to the world: 35

Stock of direct foreign investment - abroad:
$140.6 billion (31 December 2016 est.)
$141.1 billion (31 December 2015 est.)
country comparison to the world: 31

Exchange rates:
euros (EUR) per US dollar -
0.92 (2016 est.)
0.89 (2015 est.)
0.89 (2014 est.)
0.76 (2013 est.)
0.78 (2012 est.)

ENERGY

Electricity - production:
70.34 billion kWh
country comparison to the world: 39

Electricity - consumption:
84.83 billion kWh
country comparison to the world: 36

Electricity - exports:
1.645 billion kWh
country comparison to the world: 46

Electricity - imports:
19.09 billion kWh
country comparison to the world: 9

Electricity - installed generating capacity:
16.68 million kW
country comparison to the world: 43

Electricity - from fossil fuels:
52.3% of total installed capacity
country comparison to the world: 151

Electricity - from nuclear fuels:
16.2% of total installed capacity
country comparison to the world: 14

Electricity - from hydroelectric plants:
18.8% of total installed capacity
country comparison to the world: 93

Electricity - from other renewable sources:
12.7% of total installed capacity
country comparison to the world: 19

Crude oil - production:
13,530 bbl/day
country comparison to the world: 85

Crude oil - exports:
0 bbl/day
country comparison to the world: 110

Crude oil - imports:
214,700 bbl/day (2010 est.)
country comparison to the world: 32

Crude oil - proved reserves:
0 bbl
country comparison to the world: 130

Refined petroleum products - production:
282,300 bbl/day
country comparison to the world: 44

Refined petroleum products - consumption:
204,800 bbl/day
country comparison to the world: 57

Refined petroleum products - exports:
144,400 bbl/day
country comparison to the world: 38

Refined petroleum products - imports:
113,800 bbl/day
country comparison to the world: 48

Natural gas - production:
0 cu m
country comparison to the world: 129

Natural gas - consumption:
4.7 billion cu m
country comparison to the world: 64

Natural gas - exports:
0 cu m
country comparison to the world: 98

Natural gas - imports:
3.661 billion cu m
country comparison to the world: 39

Natural gas - proved reserves:
0 cu m
country comparison to the world: 136

Carbon dioxide emissions from consumption of energy:
54.06 million Mt

COMMUNICATIONS

Telephones - main lines in use:
890,000
country comparison to the world: 79

Telephones - mobile cellular:
9.32 million
country comparison to the world: 83

Telephone system:
general assessment: modern system with excellent service
domestic: digital fiber-optic fixed-line network and an extensive mobile-cellular network provide domestic needs
international: country code - 358; submarine cables provide links to Estonia and Sweden; satellite earth stations - access to Intelsat transmission service via a Swedish satellite earth station, 1 Inmarsat (Atlantic and Indian Ocean regions); note - Finland shares the Inmarsat earth station with the other Nordic countries (Denmark, Iceland, Norway, and Sweden)

Broadcast media:
a mix of publicly operated TV stations and privately owned TV stations; the 2 publicly owned TV stations recently expanded services and the largest private TV station has introduced several special-interest pay-TV channels; cable and satellite multi-channel subscription services are available; all TV signals have been broadcast digitally since September 2007; analog broadcasts via cable networks were terminated in February 2008; public broadcasting maintains a network

of 13 national and 25 regional radio stations; a large number of private radio broadcasters

Internet country code:
.fi; note - Aland Islands assigned .ax

Internet hosts:
4.763 million
country comparison to the world: 22

Internet users:
4.393 million
country comparison to the world: 55

TRANSPORTATION

Railways:
total: 5,865 km
broad gauge: 5,865 km 1.524-m gauge (2,192 km electrified; 480 km double- or multiple-track)
Highways:
total: 77,895 km
paved: 49,853 km (including 473 km of expressways)
unpaved: 28,042 km
Waterways: 6,675 km total (including Saimaa Canal); 3,700 km suitable for steamers
Pipelines: natural gas 580 km
Ports and harbors: Hamina, Helsinki, Kokkola, Kotka, Loviisa, Oulu, Pori, Rauma, Turku, Uusikaupunki, Varkaus
Merchant marine:
total: 101 ships (1,000 GRT or over) totaling 1,185,966 GRT/1,153,089 DWT
ships by type: bulk 9, cargo 23, chemical tanker 6, passenger 1, petroleum tanker 11, rail car carrier 1, roll-on/roll-off 38, short-sea passenger 12
Airports: 157
Airports - with paved runways:
total: 69
over 3,047 m: 3
2,438 to 3,047 m: 26
1,524 to 2,437 m: 10
914 to 1,523 m: 20
under 914 m: 10
Airports - with unpaved runways:
total: 88
914 to 1,523 m: 6
under 914 m: 82

MILITARY

Finnish Defense Forces (FDF): Army (Puolustusvoimat), Navy (Merivoimat; includes Coastal Defense Forces), Air Force (Ilmavoimat)

Military service age and obligation:
18 years of age for male voluntary and compulsory - and female voluntary - national military and nonmilitary service; service obligation 6-12 months; military obligation to age 60

Manpower available for military service:
males age 16-49: 1,155,368
females age 16-49: 1,106,193

Manpower fit for military service:
males age 16-49: 955,151
females age 16-49: 912,983

Manpower reaching militarily significant age annually:
male: 32,599
female: 31,416

Military expenditures:
1.47% of GDP
1.42% of GDP (2011)
1.47% of GDP (2010)
country comparison to the world: 62

TRANSNATIONAL ISSUES

Disputes - international:
various groups in Finland advocate restoration of Karelia and other areas ceded to the Soviet Union, but the Finnish Government asserts no territorial demands

Refugees and internally displaced persons:

stateless persons: 2,293 (2014)

IMPORTANT INFORMATION FOR UNDERSTANDING FINLAND

Official Name: Republic of Finland

PROFILE

GEOGRAPHY

Area: 337,113 sq. km. (130,160 sq. mi.); about the size of New England, New Jersey, and New York combined.
Cities: Capital -- Helsinki (pop. 525,000). Other cities -- Tampere (182,700), Turku (164,700).
Terrain: Low but hilly, more than 70% forested, with more than 60,000 lakes.
Climate: Northern temperate.

PEOPLE

Nationality: Noun -- Finn(s). Adjective -- Finnish.
Population: 5.13 million.
Population growth rate: 0.3%.
Ethnic groups: Finns, Swedes, Lapps, Roma, Tartars.
Religions: Lutheran 89%, Orthodox 1%.
Languages: Finnish 93%, Swedish 6% (both official); small Lapp- and Russian-speaking minorities.
Education: Years compulsory -- 9. Attendance -- almost 100%. Literacy -- almost 100%.
Health: Infant mortality rate -- 3.8/1,000. Life expectancy -- males 72 yrs., females 80 yrs.
Work force (2.5 million; of which 2 million are employed): Public services -- 32%. Industry -- 22%. Commerce -- 14%. Finance, insurance, and business services -- 10%. Agriculture and forestry -- 8%. Transport and communications -- 8%. Construction -- 6%.

GOVERNMENT

Type: Constitutional republic.
Constitution: July 17, 1919.
Independence: December 6, 1917.
Branches: Executive -- president (chief of state), prime minister (head of government), Council of State (cabinet). Legislative -- unicameral parliament. Judicial -- Supreme Court, regional appellate courts, local courts.
Subdivisions: 12 provinces, provincial self-rule for the Aland Islands.
Political parties: Social Democratic Party, Center Party, National Coalition (Conservative) Party, Leftist Alliance, Swedish People's Party, Green Party.
Suffrage: Universal at 18.

HISTORY

The origins of the Finnish people are still a matter of conjecture, although many scholars argue that their original home was in what is now west-central Siberia. The Finns arrived in their present territory thousands of years ago, pushing the indigenous Lapps into the more remote northern regions. Finnish and Lappish -- the language of Finland's small Lapp minority -- both are Finno-Ugric languages and are in the Uralic rather than the Indo-European family.

Finland's nearly 700-year association with the Kingdom of Sweden began in 1154 with the introduction of Christianity by Sweden's King Eric. During the ensuing centuries, Finland played an important role in the political life of the Swedish-Finnish realm, and Finnish soldiers often predominated in Swedish armies. Finns also formed a significant proportion of the first "Swedish" settlers in 17th-century America.

Following Finland's incorporation into Sweden in the 12th century, Swedish became the dominant language, although Finnish recovered its predominance after a 19th-century resurgence of Finnish nationalism. Publication in 1835 of the Finnish national epic, The Kalevala -- a collection of traditional myths and legends -- first stirred the nationalism that later led to Finland's independence from Russia.

In 1809, Finland was conquered by the armies of Czar Alexander I and thereafter remained an autonomous grand duchy connected with the Russian Empire until the end of 1917. On December 6, 1917, shortly after the Bolshevik Revolution in Russia, Finland declared its independence. In 1918, the country experienced a brief but bitter civil war that colored domestic politics for many years. During World War II, Finland fought the Soviet Union twice -- in the Winter War of 1939-40 and again in the Continuation War of 1941-44. This was followed by the Lapland War of 1944-45, when Finland fought against the Germans as they withdrew their forces from northern Finland.

Treaties signed in 1947 and 1948 with the Soviet Union included obligations and restraints on Finland vis-a-vis the U.S.S.R. as well as territorial concessions by Finland; both have been abrogated by Finland since the 1991 dissolution of the Soviet Union (see Foreign Relations).

GOVERNMENT AND POLITICAL CONDITIONS

Finland has a mixed presidential/parliamentary system with executive powers divided between the president, who has primary responsibility for national security and foreign affairs, and the prime minister, who has primary responsibility for all other areas. Constitutional changes made in the late 1980s strengthened the prime minister -- who must enjoy the confidence of the parliament (Eduskunta) -- at the expense of the president. Finland's 1995 accession to the European Union has blurred the line between foreign and domestic policy; the respective roles of the president and prime minister are evolving, and plans are under consideration to rewrite the constitution to clarify these and other issues.

Finns enjoy individual and political freedoms, and suffrage is universal at 18. The country's population is ethnically homogeneous with no sizable immigrant population. Few tensions exist between the Finnish-speaking majority and the Swedish-speaking minority.

Elected for a 6-year term, the president:

- Handles foreign policy, except for certain international agreements and decisions of peace or war, which must be submitted to the parliament;
- Is commander-in-chief of the armed forces and has wide decree and appointive powers;
- May initiate legislation, block legislation by pocket veto, and call extraordinary parliamentary sessions; and
- Appoints the prime minister and the rest of the cabinet (Council of State).

The Council of State is made up of the prime minister and ministers for the various departments of the central government as well as an ex-officio member, the Chancellor of Justice. Ministers are not obliged to be members of the Eduskunta and need not be formally identified with any political party.

Constitutionally, the 200-member unicameral Eduskunta is the supreme authority in Finland. It may alter the constitution, bring about the resignation of the Council of State, and override presidential vetoes; its acts are not subject to judicial review. Legislation may be initiated by the president, the Council of State, or one of the Eduskunta members.

The Eduskunta is elected on the basis of proportional representation. All persons 18 or older, except military personnel on active duty and a few high judicial officials, are eligible for election. The regular parliamentary term is four years; however, the president may dissolve the Eduskunta and order new elections at the request of the prime minister and after consulting the speaker of parliament.

The judicial system is divided between courts with regular civil and criminal jurisdiction and special courts with responsibility for litigation between the public and the administrative organs of the state. Finnish law is codified. Although there is no writ of habeas corpus or bail, the maximum period of pre-trial detention has been reduced to four days. The Finnish court system consists of local courts, regional appellate courts, and a Supreme Court.

Finland has 12 provinces. Below the provincial level, they are divided into cities, townships, and communes administered by municipal and communal councils elected by proportional representation once every four years. At the provincial level, the 11 mainland provinces are administered by provincial boards composed of civil servants, each headed by a presidentially appointed governor. The boards are responsible to the Ministry of the Interior and play a supervisory and coordinating role within the provinces.

The island province of Aland is located near the 60th parallel between Sweden and Finland. It enjoys local autonomy by virtue of an international convention of 1921, implemented most recently by the Act on Aland Self-Government of 1951. The islands are further distinguished by the fact that they are entirely Swedish-speaking. Government is vested in the provincial council, which consists of 30 delegates elected directly by Aland's citizens.

Finland's defense forces consist of 34,700 persons in uniform (27,300 army; 3,000 navy; and 4,400 air force); the country's defense budget equals about 2% of GDP. There is universal male conscription under which all men serve from eight to 11 months. As of 1995, women were permitted to serve as volunteers. A reserve force ensures that Finland can field 500,000 trained military personnel in case of need.

Finland's proportional representation system encourages a multitude of political parties and has resulted in many coalition governments. Political activity by communists was legalized in 1944, and although four major parties have dominated the postwar political arena, none now has a majority position. The Social Democratic Party (SDP) gained a plurality in Finland's parliament in the general election of March 1995. But it won far less than an overall majority and so formed a five-party governing coalition.

The SDP won 28% of the vote in 1995, mainly among the urban working class but also with some support among small farmers, white-collar workers, and professionals. The Leftist Alliance (LA) -- the SDP's rival on the left -- gained 11% of the vote in 1995 and joined the SDP-led government. The LA was formed in May 1990 and replaced the People's Democratic League, the group that represented the Finnish Communist Party in the Eduskunta.

Finland's two other major parties are the Center Party, traditionally representing rural interests, and the National Coalition -- or Conservative -- Party, which draws its major support from the business community and urban professionals. The Center won nearly 20% and the Conservatives 18% of the vote in 1995. The Conservatives are the second-largest party in the SDP-led coalition, which is rounded out by the Swedish People's Party and the Green Party. The Center Party leads the opposition in Parliament.

PRINCIPAL GOVERNMENT OFFICIALS

Portfolio	Minister	office Took	office Left	Party
Prime Minister	Juha Sipilä	29 May 2015	Incumbent	Centre
Minister of Foreign Affairs Deputy Prime Minister	Timo Soini	29 May 2015	Incumbent	Finns
Minister of Finance	Alexander Stubb	29 May 2015	Incumbent	National Coalition
Minister for Foreign Trade and Development	Lenita Toivakka	29 May 2015	Incumbent	National Coalition
Minister of Justice and Employment	Jari Lindström	29 May 2015	Incumbent	Finns
Minister of Interior	Petteri Orpo	29 May 2015	Incumbent	National Coalition
Minister of Defence	Jussi Niinistö	29 May 2015	Incumbent	Finns
Minister of Local Government and Public Reforms	Anu Vehviläinen	29 May 2015	Incumbent	Centre
Minister of Education and Culture	Sanni Grahn-Laasonen	29 May 2015	Incumbent	National Coalition
Minister of Agriculture and the Environment	Kimmo Tiilikainen	29 May 2015	Incumbent	Centre
Minister of Transport and Communications	Anne Berner	29 May 2015	Incumbent	Centre
Minister of Economic Affairs	Olli Rehn	29 May 2015	Incumbent	Centre
Minister of Social Affairs and Health	Hanna Mäntylä	29 May 2015	Incumbent	Finns
Minister of Family Affairs and Social Services	Juha Rehula	29 May 2015	Incumbent	Centre

Finland's embassy in the United States is at 3301 Massachusetts Avenue, NW, Washington, DC 20008; tel: 202-298-5800; fax: 202-298-6030.

ECONOMY

Rank	41st (nominal) / 53rd (PPP)
Currency	Euro (EUR)
Fiscal year	calendar year
Trade organisations	EU, WTO and OECD
	Statistics
GDP	$194.1 billion (PPP est.) $244.3 billion (est.)
GDP growth	▼-1.4%
GDP per capita	▲$38,271 (PPP; est.)
GDP by sector	▼Agriculture: 2.8% ▼Industry: 25.9% ▲Services: 71.2%
Inflation (CPI)	▼3.2%
Population below poverty line	17.9% at risk of poverty or social exclusion
Gini coefficient	▲28.2
Labour force	▼2,385 million
Labour force by occupation	▼Agriculture and forestry 4.4% ▼Industry 15.5% ▼Construction 7.1% ▲Commerce 21.3% ▼Finance, insurance, and business services 13.3% ▲Transport and communications 9.9% ▼Public services 28.5%
Unemployment	▼8,5% (2014)
Average gross salary	▲3,190 € / 3,988 $, monthly
Average net salary	▲2,321 € / 2,901 $, monthly
Main industries	metals and metal products, electronics, machinery and scientific instruments, shipbuilding, pulp and paper, foodstuffs, chemicals, textiles, clothing
Ease-of-doing-business rank	—12th
	External
Exports	▼$78.23 billion
Export goods	Electrical and optical equipment, machinery, transport equipment, paper and pulp, chemicals, basic metals; timber
Main export partners	Sweden 11.1% ▲Russia 10.0% ▼Germany 9.2% ▼Netherlands 6.3% ▲United States 6.3% United Kingdom 5.1% China 4.6%
Imports	▼$81.86 billion
Import goods	foodstuffs, petroleum and petroleum products, chemicals, transport equipment, iron and steel, machinery, textile yarn and fabrics, grains
Main import partners	—Russia 17.8% ▼Germany 12.3% ▼Sweden 10.7%

	▼Netherlands 5.7% ▲China 7.7% ▼Norway 3.6% ▲United States 3.4%
FDI stock	▲$100.76 billion
Gross external debt	▲$563.1 billion
Public finances	
Public debt	56.9% of GDP (est.), net debt 17.4% of GDP
Revenues	$129.4 billion
Expenses	$134 billion (2012 est.)
Economic aid	donor: ODA, $1.023 billion
Credit rating	AAA (Domestic) AAA (Foreign) AAA (T&C Assessment) (Standard & Poor's)
Foreign reserves	US$11.492 billion

Finland has a highly industrialised, mixed economy with a per capita output equal to that of other western economies such as France, Germany, Sweden or the United Kingdom. The largest sector of the economy is services at 65.7 percent, followed by manufacturing and refining at 31.4 percent. Primary production is 2.9 percent.

With respect to foreign trade, the key economic sector is manufacturing. The largest industries are electronics (21.6 percent), machinery, vehicles and other engineered metal products (21.1 percent), forest industry (13.1 percent), and chemicals (10.9 percent). Finland has timber and several mineral and freshwater resources. Forestry, paper factories, and the agricultural sector (on which taxpayers spend around 2 billion euro annually) are politically sensitive to rural residents. The Greater Helsinki area generates around a third of GDP.

In a 2004 OECD comparison, high-technology manufacturing in Finland ranked second largest after Ireland. Knowledge-intensive services have also ranked the smallest and slow-growth sectors – especially agriculture and low-technology manufacturing – second largest after Ireland. Investment was below expected. Overall short-term outlook was good and GDP growth has been above many EU peers. Finland has the 4th largest knowledge economy in Europe, behind Sweden, Denmark and the UK. The economy of Finland tops the ranking of Global Information Technology 2014 report by the World Economic Forum for concerted output between business sector, scholarly production and the governmental assistance on Information and communications technology.

Finland is highly integrated in the global economy, and international trade is a third of GDP. The European Union makes 60 percent of the total trade. The largest trade flows are with Germany, Russia, Sweden, the United Kingdom, the United States, Netherlands and China. Trade policy is managed by the European Union, where Finland has traditionally been among the free trade supporters, except for agriculture. Finland is the only Nordic country to have joined the Eurozone; Denmark and Sweden have retained their traditional currencies, whereas Iceland and Norway are not members of the EU at all.

Finland has a dynamic industrial economy based on abundant forest resources, capital investments, and technology. Traditionally, Finland has been a net importer of capital to finance industrial growth. In the 1980s, Finland's economic growth rate was one of the highest of industrialized countries.

In 1991, Finland fell into a deep recession caused by economic overheating, depressed foreign markets, and the dismantling of the barter system between Finland and the former Soviet Union. The same year, Finland devalued the markka to promote export competitiveness. This helped stabilize the economy, and the recession bottomed out in 1993.

Exports of goods contribute more than 20% of Finland's GDP; combined exports of goods and services amount to at least 25% of GDP. Exports and imports of goods equal about 40% of GDP. Timber and metalworking are Finland's main industries, but other industries produce manufactured goods ranging from electronics to motor vehicles. Finnish-designed consumer products such as textiles, porcelain, and glassware are world-famous.

Except for timber and several minerals, Finland depends on imported raw materials, energy, and some components for its manufactured products. Farms tend to be small, but sizable timber stands are harvested for supplementary income in winter. The country's main agricultural products are dairy, meat, and grains. Finland's EU accession has accelerated the process of restructuring and downsizing of this sector.

An extensive social welfare system, constituting about one-fifth of the national income, includes a variety of pension and assistance programs and a comprehensive health insurance program. Although free education through the university level also is available, only about one child in four receives a higher education in the highly competitive system. In the mid-1970s, the educational system was reformed with the goal of equalizing educational opportunities. Beginning at age seven, all Finnish children are required to attend a "basic school" of nine grade levels. After this, they may elect to continue along an academic (lukio) or vocational (ammat-tikoulu) line. But most pursue vocational studies, since the number of openings in higher educational institutions is less than the demand.

FOREIGN RELATIONS

Finland's basic foreign policy goal from the end of the Continuation War with the U.S.S.R. in 1944 until 1991 was to avoid great-power conflicts and to build mutual confidence with the Soviet Union. Although the country was culturally, socially, and politically Western, Finns realized they must live in peace with the U.S.S.R. and take no action that might be interpreted as a security threat. The dissolution of the Soviet Union in 1991 opened up dramatic new possibilities for Finland and has resulted in the Finns actively seeking greater participation in Western political and economic structures.

RELATIONS WITH THE SOVIET UNION AND WITH RUSSIA

The principal architect of the post-1944 foreign policy of neutrality was J.K. Paasikivi, who was President from 1946 to 1956. Urho Kekkonen, President from 1956 until 1981, further developed this policy, stressing that Finland should be an active rather than a passive neutral. This policy is now popularly known as the "Paasikivi-Kekkonen Line."

Finland and the U.S.S.R. signed a peace treaty at Paris in February 1947 limiting the size of Finland's defense forces and providing for the cession to the Soviet Union of the Petsamo area on the Arctic coast, the Karelian Isthmus in southeastern Finland, and other territory along the former eastern border. Another provision, terminated in 1956, leased the Porkkala area near Helsinki to the U.S.S.R. for use as a naval base and gave free access to this area across Finnish territory.

The 1947 treaty also called for Finland to pay to the Soviet Union reparations of 300 million gold dollars (amounting to an estimated $570 million in 1952, the year the payments ended). Although an ally of the Soviet Union in World War II, the United States was not a signatory to this treaty because it had not been at war with Finland.

In April 1948, Finland signed an Agreement of Friendship, Cooperation, and Mutual Assistance with the Soviet Union. Under this mutual assistance pact, Finland was obligated -- with the aid of the Soviet Union, if necessary -- to resist armed attacks by Germany or its allies against Finland or against the U.S.S.R. through Finland. At the same time, the agreement recognized Finland's desire to remain outside great-power conflicts. This agreement was renewed for 20 years in 1955, in 1970, and again in 1983 to the year 2003.

The Finns responded cautiously in 1990-91 to the decline of Soviet power and the U.S.S.R.'s subsequent dissolution. They unilaterally abrogated restrictions imposed by the 1947 and 1948 treaties, joined in voicing Nordic concern over the coup against Soviet leader Mikhail Gorbachev, and gave increasing unofficial encouragement to Baltic independence.

At the same time, by replacing the Soviet-Finnish mutual assistance pact with treaties on general cooperation and trade, Finns put themselves on an equal footing while retaining a friendly bilateral relationship. Finland now is boosting cross-border commercial ties and touting its potential as a commercial gateway to Russia. It has reassured Russia that it will not raise claims for Finnish territory seized by the U.S.S.R., and continues to reaffirm the importance of good bilateral relations.

MULTILATERAL RELATIONS

Finnish foreign policy emphasizes its participation in multilateral organizations. Finland joined the United Nations in 1955 and the EU in 1995. As noted, the country also is a member of NATO's Partnership for Peace as well as an observer in the North Atlantic Cooperation Council and the Western European Union.

Finland is well represented in the UN civil service in proportion to its population and belongs to several of its specialized and related agencies. Finnish troops have participated in UN peacekeeping activities since 1956, and the Finns continue to be one of the largest per capita contributors of peacekeepers in the world. Finland is an active participant in the Organization for Security and Cooperation in Europe (OSCE).

Cooperation with the other Scandinavian countries also is important to Finland, and it has been a member of the Nordic Council since 1955. Under the council's auspices, the Nordic countries have created a common labor market and have abolished immigration controls among themselves. The council also serves to coordinate social and cultural policies of the participating countries and has promoted increased cooperation in many fields.

In addition to the organizations already mentioned, Finland is a member of the International Bank for Reconstruction and Development, the International Monetary Fund, the World Trade Organization, the International Finance Corporation, the International Development Association, the Bank for International Settlements, the Asian Development Bank, the Inter-American Development Bank, the Council of Europe, the Organization for Economic Cooperation and Development, and INTELSAT.

U.S.-FINLAND RELATIONS

Relations between the United States and Finland are warm. Some 200,000 U.S. citizens visit Finland annually, and about 3,000 U.S. citizens are resident there. The U.S. has an educational exchange program in Finland which is comparatively large for a Western European country of Finland's size. It is financed in part from a trust fund established in 1976 from Finland's final repayment of a U.S. loan made in the aftermath of World War I.

Finland is bordered on the east by Russia and, as one of the former Soviet Union's neighbors, has been of particular interest and importance to the U.S. both during the Cold War and in its aftermath. Before the U.S.S.R. dissolved in 1991, longstanding U.S. policy was to support Finnish neutrality while maintaining and reinforcing Finland's historic, cultural, and economic ties with the West. The U.S. has welcomed Finland's increased participation since 1991 in Western economic and political structures.

Following the dissolution of the Soviet Union, Finland has moved steadily toward integration into Western institutions and abandoned its formal policy of neutrality, which has been recast as a policy of military nonalliance coupled with the maintenance of a credible, independent defense. Finland's 1994 decision to buy 64 F-18 fighter planes from the United States signaled the abandonment of the country's policy of balanced arms purchases from East and West.

In 1994, Finland joined NATO's Partnership for Peace; the country also is an observer in the North Atlantic Cooperation Council. Finland became a full member of the European Union (EU) in January 1995, at the same time acquiring observer status in the EU's defense arm, the Western European Union.

Economic and trade relations between Finland and the United States are active and were bolstered by the F-18 purchase. U.S.-Finland trade totals almost $5 billion annually. The U.S. receives about 7% of Finland's exports -- mainly pulp and paper, ships, and machinery -- and provides about 7% of its imports -- principally computers, semiconductors, aircraft, and machinery.

Finland generally welcomes foreign investment. Areas of particular interest for U.S. investors are specialized high-tech companies and investments that take advantage of Finland's position as a gateway to Russia and the Baltic countries.

KEY OFFICERS OF THE U.S. EMBASSY IN HELSINKI

Chargé d'Affaires Donna Ann Welton

Donna Welton took up her post as Deputy Chief of Mission at the U.S. Embassy in Helsinki in August 2016 following a detail to the Department of Defense as the acting Director for Southeast Asia in the Office of the Secretary of Defense (Policy). A graduate of Yale College and a native of upstate New York (where many Finnish-Americans make their home), she began her career with the United States Information Agency in 1984 and did three tours in Asian posts before returning to graduate school in 1992. After completing her coursework for a PhD in Princeton's Asian Art and Archaeology Department, she worked as a curator of Japanese art at the Metropolitan Museum of Art and as an exhibitions curator at the American Federation of Arts in New York.

Deputy Chief of Mission--Amy Hyatt
Public Affairs Counselor--Bill Davnie
Political Section Chief--Greg Thome

Labor Attache (Pol)--David Allen Schlaefer
Economic Section Chief--Jane Messenger
Management Officer--Ted Plosser
Commercial Officer--Brian McCleary
Defense Attache--Joy Shasteen
Consular Officer--Pirkko Urli
Regional Security Officer--Gerry Oman
Agricultural Officer--Roger Wentzel (resident in The Hague)

American Embassy
Address: Itäinen Puistotie 14 B, FIN-00140 Helsinki, Finland
Telephone: +358-9-171 931
E-mail: webmaster@usembassy.fi

TRAVEL AND BUSINESS INFORMATION

The U.S. Department of State's Consular Information Program provides Travel Warnings and Consular Information Sheets. **Travel Warnings** are issued when the State Department recommends that Americans avoid travel to a certain country. **Consular Information** Sheets exist for all countries and include information on immigration practices, currency regulations, health conditions, areas of instability, crime and security, political disturbances, and the addresses of the U.S. posts in the country. **Public Announcements** are issued as a means to disseminate information quickly about terrorist threats and other relatively short-term conditions overseas which pose significant risks to the security of American travelers. Free copies of this information are available by calling the Bureau of Consular Affairs at 202-647-5225 or via the fax-on-demand system: 202-647-3000. Travel Warnings and Consular Information Sheets also are available on the Consular Affairs Internet home page: http://travel.state.gov and the Consular Affairs Bulletin Board (CABB). To access CABB, dial the modem number: 301-946-4400 (it will accommodate up to 33,600 bps), set terminal communications program to N-8-1(no parity, 8 bits, 1 stop bit); and terminal emulation to VT100. The login is travel and the password is info. (Note: Lower case is required). The CABB also carries international security information from the Overseas Security Advisory Council and Department's Bureau of Diplomatic Security. Consular Affairs Tips for Travelers publication series, which contain information on obtaining passports and planning a safe trip abroad, can be purchased from the Superintendent of Documents, U.S. Government Printing Office, P.O. Box 371954, Pittsburgh, PA 15250-7954; telephone: 202-512-1800; fax 202-512-2250.

Emergency information concerning Americans traveling abroad may be obtained from the Office of Overseas Citizens Services at (202) 647-5225. For after-hours emergencies, Sundays and holidays, call 202-647-4000.

Passport Services information can be obtained by calling the 24-hour, 7-day a week automated system ($.35 per minute) or live operators 8 a.m. to 8 p.m. (EST) Monday-Friday ($1.05 per minute). The number is 1-900-225-5674 (TDD: 1-900-225-7778). Major credit card users (for a flat rate of $4.95) may call 1-888-362-8668 (TDD: 1-888-498-3648).

Travelers can check the latest health information with the U.S. Centers for Disease Control and Prevention in Atlanta, Georgia. A hotline at 877-FYI-TRIP (877-394-8747) and a web site at http://www.cdc.gov/travel/index.htm give the most recent health advisories, immunization recommendations or requirements, and advice on food and drinking water safety for regions and countries. A booklet entitled Health Information for International Travel (HHS publication number CDC-95-8280) is available from the U.S. Government Printing Office, Washington, DC 20402, tel. (202) 512-1800.

Information on travel conditions, visa requirements, currency and customs regulations, legal holidays, and other items of interest to travelers also may be obtained before your departure from a country's embassy and/or consulates in the U.S. (for this country, see "Principal Government Officials" listing in this publication).

U.S. citizens who are long-term visitors or traveling in dangerous areas are encouraged to register at the U.S. embassy upon arrival in a country (see "Principal U.S. Embassy Officials" listing in this publication). This may help family members contact you in case of an emergency.

FINLAND LEGAL SYSTEM BASICS

IMPORTANT INFORMATION

When the Finnish Parliament adopted the Declaration of the Independence of Finland on 6 December 1917, the new state already had a rich national culture and centuries of experience in managing its own affairs. The makings of an independent nation derived partly from the times of Swedish rule (from the 12th Century until 1809) and especially from the period when Finland was an autonomous Grand Duchy of the Russian Empire (from 1809 until 1917).

THE WESTERN INFLUENCES

For 700 years Finland was a Province of the Kingdom of Sweden, equal in status to any other Swedish Province. This common history is the basis of the similarities between the Finnish and Swedish societies - similarities that can be seen as well in the culture as in the political and legal structures. Swedish continues to be an official language in Finland, in addition to Finnish, even though native Swedish speakers now comprise only six per cent of the population. All legislation is published simultaneously in both languages.

The common legal heritage can be seen e.g. in the introductions to the Finnish and Swedish lawbooks, both of which still contain the ethical and judicial rules for judges compiled in the 16th Century by Olaus Petri, a Swedish clergyman and legal scholar. Furthermore, certain parts of the codification of laws completed in the Kingdom of Sweden in 1734, the first of its kind in Europe, have remained in force in Finland for over 250 years.

In addition to the western neighbour, also Central Europe and especially Germany were an early influence in the development of Finnish learning. Since 1640 Finland had a University of its own in Turku, with extensive links to a number of German and French Universities.

In Sweden, the first enacted codes were compiled already in the Middle Ages, separately for the towns and for the general law of the realm. The country had also two types of general lower courts: the Town Courts, which were based on a German model and operated in connection with the Town Councils, and the Rural District Courts. In Finland, the dual court system survived until 1993, when a unified system of lower courts was set up throughout the country. These came to be called District Courts.

The establishment in the 17th Century of the Courts of Appeal, which were meant to be the supreme judicial authorities in the country, signalled the birth of the Swedish-Finnish judiciary, even if the King in Council was vested with the supreme authority until 1789. The Svea Court of Appeal, in Stockholm, was established in 1614, and the Turku Court of Appeal in 1623. The jurisdiction of the latter covered all of Finland. The Supreme Court of Sweden - and of Finland - was established in 1789.

The separation of administrative matters and general legal affairs began on the local level as early as in the 17th Century. The County Governments, which had been set up as the general administrative authorities of the State, were empowered to hear also appeals against the decisions of the local authorities. The beginning of County administration saw also the beginning of the development of the Prison Service.

The first advocates appeared in Sweden and Finland in the beginning of the 17th Century.

THE EASTERN CONNECTION

Finland's constitutional ties with Sweden were severed in 1809, when Finland in connection with the Napoleonic wars was annexed by the Russian Empire. In spite of this, Swedish laws and the underlying legal system continued to apply in Finland - a rare and exceptional situation also in a global framework.

Over a century as an autonomous Grand Duchy was for Finland the first real step towards independence. The government and administrative machinery were created, Finland got its own representative assembly and its own currency, system of education and judiciary. The supreme administrative authority of Finland, the Senate, was also the supreme judicial authority in civil and criminal cases. The financial section of the Senate acted as the Government of Finland and the legal section as the Supreme Court. The financial section heard also appeals in administrative matters.

When the Czar gave his consent to the convocation of the Finnish representative assembly, in 1863, a time of busy social and legal development in Finland could begin. That time lasted for the remainder of the century. The reforms included e.g. an extensive programme for the construction of new prisons and the establishment of the Board of Prison Administration, in 1881.

The reform work was, however, cut short by the harsher policies of the Russian regime. The last major reform took place in 1906, when the representative assembly of four Estates, which derived already from the times of Swedish rule, was superseded by a new unicameral Parliament of 200 Representatives, at the time one of the most modern in terms of organisation and breadth of representation. The suffrage was universal; Finnish women were the second in the world to receive the vote and the first in the world to have the right to run for office.

THE RULE OF LAW

The 'russification period', as it became to be known, lasted until 1917. The attempts at oppression were countered in Finland with a steadfast reliance on the law and the rule of law. Those times further intensified the spirit of the rule of law that has been the legacy of Finnish and Scandinavian legal thinking since the Middle Ages - and remains so even today. The saying "Maa on lailla rakennettava" (By law shall this country be built) crystallises one of the basic principles of Finnish history. It is there also in the Constitution, according to which "there shall be strict compliance with the law in all official functions."

The Russian revolution made the independence of Finland finally possible. In 1919 a republican Constitution was framed, with the President of the Republic as the head of state. The President is elected by popular vote; if necessary, there are two rounds of voting, so that the two candidates with the most votes in the first round stand against each other in the second. The President's term in office is six years. A person cannot be elected for more than two consecutive terms. The Parliamentary term is four years.

The Supreme Court and the Supreme Administrative Court were established in 1918. As already noted, administrative judicial proceedings have in Finland been organised in a separate hierarchy of courts. The general courts for this purpose, the County Administrative Courts, were established as sections of the County Governments in 1955; they became also formally separate and independent entities in 1989.

After World War II the development of legislation was marked by the change of Finland from an agrarian nation into an industrialised one. The 1960's were a time of intensive co-operation between the Nordic Countries; as a result there is a body of laws that are virtually identical in Finland and in Sweden.

Similar legislation has been passed also as a result of economic co-operation and integration and common goals in the European Economic Area. It can be seen that Finnish laws and Finnish legal thinking clearly have their roots in Europe. In addition, the European Human Rights Convention has been directly applicable in Finland since 1990.

In 1995 Finland acceded to the European Union. This has naturally brought new elements into the Finnish legal system, but as a Member State of the EU Finland of course is able to participate in the enactment of new European legislation. The Finnish judiciary now applies not only Finnish, but also European law.

The roots of the Finnish legal system lie in the times when the country belonged to the Kingdom of Sweden [from the 12th Century to 1809]. These 700 years of common history form the basis of the similarities between the Finnish and Swedish societies, similarities that are evident also in their legal structures. These were retained even after Finland had been ceded to Russia, as the Swedish legislation in force at the time remained in force also during Finland's 108 years as an autonomous Grand Duchy within the Empire of the Czar. As a matter of fact, some parts of the original Swedish legislation continue to be applied to this day, even though Finland has been an independent republic since 1917.

The autonomous status that Finland enjoyed during the 19th Century also allowed for legislative self-determination. Hence, virtually nothing of the legal tradition of Russia remains, while Finland continues to display the characteristics of a continental legal tradition, with influences from Scandinavia and particularly from Germany.

One lasting effect of the Swedish times is the status of the Swedish language. For centuries, it was the language of the upper classes and the administration. Finnish, on the other hand, was taken into legislative use only in the early 20th Century. Even today Finland is a bilingual country, with Finnish and Swedish enjoying the same status as official languages (detailed information on the Ministry of Justice website). All legislation and most other official publications are available in both of them. In addition, it should be noted here that the unilingually Swedish-speaking Åland Islands, which lie between Finland and Sweden, have a far-reaching autonomy, enshrined in an Act that is "constitutional by nature" even though not formally a part of the Constitution.

Finland has been a member of the United Nations since 1955, of the Council of Europe since 1989 and of the European Union since 1995.

For further information, please refer to the English-language home page of the website of the Ministry of Justice.

CONSTITUTION

The new Constitution of Finland entered into force on 1 March 2000. It superseded the four Constitutional Acts deriving from the early times of Finnish independence, incorporating the most fundamental provisions from all of them. At the same time, many provisions were relegated to the ranks of regular parliamentary legislation. *In Finland, Sovereign Power Rests with the People*, a thorough outlook in English into the background, enactment and contents of the Constitution is available online.

THE JUDICIAL SYSTEM

The Finnish Constitution guarantees everyone the right to have his case heard appropriately and without undue delay by a court or other public authority. Everyone also has the right to have a decision affecting his rights and duties reviewed by a court or other judicial body.

In addition the Constitution contains the basic provision on fair trial and good governance. The main guarantees of these are the publicity of proceedings, the right to be heard, the right to receive a decision containing the grounds, and the right to appeal against the decision.

The independence of the judiciary is constitutionally guaranteed. The courts are under the sole obligation to apply the law in force.

The professional judges must have a higher university degree in law. They are appointed by the President of the Republic. A judge cannot be dismissed except by court order, e.g. if he has been convicted for an offence. The courts of first instance also have some locally elected lay judges.

In Finland, the constitutionality of laws is examined in advance. This mainly takes place in Parliament, and especially in its Constitutional Law Committee. The goal of this parliamentary control is to prevent in advance that laws which are in conflict with the Constitution are enacted in the ordinary legislative procedure.

No constitutional court exists in Finland, but the courts and other authorities are under an obligation to interpret legislation in such a way as to adhere to the Constitution and to respect human rights. According to the Constitution, the courts should give preference to the Constitution when they decide a case if the application of an act would be in manifest conflict with the Constitution.

PUBLIC DOMAIN

All Finnish legislation, from the Constitution to regular Acts of Parliament, Presidential Decrees, Government Decrees, Ministry Decrees and various other types of subordinate regulation, is published in print in the *Suomen säädöskokoelma*, i.e. the Statute Book of Finland.

FINLEX, the data bank for the dissemination of Finnish legislation and other legal information, was established as a subscription service in the 1980s. The newest version of FINLEX was launched in 2004 and is available on the Internet free of charge. Most of the material on the website is available only in Finnish and Swedish, but there is also some material in English. FINLEX consists of five subject areas:

- *Legislative information*, containing translations of Finnish Acts and Decrees, mostly into English; consolidated and original texts of Acts and Decrees; a reference database of changes made to any Act or Decree; and all Sámi language legislation. The most recent legislation is available also as pdf files in the "Electronic Statutes of Finland".

- *Case-law* from the following courts: The Supreme Court, the Supreme Administrative Court, the Courts of Appeal, the regional Administrative Courts, the Market Court, the Labour Court and the Insurance Court. In addition, there are summaries of judgments of the European Court of Human Rights and the Court of Justice of the EC, as well as a reference database on case-law in legal literature.

- *Secondary legislation*: The decrees, decisions and regulations of Ministries and Central Agencies; the decisions of the Chancellor of Justice and of the Data Protection Board; Collective Agreements concluded by registered associations of employers and employees.

- *Treaties* concluded by Finland, including a reference database of the date of entry into force, date of ratification, parties and the reservations made by the parties. The most recent treaties are available also as pdf files in the "Electronic Treaty Series of Finland", including the texts in the original languages, e.g. English or French.

- *Government Bills* (draft legislation) are available from 1992.

COMMERCIAL LAW

A comprehensive two-volume edition of Finnish legislation, *Suomen Laki I-II*, i.e. the Laws of Finland, is published annually by a commercial enterprise, Talentum. This work is available also as an online version.

A more recent entry in the field of legal information service is Edilex, which contains a database of national legislation, a daily news service, law books, articles, journals and other material. Subscription is required for most of the services. Edilex is provided by Edita Publishing.Another similar service is WSOYPro, which is provided by WSOY, the largest publishing house in Finland.

THE COURT SYSTEM

DISTRICT COURTS

Finland is divided into a number of judicial districts, each with a District Court (käräjäoikeus). The districts vary greatly in size, both in terms of population and of area. A District Court is made up of a Chief Judge (laamanni) and a number of other professional judges (käräjätuomari).

In civil cases the proceedings start with the pre-trial phase of the procedure, after which the case is adjourned to the main hearing. The case also can be resolved already in the course of the partly written and partly oral pre-trial procedure.

Also in criminal procedure the principles of orality, directness and concentration of the trial are stressed. The main hearing is divided into the opening statements of the parties, the presentation of evidence and the conclusions.

The rights of the accused are respected as stated in the European Convention of Human Rights. In Finland the victim has the right to claim damages from the accused in connection with the criminal proceedings and it is the public prosecutor´s duty in certain situations to present the claim for damages on behalf of the victim.

In ordinary civil cases the court consists of three professional judges. One single judge, however, presides over the pre-trial procedure of a civil case. In criminal cases (and in some cases concerning family law) the court is composed of one presiding professional judge and three lay members (volunteers elected by the municipal councils). Minor cases are tried by one judge alone.

The greatest volume of cases dealt with by the district courts is that concerning petitionary matters. These include e.g. divorce, registration of titles and mortgages over real property, bankruptcies and the adjustment of the debts of private individuals. Such matters are normally decided in chambers without a hearing being held.

COURTS OF APPEAL

The second instance in an ordinary case is the Court of Appeal (hovioikeus). These courts hear civil and criminal appeals.

All decisions by the District Courts may be appealed to the Court of Appeal. The parties have a right to refer both questions of fact and questions of law.

In the Courts of Appeal the cases are heard by three judges. The Court of Appeal first carries out a screening procedure, where it is determined if the matter is to be taken up for further consideration. If the Court of Appeal considers that the decision has been correct already in the district court, the appeal will not be entertained.

The appeal procedure is similar in both civil and criminal cases. After preliminary preparation the case can be resolved either after hearing or in written procedure. The Courts of Appeal have to arrange an oral hearing if the evidence of the case has to be evaluated again or when a party so requests unless the appeal is e.g. clearly without merit.

THE SUPREME COURT

The third and final instance is the Supreme Court (korkein oikeus), which has its seat in Helsinki. Its most important task is to establish precedents, thus giving guidelines to the lower courts on the application of the law.

The Supreme Court hears both civil and criminal appeals, but cases are admitted only under certain conditions.

The Supreme Court may grant a leave to appeal in cases in which a precedent is necessary for the correct application of the law, a serious error has been committed in the proceedings before a lower court or another special reason exists in law.

Normally two members decide whether leave should be granted. If leave is granted, the case is decided in a composition of five members. If the matter is important in principle and has far-reaching consequences, it is decided in a plenary session or in a reinforced composition of eleven members.

Usually, the cases are decided on the basis of written materials; the Supreme Court may, however, also conduct oral hearings and inspections.

Finland has a dual court system. There are the general courts, which are in charge of civil and criminal law, and the administrative courts, which review the actions of public authorities on the basis of appeals filed by private individuals and corporations.

There are three tiers of general courts. The 59 District Courts operate as the courts of first instance, with jurisdiction over all civil and criminal cases within their territorially limited districts.

In addition, there is the appellate level of six Courts of Appeal, and finally theSupreme Court in Helsinki, as the court of final appeal.

The administrative courts operate on two tiers. Firstly, there are eight regional Administrative Courts, which deal with appeals against administrative acts. The judgements of these courts can then be appealed in the Supreme Administrative Court in Helsinki.

ADMINISTRATIVE JURISDICTION

A general right of administrative appeal exists in Finland. This right can only be restricted with a specific legislative provision to that effect. The administrative courts hear appeals of private individuals and corporate bodies against the acts of the authorities. In certain cases the State and municipal authorities also have the right of appeal.

An appeal is usually first heard by a regional Administrative Court (hallinto-oikeus). The administrative courts hear tax, municipal, construction, social welfare, health care and alien cases as well as other administrative cases. In certain of these the appeal must be preceded by a complaint to a separate lower appellate body.

The administrative court consists of three judges. The procedure is mainly written. The administrative courts also conduct oral hearings. They have to be held whenever it is necessary for the resolution of the case or when a party so requests.

The Supreme Administrative Court (korkein hallinto-oikeus) finally decides the legality of the acts of the authorities. The bulk of its case-load consists of appeals against the decisions of the Administrative Courts.

Usually no leave to appeal is required. The main exception to this rule is an appeal against a decision in a tax case, for which leave is required. The Supreme Administrative Court itself grants the leave. The cases are heard by five judges. The Supreme Administrative Court may conduct also inspections or oral hearings.

In addition to its purely judicial tasks, the Supreme Administrative Court supervises the lower judicial authorities in the field of administrative law.

SPECIAL COURTS

The High Court of Impeachment (valtakunnanoikeus), which has been convened only a few times, hears criminal cases relating to offences in office allegedly committed by a member of the Council of State, the Chancellor of Justice, the Parliamentary Ombudsman or a member of either the Supreme Court or the Supreme Administrative Court. In such cases the prosecution is the responsibility of the Prosecutor General, the Chancellor of Justice or the Parliamentary Ombudsman.

The Market Court (markkinaoikeus) hears i.a. disputes regarding public acquisition, competition between firms and improper marketing. Depending on the nature of the case, the rulings of the Market Court are open to appeal before the Supreme Administrative Court or the Supreme Court.

The Labour Court (työtuomioistuin) hears disputes relating to collective agreements on employment relationships and on civil service relationships. Its decisions are not subject to appeal. Disputes relating to individual employment relationships are heard by the general courts and individual civil service relationships by the administrative courts.

The Insurance Court (vakuutusoikeus) considers certain cases falling within the field of social insurance, e.g. occupational accident insurance and pensions. Such cases are usually first heard by an appellate board, whose decisions are then subject to appeal to the Insurance Court. In certain cases related to accident insurance, the decisions of the Insurance Court are open to appeal before the Supreme Court, subject to leave by the Supreme Court.

The Prison Court (vankilaoikeus) makes decisions on the isolation of dangerous repeat offenders and orders young offenders to serve their sentence in the juvenile prison.

PROSECUTORS

The highest prosecuting authority in Finland is the Prosecutor General (valtakunnansyyttäjä), who is appointed by the President. As the director of the prosecution service, the Prosecutor General manages and supervises its operation and work.

The State Prosecutors (valtionsyyttäjä) who work in the Office of the Prosecutor General, appraise the evidence and decide whether charges should be brought in cases with wider national significance. The State Prosecutors have the right to act throughout the country. They are appointed by the Government.

The local prosecuting authorities are in Finland District Prosecutors (kihlakunnansyyttäjä). They are appointed by the Prosecutor General.

The prosecutors make their decisions to bring charges on the basis of preliminary investigations carried out by the police; it is their duty to appraise the available evidence and determine whether there is a prima facie case. If not, the prosecutor will make a decision not to prosecute. Prosecution may similarly be refused e.g. in cases in which the alleged offence is of minor significance.

Finland is a member of Eurojust, established by the European Union Member States in 2002 to support cooperation between prosecuting authorities and investigation of serious international crimes.

ADVOCATES AND LEGAL AID

A party to proceedings before a court usually uses the services of a counsel, even though this is strictly speaking not required by law. The duties of counsel are performed by an advocate, a public legal aid attorney, or another lawyer. Public legal aid attorneys (julkinen oikeusavustaja) are employed by the State to assist people in their legal affairs.

Legal aid is there to give individuals the possibility to obtain assistance for legal matters fully or partially at the expense of the State. It is granted on the basis of the applicant's income, expenditures and wealth. When these exceed a certain amount, legal aid will not be granted. Legal aid will not be granted if the applicant has legal expenses insurance covering the matter at hand.

Legal aid can be given both in court proceedings and in other matters.
In criminal proceedings, the defendant is under certain circumstances provided with a public defender at the expense of the State, regardless of his or her financial status.

The victim of domestic violence or sexual crime may be provided with a trial counsel at the expense of the State, regardless of his or her financial status.

In Finland a crime victim can recieve compensation from the State for damages caused by the crime, for instance for costs of medical care. If the victim has received compensation from the offender or an insurance company, it will be deducted from the compensation paid by the State.

ENFORCEMENT OF JUDGEMENTS

In Finland the enforcement of civil judgements is the duty of the District Bailiffs (kihlakunnanvouti), who are administratively within the ambit of the Ministry of Justice.

The bailiffs have general jurisdiction to ensure compliance with obligations laid down in court judgements. In practice these most often take the form of judgement debts. If the judgement is not heeded voluntarily, it is carried out compulsorily, by way of enforcement. Due taxes and public fees, as well as certain comparable civil debts, are executable without need for a judgement.

Also criminal sanctions of a monetary nature, such as fines, are collected by way of enforcement. In addition, the enforcement authorities are charged with the carrying out of evictions, court-ordered asset seizures and court orders on child custody and right of access.

The decisions of the bailiffs are subject to appeal in a District Court.

SYSTEM OF SANCTIONS

In Finland, the punishment imposed on a convicted criminal takes the form of imprisonment, fine, fixed-sum fine or community service. Community service can be imposed instead of unconditional imprisonment for at most eight months. Community service places are offered by various non-profit public or voluntary organisations.

A special juvenile punishment can be imposed on a young person, if a fine is considered insufficient and unconditional imprisonment too severe. Juvenile punishment consists of supervision and work and an educational program.

Mediation is still an unofficial system in Finland. Successful mediation may result in a decision not to prosecute or less severe sentencing by a court. Notwithstanding mediation, serious offences are likely to be considered by a court of law.

A sentence of imprisonment is passed either for a fixed period or for life. The minimum fixed period is fourteen days and the maximum twelve years. Under certain circumstances the sentence can be made conditional. In addition, there is an opportunity for parole after a given proportion of the sentence has been served. An offender serving a term of imprisonment for life can only be released by Presidential pardon.

The Prison Service (Vankeinhoitolaitos) enforces prison sentences and fine conversion sentences passed by the courts and takes care of the enforcement of remand imprisonment. The enforcement of community service and juvenile punishment is carried out by the Probation Service (Kriminaalihuoltolaitos). The Probation Service also sees to the supervision of conditionally sentenced young offenders and prisoners out on parole.

The Criminal Sanctions Agency (Rikosseuraamusvirasto) is in charge of the direction , administration and final enforcement of sentences.

SUPERVISION OF THE ADMINISTRATION OF JUSTICE

The Chancellor of Justice of the Council of State (oikeuskansleri) monitors the legality of the operations of the Council of State and other authorities, as well as of other public agencies. He also monitors the activities of the members of the Finnish Bar Association. The Chancellor of Justice is appointed by the President of the Republic.

The Finnish administrative machinery is also overseen by the Parliamentary Ombudsman (eduskunnan oikeusasiamies). The duties of these senior authorities differ in practical terms only in that the overseeing of the legality of the activities of the Council of State is entrusted mainly to the Chancellor of Justice. Matters pertaining to conscripts and convicts are within the ambit of the Ombudsman.

The overseers of legality have no jurisdiction to alter the decisions of other authorities, nor to award damages on the basis of complaints. Their rulings are not subject to appeal.

In addition to the senior overseers of legality, there are certain specialised authorities who have similar duties in more limited fields. These include the Consumer Ombudsman, the Ombudsman for Equality, the Data Protection Ombudsman, the Ombudsman for Minorities and the Bankruptcy Ombudsman.

PARLIAMENTARY INFORMATION

The Parliament of Finland website contains an extensive amount of material also in English. Parliamentary papers, such as bills, committee reports, session minutes etc. are, however, available only in one or both of the official languages. From this site can be accessed*Bibliographia Iuridica Fennica*/Legal Literature in Finland (*Suomen lainopillinen kirjallisuus /Finlands juridiska litteratur / Litterature juridique de la Finlande / Legal literature in Finland*) via the Jussi database which covers 1982-2001. It's online from 2001 to date via the SELMA database in English and in Finnish. See also the SELMA database main page.

GOVERNMENT INFORMATION

The Finnish Government web service has also a dedicated English-language area. The site offers an extensive view into how the executive branch of government operates in Finland. Of course, much of the content is political or otherwise topical, rather than legal, in nature, but the site does contain information e.g. on the legislative programme of the government currently in charge. In due course, this policy paper and the others available on the site have an effect also on the contents of the law in Finland.

Suomi.fi, the portal for public sector services in Finland, has been in existence since 2002. It contains information relevant to everyday life, collected in different subject areas. It covers also all aspects of legislation, government and judicial affairs in Finland, and naturally offers a full complement of links to all relevant sites, including the ones provided in this article.

THE LEGAL PROFESSION

The website of the Finnish Bar Association contains information on the regulations governing the practice of law in Finland, as well as on the activities of the Bar Association. There is also an extensive legal links selection, as well as an "Advocate Finder" service for searching attorneys and law firms e.g. on the basis of location, specialisation and language skills.

The Association of Finnish Lawyers is the general professional organisation of most lawyers in Finland, not only those admitted to the Bar.The Association's website contains information on the activities of the association and on lawyer's employment situation in Finland. Again, there is a long list of links that may be of interest to the legal profession.

FINLAND LAND AND PROPERTY OWNERSHIP SYSTEM - STRATEGIC INFORMATION AND DEVELOPMENTS

Finland operates a cadastral system operated by the National Land Survey of Finland

BASIC INFORMATION ON REAL ESTATE AND LAND OWNERSHIP IN FINLAND

REAL ESTATE MARKET

The structure of the Finnish real estate market has gone through some significant changes in recent years. The market share of offices has decreased due to, among other things, the expansion of the investor base in other sectors. At the same time, the residential properties market has become stronger due to, for example, increased demand for rental apartments. It has also become more attractive to invest in public property in Finland, such as healthcare and educational properties.

OWNERSHIP RIGHTS

Finland has Direct ownership of real estate. The law grants the owner an exclusive right to:

possess, use and manage the land; and

own any components or substances derived from the real estate.

However, some restrictions may limit the owner's rights – for example, planning legislation regarding land use.

Real estate can be jointly owned by more than one person or entity. The co-owners are subject to the detailed provisions set out in the Act on Co-ownership (180/1958, as amended).

Ownership of housing and corporate buildings in Finland is frequently arranged through indirect ownership by way of a limited liability company with the express purpose of owning the relevant real estate, including the buildings on it.

If the land and buildings on it are owned by different persons, the owner of the building or buildings usually has a tenancy right to use the land granted by the landowner under a fixed-term lease.

If the land and buildings are owned by the same entity, they are in the same real estate unit. Hence, the buildings are not registered as separate units.

Private individuals and legal entities may hold and exercise rights over real estate.

OWNERSHIP BY FOREIGNERS

Under Finnish law, there are no general restrictions on foreign ownership or occupation of Finnish real estate. However, in relation to indirect property investment (and as further defined in the Act on the Monitoring of Foreigners' Corporate Acquisitions in Finland, 172/2012, as amended)), foreign buyers must apply for prior approval from the Ministry of Employment and the Economy for an acquisition resulting in the buyer holding more than one-tenth, one-third or one-half of the voting power (or corresponding dominant control) of either:

a Finnish defence company; or any other company or business that holds a key position in relation to maintaining vital functions of Finnish society.

Further, foreign persons are restricted from buying real estate located on the Aland Islands (an autonomous region of Finland), unless specifically allowed by the government of those islands.

IMPORTANT INFORMATION

Real estate mortgage holders have priority based on the filing date of the relevant mortgage. A mortgage with an earlier filing date is satisfied before mortgages with a later date.

REGISTRATION

Title transfers to the buyer in accordance with the parties' agreement and is not dependent on registration of the buyer's title. However, a transfer of title must be registered with the Title and Mortgage Register maintained by the National Land Survey of Finland (www.maanmittauslaitos.fi) and prior registration has priority in case of conflicting transfers of title.

Also, certain land lease agreements and transfers of such leases must be registered with the Title and Mortgage Register.

Under the Land Code (540/1995, as amended), title must be applied for within six months of signing a document transferring ownership, such as an acquisition agreement.

It is the buyer's responsibility to provide evidence of the acquisition, by providing the original agreement or a true copy of the agreement certified by an official representative or registration authority.

Electronic documentation and transfer of title are possible through electronic service systems.

The Title and Mortgage Register contains information on, for example:

ownership of real estate;

mortgages; and

rights over property.

Information submitted to the Title and Mortgage Register is public. The registration authorities are obliged to provide certificates from it on request.

Is there a state guarantee of title?

Under the Land Code, the state is liable for damages caused by:

an obvious spelling or calculation mistake;

a mistake caused by a technical error; and

other similar errors or defects in the Title and Mortgage Register's records, or in extracts obtained from the relevant register.

If the damage is caused by an error in the information sent to the Title and Mortgage Register, the damage is not compensated by the state.

Errors in the Land Register are compensated by the registrar.

If an authority other than the National Land Survey of Finland has given an incorrect or inadequate certificate from the Title and Mortgage Register, and the error or defect is not caused by incorrect information in the register, that other authority is liable for compensating any damage incurred.

SALE AND PURCHASE

Brokerage

Real estate brokerage is regulated under the Act on Real Estate Brokerage Firms and Brokerage Firms of Rental Apartments (1075/2000, as amended). According to this act, only private traders or legal persons registered as real estate agencies may operate as real estate agents.

Also, the Brokerage Act (1074/2000, as amended) sets out provisions in relation to real estate brokers. The provisions in the Brokerage Act include, for example, limitations as to the maximum length of the relevant assignment agreement between the client and broker.

The Brokerage Act provides no cap, but a broker's commission must be reasonable with regard to, among other things, the nature of the assignment and the relevant workload relating to the assignment.

When performing the assignment, the broker must take into consideration the interest of both the client and the client's counterparty. Further, the broker has certain disclosure obligations both to the client and to the client's counterparty as to relevant information that the broker knows, or should know, has an impact on the decision regarding the relevant sale purchase or lease.

DUE DILIGENCE

Real estate due diligence is typically performed by the relevant professionals (eg, legal, technical, financial and tax advisers). The results of due diligence are often presented in reports, which include relevant findings and related recommendations.

Due diligence typically covers:

public registers relating to the real estate (including review of any possible encumbrances registered over the real estate);

leases relating to the real estate;

pending or threating litigation or other claims relating to the real estate;

environmental issues such as zoning provisions, building permits and contamination in the soil and groundwater;

technical investigations; and

tax and financial issues.

Preliminary agreements

Are any preliminary agreements typically entered into before conclusion of a sale contract?

Preliminary agreements typically entered into between the parties during the initial phase of the sale negotiations include:

letters of intent;

exclusivity agreements; and

non-disclosure agreements.

Unlike exclusivity agreements and non-disclosure agreements, a letter of intent mainly reflects the intention of the parties to agree on the proposed sale and is not usually legally binding. If any of the terms and conditions of the letter of intent are meant to be legally binding, this should be clearly stated in the letter of intent.

Real estate agents are often involved in the early marketing of real estate sales and usually prepare, for example, the information memorandum and other sales material.

Contracts

Must sale contracts be concluded in writing? If so, must they be notarised?

The sale of real estate must be concluded in writing. The acquisition agreement must be signed by both parties and attested by a notary in the presence of all the signatories to the agreement.

The acquisition agreement must include details of:

the parties' intention to sell and purchase the real estate;

the real estate to be sold and purchased;

the identity of the seller and the buyer; and

the price (to be paid in cash or other consideration).

If these provisions are not included or the agreement lacks other legal requirements, the sale will not be binding.

Further, the acquisition agreement usually also includes other provisions, such as:

warranties;

indemnities;

limitations of liability;

taxes;

insurance;

governing law; and

dispute resolution.

Obligations and liabilities

DISCLOSURE OBLIGATIONS

Under the Land Code, the seller must disclose to the buyer relevant information which could have an impact on the use or value of the real estate or on the transaction as a whole. In addition, if the seller notices before entering into the sale agreement that the buyer has an incorrect understanding of relevant characteristics of the real estate, the seller must correct this.

Under the Land Code, the buyer has the right to price reduction and, in certain situations, damages as a result of the defect. In addition, the buyer may also terminate the sale of real estate in case the defect is material.

CONTRACTUAL WARRANTIES

The seller is bound under Finnish law by certain statutory warranty obligations regarding the sale of real estate, including those relating to:

valid title to the real estate; and

accuracy of the information disclosed to the buyer.

Additional warranties given to the buyer include those relating to:

the validity of any lease(s) relating to the real estate;

compliance with relevant laws and permits, such as environmental laws and building permits;

the condition of buildings located on the real estate; and

the absence of any encumbrances.

The buyer has no obligations at the outside aside from paying the purchase price, unless the acquisition agreement states otherwise. Further, under certain circumstances, the buyer may inherit certain environmental liability.

TAXES

A direct acquisition of real estate is subject to transfer tax at a rate of 4% of the purchase price.

The acquisition of shares in a Finnish real estate company, housing company or real estate holding company is generally subject to transfer tax at a rate of 2% of the purchase price (or other consideration) payable by the buyer.

The transfer tax base also includes any debts or liabilities assumed by the buyer based on the transfer agreement, provided that the seller benefits from this.

The most common method is to acquire the corporate vehicle which owns the real estate rather than the real estate itself (as transfer tax on a share transfer in a Finnish real estate company is 2%, while transfer tax on the direct acquisition of real estate is 4%).

Further, if shares in a non-Finnish holding company (indirectly holding Finnish real estate) are transferred between non-residents, transfer tax can be avoided.

TRANSFER OF TITLE

Title transfers to the buyer in accordance with what the parties have agreed and is not dependent on registration of the buyer's title.

The duration of sale transactions varies depending on, for example, the characteristics of the object of sale and the issues which may arise during the due diligence. The duration may therefore range from a few weeks to several months (or even longer).

LEASES

Under the Land Tenancy Act (258/1966, as amended), all of the provisions of the lease, together with any amendments and assignments of the lease, must, as a rule, be in writing.

However, a lease can be made orally in some circumstances – for example, if it relates to certain types of agricultural land and the lease period is for less than two years.

Are there any regulations setting out mandatory or prohibited provisions in lease agreements?

Most lease provisions are freely negotiable but in situations where a particular matter has not been agreed on by the parties, the Land Tenancy Act applies. Where a provision under the Land Tenancy Act is mandatory, any provision which departs from that provision is void.

What provisions are typically included in lease agreements?

Lease agreements typically include at least provisions regarding the parties, intent of the lease, rent and term of the lease.

What are the standard forms of lease agreement used in your jurisdiction?

Most lease agreements are made in writing and signed by both parties.

Length of term

Are there any regulations on minimum and maximum terms of leases?

In general, the parties are free to agree on the length of the lease term. However, the Land Tenancy Act provides for certain limits on the lease term, depending on the type of lease. For example, a lease of an urban plot must be for a fixed term of at least 30 years, up to a maximum of 100 years. If the parties have not agreed the term of the lease of an urban plot, the term is deemed to be 30 years.

When a lease of a residential area concerns an area which, according to the purpose of the lease, must be occupied mainly by buildings built by the tenant, the lease term must be at least 30 years. The lease term is deemed to be 30 years if not agreed otherwise by the parties.

If the parties agree on a lease for a longer term than allowed under the Land Tenancy Act, the term of the lease is considered to be the maximum length allowed for that type of lease.

Are long-term tenants accorded any special rights as to extension or renewal of leases?

The parties to a lease are free to agree on terms for the renewal of the lease. Long-term tenants are not automatically provided rights to extend the lease term under law.

Rent

What regulations (if any) govern rent increases?

The parties are, at the outset, free to agree the rent level as well as the rent increases under the lease. However, the rent level can be adjusted in court or in arbitration if considered unreasonable, taking into account:

the general market rental value;

the use of the land;

the value of the land in the area; and

other relevant factors affecting the amount of the rent.

Further, under the Land Tenancy Act, the landlord has the right to increase the rent if the leased area has been essentially increased due to a reason not attributable to the parties.

What regulations (if any) govern rent security deposits?

A rent security deposit is not a legal requirement, but it is usually required by the landlord.

Can the tenant withhold rent payments on any legal grounds?

The tenant may be released from rent payments or receive a reasonable reduction of the same in situations where the tenant has the right to terminate the lease with immediate effect – for example, if the leased real estate is not in the state of repair as agreed in the lease or if a public authority restricts the intended use of the real estate.

Sub-letting

Under what circumstances is sub-letting typically allowed?

Finnish law does not per se recognise the sub-letting of land areas.

However, the tenant may always assign the lease with the landlord's consent. In some cases the Land Tenancy Act provides for an assignment of the lease without the landlord's consent unless otherwise expressly agreed. Further, a lease of an urban plot may always be assigned without the landlord's consent and an agreement to the contrary is void.

Obligations and liabilities

What are the general obligations and liabilities of the landlord in respect of the property and what are the consequences of breach?

The Land Tenancy Act sets out certain obligations of the landlord, such as to convey the leased real estate to the tenant at the date agreed by the parties and to convey the leased real estate to the tenant in the state of repair as agreed in the lease. The general consequences of a breach by the landlord are that the tenant is released from payment of rent or, in case of a material breach, the tenant may have a right to terminate the lease.

Most of the obligations and liabilities of the landlord may be agreed on by the parties under the lease. Therefore, the obligations and liabilities as set out in the Land Tenancy Act mainly apply in cases where the parties have not agreed on the relevant matter. As an example, the landlord is responsible for certain mandatory costs relating to the real estate unless otherwise agreed by the parties.

What are the general obligations and liabilities of the tenant in respect of the property and what are the consequences of breach?

Most of the general obligations and liabilities of the tenant as well as the consequences of a breach thereof may be agreed on by the parties. The main obligation of the tenant is to perform the agreed rent to the landlord. In addition, the tenant cannot, for example, use the leased real estate contrary to the purpose of the lease. Except for leases of urban plots, a landlord can terminate a lease (and claim compensation for possible damages) where the tenant has, among other things, not paid the rent on time or failed to keep the leased real estate in good repair.

Taxes

Are any taxes payable on rental income? If so, are any exemptions available?

Rental income is considered as regular business income for a corporation and taxed at a rate of 20% and capital income for individuals taxed at a rate of 30% (34% for income exceeding €30,000 a year).

Value added tax (VAT) is not payable on rent paid under a lease unless the lessor of a real estate opts for VAT.

Insurance

Are the landlord and tenant bound by any insurance requirements?

At the outset, the parties are free to agree on the insurance. However, some activities by the tenant might require insurance by law. For example, according to the Environmental Damage Insurance Act (81/1998, as amended), environmental damage insurance must be obtained by private corporations whose operations involve a material risk of environmental damage or whose operations cause harm to the environment in general.

Termination and eviction

What rules and procedures govern termination of the lease by the landlord and the tenant's eviction from the property?

Except for leases of urban plots, landlords can terminate a lease where the tenant has:

unlawfully or contrary to the provisions of the lease, assigned the lease or the right of possession of the leased real estate (wholly or partly) to another;

not paid the rent on time;

failed to keep the leased real estate in good repair; or

used the real estate unlawfully or contrary to the provisions of the lease.

The termination of the lease must be made by written notice stating, among other things, the grounds for the te

INFORMATION FOR PROPERTY OWNERS

As a property owner, you need to know about the rights and obligations that concern your property. Sometimes, it may be in your interest to consolidate two properties you own or to exchange properties with someone else.
You can change the name of your property (in Finnish)

INFORMATION ABOUT YOUR PROPERTY

You can order a report on information about your property from our customer service. The report carries a charge and contains, for example, information about the rights of way that apply to your property. If you need information about building permits, contact your municipality.

It is possible for a property not to have a right of way. The width of the right of way, or its location, may also be unclear. In such cases, as the landowner you can apply for a private road survey. From our customer service, you can also order an investigation into the archives to find out matters related to a right of way by studying old cadastral survey documents and maps. Such an investigation is subject to a charge.

If a boundary marker has been lost or the location of the boundary is otherwise unclear, you need to apply for a boundary demarcation.

When you need to know your property's shares in jointly-owned areas, order an extract from the cadastre.

SELLING A PROPERTY

You can sell your property through the Property Transaction Service. In such cases, the sale does not have to be authenticated by a public purchase witness. You can also convey properties in other ways through the Property Transaction Service.

When you are selling your property or an unseparated parcel, that is a part of the property, you need to let the buyer check the following documents: certificate of title, certificate of mortgages and encumbrances and if necessary, an extract from the cadastre.

The certificate of title shows ownership information. If you have not applied for the registration of title, you need to give the buyer the contracts, through which you acquired the property. The certificate of mortgages and encumbrances contains information about any mortgages on the property as well as registered leases and other special rights. The extract from the cadastre contains information about the area of the property and any shares in jointly-owned areas.

Property information is available from the National Land Survey. Read more about ordering extracts subject to a charge. You can also order extracts and certificates from the Property Transaction Service.

INFORMATION ABOUT SOMEONE ELSE'S PROPERTY

You need information about someone else's property when:

- You intend to buy a property.
- You are investigating rights of passage.
- You are constructing a building on your own property.

Get this information by ordering an extract or a certificate. You can also contact our customer service.

The Official purchase price register provides information about actual purchase prices. If you wish, you can compare the property you are buying with information in the register. Information about individual property purchases is available from our customer service.

PRACTICAL INFORMATION FOR BUYING PROPERTY IN FINLAND

You should prepare carefully before buying a property, an unseparated parcel or a designated share of a property.

BEFORE THE PURCHASE

Always check the certificate of title and the certificate of mortgages and encumbrances. Ask the seller to provide you with the certificates or order them from the National Land Survey. The certificates are subject to a charge.

Visit the property that you consider buying, make sure you know where its boundaries are and the condition it is in.

The municipal building inspection authority can provide you with more information about building permits and zoning.

The Official purchase price register provides information about actual purchase prices. If you wish, you can compare the property you are buying with information in the register. Information about individual property purchases is available from our customer service.

PURCHASE

Draft a bill of sale

a) As the buyer, you can together with the seller draft the bill of sale in the Property Transaction Service. (in Finnish)

b) It is also possible to draft the bill of sale on paper. In such cases, both the buyer and seller must be present in one location to sign it and have it witnessed by a public purchase witness.

The municipality may have the right of pre-emption in a property sale. The right of pre-emption is valid for three months following the date of sale.

Register your right of ownership that is apply for registration of title within six months of signing the bill of sale. At the same time, you can apply for a mortgage.

When the registration of title is complete, the unseparated parcel is converted into a new property in a parcelling procedure, which is initiated automatically.

Sometimes it is necessary to find out the information related to the owner of a property. You can order a specification of ownership from our customer service. The specification of ownership contains information about the property identifier, the name of the property and the property owner's name and address. Specifications of ownership carry a charge.

To find out who owns a property, you must know its property identifier.

When you know the property identifier, you can:

- Order a certificate of title, which carries a charge.
- By phone, it is possible to request ownership information about a maximum of ten properties without charge during a twelve-month period. Please note: Our telephone service is only available in Finnish and Swedish.
- Request property information about several property units by e-mail for a fee.

Please note that we do not provide property ownership information

- for use in direct marketing or opinion polls or market surveys or
- to enable contacting a property owner for the purpose of purchasing the property

PROPERTY OWNERSHIP REGISTRATION

When a piece of land is transferred from one owner to the next, the new owner must register his or her ownership of, or title to, the property. This is done by applying for a registration of title. Only a property whose ownership has been registered can be used as security for a loan. The

registration of title is entered into the public title and mortgage register. Once title to a property has been registered, the new owner is shown on the certificate of title.
A piece of land is a property or an unseparated parcel or designated share of a property. Ownership can be transferred through a sale, as a gift, through the distribution of matrimonial assets or by inheritance.

APPLY FOR REGISTRATION OF TITLE ON TIME

The new owner is expected to apply for registration of title within six months of signing the contract of conveyance, even if ownership has not yet been transferred to the new owner.
The six-month period starts on the day the contract, such as a bill of sale, is signed. If this period is exceeded, each six-month period of further delay increases the amount of transfer tax. The maximum total transfer tax is the double of the amount due within six months of signing the contract.
When the registration of title has been granted, the National Land Survey will initiate a parcelling procedure to convert the unseparated parcel into a new property. The parcelling procedure is initiated automatically.
With one application, you can apply for the registration of title to more than one property. The price is determined by the number of properties.

APPLY FOR A PRO FORMA REGISTRATION OF TITLE

It is not compulsory to apply for a pro forma registration of title, but doing so makes it easier to handle matters related to the conveyance of property. You should apply for a pro forma registration of title in at least the following cases:

- When the estate of a deceased person wants to sell a property belonging to the deceased. With a pro forma registration of title, it is not necessary to give the estate inventory deed to the subsequent buyer of the property for him or her to append to the application for registration of title.
- When a company has undergone changes, such as a split or a merger.

PROCESSING TIME

From initiation to decision, the entire process takes approximately 2 months.

APPLYING FOR TITLE REGISTRATION

1. Assemble all necessary appendices (in Finnish).
2. Fill in the form (in Finnish).
3. You can send your application by e-mail or by post, or bring it in person to our customer service. Physical documents will be returned to you when your case has been initiated.

NECESSARY APPENDICES

The most common ones are the receipts for payment of the purchase price and transfer tax. You do not need to use original copies of contracts that have been signed by a public purchase witness as appendices to the application for registration of title. Other contracts must be sent by post as original copies. A list of other necessary appendices is included in the instructions on how to fill in an application for registration of title (in Finnish).

When you apply for a pro forma registration of title, include a copy of the estate inventory deed and a certificate of succession concerning the deceased.

In changes related to company law, include the companies' plan for splitting up and its appendices.

APPLYING FOR A MORTGAGE

If you want to use your property or leasehold as security for a loan, you need to apply for a mortgage. The mortgage can only be granted if the title or leasehold has been registered in the title and mortgage register. You can apply for a mortgage and a registration of title at the same time. When the mortgage has been granted, it is shown on the certificate of mortgages and encumbrances.

The mortgage can be directed at a property, at an unseparated parcel or a specified share of a property. A lease can be mortgaged if it meets certain conditions.

You will be notified when the mortgage has been decided and the electronic mortgage deed has been registered in the title and mortgage register.A mortgage is valid until further notice. It must be terminated when it is no longer needed.

Fill in an application form online by using the Property Transaction Service (in Finnish) or download an application form (in Finnish) here. Sign your application and send it by post or e-mail.

PROCESSING TIME

A mortgage application will be processed within 20 days.

HOW MUCH DOES A MORTGAGE COST?

Each registered mortgage is subject to a charge.

If you apply for a mortgage through the Property Transaction Service, you will be expected to pay as you apply. In other cases the charge becomes payable when the decision has been given.

IMPORTANT CONTACTS

Central Administration

Opastinsilta 12 C, 00520 Helsinki

National Land Survey Registry
Opastinsilta 12 C, 00520 Helsinki
Mailing address: PL 84, 00521 Helsinki
Opening hours: Mon-Fri 8:00-16:15
Phone: 029 530 1115
Email: kirjaamo@nls.fi

Pasila Office Centre (Pasilan virastokeskus)
Opastinsilta 12 C, 00520 Helsinki

Finnish Geospatial Research Institute (FGI) / Masala
Geodeetinrinne 2, 02430 Masala

IMPORTANT LAWS AND REGULATIONS ON LAND AND REAL PROPERSY OWNERSHIP AND MANAGEMENT

LAND AND REAL ESTATE CODE

(540/1995; AMENDMENTS UP TO 964/1998 INCLUDED)

PART 1 — ACQUISITION OF REAL ESTATE

Chapter 1 — **General Provisions**

Section 1 — *Conveyance of Real Estate* Title to real estate is acquired by sale, trade, gift or other conveyance, as provided in this Code. Separate provisions apply to the acquisition of real estate by inheritance, will, distribution of matrimonial assets, expropriation or otherwise not by conveyance.

Section 2 — *Conveyance of Part of Real Estate* The provisions on the conveyance of real estate apply also to the conveyance of a share and a parcel of real estate, a common, a parcel and a share of a common.

CHAPTER 2 — SALE OF REAL ESTATE

Section 1 — *Form of Deed of Sale*

(1) A sale of real estate shall be concluded in writing. The seller and the buyer or their attorneys shall sign the deed of sale. A notary shall attest the sale in the presence of all the signatories of the deed of sale.

(2) The deed of sale shall indicate:

(1) the intent to convey;

(2) the real estate to be conveyed;

(3) the seller and the buyer; and

(4) the price or other consideration.

(3) The sale shall not be binding unless it is concluded as provided in this section. If the seller and the buyer have agreed on a price or other consideration in excess of that taken into the deed of sale, the seller shall not have the right to collect the excess amount.

Section 2 — *Cancellation and Suspension Clauses*

(1) A clause may be taken into the deed of sale to the effect that the sale can be cancelled for a reason not mentioned in this Code or that the seller retain title to the real estate until the price has been paid or another condition fulfilled.

(2) A clause referred to in paragraph (1) above shall not be binding unless it has been taken into the deed of sale, nor in so far as it is intended to remain valid for longer than five years from the conclusion of the sale. If no validity period for the clause has been taken into the deed of sale, the clause shall remain valid for five years. An action for the return of the real estate to the seller shall be brought at the latest in three months from the end of the validity of the clause.

Section 3 — *Power of Attorney* The power of attorney for a sale of real estate shall be in writing. The seller shall sign the power of attorney, which shall indicate the attorney and the real estate to be sold.

Section 4 — *Sale in Name of Company to Be Established*

(1) If a sale of real estate has been concluded in the name of a limited-liability company to be established and the company has not become responsible for the sale within two years of its conclusion, or the establishment of the company has been discontinued before that time, the person concluding the sale in the name of the company shall be deemed the buyer.

(2) The seller shall forfeit his right to renounce the sale, as provided in chapter 2, section 14(3) of the Limited-Liability Companies Act (734/1978), if no action for the same has been brought within two years of the conclusion of the sale.

Section 5 — *Agreement on Cancellation of Sale* An agreement on the cancellation of a sale of real estate or the return of the real estate to the seller shall be concluded in accordance with the provisions in sections 1 and 3.

Section 6 — *Notary*

(1) Provisions on notaries and their duties are issued by Decree.

(2) The provisions in chapter 17, section 43 of the Code of Judicial Procedure on the disqualification of witnesses apply to the disqualification of notaries.

(3) Provisions on the charges for the performances of notaries and the compensation for their travel expenses are issued by Decree. The charges shall be fixed at the average cost incurred to the State by the performance of the pertinent duties. A public official shall forward the payment to the State or the municipality in question. Otherwise, the provisions of the Act on the Charge Criteria of the State (150/1992) apply.

Section 7 — *Precontract*

(1) The parties may conclude a precontract on an intended sale of real estate. The precontract may be binding on one of the parties only.

(2) The precontract shall be concluded in accordance with the provisions in sections 1 and 3; also the other provisions on the sale of real estate apply to a precontract, where applicable. The precontract shall also indicate the deadline for the conclusion of the sale of real estate and the conditions whose fulfillment triggers the sale. However, the price and other consideration may be left to be agreed later, on the basis referred to in the precontract. If the time of validity of the precontract has not been indicated, it shall be five years from the conclusion of the precontract.

(3) A party to the precontract shall have the right to bring an action within the time limit provided in section 2(2) and demand that the other party conclude the sale as agreed in the precontract.

Furthermore, a party shall have the right to due compensation for breach of precontract. If the real estate has in breach of the precontract been conveyed to a third party, the buyer referred to in the precontract shall have the right to due compensation from the seller.

Section 8 — *Compensation for Non-conclusion of Sale* If the parties have agreed on a sale of real estate, but the agreement has not been concluded in accordance with section 7(2), the party liable for the non-conclusion of the sale shall compensate the other party for the reasonable costs incurred by advertising, visiting the real estate and the other activities necessary for the conclusion of the sale. If a down payment has been made, the part exceeding the costs referred to above shall be returned.

Section 9 — *Freedom of Agreement*

(1) The seller and the buyer shall fulfill their obligations as agreed, unless otherwise provided below.

(2) The rights and obligations of the seller and buyer provided in this Code may be derogated from by agreement. The rights of the buyer provided in sections 17–34 may be restricted only by an agreement which indicates in detail how the status of the buyer differs from that provided by law.

Section 10 — *Acquisition of Residential Real Estate from Merchants* If the buyer has acquired real estate to serve as residence or leisure residence for himself or his family, from a merchant who develops or sells real estate professionally:

(1) a clause derogating from the provisions in sections 17–34 to the detriment of the buyer shall not be binding;

(2) the seller cannot invoke the time limit provided for a notice in section 25(2);

(3) the seller shall be liable to compensate for repair costs, other necessary costs and the costs of measures that have become unnecessary due to a breach of contract, even if the matter concerns a hidden defect referred to in section 17(1), or if the seller can prove that his conduct has been careful;

(4) the buyer's liability for compensation may be adjusted, if late payment is a result of insolvency arising from illness, unemployment or other special circumstance which is not primarily the fault of the buyer.

Section 11 — Invalid Clauses

(1) Unless otherwise provided, the following clauses shall not be binding in a sale of real estate:

(1) a clause under which the seller or a third party has the right to redeem the real estate at will or under which the seller or a third party has the right of first refusal before the real estate is conveyed to a new titleholder;

(2) a clause which restricts the right of the buyer to reconvey the real estate, to raise a lien over it, to agree on a lease on or other special right to it or to otherwise dispose of it in a comparable manner;

(3) a clause which restricts the liability of the seller or a previous titleholder in cases of contesting of title; and

(4) a clause which restricts the personal freedom of the buyer or is otherwise improper or illegal.

(2) Without prejudice to paragraph (1)(2) above, a clause under which the buyer cannot without the consent of the seller reconvey undeveloped real estate or sell it below a set price shall be allowed. Such a clause shall not be binding unless it is taken into the deed of sale. The provision in section 2(2) applies to the time of validity of the clause.

(3)

Section 36 of the Contracts Act applies to the adjustment of an unreasonable clause.

Section 12 — *Seller's Obligation to Convey*

(1)

If the time of conveyance has not been set, the buyer shall have the right to gain possession of the real estate at once after the conclusion of the sale. The real estate shall be conveyed to the buyer in the condition that is to be deemed agreed upon.

(2)

The seller shall hand over to the buyer those title documents in his possession that are necessary for the registration of title. The same applies to mortgage instruments, lease agreements and other comparable documents that are necessary for the buyer as the titleholder of the real estate.

Section 13 — *Produce of Real Estate During Seller's Possession*

(1)

The produce gained from real estate prior to the agreed time of conveyance shall belong to the seller. However, the seller shall not take timber or extract land resources in excess of the domestic use of the real estate sold, nor attach special rights to it.

(2)

The buyer shall not dispose of the real estate so that the use of the rights due to the seller by virtue of paragraph (1) or by virtue of agreement is precluded.

Section 14 — *Use of Real Estate Before Transfer of Title*

(1)

The buyer may after the conclusion of the sale use the real estate and dispose of it, as well as reconvey his right, even if the retention or transfer of title has in the deed of sale been made conditional.

(2)

However, prior to the final transfer of title the buyer shall not without the consent of the seller take timber or extract land resources or other things affixed to the real estate so that its value diminishes significantly. Furthermore, the buyer shall not

raise liens over or attach special rights to the real estate without the consent of the seller.

Section 15 — *Liability for Public Debts*

(1)

The seller shall be liable for debts and fees under public law and for other similar debts incurred prior to the conclusion of the sale.

(2)

The buyer shall be liable for the transfer-of-assets tax levied on the sale. (933/1996)

Section 16 — *Risk of Damage to Real Estate* Damage caused to real estate by fire, storm, criminal damage or other reason not dependent on the seller after the conclusion of the sale shall be at the risk of the buyer, even if the seller retains possession of the real estate or the retention or transfer of title has in the deed of sale been made conditional.

Section 17 — *Defect in Quality*

(1) Real estate shall have a defect in quality if:

(1)

the characteristics of the real estate are not as agreed;

(2) the seller has prior to the conclusion of the sale provided the buyer with false or misleading information on the area of the real estate, the condition or structure of the buildings, or other characteristic of the real estate pertinent to its quality and there is reason to believe that the information has had an effect on the sale;

(3) the seller has prior to the conclusion of the sale failed to provide the buyer with information on a characteristic referred to in subparagraph (2), which typically has an effect on the use or value of similar real estate and of which the seller knew or should have known, and there is reason to believe that the failure has had an effect on the sale;

(4) the seller has prior to the conclusion of the sale noticed but failed to rectify the buyer's misconception of a characteristic having an effect on the intended use of the real estate; or

(5) due to a hidden defect, the real estate is of significantly lower quality than what can justifiably be expected in view of the price and the other circumstances.

(2) In case of a defect in quality the buyer shall have the right to a price reduction or, in case of an essential defect, to cancel the sale. Furthermore, in case of a defect referred to in paragraph (1)(1)–(4) the buyer shall have the right to due compensation.

Section 18 — *Defect in Possession*

(1) Real estate shall have a defect in possession if:

(1) the seller has prior to the conclusion of the sale provided the buyer with false or misleading information on a current plan, building prohibition, conveyance restriction or other official decision restricting the use or possession of the real estate and there is reason to believe that the information has had an effect on the sale;

(2) the seller has prior to the conclusion of the sale provided false or misleading information on an official permit or decision relating to the use of adjoining real estate and there is reason to believe that the information has had an effect on the sale;

(3) the seller has prior to the conclusion of the sale failed to provide the buyer with information on a decision, or a permit or decision in his knowledge, referred to in subparagraph (1) and (2), respectively, which typically has an effect on the use or value of similar real estate, and there is reason to believe that the failure has had an effect on the sale;

(4) the seller has prior to the conclusion of the sale noticed but failed to rectify the buyer's misconception of a decision referred to in subparagraphs (1) and (2) or a comparable circumstance, which prevent the buyer from using or possessing the real estate as intended;

(5) the necessary permit for a building on the real estate or for the activity carried out on the real estate has not been obtained; or

(6) a share or a parcel of the real estate cannot due to the restrictions in chapter 4 of the Real Estate Formation Act (554/1995) be formed into a new real estate or, when the share or parcel has been acquired for building purposes, into a new real estate to be used as a building site.

(2) In case of a defect in possession the buyer shall have the right to a price reduction or, in case of an essential defect, to cancel the sale. Furthermore, the buyer shall have the right to due compensation.

Section 19 — *Defect in Title*

(1) Realestate shall have a defect in title if:

(1) the buyer may lose title to the real estate in favour of the rightful titleholder or the sale may be voided upon the request of a third party;

(2) the seller has prior to the conclusion of the sale provided the buyer with false or misleading information of the registered titleholder, a lien over, lease on or other special right to the real estate in favour of a third party, or the ownership of a building, facility, or other object customarily affixed to the real estate, and there is reason to believe that the information has had an effect on the sale;

(3) the seller has prior to the conclusion of the sale failed to provide the buyer with information referred to in subparagraph (2) and there is reason to believe that the failure has had an effect on the sale; or

(4) the buyer cannot have his title registered due to the title documents of the seller being defective or incomplete, or due to another irregularity in the acquisition of the seller.

(2) The buyer may invoke a defect in title also if a third party claims that he has a right referred to in paragraph (1) and there are likely grounds for the validity of the claim.

(3) In case of a defect in title the buyer shall have the right to a price reduction or, in case of an essential defect, to cancel the sale. Furthermore, the buyer shall have the right to due compensation.

Section 20 — *Information Provided by Third Parties*

(1) The seller shall be responsible also for the information provided by a real estate agent or other representative acting on his behalf and for the failure of such persons to provide information.

(2) Separate provisions are enacted on the liability of a real estate agent for compensation and on the information that a real estate agent or a merchant is to provide when advertising real estate for sale.

Section 21 — *Timing of Defects*

(1) Any defects in real estate shall be determined on the basis of the condition of the real estate at the conclusion of the sale. The seller shall be responsible for a defect extant at that time, even if the defect becomes apparent only later.

(2) The buyer shall not invoke a defect which the seller has rectified prior to the transfer of the possession of the real estate to the buyer.

Section 22 — *Buyer's Knowledge of Defects*

(1) The buyer shall not invoke a defect in quality which could have been noticed in an inspection of the real estate prior to the conclusion of the sale. The buyer need not verify, without a special reason, the correctness of the information on the real estate provided by the seller, nor extend the inspection to such circumstances whose inspection requires technical or other extraordinary measures.

(2) The buyer shall not invoke a defect of which he must have known at the conclusion of the sale.

(3) The seller shall not be released from responsibility by virtue of paragraphs (1) and

(2) if his own conduct has been in bad faith or grossly negligent.

Section 23 — *Criminal Damage and Wrongful Use*

(1) If the seller has after the conclusion of the sale neglected the appropriate maintenance of the real estate, wrongfully used it or otherwise caused damage to it through negligence, the buyer shall have the right to a price reduction or, if the

damage is essential, to cancel the sale. Furthermore, the buyer shall have the right to due compensation.

(2) If the seller has after the conclusion of the sale wrongfully raised a lien over or attached a special right to the real estate, the provision in paragraph (1) applies.

Section 24 — *Seller's Failure to Perform* If the seller does not fulfill a building obligation or other performance obligation connected to a sale of real estate, the buyer shall have the right to a price reduction or, if the failure is essential in view of the entire sale, to cancel the sale. Furthermore, the buyer shall have the right to due compensation.

Section 25 — *Notice of Defects*

(1) The buyer shall not invoke a defect if he does not give notice of it and of his claims based on it to the seller in a reasonable time from finding out about the defect or from the time when he should have found out about it. The same applies if the buyer wants to invoke a breach of contract referred to in section 23 or 24.

(2) If the buyer does not give notice of a defect in quality or a breach of contract referred to in section 23(1) or section 24 within five years from the transfer of the possession of the real estate, he shall forfeit his right to do so.

(3)

The seller shall not be released from responsibility by virtue of paragraphs (1) and

(2) if his own conduct has been in bad faith or grossly negligent.

Section 26 — *Claims against Merchants*

(1) If the buyer has acquired real estate to serve as residence or leisure residence for himself or his family, he shall have the right to make a claim based on a defect in quality, instead of the seller, against:

(1) a merchant who develops or sells real estate professionally and who has conveyed the real estate to the seller or a previous titleholder for the purpose referred to above; or

(2) a building element dealer, developer or other merchant who is responsible for defects to the seller or a previous titleholder by virtue of an agreement or chapter 9 of the Consumer Protection Act.

(2) A merchant shall be responsible, by virtue of this section, only for defects for which he would have been responsible to his counterpart, and only to the extent of his liability towards that counterpart. The merchant shall be released from responsibility if compensation for the defect has been paid to a previous titleholder of the real estate or if the titleholder has due to a failure to give notice of the defect forfeited his right to invoke it.

(3) The buyer shall give notice of a defect that he has found out about and his claim based on it to the merchant. The provisions in section 25(1) and (3) apply to the notice of defect.

Section 27 — *Seller's Delay*

(1) If the seller does not transfer the possession of real estate at the time agreed, the buyer shall have the right to demand that the agreement be fulfilled or, if the delay is essential and the buyer

will not accept possession of the real estate, that the sale be cancelled. Furthermore, the buyer shall have the right to due compensation.

(2) If the seller does not hand over the documents referred to in section 12(2) to the buyer at the time agreed, the provision in paragraph (1) applies.

Section 28 — *Buyer's Delay*

(1) If the buyer does not pay the price, a part thereof or other agreed consideration at the time agreed, the seller shall have the right to demand that the agreement be fulfilled and, in addition, the payment of compensation. If the delay is essential and the buyer does not pay the full price, the seller may cancel the sale and demand compensation provided that it has been agreed in the deed of sale that the payment of the price is a condition on the retention or transfer of title to the real estate.

(2) If the buyer's payment delay is a result of a legal provision, an interruption in communications or other similar *force majeure*, which the buyer cannot reasonably be expected to overcome, the seller shall not have the right to compensation or cancellation of sale.

(3) The Interest Act (633/1982) applies to the right of the seller to interest for delay.

Section 29 — *Buyer's Anticipatory Breach*

(1) Even if the price or a part thereof has not yet become due and payable, the seller shall have the right to cancel the sale, if it has in the deed of sale been agreed that payment is a condition for the retention or transfer of title and if:

(1) the buyer has after the conclusion of the sale been declared bankrupt;

(2) the buyer has after the conclusion of the sale been found without means in execution proceedings; or

(3) it is otherwise evident that the buyer will not fulfill his obligation to pay.

(2) However, the seller shall not cancel the sale unless the part of the price remaining unpaid is essential or if an acceptable security for its payment is given in a reasonable time after an exhortation to pay. Furthermore, if the sale is cancelled, the seller shall have the right to due compensation.

Section 30 — *Right to Withhold Performance*

(1) If the buyer has a claim based on the seller's breach of contract, the buyer may withhold payment of the price for the part corresponding to his claim.

(2) If the seller has a claim based on the buyer's breach of contract, the seller shall have the right to withhold possession of the real estate. If the seller has retained possession of the real estate, he may continue using the real estate as provided in section 13.

Section 31 — *Price Reduction*

(1) A price reduction shall be calculated by subtracting the value of the defective real estate at the conclusion of the sale from the agreed price. If the agreed price is not equal to the market value of the real estate, in the agreed condition, the price reduction shall be calculated taking into account the ratio between the agreed price and the market price.

(2) The seller shall return the part of the price constituting the price reduction with interest, as provided in section 3(2) of the Interest Act, said interest as from the date when the seller received payment of the price.

Section 32 — *Compensation*

(1) *Due compensation* shall mean full compensation for any damage incurred by a breach of contract.

(2) If the seller shows that a defect or a breach of contract referred to in section 24 is not due to his negligence, the seller shall not be liable for compensation.

(3) The compensation may be adjusted, if it is unreasonable in view of the reason of the breach of contract, the opportunity of the party causing the damage to prevent it, the contribution of the other party and the other circumstances.

Section 33 — *Cancellation of Sale*

(1) If the sale is cancelled, the buyer shall return the real estate to the seller and the seller shall return the price already paid to the buyer.

(2) If the buyer has gained noteworthy profit or benefit from the real estate, he shall compensate the seller for the same. The seller shall pay a reasonable compensation to the buyer for the necessary expenses incurred by the maintenance of the real estate and for those useful expenses that have added to the value of the real estate. The seller shall return the price already paid with interest, as provided in section 3(2) of the Interest Act, said interest as from the date when the seller received payment of the price.

(3) The buyer shall have the right to remove, within a reasonable time, the buildings and facilities that he has built, where these are not necessary for the regular use of the real estate and where their removal does not cause significant damage to the real estate.

(4) A party may withhold his own return performance until the other party fulfills his obligations and pays the compensation and interest for which he is liable, or gives an acceptable security for their payment.

Section 34 — *Restrictions to Right to Cancel*

(1) The buyer shall have the right to cancel the sale only if he can return the real estate to the seller.

(2) A buyer who has attached a special right to the real estate, or whose activity or failure to act has decreased the value of the real estate, may cancel the sale only if he compensates the seller by an amount corresponding to the decrease in value. If the real estate is encumbered by a lien raised by the buyer, the buyer may cancel the sale only after paying to the seller the amount recoverable on the basis the lien.

(3) The sale shall not be cancelled unless the pertinent action has been brought within ten years from the transfer of possession of the real estate. The provisions in this section are without prejudice to the right of the buyer to claim for his rights if his acquisition has been voided.

CHAPTER 3 — CONTESTING OF TITLE AND PERMANENCE OF SPECIAL RIGHTS IN SALES OF REAL ESTATE

Section 1 — *Contesting of Title*

(1) The rightful titleholder of real estate may demand that the acquisition of the buyer be voided on the basis of a defect encumbering the acquisition of the seller and that the real estate be returned to the rightful titleholder.

(2) Chapter 13, sections 4, 5, 9, and 10 contain provisions on the grounds precluding the contesting of title.

Section 2 — *Liability of Previous Titleholders* A buyer who has lost real estate through the contesting of title shall have the right to bring his claim pertaining to this, instead of the seller, against the previous titleholder in whose acquisition there has been a defect resulting in the voiding of the acquisition of the buyer. If the buyer has brought his claim against the seller in accordance with chapter 2, section 19, the seller shall have a corresponding right.

Section 3 — *Buyer's Rights and Obligations*

(1) A buyer who has lost real estate through the contesting of title may keep the profit and benefits gained from the real estate if he at the conclusion of the sale did not know nor should have known that the seller was not the rightful titleholder.

(2) If the value of the real estate has decreased as a result of the buyer's activity or failure to act, he shall compensate the rightful titleholder by an amount corresponding to the decrease in value, unless the payment of compensation is under the circumstances to be deemed unreasonable.

Section 4 — *Liability of Rightful Titleholder for Compensation*

(1) The rightful titleholder shall compensate the buyer by a reasonable amount for the necessary expenses incurred by the maintenance of the real estate and, if the buyer at the conclusion of the sale did not know nor should have known that the seller was not the rightful titleholder, also for those useful expenses that have added to the value of the real estate.

(2) The buyer shall have the right to remove, within a reasonable time, the buildings and facilities that he has built, where these are not necessary for the regular use of the real estate and where their removal does not cause significant damage to the real estate.

(3) The buyer may retain possession of the real estate until the compensation referred to in paragraph (1) has been paid or an acceptable security for payment given.

Section 5 — *Time Limit for Claims* An action based on sections 3 and 4 shall be brought within three years from the return of the real estate to the rightful titleholder through the contesting of title in court. The lapsing of this time limit shall not preclude a claim for set-off in proceedings initiated by the opposing party.

Section 6 — *Precedence of Acquisitions*

(1) f the same real estate is sold to two buyers, the former acquisition shall prevail. The same applies to the order of precedence between a sale and another acquisition. However, the latter acquisition shall prevail under the circumstances referred to in chapter 13, section 3.

(2) The provisions in chapter 2, section 19 apply to the liability of the seller towards the buyer whose acquisition does not prevail. The provisions in sections 3 and 4 apply, where appropriate, to the mutual liability of the buyers.

Section 7 — *Permanence of Registrable Special Rights*

(1) A special right established prior to the conclusion of the sale and registrable under chapter 14, section 1, shall be binding on the buyer. Chapter 13, section 3 contains provisions on the grounds on which such special rights are not binding.

(2) A registrable special right attached to the real estate by the seller after the conclusion of the sale shall not be binding on the buyer, unless otherwise provided in chapter 13, section 3.

Section 8 — *Permanence of Other Special Rights* Unless otherwise provided, a contractual special right not referred to in chapter 14, section 1 shall be binding on the buyer of real estate only if he knew of the special right at the conclusion of the sale.

Section 9 — *Liability of the Seller*

(1) If the holder of a special right loses the special right through a sale, he shall have the right to due compensation from the seller.

(2) If the special right is binding on the buyer, he shall have rights with respect to the seller, as provided in chapter 2, sections 19 and 23.

Section 10 — *Protection from Enforcement* A sale of real estate shall be permanent even if the seller has lost his competence to convey because of execution, precautionary measure or bankruptcy, unless the restriction of competence was at the conclusion of the sale entered into the title and mortgage register and the buyer also otherwise did not know nor should have known that the seller no longer was competent to convey the real estate.

CHAPTER 4 — APPLICATION OF PROVISIONS ON SALE OF REAL ESTATE TO OTHER CONVEYANCES

Section 1 — *Trades of Real Estate* The provisions in chapters 2 and 3 on the sale of real estate apply, where appropriate, to trades of real estate.

Section 2 — *Gifts of Real Estate*

(1) The provisions in chapter 2, sections 1–7, section 9(1) and section 11 as well as in chapter 3 on the sale of real estate apply, where appropriate, to gifts of real estate.

(2) If the donee breaches a condition relating to the use of the gift or another essential condition or prerequisite, the donor shall have the right to revoke the gift, unless the donee has conveyed the real estate to a third party. An action for the revocation of gift shall be brought within one year from the donor's gaining knowledge of the grounds for revocation.

Section 3 — *Other Conveyances* The provisions in chapter 2, sections 1–8, section 9(1) and section 11 as well as chapter 3 on the sale of real estate apply, where appropriate, to the conveyance of real estate to a company in exchange of stock or other shares, to an agreement on the splitting of real estate held in shares and to the transfer of title to real estate by other, comparable contracts.

Section 4 — *Transfer of Usufruct*

(1) The provisions in chapter 2, sections 9–34, chapter 3 and this chapter on the conveyance of real estate apply, where appropriate, to the transfer of a lease or other usufruct on the land and waters of a third party, if the area contains a

building or a permanent facility or construction belonging to the usufructuary or if it is agreed that one may be built.

(2) An agreement on the transfer of usufruct shall be in writing and it shall contain the information referred to in chapter 2, section 1(1), if the transfer is to be registered. The transfer shall also in other cases be made in writing, if either party so demands.

PART II — REGISTRATION

CHAPTER 5 — GENERAL PROVISIONS ON REGISTRATION

Section 1 — *Registration*

(1) In this Code, *registration* means the registration of titles and special rights, as well as mortgaging.

(2) The title and mortgage register shall be kept for registration purposes.

(3) Entries on other rights to and encumbrances over real estate shall also be made in the title and mortgage register.

Section 2 — *Register Authority*

(1) The District Court in whose jurisdiction the real estate is located shall be the competent register authority.

(2) Unless otherwise provided, the District Court shall have a quorum, for purposes of registration, with one judge qualified in law. Registration matters shall be considered in the office of the District Court.

CHAPTER 6 — APPLICATION FOR REGISTRATION

Section 1 — *Application*

(1) The application for registration shall indicate:

(1) the real estate or other registrable object to which the application pertains;

(2) the claim or request of the applicant and, where necessary, a justification for the same;

(3) the name and domicile of the applicant, a personal identity number, trade register number or other corresponding identifier; and

(4)

the telephone number of the applicant, his legal representative or attorney, as well as the address for service.

(2) The application shall be in writing and signed by the applicant or the person drawing up the application. The necessary documents shall be attached to the application. The applicant may present his application orally, if the matter appears clearly from the documents and if not otherwise provided below.

(3) The tax payable when presenting an application for registration is governed by the Act on the Transfer-of-Assets Tax (931/1996) and, as regards mortgages, by the Stamp Duty Act (662/1943). (933/1996)

Section 2 — *Delivery of Application*

(1) The application shall be presented to the register authority or delivered by post or courier.

(2) If the application has been delivered to a register authority which is not competent in the matter, the application shall be forwarded to the competent authority. The applicant shall be notified of the same.

Section 3 — *Lis Pendens*

(1) A registration becomes pending when the application has been presented or delivered to the competent register authority.

(2) The application shall be accepted, even if unaccompanied by a tax receipt. (933/1996)

(3) An entry on the pending registration shall be made in the title and mortgage register without delay.

Section 4 — *Official Information* The register authority shall on its own initiative obtain the necessary information on circumstances relevant in the consideration of the matter as is available from the title and mortgage register and the other registers accessible to the register authority.

Section 5 — *Supplementing the Application*

(1) If the application is incomplete, the applicant shall be exhorted to supplement his application. The applicant shall be informed as to how his application is incomplete, the deadline for supplements and the consequences of a failure to heed the exhortation. The exhortation shall not be given if it is evident that no registration can be made on the basis of the application. Where necessary, another exhortation may be given.

(2) An exhortation to supplement the application shall be given also if it is unaccompanied by a tax receipt or an account on the circumstances affecting the assessment of the tax, or if the tax paid does not correspond to the information contained in the application. (933/1996)

(3) If the applicant fails to heed the exhortation, the application shall be dismissed.

Section 6 — *Hearings*

(1) In order to clarify the circumstances pertaining to the registrable right, the register authority may reserve the applicant or another person the opportunity to submit a written statement or invite him to be heard, at a set time, before the court in person or represented by an attorney.

(2) If it is claimed that there is a right of a third party precluding the registration and the claim is reasonably substantiated, or the right of the applicant is otherwise subject to dispute, the register authority shall exhort the person with the burden of proof to have the matter resolved in a trial within a set time limit. The claimant shall be exhorted under threat of having the registration made regardless and the applicant under threat of dismissal of the application.

Section 7 — *Consent*

(1) A consent required for registration shall be given in writing or orally to the register authority.

(2) A lienholder giving his consent to registration shall present the mortgage instrument. If the consenting party has been entered in the title and mortgage register as the holder of the mortgage instrument, said instrument need not be presented unless the register authority decides otherwise.

Section 8 — *Applications in Abeyance*

(1) If the application is left in abeyance, the applicant shall be exhorted to show, within a set time limit, whether a barrier for registration still exists. The exhortation shall not be given if the applicant has requested a postponement or if this is otherwise unnecessary with regard to the consideration of the matter. The provisions in section 5 apply to the exhortation and the consequences of failure to heed it.

(2) The register authority may on its own initiative take an application in abeyance under consideration. However, the application shall not be rejected before the applicant has been reserved an opportunity to be heard.

Section 9 — *Decision and Instrument*

(1) A registration decision shall be made without delay and in accordance with the application, unless there is a barrier for the same. A legal circumstance arising after the application has become pending shall not preclude registration.

(2) The registration decision shall be made by entering it into the title and mortgage register. The content of the decision is indicated by the register. If the matter is not decided in accordance with the application, the applicant shall, in addition, be issued a separate copy of the decision. A copy of the decision shall be issued also if the application is left in abeyance or another corresponding procedural decision is made.

(3) A certificate on the register entry or a separate decision issued to the applicant shall be the final instrument in the matter.

Section 10 — *Notification of Decision*

(1) If the matter has not been decided in accordance with the application and the applicant is not present at the conclusion of the consideration, or the decision is not delivered to him by post, the date of the decision shall without delay be notified to the applicant. The same applies to other interested parties who have been heard, unless the matter is decided in accordance with their demands.

(2) The decision shall be available at the register authority office when the date of the decision is to be notified to the parties.

Section 11 — *Dossier* The documents compiled during the consideration of a registration shall be collected into a dossier. If the grounds for the decision are not sufficiently clear in the copy of the instrument or the other materials in the dossier, also the justification of the decision shall be entered into the dossier.

Section 12 — *Notifications*

(1) The provisions on the application for registration apply, where appropriate, to the notifications delivered to the register authority and their consideration.

(2) Provisions on the delivery of notifications to the title and mortgage register as a computerized file transfer are issued by Decree.

Section 13 — *Pending Trials* A court shall notify the register authority on any pending trial concerning the cancellation or invalidity of an acquisition of real estate or a conflict of rights to the real estate, as well as on its decision and whether the decision has become final. The same applies to an action for the deletion of a register entry or its correction.

Section 14 — *Supplementary Provisions*

(1) Unless otherwise provided in this Code, the provisions of the Code of Judicial Procedure on the consideration of civil cases in a District Court apply, where appropriate, to the consideration of registrations.

(2) If the register authority has invited someone else than the applicant to be heard, the party heard shall have the right to due compensation from State funds, as provided in the Act on Compensation to Witnesses from State Funds (666/1972). The register authority may obligate the applicant to reimburse the State for the compensation paid, if the hearing has been necessary in order to clarify an issue that should have been clarified by the applicant.

CHAPTER 7 — TITLE AND MORTGAGE REGISTER

Section 1 — *Information Entered into the Title and Mortgage Register*

(1) The applications for registration, information on their consideration and the registration decisions shall be entered into the title and mortgage register.

(2) In addition, information on execution, precautionary measures and the bankruptcy of the titleholder of the real estate, as well as other information on rights to and encumbrances over the real estate, if they by virtue of this Code or another Act or Decree are to be notified to the register authority, shall be entered into the title and mortgage register when notified.

Section 2 — *Access to Register*

(1) The information in the title and mortgage register shall be subject to public access. The register authorities shall issue certificates from the register upon request.

(2) The Ministry of Justice may provide access to information as a mass delivery referred to in the Personal Data File Act (471/1987), where the party to whom the information is provided has the right to enter it into a personal data file. Provisions are issued by Decree on the delivery of information by computerized file transfer for the purposes of real estate agency, credit extension or other comparable activities.

(3) Provisions on the format of the certificates issued from the title and mortgage register and on their issuance by others than the register authorities are issued by Decree. Separate provisions are enacted on the charges collected for the certificates.

Section 3 — *Publicity of Registrations* An entry in the title and mortgage register shall be deemed public knowledge as from the first weekday after the date of entry. After that time no protection shall be provided by good faith, except in cases referred to in chapter 17, section 10.

Section 4 — *Compensation for Damage Caused by Technical Errors*

(1) A person who has suffered damage as a result of an evident misprint or miscalculation, error caused by a technical fault or another comparable error or defect in the title and mortgage register or an instrument or certificate issued from it shall have the right to due compensation from State funds.

(2) If the damage is caused by an error in the information entered into the title and mortgage register, compensation shall not be covered by this Code. The keeper of the land register shall be liable for compensation for damage caused by errors in the contents of that register. If another authority than the register authority has issued an erroneous or incomplete certificate from the title and mortgage register and the error or incompleteness is not a result of an error in the contents of the register, the compensation shall be paid from the funds of the relevant public authority.

(3) The provisions in chapter 13, sections 6–8 apply, where appropriate, to the compensation for damage.

Section 5 — *Acquisition Information*

(1) Information on the conveyance of real estate and other acquisitions may be entered into the title and mortgage register before an application for the registration of title is made.

(2) No claims shall be made against the register keeper on the basis of an error in or the incompleteness of the acquisition information.

Section 6 — *Archiving* The register authority may send the information on a special right or restriction that apparently has lapsed, on an application that has been rejected or dismissed and on other entries that apparently no longer have an effect, to be archived.

Section 7 — *Register Keeping* The Act on the Title and Mortgage Register (353/1987) contains provisions on the establishment, opening and keeping of the title and mortgage register.

CHAPTER 8 — CORRECTION OF ERRORS

Section 1 — *Correction of Material Errors*

(1) If the decision of the register authority is based on evidently erroneous or incomplete information or evidently mistaken application of the law, the register authority may erase its erroneous decision and decide the matter anew.

(2) A material error may be corrected only if all parties whose right is affected by the correction have been heard and all parties whose right decreases due to the correction have given their consent to it.

Section 2 — *Correction of Technical Errors*

(1) If there is an evident misprint or miscalculation, error caused by a technical fault or another comparable error or defect in the title and mortgage register, the register authority shall make the necessary corrections to the entries.

(2) Before the correction those interested parties who are known to the register authority and who may suffer damage from the correction shall be reserved an opportunity to be heard.

Section 3 — *Correction Procedure*

(1) The provisions in chapter 6, section 9 apply, where appropriate, to the correction of errors. If a correction matter is not decided at once, an entry on its pending status shall be made in the register.

(2) If an appeal has been lodged against a registration decision, the pending status of the correction matter shall be notified to the appellate court and the decision in the matter delivered to it.

(3) A decision rejecting an application for the correction of an error shall not be subject to appeal.

Section 4 — *Correction Markings in Instruments and Certificates*

(1) The correction of an error shall as soon as possible be marked to an instrument issued prior to it or, alternatively, a new instrument shall be issued. Furthermore, the register authority shall try and mark the corrections in an erroneous certificate issued from the register, or issue a new certificate.

(2) An erroneous instrument or certificate shall be presented, upon exhortation, to the register authority for correction. The register authority may obligate, under threat of a fine, the possessor of the document to fulfill his duty to present it. If the party concerned fails to fulfill his duty, the register authority may enforce the fine.

CHAPTER 9 — REGISTRATION APPEALS

Section 1 — *Appeal*

(1) A final registration decision made by the register authority shall be subject to appeal before a Court of Appeal.

(2) A decision transferring the application to another register authority shall not be subject to appeal.

Section 2 — *Appeal Instructions* When a registration matter has not been decided in accordance with the application or the demand of another party, written appeal instructions shall be attached to the instrument.

Section 3 — *Appeal Deadline* The deadline for appeal shall be 30 days from the decision of the matter. The appealing party shall deliver his appeal documents to the relevant register authority on the day of the deadline at the latest, under threat of forfeiting his right of action.

Section 4 — *Application of Code of Judicial Procedure*

(1) The provisions in chapter 25 of the Code of Judicial Procedure apply, in addition to the provisions of this Code, to an appeal against the decision of a registration authority. However, the intent to appeal need not be announced.

(2) The decision of a Court of Appeal in a registration matter shall be subject to appeal before the Supreme Court, as provided in chapter 30 of the Code of Judicial Procedure.

Section 5 — *Notification of Appellate Court Decision and Return of Matter*

(1) The appellate court shall without delay notify the register authority of its decision and whether the decision has become final.

(2) The register authority shall on its own initiative reconsider a matter returned by the appellate court, make a new decision, if necessary, and make the appropriate entries in the title and mortgage register.

PART III — REGISTRATION OF TITLES AND SPECIAL RIGHTS

CHAPTER 10 — GENERAL PROVISIONS ON REGISTRATION OF TITLES AND SPECIAL RIGHTS TO REAL ESTATE

Section 1 — *Registration of Title*

(1) The acquisition of title to real estate shall be registered.

(2) The provisions on the registration of title apply also to the registration of the acquisition of a share and a parcel of real estate, a common, a parcel and a share of a common.

Section 2 — *Registration of Special Right*

(1) A contractual right to use real estate owned by another person shall be registered as a special right.

(2) Registration may be used also for the determination of whether business property located on the real estate is affixed to the real estate.

CHAPTER 11 — OBLIGATION TO REGISTER TITLE

Section 1 — *General Obligation to Register Title*

(1) Everyone shall apply for the registration of title after having acquired real estate or a share or parcel thereof.

(2) Registration of title shall be applied for within six months of the drawing up of the deed of conveyance or another document on which the acquisition is based, unless otherwise provided below.

Section 2 — *Start of Registration Period for Acquisitions under Family and Inheritance Law*

(1) If title to real estate has been acquired by inheritance, the registration period shall begin when the estate distribution has become final. If no estate distribution is necessary for the acquisition of title, the registration period shall begin at the end of the period reserved for an estate inventory or, if a distribution of matrimonial assets is necessary for the separation of the real estate, when that distribution has become final.

(2) The registration period for an acquisition based on a will shall begin when the will becomes final or when the estate distribution or distribution of matrimonial assets becomes final, should one or the other be necessary for the separation of the bequeathed real estate.

(3) The registration period for an acquisition based on the distribution of matrimonial assets shall begin when the distribution has become final.

Section 3 — *Start of Registration Period for Acquisitions Based on Official Decisions*

(1) If the acquisition is based on an official real estate formation measure, the registration period shall begin when the measure has been entered into the land register. If the real estate has not previously been entered into the land register, the registration period shall begin at the time of first entry. The registration period for an acquisition based on the decision of an authority not involved with the formation of real estate shall begin when the decision becomes final.

(2) The period for the registration of title to real estate sold by enforced auction shall begin when the deed of sale is handed over to the buyer.

Section 4 — *Real Estate Not Subject to Obligation to Register Title* Title to State forests, expropriated units, lands separated for public use, accretions and relictions, common waters and commons shall not be registered. If such real estate or a share or parcel thereof is conveyed, the acquisition shall be subject to the obligation to register title.

Section 5 — *Threat of Fine* If the titleholder of a real estate has not applied for the registration of his title within the period provided in sections 1–3, the register authority may obligate him to do so within a set time limit under threat of a fine. If he fails to do so within the time limit, the register authority may enforce the fine.

Section 6 — *Pro Forma Registration of Title*

(1) The shareholders of an undistributed decedent's estate may apply jointly for a pro forma registration of title to real estate belonging to the decedent's estate.

(2) A titleholder of real estate, whose title has already once been registered, may apply for a pro forma registration of title for the purpose of clarifying his legal status.

Section 7 — *Registration of Title on Official Initiative*

(1) The register authority shall on its own initiative amend the registration of title to a share or parcel of real estate to cover the real estate formed from it, after the newly formed real estate has been entered into the land register. The person whose title to

the share or parcel has last been registered shall be deemed titleholder of the newly formed real estate.

(2) The register authority may on its own initiative amend the registration of title to real estate to cover also real estates formed from it by parcelling, partitioning or surveying of an urban plot.

(3) The register authority shall on the notification of a court enter as the new titleholder of real estate the person to whom the real estate belongs according to a final judgment.

CHAPTER 12 — PROCEDURE

Section 1 — *Proof*

(1) The applicant for registration of title shall present proof of the legality of his acquisition. The document on which the acquisition is based shall be attached to the application in the original or as a copy authenticated by a notary or a register authority.

(2) If the title of the previous titleholder has not been registered, the proof that would have been required for the registration of his acquisition shall be presented at the same time. If the acquisition of the previous titleholder was not subject to the obligation to register title, the applicant shall present the other required proof of the title of the previous titleholder. Proof of the title of the previous titleholder shall not be required if the real estate has been sold by enforced auction or acquired through an official real estate formation measure.

Section 2 — *Leaving Application to Register Title in Abeyance*

(1) The application shall be left in abeyance, if it otherwise could be granted, but:

(1) the acquisition of real estate or its permanence is according to the contract or otherwise conditional;

(2) the contract or official measure on which the acquisition is based has not become final or the deadline for the use of the right of municipal pre-emption has not passed;

(3) the consent or decision of a third party, competent body of a corporation, court or other authority is required for the acquisition of real estate;

(4) the real estate has been acquired in the name of a company to be established;

(5) an entry on execution or precautionary measures directed at the real estate has been made in the title and mortgage register prior to the conveyance of the real estate;

(6) the register authority has directed a disputed issue to be resolved in a trial or the applicant has been granted a public notice in order to obtain the registration of title; or

(7) an action relating to the permanence of the acquisition or a better right to the real estate is pending.

(2) If the application has been left in abeyance because of a clause in the conveyance contract and no proof on the return of the title to the conveyor has been presented within the time limit provided for the bringing of an action, the application shall be granted. If no proof has been presented of a company to be established having become responsible for the conveyance of real estate within two years of the conclusion of the contract of conveyance, the person concluding the contract in the name of the company shall be registered as the titleholder.

Section 3 — *Registration of Title by Public Notice*

(1) The applicant shall be granted a public notice in order to obtain the registration of title, if:

(1) the applicant does not present an acquisition document or an authentic copy thereof, as provided in section 1, but he presents likely grounds for the legality of the acquisition; or

(2) the applicant shows that he or the previous titleholders have possessed the real estate as titleholders for the preceding ten years and there is no reason to believe that another person has a better right to the real estate.

(2) The register authority shall issue a public notice, as provided in chapter 11, section 10 of the Code of Judicial Procedure, and exhort those persons who deem themselves to have a better right than the applicant to the real estate, to make their claim before the register authority within six months of the publication of the public notice in the *Official Gazette*. In addition, the public notice shall be notified to those known persons whose right may be affected by the registration of title.

(3) If no claim has been made or action brought within the set time limit, the application may be granted.

Section 4 — *Rejection of Application to Register Title* The application shall be rejected, if:

(1) no acquisition document or an authentic copy thereof, as provided in section 1, has been presented;

(2) the acquisition document has not been drawn up as provided by law;

(3) no proof of the title of the conveyor or another previous titleholder of the real estate has been presented;

(4) the required consent or decision of a third party, competent body of a corporation, court or other authority has not been obtained for the applicant's acquisition;

(5) title to the real estate is returned to the conveyor because of a cancellation or suspension clause in the conveyance contract and a judgment or agreement to this effect is presented;

(6) the real estate belongs to a bankruptcy estate and this has been entered in the title and mortgage register prior to the acquisition; or

(7) the applicant's acquisition is otherwise not valid or will evidently not be permanent.

Section 5 — *Entry on Restriction of Possession* If a usufruct based on law or a will or a condition attached to the applicant's acquisition restricts the right of the applicant to convey the real estate, or to attach special rights to or raise liens over it, the restriction of possession shall be entered into the title and mortgage register at the same time as the decision in the registration matter is made or otherwise upon request.

Section 6 — *Delivery of Notifications* The register authority shall notify the registration of title to a parcel of real estate to the surveying office or surveyor in whose jurisdiction the parcel is located.

CHAPTER 13 — LEGAL EFFECTS OF REGISTRATION OF TITLE

Section 1 — *Defect of Form* No claim regarding a defect of form in the deed of acquisition shall be made after a registration of title based on it has been completed or the application for one has been left in abeyance.

Section 2 — *Disputed Title* The registration of title shall not preclude the consideration of a dispute over title to real estate or the validity of an acquisition in a trial or by official real estate formation measure, as separately provided.

Section 3 — *Protection in Cases of Double Conveyance*

(1) If the same real estate has been conveyed to two persons, the later conveyance shall take precedence, if registration of title to it is first applied for and the conveyee, at the time of acquisition, did not know nor should have known of the previous conveyance. If registrations of title to several acquisitions are applied for on the same day, the earliest conveyance shall take precedence.

(2) If the application is rejected or if a registered acquisition is invalidated or if the conveyee otherwise loses his right based on the acquisition, the precedence shall lapse.

(3) The provisions in paragraphs (1) and (2) apply, where appropriate, to the effects of registration on the precedence order of a conveyance of real estate and a special right attached to the real estate. The conveyance or special right takes precedence under the conditions laid down above also in relation to a previous acquisition of real estate not based on a conveyance.

Section 4 — *Protection against Rightful Titleholder*

(1) An acquisition of real estate based on a conveyance shall be permanent even if the conveyor was not the rightful titleholder of the real estate due to a defect in his acquisition or that of a previous titleholder, if the title of the conveyor was registered at the time of acquisition and the conveyee, at that time, did not know nor should have known that the conveyor was not the rightful titleholder.

(2) A special right to or lien over real estate shall be binding even if the person effecting one was not the rightful titleholder of the real estate, if his title was registered at the time of acquisition and the person holding the lien or special right, at that time, did not know nor should have known that he was not the rightful titleholder.

(3) The provisions in paragraphs (1) and (2) apply, where appropriate, if the acquisition of the conveyor or the other person is invalid regarding third parties. The provisions in this section on the registration of title apply also to a pending application on the basis of which a registration of title later takes place.

Section 5 — *Exceptions to Protection of Conveyees* The conveyee or person holding a title or special right shall not receive the protection referred to in section 4, if:

(1) the deed of title or other acquisition document of the rightful titleholder or the power of attorney or other competence document of his representative has been forged;

(2) the conveyance of the rightful titleholder is invalid because he has been coerced into it in a manner referred to in section 28 of the Contracts Act; or

(3) the conveyor of the real estate or the establisher of a lien over or special right to it has been registered as titleholder by mistake or if the entry in the register is not based on a decision of the register authority.

Section 6 — *State's Liability for Compensation*

(1) A person in relation to whom an acquisition of real estate or a lien or special right remains valid by virtue of section 4 shall have the right to due compensation from State funds.

(2) A conveyee or a person holding the lien or special right who loses his right to the real estate by virtue of section 5 shall have the right to due compensation from State funds.

(3) If a person suffering damage has without a valid reason failed to apply for the registration of his right or to invoke his good faith or another circumstance affecting the permanence of his right, or otherwise contributed to the damage, the compensation may be reasonably adjusted.

Section 7 — *State's Right of Recourse*

(1) The right to compensation of a person receiving compensation by virtue of section 6 shall be transferred to the State to the amount of compensation paid.

(2) The right to compensation referred to in paragraph (1) shall be transferred on the day when the State has assumed the liability or a court judgment to this effect has become final. The State may bring its claim for recourse in the same trial where compensation is sought from it.

Section 8 — *Procedural Provisions*

(1) The Ministry of Justice shall grant and pay the compensation and represent the State in cases relating to compensation or recourse.

(2) The court shall on its own initiative notify the State when a case relating to title to real estate has become pending and may result in the State being held liable for compensation by virtue of section 6.

(3) An action for compensation against the State shall be brought within two years from the date when the court decision on the title to real estate has become final.

The action shall be considered in the court in whose jurisdiction the real estate is located.

Section 9 — *Protection in Acquisitions Not by Conveyance*

(1) A person who has acquired real estate by inheritance, will, distribution of matrimonial assets or otherwise not by conveyance shall not enjoy the protection of good faith provided in sections 3 and 4 against an earlier conveyee, holder of a special right or the rightful titleholder.

(2) Chapter 5, section 50 of the Enforcement Act contains provisions on the permanence of an acquisition by enforced auction.

Section 10 — *Protection of Enjoyment*

(1) A person whose title to real estate has been registered and who thereafter has possessed the real estate for ten years may keep the real estate, if he at the time of acquisition did not know nor should have known that the real estate had been taken from the rightful titleholder. If no action for a better right to the real estate is brought during this time, the rightful titleholder shall forfeit his right to demand the return of the real estate.

(2) If the real estate has during the time referred in paragraph (1) been conveyed to another person, this person may invoke the registration of the title and the possession of the conveyor and the good faith of himself or one of the previous titleholders at the time of acquisition.

Section 11 — *Answerability*

(1) An action for a better right to real estate may be brought against the person whose title to it has been registered. If he has conveyed the real estate before the action has become pending, also the conveyee shall be summoned to answer in the trial.

(2) The provision in paragraph (1) applies, where appropriate, to claims for payment off the real estate on the basis of a lien or directly by virtue of law.

CHAPTER 14 — REGISTRATION OF SPECIAL RIGHTS

Section 1 — *Registrable Special Rights*

(1) The following special rights, based on a contract or another transaction, over the real estate of another may be registered:

(1) a lease or other usufruct;

(2) a right to a pension off the real estate;

(3) a right to take timber; and

(4) a right to extract land or mineral resources or another comparable right of extraction.

(2) A special right shall not be registered if it is permanent, if it is for the benefit of a given real estate or area or if it has been established by an official real estate formation measure or otherwise by a decision of the authorities. A right to take timber shall be registered to remain valid

for at most five years and an extraction right for at most 50 years from the attachment of the right; a usufruct shall be registered for at most the statutory maximum period.

Section 2 — *Obligation to Register*

(1) The holder of a lease or another usufruct on the real estate of another shall apply for the registration of his right, if the usufruct is transferable to a third party without hearing the titleholder or if there are buildings or other constructions belonging to the usufructuary on the real estate or it has been agreed that they may be built. The registration shall be applied for when the usufruct has been established or when the usufructuary has received the usufruct by conveyance or other acquisition.

(2) The provisions in chapter 11, sections 1–6 apply to the application deadline and a threat of a fine.

Section 3 — *Agreement of Joint Possession*

An agreement between the joint titleholders of a real estate on the possession of the

real estate may be registered.

Section 4 — *Registration of Rights Relating to Buildings or Constructions*

(1) A right belonging to someone else than the titleholder and relating to a building, construction, machine or facility used in business and contributing to the purpose of the real estate may be registered, if:

(1) the object has been built or brought on the real estate subject to a reservation or repossession clause or on the basis of a lease contract or another comparable agreement; or

(2) the object has been transferred to the usufructuary of the real estate as a part of the usufruct.

(2) A right subject to a reservation or repossession clause shall be registered to be in force for at most five years from the conclusion of the agreement.

Section 5 — *Delimitation of Components and Accessories* For the purpose of delimiting the components and accessories of real estate, the declaration of the titleholder may be registered to the effect that a building or facility used in business, owned or later obtained by him, and permanently located on the real estate, said object to be identified in the declaration or otherwise defined as to its characteristics,

(1) does not belong to the real estate, even if it otherwise would be deemed a component or an accessory; or

(2) belongs to the real estate, even if it otherwise would not be deemed a component or an accessory.

Section 6 — *Object of Registration*

(1) The registration may concern:

(1) a real estate or a common entered into the land register;

(2) a parcel, the title to which has been registered; or

(3) a registered usufruct referred to above in section 2.

(2) The provisions in this chapter on real estate, a titleholder and the registration of title apply, where appropriate, also to other subjects of registration, as well as the attacher of a right and its registration. If a special right is attached to a real estate not subject to registration, other proof than a registration shall be presented of the validity of the title to it.

Section 7 — *Legal Effects of Registration of Special Rights*

(1) The registration of a special right shall have the legal effects provided in chapter 13, sections 1–3 for a registration of title.

(2) If several registrable special rights have been attached to a real estate and they cannot be simultaneously fulfilled, the right first attached shall prevail, unless otherwise follows from chapter 13, section 3.

(3) The provisions in chapter 4, sections 4–9 and 11 on the legal effects of the registration of title apply also to the legal effects of a registration of a usufruct referred to in section 2.

Section 8 — *Precedence*

(1) The legal effects of the registration of a special right begin on the day when the registration application has become pending. A registration earlier applied for shall take precedence in relation to a registration or mortgage later applied for. A special right shall take precedence to a lien, based on a mortgage, applied for on the same day.

(2) Only the precedent right shall be registered under section 3, section 4(1)(2), or section 5 above; the precedence shall not be altered subsequently so that another registration referred to in this paragraph is made to prevail over it.

(3) The provisions in chapter 18, section 1 apply to the alteration of precedence.

Section 9 — *Registration Procedure*

(1) Registration may be applied for by the holder of the registrable right and by the titleholder of the real estate.

(2) The applicant shall present the contract or other document relating to the attachment or transfer of the registrable right.

Section 10 — *Consent*

(1) The consent of the titleholder shall be a prerequisite for the registration referred to above in section 4.

(2) The consent of all lienholders over the real estate to the registration and the alteration of precedence shall be a prerequisite to a registration referred to in section 3, section 4(1)(2), or

section 5 above. However, no consent shall be required for a registration referred to in section 3, if the alteration has only a minor effect.

(3) If the property of the titleholder is under a business mortgage, the registration referred to in section 5(2) may be made only if all the holders of the business mortgage consent to the same.

Section 11 — *Leaving Application to Register in Abeyance* The application shall be left in abeyance, if it otherwise could be granted, but:

(1) the title of the attacher of the right to the real estate has not been registered;

(2) the attachment of the right is according to a contract or otherwise conditional, or it has not yet become final;

(3) the consent or decision of a third party, competent body of a corporation, court or other authority is required for the attachment of the right;

(4) an entry on execution or precautionary measures directed at the real estate has been made in the title and mortgage register prior to the establishment of the right; or

(5) the register authority has directed a disputed issue to be resolved in a trial or an action relating to the permanence of the right or a better right to the real estate is pending.

Section 12 — *Rejection of an Application to Register* The application shall be rejected, if:

(1) the right is not registrable;

(2) the attachment or transfer document has not been presented or it has not been drawn up as provided by law;

(3) no proof of the title of the attacher has been presented;

(4) the required consent or decision of a third party, competent body of a corporation, court or other authority has not been obtained for the attachment of the right;

(5) the real estate belongs to a bankruptcy estate and this has been entered in the title and mortgage register prior to the attachment of the right;

(6) an entry on execution or precautionary measures directed at the real estate has been made in the title and mortgage register before the application referred to in section 4 or 5 has become pending;

(7) someone else than the attacher has applied for the registration of his title to the real estate on the basis of an acquisition before the registration of the special right has been applied for, and he does not consent to the registration; or

(8) the registrable right is otherwise not valid or will evidently not be permanent.

Section 13 — *Registration of Alteration, Transfer and Lapse of Rights*

(1) If a special right has been registered, its alteration, transfer and lapse may be registered applying, where appropriate, the provisions on the registration of special rights.

(2) The legal effects of registration apply to an alteration of a special right by agreement or other transaction only if it has been registered.

Section 14 — *Prerequisites for Alteration of Registration*

(1) If it has been agreed that a registered special right is to be altered and if a mortgage or the registration of another special right has been applied for the real estate after

the registration, the alteration may be registered if those rightholders whose right decreases as a result of the alteration consent to the same. However, no consent shall be required if the alteration has only a minor effect.

(2) The provisions in paragraph (1) apply also to the alteration of a registered right that is subject to a mortgage or to another special right.

Section 15 — *Deletion of Registration of Special Rights*

(1) The registration of a special right may be deleted on the request of the titleholder or, if the agreed time of validity of the registered right has expired, on the initiative of the register authority. However, the registration shall not be deleted, if the time of validity of the right has been extended or it has been immediately given back to the same rightholder, and proof of the same is presented during the time of validity of the right.

(2) The registration of a right to a pension off the real estate may be deleted on the initiative of the register authority after six months from the death of the rightholder, unless his successors have during this time declared that they wish to retain the registration.

(3) The registration referred to in section 5 above may be deleted on the notification of the titleholder, if those mortgage or business mortgage holders, whose status is diminished, consent to the same.

Section 16 — *Effect of Liens on Deletion of Registration*

(1) The registration of a special right shall not be deleted, even if it has lapsed before the full term due to termination, agreement or another reason, before the mortgages and registrations of special rights to it have been cancelled.

(2) If the special right is subject to mortgages, the application for the deletion of the registration shall be left in abeyance and notified to the lienholder. In the decision the lienholder shall be exhorted to bring an action for the collection of the debt within three months of the notification. If the creditor fails to seek payment from the real estate in the set time limit and notify the same to the register authority, the mortgage shall be cancelled and the registration of the special right may be deleted.

(3) A lienholder who has sought payment shall be liable to the lessor for the lease payments becoming due after the notification of the decision referred to in paragraph (2) until the transfer of the lease.

PART IV — REAL ESTATE LIENS

CHAPTER 15 — GENERAL PROVISIONS ON REAL ESTATE LIENS

Section 1 — *Applicability*

(1) A real estate lien may be raised over real estate, a share or parcel of real estate, a lease and another usufruct on the real estate of another, as provided in this Code.

(2) The provisions on real estate mortgages and liens apply also to the mortgages and liens over shares and parcels of real estate.

Section 2 — *Raising Liens*

(1) A real estate lien shall be raised by creating a mortgage over the real estate or the other property and handing the mortgage instrument over to the creditor as security for a debt.

(2) A real estate lien as security for the payment of a debt or fee under public law shall be raised by entering it into the title and mortgage register.

Chapter 16 — **Mortgage**

Section 1 — *Applicability*

(1) A mortgage may be created over real estate, a share in jointly held real estate and a parcel not belonging to the titleholder of the real estate. The possibility of the registration of title to the property shall be a prerequisite for a mortgage.

(2) An urban plot subject to a registered lease shall not be mortgaged.

Section 2 — *Joint Mortgage*

(1) A joint mortgage over two or more real estates may be created only if:

(1) they belong to the same titleholder or the same titleholders in equal shares;

(2) they are located in the jurisdiction of the same register authority; and

(3) they are not subject to mortgages or they are subject only to mortgages of the same amount and seniority.

(2) No separate mortgages shall be created over real estates subject to a joint mortgage as long as they belong to the same titleholder.

(3) The joint mortgage may be created over the entire real estate even if it is held by shares, unless the agreement on joint possession has been registered and unless a separate mortgage has already been created over a share of the real estate.

Section 3 — *Applicant*

(1) The titleholder who has last applied for the registration of his title may apply for a mortgage over the real estate.

(2) If the title of the applicant has not been registered, the mortgage shall be created only if his registration application has been left in abeyance because of a cancellation or suspension clause or because the real estate has been acquired in the name of a company to be established, and the conveyor of the real estate consents to the mortgage.

Section 4 — *Application*

(1) The application for a mortgage shall be in writing. The application, signed by the applicant, shall indicate the property to be mortgaged and the amount of the mortgage in [FIM]. If the application is for the creation of several mortgages over the same real estate, their order of seniority may be determined in the application.

(2) The application may contain instructions for the register authority as to whom, instead of the applicant, the mortgage instrument is to be handed over. If the recipient of the mortgage instrument has been indicated in the application, the application shall not be altered or withdrawn without his consent.

(3) The titleholder of real estate may appoint an attorney to apply for a mortgage. The titleholder shall sign the power of attorney, which shall indicate also the name of the attorney, the property to be mortgaged and the amount of the mortgage.

Section 5 — *Mortgage Instrument* When the mortgage has been created, the applicant is issued a mortgage instrument as a certificate of the mortgage.

Section 6 — *Leaving Application in Abeyance* The application shall be left in abeyance, if it otherwise could be granted, but:

(1) the consideration of the applicant's registration application is pending and, in a case referred to in section 3(2), the conveyor of the real estate has not consented to the mortgage;

(2) a dispute on title to the real estate is pending in a court; or

(3) an entry on execution or precautionary measures directed at the real estate has been made into the title and mortgage register before the application has become pending.

Section 7 — *Rejection of Application* The application shall be rejected, if:

(1) the applicant is not the titleholder, or his title to the real estate has not been registered and he has not applied for the same;

(2) the application has not been drawn up as required by law;

(3) no mortgage can be created over the property to which the application relates;

(4) the real estate belongs to a bankruptcy estate and this has been entered in the title and mortgage register before the application;

(5) the real estate cannot, due to a restriction of possession which has been entered into the title and mortgage register, be subject to a mortgage; or

(6) the applied mortgage cannot be created for another reason.

Section 8 — *Seniority and Validity of Mortgages*

(1) The legal effects of a mortgage that has been created begin on the day when the application has become pending.

(2) A mortgage earlier applied for shall be senior to one later applied for. Mortgages applied for on the same day shall have equal seniority, unless otherwise declared, on the basis of the application, when the mortgages are created.

(3) A mortgage shall remain valid until it is cancelled. A mortgage decision may be repealed or the mortgage annulled only if the acquisition of the applicant is not permanent by virtue of chapter 13, section 5 or if the mortgage is based on a forged document or it has otherwise been obtained under circumstances referred to in the said section.

Section 9 — *Entry on Holder of Mortgage Instrument*

(1) Upon notification, an entry shall be made into the title and mortgage register on the person holding the mortgage instrument. Where necessary, the register authority may require the holder to present the mortgage instrument.

(2) The register authority shall notify the person who was previously entered as the holder of the mortgage instrument of an entry on a new holder, unless the instrument is presented to the authority at the notification of the new holder.

(3) The register authority shall delete an entry on the holder of the mortgage instrument upon the notification of the person so entered.

Section 10 — *Effects of Real Estate Formation on Mortgages*

(1) A mortgage created over a share or parcel of real estate shall after real estate formation be over the real estate that is formed from the share or parcel. If a mortgaged share is included in a formed real estate, the mortgage shall be over the part of the real estate belonging to the shareholder.

(2)

A mortgage over real estate shall completely cover the real estates formed from it by parcelling, partitioning or surveying of an urban plot. However, the mortgage shall not cover a parcel or a real estate formed from a parcel, where the registration of title to it has been applied for before the mortgage application.

(3) Separate provisions are enacted on the effects on mortgages of a partitioning where a real estate is formed from parts of a number of real estates or where a parcel is moved from one real estate to another, as well as expropriation and other real estate formation measures.

CHAPTER 17 — REAL ESTATE LIENS

Section 1 — *Right to Raise Liens*

(1) The titleholder shall have the right to raise liens over the real estate.

(2) The titleholder may appoint an attorney to raise a lien. The titleholder shall sign the power of attorney, which shall indicate the name of the attorney and the mortgage instrument concerned.

Section 2 — *Raising Liens*

(1) A lien over real estate shall be raised by handing the mortgage document over to the creditor as security for a debt.

(2) If the mortgage instrument has been handed over as security of an eventual debt, the lien shall be raised when the debt becomes active.

(3) If the mortgage instrument has been handed over to a third party, the lien or second lien shall be raised by the titleholder notifying the same to the third party, or by the lienholder presenting the titleholder's written certificate of the same to the third party. If instructions have been given in the mortgage application to the effect that the mortgage instrument is to be handed over to a named creditor as security for a debt, the lien shall be raised by creating the mortgage.

Section 3 — *Lien Commitment*

(1) The provisions in chapter 10, sections 14 and 15 of the Commercial Code apply to lien commitments.

(2) If a lien commitment has been made, the creditor shall have the right to demand the titleholder to hand over the mortgage instrument. If the real estate no longer belongs to the person who made the lien commitment, if the mortgage instrument has been handed over to another creditor or if the person who made the commitment otherwise no longer has the right of decision over it, the creditor shall have the right to due compensation.

Section 4 — *Preclusion of Right to Raise Liens*

(1) If a real estate subject to a joint mortgage or a parcel of a mortgaged real estate is conveyed to another person, the mortgage instrument based on the earlier mortgage may be handed over as security of a new debt only if the mortgage has been lifted from the properties owned by other persons than the one raising the lien.

(2) Without prejudice to paragraph (1), the titleholder may hand over a mortgage instrument based on the mortgage of the entire real estate before the application is made for the registration of title on the acquisition of a parcel from that real estate, but in such cases the lien is backed only by the part owned by the titleholder.

Section 5 — *Significance of Liens*

(1) The creditor shall have the right to receive payment of a debt backed by a lien when the assets from the real estate are being distributed because of execution or redemption, or

otherwise by the authorities. The lien gives the debt precedence in accordance with the seniority of the mortgage, at most to the amount indicated in the mortgage instrument.

(2) The creditor shall have the right to seek payment of the debt from the mortgaged real estate regardless of a transfer of title. The creditor may convey the mortgage instrument only if he at the same time transfers the debt which is backed by the lien.

(3) A mortgage instrument shall not be taken in execution.

Section 6 — *Effects on Liens of Cancellation of Mortgages and Extinguishment of Debts*

(1) The mortgage instrument shall be void and the lien lapse, if the mortgage is cancelled or lifted. If the mortgage is altered as to its amount or the property subject to it or otherwise, the lien shall correspond to the altered mortgage.

(2) The creditor shall have the right to payment from the mortgaged real estate even if the debt has been extinguished due to the statute of limitations, non-declaration in bankruptcy proceedings or non-declaration in proceedings for the identification of unknown creditors.

Section 7 — *Decrease in Value of Security*

(1) If the security for the payment of a debt from a mortgaged real estate is put in jeopardy because the value of the real estate decreases to an essential degree due to a fire, natural disaster, activity of the titleholder or another comparable reason, the creditor may seek payment of the debt from the real estate even if the debt has not yet become due and payable.

(2) If the creditor does not bring an action for the payment of the debt within six months of gaining knowledge of a circumstance referred to in paragraph (1), he shall not have the right to payment before the debt becomes due and payable.

Section 8 — *Right to Compensation for Insurance and Redemption*

(1) The creditor shall have the right to receive payment from an insurance compensation before the debt has become due and payable, unless the compensation is by virtue of paragraph (2) to be paid to the titleholder. If the debt backed by the lien is subject to a dispute or it is otherwise unclear as to whom the compensation should be paid, the insurer shall withhold payment.

(2) The titleholder shall have the right to collect the insurance compensation, if he has repaired the damage in a reasonable time or given security for the use of the insurance compensation for the restoration or repair of the damaged real estate. The titleholder shall have the right to collect the compensation also if the amount of the compensation is minor in proportion to the value of the real estate or if it is otherwise evident that the collection of the compensation does not decrease the security of the debt.

(3) Separate provisions are enacted on the right of a lienholder to compensation for redemption and compensation set in real estate formation.

Section 9 — *Order of Liability of Real Estates Subject to Joint Mortgage*

(1) A lien shall be backed in full by all real estates subject to a joint mortgage and all real estates formed from a mortgaged real estate by parcelling, partitioning or surveying of an urban plot.

(2) If the mortgaged real estates belong to different titleholders, the lien shall be primarily backed by the real estate belonging to the debtor and secondarily by the other real estates, to the amount not recoverable from the primarily liable real estate.

(3) If several real estates belonging to different titleholders have been formed from a mortgaged real estate and the debt cannot be fully recovered from the real estate belonging to the debtor, or none of the titleholders is the debtor, the source real estate shall be primarily liable for the lien. The order of liability of partitioned real estates and urban plots shall be determined so that a real estate with a later application for the registration of title shall be liable before one with an earlier application. If no application for the registration of title has been made or if they have been made on the same day, the real estate later conveyed shall be primarily liable. The provisions in this section on a partitioned real estate apply also to a parcel conveyed from a mortgaged real estate.

(4) The Enforcement Act contains provisions on the effect of the order of liability to the order in which the real estates are to be sold and on the right of the titleholder of a real estate secondarily liable to a lien for the security of his claim of recourse.

Section 10 — *Protection in Cases of Conveyance*

(1) A lien over a real estate shall remain valid even if the person raising the lien had before that time conveyed the real estate, if the creditor did not know nor should have known of the conveyance. The same provision applies if title to the real estate has otherwise been transferred to another or if the right of the person raising the lien to hand over a mortgage instrument based on an earlier mortgage has been precluded in accordance with section 4.

(2) The creditor shall not invoke his good faith if the information on the transfer of the title to the real estate has been available in the title and mortgage register for at least one month before the raising of the lien.

(3) If the mortgage instrument has been handed over to the creditor as security for an eventual debt and the person handing it over had at that time the right to raise liens over the real estate, the lien shall remain valid, if the creditor did not know nor should have known of the transfer of title prior to the activation of the debt. The same provision shall apply if the creditor was in good faith when receiving the mortgage instrument, as referred to in paragraphs (1) and (2).

Section 11 — *Protection against Rightful Titleholder and State's Liability for Compensation*

(1) The provisions in chapter 13, sections 4, 5 and 9 apply to the validity of a lien in cases where the person raising it was not the rightful titleholder of the real estate.

(2) The provisions in chapter 16, sections 6–8 apply to the State's liability for compensation. The right of the creditor to compensation for the loss of the lien shall not be precluded by the fact that the mortgage decision has been repealed or annulled.

Section 12 — *Protection against Enforcement*

(1) A lien over real estate shall remain valid even if the titleholder has prior to the raising of the lien lost his right of decision over it because of execution, precautionary measures or bankruptcy, unless the loss of that right was entered into the title and mortgage register at the time of the raising of the lien and the creditor also otherwise did not know nor should have known that the titleholder no longer had the right to raise a lien over the real estate.

(2) If the mortgage instrument has been handed over to the creditor as security for an eventual debt and the person handing it over had at that time the right to raise liens over the real estate, the lien shall remain valid, unless the loss of that right

was entered into the title and mortgage register prior to the activation of the debt and the creditor also otherwise did not know nor should have known that the titleholder no longer had the right to raise a lien over the real estate.

Section 13 — *Cancellation of Conveyance of Real Estate and Its Effect on Liens*

(1) A lien over real estate shall remain valid even if the real estate is returned to the conveyor by virtue of a clause in the deed of conveyance or if the conveyance on the basis of which the person raising the lien acquired title to the real estate is revoked, by an agreement or a court judgment, for breach of contract.

(2) A registration of title based on the conveyance of a share or parcel of real estate shall not be deleted even if the conveyance is cancelled or if the title to the share or parcel is otherwise returned to the titleholder of the real estate before the mortgages and the registrations of special rights have been cancelled. A pro forma registration of title to the entire real estate may be granted in order to clarify the legal status of the titleholder.

CHAPTER 18 — MORTGAGE ALTERATION

Section 1 — *Alteration of Seniority*

(1) The seniority of mortgages may be altered upon the application of the titleholder, if the lienholders and holders of special rights whose right decreases due to the alteration consent to the same. An alteration of seniority may be effected also upon the application of a lienholder, with the consent of the titleholder and the other rightholders.

(2) The seniority of a joint mortgage may be altered only so that the alteration affects all the real estates equally. The seniority shall not be altered so that a mortgage over some of the real estates only becomes more senior than the joint mortgage.

Section 2 — *Mortgage Extension* A mortgage may, upon the application of the titleholder and with the consent of the lienholder, be extended to cover also other real estate belonging to the titleholder, subject to the provisions in chapter 16, section 2.

Section 3 — *Mortgage Merger*

(1) Mortgages of equal seniority, or one immediately after or separated only by the registration of a special right from the other in the order of seniority, may upon the application of the titleholder and with the consent of the lienholder be merged into one mortgage. The merged mortgage shall have the same seniority as the least senior of the original mortgages.

(2) The amount of a merged mortgage may upon the application of the titleholder and with the consent of the lienholder be lowered so that it is less than the sum of the amounts of the original mortgages.

Section 4 — *Mortgage Split*

(1) A mortgage may upon the application of the titleholder and with the consent of the lienholder be split into two or more mortgages so that the sum of the amounts of the split mortgages is at most equal to the amount of the original mortgage.

(2) The split mortgages shall have equal seniority, unless it is otherwise determined upon the request of the applicant.

Section 5 — *Mortgage Cancellation* A mortgage may upon the application of the titleholder and with the consent of the lienholder be cancelled entirely or to a given amount. The cancellation of a joint mortgage may be applied for by any of the titleholders of the real estates subject to the joint mortgage, even without the consent of the other titleholders.

Section 5a — *Conversion of Mortgage into Euros* (964/1998)

(1) On the application of the lienholder, the nominal value of a mortgage may be converted from Finnish marks (FIM) into euros (EUR) as provided in Articles 4 and 5 of the Council Regulation (EC) No 1103/97 on certain provisions relating to the introduction of the euro.

(2) With the conversion, the nominal value of the mortgage may at the request of the lienholder be decreased at most to the closest EUR 100; the consent of the titleholder shall not be needed for such a decrease.

(3) As from 1 January 2002, the register authority shall convert the nominal values of mortgages from FIM into EUR as provided above when the mortgages are otherwise to be altered or when a new instrument is to be issued for an existing mortgage.

Section 6 — *Dissolution of Joint Mortgage*

(1) If real estates belonging to the same titleholder are subject to a joint mortgage, the mortgage may upon his application and with the consent of the lienholder be lifted from a given real estate. The joint mortgage shall not be dissolved, if the real estates remain subject to another joint mortgage.

(2) A joint mortgage over real estates belonging to different titleholders may upon the application of a titleholder and with the consent of the lienholder be lifted from the real estate belonging to that titleholder. It shall also be a prerequisite for such lifting that the titleholders of the remaining real estates and the holders of liens and special rights, of equal or less seniority, over these real estates consent to the same.

(3) However, the consent of the titleholder or the titleholder of a primarily liable real estate shall not be required for the lifting of a mortgage from a parcelled real estate or another real estate that is liable only secondarily or not liable at all, in accordance with chapter 17, section 9(2) or (3). Neither shall the consent of the holder of a right to a primarily liable real estate be required. The lienholder shall not consent to the lifting, if the intention is to lift the joint mortgage from a real estate belonging to the debtor. The dissolution of a joint mortgage may, in cases referred to in this paragraph, be applied for by a titleholder whose real estate is subject to the joint mortgage or by a lienholder. The provisions in this section on a parcelled real estate apply also to parcels conveyed from a mortgaged real estate.

Section 7 — *Alteration Procedure*

(1) The provisions on the creation of mortgages apply, where appropriate, to an application for the alteration of a mortgage and to the consideration of the matter.

(2) The original mortgage instruments based on the mortgages to be altered shall be attached to the application. When the mortgage alteration has been completed, the register authority shall, where necessary, issue a new mortgage instrument as a certificate of the altered mortgage or make the relevant correction to the original mortgage instrument.

(3) If the mortgage is to be cancelled or otherwise altered by virtue of another Act, the register authority shall make an entry on the same to the title and mortgage register when the notification of a final decision on the matter has arrived to it. A mortgage instrument based on the altered mortgage shall be issued only if the original mortgage instrument has been delivered to the register authority.

Section 8 — *Replacement and Cancellation of Mortgage Instrument*

(1) The holder of a mortgage instrument shall have the right to receive a new mortgage instrument from the register authority to replace a spoiled one. The mortgage instrument may be replaced, upon request, also when the registration number of the object of the mortgage has changed.

(2) The provisions in the Act on the Cancellation of Documents apply to the cancellation of a mortgage instrument. The register authority shall issue, upon request, a new, corresponding mortgage instrument to the person upon whose application the mortgage instrument was cancelled.

(3) The issue of a new mortgage instrument shall be entered into the title and mortgage register.

Section 9 — *Right to Altered Mortgage Instrument* The lienholder shall have the same right to the mortgage instrument referred to in section 7(3) and section 8 as he had to the replaced mortgage instrument.

CHAPTER 19 — MORTGAGES AND LIENS OVER USUFRUCT AND BUILDINGS

Section 1 — *Object of Mortgage over Usufruct*

(1) A lease and another fixed-term usufruct on the land of another person may be mortgaged, if the right can be transferred to a third party without hearing the titleholder and if the area contains a building or facility belonging to the usufructuary or if it is agreed that one may be built. It shall be a prerequisite for the mortgage that the usufruct is entered into the title and mortgage register. Also a share of the usufruct may be mortgaged.

(2) The same mortgage shall not cover two or more usufructs or a real estate and a usufruct.

Section 2 — *Applicant for Mortgage over Usufruct* The mortgage shall be created upon the application of the usufructuary whose right has last been registered.

Section 3 — *Application of Provisions on Real Estate Mortgages and Liens*

(1) The provisions in chapter 16, sections 4–9 and chapter 18, section 1, sections 3–5 and sections 7–9 on real estate mortgages apply, where appropriate, to mortgages over usufruct.

(2) The provisions in chapter 17, sections 1–8 and sections 10–13 on real estate liens apply, where appropriate, to liens over usufruct and the buildings and facilities concerned.

(3) The provisions in the sections referred to above in paragraphs (1) and (2) on real estates apply to usufruct and the respective provisions on the registration of title, to the registration of the right.

Section 4 — *Alteration of Usufruct* An agreement on the alteration of usufruct shall not be binding on the lienholder before the registration of the alteration. Chapter 14, section 14 contains provisions on the prerequisites for the registration of alterations.

Section 5 — *Cessation of Usufruct*

(1) A lien over a usufruct shall lapse when the term fixed for the usufruct expires. However, the lien shall remain valid, if the usufruct is extended or it is immediately given back to the same usufructuary and an entry to this effect is made into the title and mortgage register during the term of the usufruct.

(2) If the usufruct expires prematurely because of termination, agreement or another reason, the lien over the usufruct, as registered, shall remain valid until the mortgage has been cancelled. The same applies, if the same person becomes the titleholder and the usufructuary. Chapter 14, section 16 contains provisions on the prerequisites for the deletion of the registration and the cancellation of the mortgage.

(3) If the titleholder has become the usufructuary or the usufruct has otherwise lapsed, it shall not be mortgaged nor the mortgage instrument based on such mortgage handed over as security for a debt. However, the lien shall remain valid if the creditor did not know nor should have known of the lapsing of the usufruct at the time of the raising of the lien.

Section 6 — *Transfer of Mortgage to Cover Real Estate*

(1) If the titleholder has become the usufructuary or the usufruct has otherwise lapsed, the mortgages over the usufruct may upon the application of the titleholder and with the consent of the lienholder be transferred to cover the entire real estate, so that they have the same seniority as the registration of the usufruct and are among themselves in the same order of seniority as previously. It shall be a prerequisite for this that all mortgages over the usufruct are transferred at the same time. If the real estate is subject to mortgages or registrations of special rights, the consent of those rightholders whose registration is equally or less senior than the registration of the lapsed usufruct shall be required.

(2) The lapsing of the usufruct shall not affect the object of the mortgages over the real estate until the registration of the usufruct has been deleted. Thereafter, the

mortgages over the real estate shall cover also the property previously subject to the usufruct.

Section 7 — *Conveyance of Buildings to Usufructuary* The conveyance of a building on the real estate or the conveyance of other property affixed to the real estate shall not affect the object of the mortgages over the real estate, unless the conveyed property has been registered as a part of the usufruct in accordance with chapter 14, section 4(1)(2). The mortgages over the usufruct cover after such registration also the property referred to therein.

CHAPTER 20 — STATUTORY LIENS

Section 1 — *Scope of Application of This Chapter*

(1) A real estate that by virtue of another Act is liable for the payment of a debt or fee under public law or another similar debt shall be security for the debt, as provided in this Code.

(2) The provisions on statutory liens over real estate shall apply also when the statutory lien covers a share or parcel of real estate, a lease or another usufruct on the land of another person.

Section 2 — *Registration of Statutory Liens*

(1) A statutory lien shall be notified to be entered into the title and mortgage register. If the notification has not been presented to the register authority within one year from the activation of the debt, the lien shall lapse.

(2) The notification may be made when the decision granting a loan or imposing an obligation to pay has been made, even if it is not yet final. A recurring payment from real estate, not based on a court judgment, may be notified for registration only if the payment of an installment has been neglected.

(3) Provisions on the notification and the minimum amount registrable as a statutory lien are issued by Decree.

Section 3 — *Effect of Conveyance and Enforcement*

(1) A statutory lien shall not be binding on the conveyee, if it has not been entered into the title and mortgage register before the application of the registration of the title of the conveyee and the conveyee did not know nor should have known of the debt or the basis for one.

(2) If the conveyor has failed to inform the conveyee of a debt payable from the real estate and the statutory lien does not remain valid, the creditor shall have a right to due compensation from the conveyor.

(3) A statutory lien shall have no effect in respect to the creditors of the titleholder, unless it has been entered into the title and mortgage register before the register authority has been notified of execution, precautionary measures or bankruptcy.

Section 4 — *Effects of Registration*

(1) The registration of a statutory lien shall be valid from the date when the pertinent notification is made to the register authority.

(2) On the basis of a registered statutory lien, the creditor shall have the right to payment of the debt from the real estate before the payment of debts backed by mortgages. The same shall apply to interest, as registered, and other additional expense for at most three years from the date of execution to the date when the interest is paid.

(3) Registration shall not preclude the investigation of the existence of the statutory lien and the amount of the debt.

Section 5 — *Barriers to Registration*

(1) A statutory lien shall not be registered, if:

(1) the notification has not been made in the prescribed time;

(2) someone else than the debtor has applied, before the notification, for the registration of his title on the basis of a conveyance and he does not consent to the registration;

(3) an entry on execution or precautionary measures on the real estate or the bankruptcy of the titleholder has been made into the title and mortgage register prior to the notification; or

(4) the real estate is by law not liable for the debt or the registration is otherwise not possible.

(2) The notification may be left in abeyance until the basis or the permanence of a statutory lien has been clarified.

Section 6 — *Deletion of Registration* The lienholder shall notify the registration of a statutory lien to be deleted, when the debt has lapsed or when the lien is no longer valid. In such cases, the registration may be deleted also upon the request of the titleholder.

Section 7 — *Application of Provisions on Real Estate Liens* The provisions on real estate liens and mortgages apply, where appropriate, to statutory liens and the registration thereof.

PART V — MISCELLANEOUS PROVISIONS

CHAPTER 21 — DETAILED PROVISIONS AND ENTRY INTO FORCE

Section 1 — *Detailed Provisions* Detailed provisions on registration, the maintenance of the title and mortgage register and the other implementation of this Code are issued by Decree.

Section 2 — *Entry into Force* This Code shall enter into force as provided by Decree.

REAL ESTATE FORMATION ACT

(554/1995; amendments up to 111/2003 included)

CHAPTER 1 -SCOPE OF APPLICATION AND DEFINITIONS

SECTION 1

(1) The present Act applies to: 1) formation of real estate and other register units; 2) changing the property division in other ways; 3) confirmation of matters concerning the dimensions of a register unit or other

property division matters; and 4) registration and amalgamation of real estate and other register units.

(2) The present Act does not apply to a matter concerning the formation of real estate referred to in subsection 1 which is otherwise provided for in the legislation.

SECTION 2

(1) In this Act: 1) real estate refers to an independent unit of land ownership which under the Real Estate Register Act (392/85) is to be entered into the Real Estate Register as real estate, and other register unit refers to another separate unit to be entered into the Real Estate Register under the said Act. The real estate comprises the area belonging to it, the shares of the joint property units and of the joint special benefits as well as the easements and the private special benefits belonging to the real estate (dimensions of the real estate);

2) joint property unit refers to an area which jointly belongs to two or more real estates in shares based on specific grounds;

3) plot refers to a real estate formed in accordance with a binding subdivision plan and entered into the Real Estate Register as a plot; (322/1999)

4) public area refers to a real estate owned by the municipality and formed out of an area or a part of an area assigned as a street area, a market or square, a recreational area, a traffic area, a danger area, a special area or a water area in the town plan and entered as a public area in the Real Estate Register;

5) register village refers to an entity formed from register units which have been entered into the Real Estate Register as belonging to the same village;

6) land law village refers to a village inhabited before Basic Land Consolidation, an equivalent group of houses, any other equivalent single unit of ownership land area considered original and not partitioned in Basic Land Consolidation; and

7) water law village refers to an inhabited village before Basic Land Consolidation, an equivalent group of houses, a lone-standing house, a granted parcel of land established before Basic Land Consolidation, excess land separated for the State in Basic Land Consolidation, a new house established on excess land after Basic Land Consolidation, State forest land excluded from Basic Land Consolidation and any other equivalent water area ownership unit considered original whose ownership has not been divided.

CHAPTER 2 -CADASTRAL PROCEDURES AND EXECUTORS

SECTION 3

(1) The measures referred to in section 1 above are carried out in the cadastral procedure excluding the registration and amalgamation of real estates.

(2) The land survey offices of the National Land Survey of Finland undertake the execution of the cadastral procedures and other measures referred to in subsection 1. However, the authority which under section 5 of the Real Estate Register Act keeps the Real Estate Register in the area concerned, as provided in section 5 below, undertakes the execution of the cadastral procedures and other measures in areas covered by a town plan. If the cadastral procedure concerns both an area covered by a town plan and an area outside of it the land survey office undertakes the execution of the procedure. (322/1999)

SECTION 4

(1) The cadastral procedure is executed by a land surveyor and two trustees (executors). A cadastral procedure other than the partitioning of a joint property unit, re-allotment, urban land replotting and the forming of jointly owned forest may be executed by the land surveyor without the trustees if use of the trustees is not necessary and the use of trustees is not demanded by an interested party.

SECTION 5 (322/1999)

(1) The land surveyor shall be a graduate engineer in the service of the National Land Survey of Finland, graduated with an appropriate degree from the Department of Surveying of a University of Technology, an engineer or technician graduated with an appropriate degree from a Polytechnic or School of Technology, a cadastral surveyor of the municipality, or an engineer or technician in the service of the municipality graduated with the abovementioned degree.

(2) An engineer or a technician employed by the National Land Survey of Finland may act as the land surveyor in a subdivision, a voluntary land exchange, a demarcation, an easement survey, the formation of a separate area into a real estate unit, the transfer of an interest within a joint property unit and its formation into a real estate unit, the formation of a joint property unit and in administrative procedures for the execution of a road construction plan under the Act on Private Roads (358/1962).

(3) If the municipality undertakes the keeping of the Real Estate Register under section 5 of the Real Estate Register Act in areas covered by a town plan, the land surveyor in the said area shall be the cadastral surveyor, engineer or technician employed by the municipality for purposes of subdivision, voluntary land exchange, demarcation, easement survey, formation of a separate area into a real estate unit, transfer of an interest within a joint property unit and its formation into a real estate unit, formation of a joint property unit and administrative procedures for the execution of a road construction plan under the Act on Private Roads. The cadastral surveyor also acts as the land surveyor in mandatory land exchanges, in procedures executed in connection with subdivision as referred to in section 62 and, in addition to demarcation, in all other property definitions.

(4) The land surveyor shall be a graduate engineer if procedures other than definition of real estate or easement procedures or procedures referred to in section 156(3) are necessary in connection with the procedure referred to in subsection 2 or 3.

Section 5a (322/1999)

(1) In the territory of his/her own municipality and with the consent of the municipality a cadastral surveyor, engineer or technician employed by the municipality may be appointed as the land surveyor in a cadastral procedure outside the area referred to in section 5(3).

(2) A cadastral surveyor referred to in section 5(1) in the service of the National Land Survey of Finland may be appointed as the land surveyor for a procedure under section 5(3).

SECTION 6

(1) The municipal council shall appoint as trustees at least six persons for the period equivalent to that of the term of the council.

(2) The trustee shall be versed in real estate matters and knowledgeable in local affairs. The provisions on the lay members of the local court also apply to the eligibility of persons as trustees.

(3) The central administration of the National Land Survey of Finland shall determine the fee, compensation for travel expenses and daily allowance to be paid to the trustee.

(4) The provisions of the Municipal Act concerning municipal delegates otherwise apply to the trustee, unless otherwise provided below.

SECTION 7

(1) The trustee performs all tasks under public liability.

(2) Before commencing his/her duties, the trustee shall give affirmation in the District Court or Land Court to honestly fulfil his/her tasks as a trustee to the best of his/her ability and according to his/her conscience, pledging to not bring about any injustice to any person under any circumstances.

SECTION 8

(1) Trustees shall be summoned to a cadastral procedure by the land surveyor.

(2) If trustees are summoned as executors during the course of the procedure, any rulings already set in place during the procedure shall not be subject to review as a result.

SECTION 9

(1) If the trustees appointed from within the municipality are disqualified or prevented from participating in the procedure, trustees from a neighbouring municipality may be summoned.

(2) If the procedure concern areas within several municipalities, the trustee may act in areas beyond the jurisdiction of his/her own municipality.

SECTION 10

(1) If a summoned trustee remains absent from the procedure or is found to be disqualified and another trustee cannot be brought in to replace him/her without difficulty, the land surveyor may summon as executor a person deemed competent to stand in as a trustee until a more permanent trustee can be brought into the proceedings. The stand-in trustee shall undertake the affirmation to the land surveyor as referred to in section 7.

(2) The presence of trustees is not required when performing technical tasks involved in the procedure.

SECTION 11

(1) The provisions of the Code of Judicial Procedure on the disqualification of a judge apply also to the disqualification of a trustee.

(2) If the trustee knows him/herself to be disqualified he or she shall notify the other executors of his/her disqualification. An interested party who considers a trustee to be disqualified shall make an objection to the executors without delay once having learnt of the disqualification.

SECTION 12

(1) The executors shall decide on the disqualification of an executor. A decision that finds an executor to be disqualified cannot be appealed.

(2) If the land surveyor is found to be disqualified the procedure shall be interrupted and the matter shall be notified without delay to the land surveyor appointee. The appointee shall thereby appoint another land surveyor to continue the procedure. The cadastral surveyor shall summon another trustee to replace the disqualified trustee without delay.

(3) Any matters already resolved in the procedure prior to notification of disqualification of an executor shall not be taken up again due to the said disqualification.

SECTION 13

(1) The executors may summon an expert to assist in handling a matter which requires special expertise. The fee payable to the said expert shall also be determined in conjunction with the summoning decision.

CHAPTER 3 - COMMENCEMENT OF A CADASTRAL PROCEDURE, INTERESTED PARTIES AND OTHER PARTIES WITH A RIGHT TO BE HEARD

Section 14 (322/1999)

(1) Application for a cadastral procedure shall be submitted in writing to the land survey office in whose area the object of the procedure or the main part of it is located. The application for the procedure referred to in section 5(3), however, is presented to the Real Estate Register keeper of the municipality concerned. Provisions on the commencement of the procedure without application are laid down separately below.

(2) Further provisions on the application and the reports to be attached to it are given by Government decree.

Section 15

(1) If the application has been drafted in accordance with the present Act and the provisions and regulations pursuant to it, the land survey office or the keeper of the Real Estate Register shall give an order to execute the procedure.

(2) If the application has a defect due to which the order to execute cannot be given and the authority does not have access to the information necessary to correct the defect the applicant shall be given an opportunity to supplement the application.

(3) The application shall be rejected if it does not fulfil the requirements laid down in subsection 1 even after the supplementation.

Section 16

(1) A cadastral procedure is pending from the issuing of the order to execute.

(2) The procedure executed in the cadastral procedure shall be the one referred to in the application. Another procedure or measure in place of the procedure referred to in the application may be executed with the consent of the applicant if it is necessary for the fulfilment of the purpose of the application. Furthermore, an additional measure may be executed as a cadastral procedure in connection with the procedure.

(3) A measure other than the measure executed as the cadastral procedure referred to in subsection 2 may be executed at the request of the interested party in connection with the cadastral procedure if the execution of the said measure does not cause any appreciable delay in the closing of the procedure referred to in the application.

Section 17

(1) The applicant and any other person whose rights the procedure immediately concerns constitutes an interested party in the procedure. The holder of a lien constitutes an interested party when the subdivided real estate or area is released from mortgages under section 28 or section 134 without the consent of the holder of a lien.

(2) The municipality has a right to be heard in the procedure referred to in section 168(3) within its territory.

Section 18

(1) The right to be heard of the owner of the real estate or of the area is exercised in a cadastral procedure by the party with the title or the party governing the real estate or area as the owner.

(2) If the real estate or area has been transferred to a new owner during the procedure the new owner is obliged by what the previous owner has agreed to or accepted in the procedure.

(3) The provisions of the present section for a real estate or area also apply, as appropriate, to a specified share of a real estate or area as well as to an easement and a lease or to another special right.

Section 19

(1) A joint-owner of the joint property unit has the right to be heard as an interested party for the part of the real estate, the unseparated parcel or area if the procedure concerns a joint property unit or a real estate or an unseparated parcel owned jointly by several persons. If several joint-owners of a joint property unit are present and if their claims conflict with each other the executors shall decide in which way each claim will be taken into consideration. An agreement concerning a jointly owned real estate or an unseparated parcel requires authorisation from all joint-owners and the provisions of the Act on Joint Property (758/89) apply to the joint property unless otherwise provided below.

(2) The provisions of subsection 1 apply, as appropriate, if the procedure concerns a right or benefit belonging jointly to several persons or real estates.

CHAPTER 4 - SUBDIVISION

Section 20 (322/1999)

(1) An area with specific borders (unseparated parcel) may be formed out of a register unit to form a different real estate or it may be transferred into an already existing real estate by subdivision. A plot in accordance with a binding subdivision plan is formed by subdivision or through some other real estate forming procedure. When forming the plot, slight deviation from the subdivision plan may be allowed as set down in further provisions given by Government decree.

(2) The real estate to be formed by subdivision may contain unseparated parcels from several real estates or joint property units. A plot or a public area to be formed by subdivision may also contain entire real estates (joint subdivision).

(3) A conveyed joint property unit is formed into a real estate or transferred to an already existing real estate by subdivision. A rapids property may be formed out of a jointly owned rapid or a part of it by subdivision.

Section 21

(1) The real estate or the joint property unit to be subdivided is called an original property unit in the present Act, the real estate formed out of a unseparated parcel is called a subdivided real estate unit and a real estate or a joint property unit formed out of the remaining pieces of land of the original property unit is called a residual property unit. The real estate to which the unseparated parcel is transferred is called a receiver property unit.

(2) The subdivision shall note which one of the formed real estates is the residual property unit. The real estate ordered to be the residual property unit is the one formed for the owner of the original property unit in accordance with the Register of Titles and Mortgages. The subdivision shall note the unseparated parcel or the parcels from whose area the subdivided real estate has been formed. The information referred to here shall be entered into the Real Estate Register. If several real estates have been formed for the real estate owner referred to above, the real estate ordered to be the original real estate is the one he or she notifies.

(322/1999)

(3) The provisions concerning real estate and its owner set down below in this Chapter apply, as appropriate, to a joint property unit and its joint-owners.

SECTION 22

(1) A subdivision may be applied for by the owner or the part-owner of an unseparated parcel or an original property unit who has the title to an unseparated parcel or real estate, and by the holder of a special right concerning a plot in accordance with a binding subdivision plan if buildings belonging to the holder of the right may be built on the plot based on the right.

(322/1999)

(2) If the owner has conveyed an unseparated parcel to another party, the subdivision procedure is pending when the notice of the legal registration authority on the acquisition of title to an unseparated parcel has arrived at the real estate registration authority whose task it is to see to the keeping of the Real Estate Register in the area. The beginning of the subdivision procedure may be postponed or a commenced procedure shall be interrupted if the owner of the unseparated parcel presents a report according to which the subdivided real estate is not intended to be formed only out of the specified share of the real estate concerned or if there are other relevant grounds for postponement or interruption. (322/1999)

(3) The provisions of subsections 1 and 2 concerning the subdivision of an unseparated parcel out of a real estate apply, as appropriate, to a joint property unit, to an unseparated parcel of joint property and to an unseparated parcel reserved by the seller to him/herself in connection with conveyance of a real estate. If the title to a joint property unit or to a specified share of it cannot be granted the applicant shall present another necessary report concerning the ownership of the joint property and the owner of an unseparated parcel shall present a report concerning his/her right to the specified share of the real estate. (273/1998)

Section 22a (322/1999)

(1) Subdivision of a joint property unit is executed based on the application of the municipality or the owner or joint-owner of the area.

(2) If necessary, the keeper of the Real Estate Register may order subdivision concerning a joint property to be executed without an application.

SECTION 22 B (322/1999)

(1) In a subdivision, an area assigned to be a joint property or a part of it may be transferred to an already existing area of similar type.

SECTION 23

(1) The unseparated parcel to be subdivided shall belong in its entirety to the same owner or the same owners. If the unseparated parcel consists of two or more areas the joint-owner's share of each area shall be the same. A rapids property may be formed if the joint-owners who have requested the formation own at least one third of the joint rapids area.

(2) If the joint-owners of a real estate have not jointly applied for subdivision of their property, the condition for the subdivision is that none of the joint-owners present at the cadastral procedure oppose the subdivision in the requested manner. (273/1998)

Section 23a (322/1999)

(1) The condition for subdivision of a public area is that the municipality has the title to the area to be subdivided or the area will be the property of the municipality under section 94 of the Land Use and Building Act (132/1999) and that the real estates out of which the public area is formed are free of mortgages or the area will be free of them under section 29(3) of this Act or section 107 of the Land Use and Building Act.

SECTION 24

(1) A joint subdivision of several cadastral units in one legal survey may be executed if: 1) the original property units are located in the same municipality; 2) the unseparated parcels belong to the same owner or joint-owners in such a way that each joint-owner's share of each unseparated parcel is equally large; 3) the unseparated parcels are owned with the same rights and the owners consent to joint subdivision; 4) the formation of unseparated parcels into one real estate unit does not cause confusion in the Real Estate System nor the Registration System; (1188/1996) 5) there are no mortgages on the unseparated parcels or they are only subject to joint mortgages of the same quantity and priority or, in addition to these, only one unseparated parcel is subject to joint mortgages with an inferior priority; and

6) no unseparated parcel is foreclosed or part of an estate in bankruptcy, nor is any unseparated parcel subject to precautionary measures.

(2) A joint subdivision may also be executed when the subdivided real estate is released from liability for mortgages entirely or in such a way that only the mortgages referred to in subsection 1(5) remain to encumber it. A plot under a binding subdivision plan may also be subdivided when an agreement on the order of priority in which the mortgages and the other recorded rights have bearing on the plot has been reached between the holders of a lien and of the special rights concerning different parts of the plot. (322/1999)

SECTION 25

(1) A subdivision out of a joint property may be executed if there are no mortgages on the participating property units or they are only subject to joint mortgages of the same quantity and priority or, in addition to these, only one participating property unit is subject to joint mortgages with an inferior priority.

(2) A subdivision out of a joint property may also be executed when the subdivided real estate unit is released from liability for the mortgages of the participating property units entirely or in such a way that only the mortgages referred to in subsection 1 remain to encumber it.

(3) In accordance with section 4(1) of the Jointly Owned Forest Act (37/1991), a subdivision concerning an area conveyed from a jointly owned forest and concerning a jointly owned forest sold under section 5(1) of the said Act may be executed notwithstanding the provisions of subsections 1 and 2. (1188/1996)

SECTION 26

(1) An unseparated parcel or several unseparated parcels may be transferred into a real estate by subdivision. The provisions of section 24 on the conditions of a joint subdivision apply to the conditions of the transfer. The provisions of the said section on the original property unit and on the unseparated parcel also apply to the receiver property unit.

SECTION 27

(1) The provisions of section 24(1)(5) and section 25 also apply to a recorded special right concerning the unseparated parcel to be subdivided.

SECTION 28

(1) In a subdivision, the subdivided real estate may be released from liability for the registered mortgages of the original property unit if there is no lien based on the mortgage in question concerning the unseparated parcel from which the subdivided real estate is formed or if the holder of a lien gives his/her consent to it. If the residual property unit is clearly sufficient to cover all mortgages concerning the original property unit, the subdivided real estate may be released from the registered mortgages of the original property unit even without the consent of the holder of a lien. In this case the subdivided real estate unit shall be released from all the registered mortgages of the original property unit. (273/1998)

(2) A subdivided property unit formed out of a joint property unit may be released from liability for mortgages registered to a participating property unit with the consent of the holder of a lien or without the consent of the holder of a lien if the participating property unit is clearly sufficient to cover the mortgages directed to it after the subdivision or if the lowering of value of the participating property unit caused by the subdivision is insignificant. The above provisions of this subsection concerning a registered mortgage pertaining to a participating property unit also apply to a registered pension entitlement concerning the participating property unit. (273/1998)

(3) The land surveyor shall notify without delay the land register authorities about the decision on the release of a mortgage. The land register authorities shall delete the mortgage for the subdivided property unit when the decision on the release referred to in subsections 1 or 2 has gained legal force.

(4) The provisions on subdivided real estate as stated above in this section correspondingly apply to the real estate which is formed out of an unseparated parcel and a receiver property unit.

SECTION 29

(1) The mortgages concerning an unseparated parcel or a receiver property unit from which the subdivided real estate or the unseparated parcel and the receiver property unit have not been released shall extend to concern the real estate to be formed. (322/1999)

(2) If a subdivided real estate is separated from a joint property unit or if a real estate is formed out of a separated joint property unit and a receiver property unit, the mortgages of the participating property units also concern the formed real estate after the subdivision.

(3) If a joint property unit is contained within a plot or a public area, those mortgages are not taken into consideration in the subdivision which concern the participating property units of the joint property unit and, furthermore, if some of the joint property unit has become part of a plot or

a public area the said plot or public area shall be released from the mortgages concerning the participating property units of the joint property unit. (322/1999)

Section 30 has been repealed by Act 273/1998.

Section 31

(1) The demarcation of the unseparated parcel to be subdivided shall be executed in accordance with the deed of conveyance or other title deed and other available report or, if the unseparated parcel is separated for the owner of the original property unit, according to his/her assignment.

(2) If the interested parties agree on an addition or a change in the document which the cadastral procedure is based on during the subdivision procedure and the addition or the change requires conveying an additional area or an additional share, the agreement shall be drafted in accordance with the provisions of Chapter 2(1) of the Land Code (540/1995). The subdivision is not hindered by the title of such an additional area or share not having been registered if a report of the title which would have been required in the registration of title is presented.

(3) Executors may decide on an insignificant change of an unseparated parcel without the consent of the interested parties if the change does not influence the value of the unseparated parcel and if the change is important for the accomplishment of a functional property division and no considerable inconvenience is caused to any interested party. In accordance with the demand of an interested party, the boundaries of the unseparated parcel to be subdivided may be checked if the checking is such that it can be executed as a mandatory land exchange following the completion of the subdivision.

Section 32 (322/1999)

(1) In an area with a binding subdivision plan, the subdivision can be executed only to form a plot in accordance with the subdivision plan unless the municipality grants permission for the subdivision on special grounds. Otherwise in a town plan area the subdivision may not be executed in such a way that it hinders the implementation of the said plan.

Section 33 has been repealed by Act (322/1999).

Section 34

(1) In an area assigned to be a recreational area or conservation area in a master plan with legal consequence a real estate intended to be a building site may not be formed by subdivision if it considerably hinders the use of the area for the assigned purpose. (322/1999)

(2) In an area which does not have a town plan or which has not been assigned to be a recreational area or a conservation area in a master plan with legal consequence a real estate intended to be a building site may be formed by subdivision if the real estate to be formed meets the requirements of the provisions laid down for a building site in the Land Use and Building Act and the decrees pursuant to it. (322/1999)

(3) In an area requiring planning, an unseparated parcel intended to be a building site may be formed into a separate real estate by subdivision only if the unseparated parcel has a valid building permit when beginning the cadastral procedure or if during the cadastral procedure a building permit for other than a temporary building is received, or if the municipality gives its consent to the formation of a real estate. (322/1999)

(4) Notwithstanding the above provisions of this section, unless otherwise required due to a change of circumstances or other special reasons, an unseparated parcel may be subdivided into a real estate if a building permit for other than a temporary building exists for the area to be subdivided at the beginning of the cadastral procedure or if during the cadastral procedure one is received or if a building has already been built based on such a permit.

Section 35 (322/1999)

(1) In an area where a building ban is in force, an unseparated parcel intended as a building site may be subdivided into a separate real estate only if a building permit is in force for the unseparated parcel when beginning the cadastral procedure, or a building permit for other than a temporary building or an exception to build notwithstanding the building ban referred to in section 171 of the Land Use and Building Act is received during the cadastral procedure, or if the municipality gives its consent to the formation of real estate.

(2) In a building ban area referred to in subsection 1 above, an unseparated parcel may be transferred to an already existing real estate by subdivision and an unseparated parcel intended for other uses than a building site may be subdivided into different real estates if the subdivision does not considerably hinder the drafting of a plan.

Section 36 (322/1999)

(1) On a shoreline area as referred to in section 72 of the Land Use and Building Act, an unseparated parcel intended for a building site may not be subdivided before the entry into force of a town plan or a master plan with legal consequence which gives particular provisions on the possibility of building. If there is uncertainty during the subdivision about whether the unseparated parcel is located on a shoreline area the land surveyor shall assign the matter to be decided in the regional environment centre. The unseparated parcel intended for a building site may, however, be subdivided if: 1) it is evident that building on the unseparated parcel does not hinder the drafting of a town plan; 2) the municipality has given its consent to the subdivision for a justifiable reason; 3) an exception referred to in section 17 of the Land Use and Building Act or a building permit for other than a temporary building is in force when beginning the cadastral procedure, or one is received during the cadastral procedure for an unseparated parcel to be formed into a real estate or, when the matter concerns the transfer of an unseparated parcel to an already existing real estate, for a real estate to be formed out of an unseparated parcel and a receiver property unit, or a building based on such a permit has already been built; or

4) the real estate to be formed is intended to be used for building as referred to in section 73(3) of the Land Use and Building Act.

SECTION 37

(1) A subdivision may be executed in an area where land consolidation, partitioning or other division is pending if the subdivision does not considerably delay the execution of the division and there is no special reason not to execute the subdivision.

(2) If a joint-owner of a real estate has conveyed an unseparated parcel with the intention of having it separated for him/her from a real estate to be formed by partitioning, the subdivision may be executed in connection with the partitioning after the partitioning plan has gained legal force if the unseparated parcel has become part of the piece of land received by the conveyor.

Section 37a (322/1999)

(1) The provisions on an unseparated parcel as mentioned above in this **Chapter** apply, as appropriate, to a plot to be subdivided or a real estate contained in a public area.

Chapter 5 - Formation of a separate reliction area or other separate area into a real estate unit and annexation thereof to a real estate

Section 38

(1) A reliction area formed from authorised land drainage which has become private property through partitioning, either as executed by an authority or a private party or under an order contained in the drainage permit and which does not belong to any real estate unit, and a reliction area which has belonged to a real estate unit and which has been conveyed to another owner without separating it from the real estate unit may be formed into a real estate unit or joined to a real estate unit. The separate reliction areas referred to above may be formed into a real estate unit or joined to a real estate only if the conditions mentioned above have existed before 13 November 1911 and still exist. The ownership of a reliction area shall be resolved in a cadastral procedure. Provisions of section 184 apply to disputes over ownership.

Section 39

(1) Formation of a reliction area into a real estate unit or annexation to a real estate may be applied for by the party who him/herself or whose title holder has received the reliction area in a manner referred to in section 38 or who governs the reliction area as the owner.

Section 40

(1) In addition to the provisions of sections 38 and 39, the provisions on the transferral of an unseparated parcel into another real estate by subdivision apply, as appropriate, to joining a separate reliction area to a real estate, and provisions on subdividing a separate parcel into a separate real estate unit apply to the formation of a separate reliction area into a real estate unit. The provisions of sections 32-36 above, however, only apply if several different real estates are formed out of the reliction area for the same owner.

(2) When granting the title to the party who is the owner of the real estate unit formed from a separate reliction area or an area joined to the real estate unit based on a resolution reached in the cadastral procedure referred to in this Chapter, an excerpt of the report drafted in the cadastral procedure is adequate as documentation of his/her title.

Section 41 (273/1998)

(1) The provisions on subdivision apply, as appropriate, to the formation of a separate area not belonging to a register unit into a real estate unit or annexation of it to a real estate.

Chapter 6 has been repealed by Act 322/1999.

CHAPTER 7 - PARTITIONING

Section 47

(1) The right to have a real estate unit divided by partitioning belongs to the owner of the real estate unit or an unseparated parcel thereof who also holds the title to the real estate unit or an unseparated parcel thereof.

(2) If several real estate units have the same owners, the real estates may be partitioned at the same time in such a way that the provisions below for the real estate to be partitioned apply to the entity formed by the real estates to be partitioned (joint partitioning). (273/1998)

(3) If a number of real estate units are primarily under the same ownership, partitioning of these real estate units may be executed at the same time. In such a case, each joint-owner receives pieces of land for the real estate units to be formed for him or her only from the pieces of land of those real estate units in which he or she has a share, unless all interested parties agree otherwise. Otherwise the provisions on joint partitioning apply to the partitioning referred to in this subsection. (273/1998)

(4) A rapids property may not be partitioned. In addition to the general conditions for partitioning, the provisions on the conditions for dividing a water area apply, as appropriate, to the conditions for partitioning of a real estate unit which includes only insignificant quantities of other pieces of land in addition to water areas.

SECTION 48 (2731998)

(1) The condition for joint partitioning is that all joint-owners are in agreement on it or, if not all joint-owners are in agreement, one joint-owner demands partitioning, thus rendering joint partitioning necessary in order to reach a feasible partitioning result.

(2) In joint partitioning, the shares of one joint-owner in two or more real estate units may be amalgamated if the joint-owner so requests. Furthermore, the provisions on the conditions for amalgamating real estates apply to the conditions for amalgamating shares.

Section 49

(1) The share owned by a joint-owner is the basis of division in partitioning. If the partitioning is executed on behalf of the owner of the real estate unit, the shares he or she has ordered are the basis of division.

(2) If the unofficial partition concerning a real estate unit has been valid for a long time, the joint-owner's usufruct is, however, the basis of division of a real estate unit governed by unofficial partition if all joint-owners agree on it or if it is reasonable.

SECTION 50

(1) The real estate unit to be formed for the joint-owner shall receive the number of pieces of land that belong to it in accordance with the assessment and the basis of division.

(2) Notwithstanding the provisions of subsection 1, the partitioning may be executed in such a way that the total value of the pieces of land, growing stock, buildings, fixed equipment and structures, interests in joint property units and special benefits of the real estate unit to be formed for each joint-owner corresponds to the share of the equivalent total value of the real estate unit to be partitioned belonging to the joint-owner in accordance with the basis of division. The partitioning shall be executed in a manner referred to in this subsection if all joint-owners have agreed on it or, if the joint-owners have not agreed on the manner of partitioning, execution of

partitioning in a manner referred to in this subsection is necessary in order to reach a functional partitioning result.

SECTION 51

(1) If all joint-owners agree and if it is necessary for the formation of functional real estates, departing from the number of pieces of land or total value of property allocated to the real estate unit according to the basis of division to be formed may be allowed. Departing from the basis of division may be allowed even without the consent of the joint-owners if it is important in order to form functional real estate units and if no joint-owner suffers considerable damage and the amount of pieces of land and total property allocated to any of the real estate units does not exceed the amount which would belong to it in accordance with the basis of division by more than 20 per cent or fall below it by more than 10 per cent.

(2) Compensation shall be paid for the difference if the property belonging to the real estate unit to be partitioned does not divide in accordance with the basis of division between the real estate units to be formed.

SECTION 52

(1) The pieces of land shall be placed in such a way that each real estate unit to be formed receives, if possible, pieces of land suitably located with respect to its use. If the partitioning is executed in a manner referred to in section 50(1), each real estate unit is given pieces of land for different purposes in accordance with the basis of division, as far as possible, unless the joint-owners agree otherwise or other special reason demands otherwise.

(2) The pieces of land shall be divided in such a way that the compensation referred to in section 51(2) does not become excessive.

Section 53

(1) Provisions of sections 32-34 apply to partitioning, as appropriate.

(2) In partitioning in an area as referred to in sections 35-36 the real estates shall be formed, as far as possible, in such a way that the plan to be drafted and other organisation of settlement is taken into consideration.

Section 54

(1) During the partitioning proceedings, a partitioning plan is drafted presenting the basis of division, the real estate units to be formed, the joint areas to be formed and the real estates' shares in joint areas and in special benefits, private special benefits, easements, rights of way and compensations to be paid due to the partitioning. At the proceedings, the interested parties shall be provided with a detailed explanation of the division plan and its grounds and with the opportunity to acquaint themselves with the division plan and to voice any objections to it. Once all objections have been dealt with, a decision shall be made on how the partitioning is to be executed, after which the partitioning is completed.

(2) If it is expedient from the point of view of execution of partitioning, a decision is made in connection with the handling of the division plan only on the division of pieces of land, joint areas and the real estate units' shares of them, special benefits as well as easements and rights of way. Only a preliminary estimate of the compensations is presented in such a case. The definite

compensations are ordered and other necessary measures to complete the partitioning are taken only after the division plan has gained legal force.

(3) If the division plan has gained legal force during the cadastral procedures, the real estates which have been formed may be registered before the closing of the cadastral procedure.

Section 55

(1) If shares are the basis of division in the partitioning of a real estate unit divided by unofficial partitioning and a joint-owner has improved the cultivability of the pieces of land under his or her management or in other ways raised their value more than the other joint-owners have, the other joint-owners are liable to compensate him or her for the added value produced by the improvement measures according to their basis of division.

CHAPTER 8 - LAND EXCHANGE AND AREA TRANSFERRAL

Section 56

(1) Areas may be exchanged between real estates by executing a land exchange.

(2) Land exchange may also be executed in such a way that the real estate receives some share of the joint property unit belonging to another real estate as compensation for the area it has conveyed.

Section 57

(1) Land exchange may not be executed in such a way that it causes harm to the clarity of the Real Estate System or relevant hindrance to the use of a real estate involved in the land exchange.

(2) In an area covered by a town plan, the condition for land exchange is that it furthers the formation of plots or functional building sites or realisation of other area reservations in accordance with the plan. (322/1999)

Section 58

(1) An exchange of land may be executed if the owners of the real estates have agreed on it.

(2) A land exchange may be executed without the agreement of the owners if the area to be exchanged is insignificant and causes considerable hindrance to the use of the real estate bordering it, or is an area separated from the other pieces of land of the real estate by a brook, road or other such obstacle, or is otherwise a separate area which cannot be used in a functional manner by the owner but which can clearly be used more functionally in connection with the pieces of land of another real estate, as well as when the land exchange is necessary in order to remove a detrimental curve in boundaries (mandatory land exchange).

(3) A land exchange may be executed without the agreement of the joint-owners on the formation into a real estate of a plot or a building site fitting the town plan only if the areas to be exchanged have been assigned for the same use in the town plan. (322/1999)

(4) A land exchange may be executed in the manner referred to in section 56(2) above only if the owners agree on it.

Section 59

(1) The grading values of the areas to be exchanged must correspond approximately to each other. If the areas to be exchanged are of insignificant value, the land exchange may be executed even if their grading values do not correspond to each other. The same applies to a land exchange executed in the manner referred to in section 52(2).

(2) Based on the owners' agreement, a land exchange may be executed in such a way that the total value of the areas, growing stock, buildings, fixed equipment and structures coming to each real estate corresponds approximately to the total value of the equivalent property conveyed by the real estate.

(3) Compensation shall be paid if the value of the share coming to a real estate in the land exchange does not fully correspond to the value of the property it has conveyed.

SECTION 60

(1) If there is a jointly owned reliction area in the property or a private reliction area has appeared after the real estate has been formed which considerably hinders the use of the real estate or which can functionally only be used in connection with the real estate, the owner of the real estate has the right to claim the reliction area or a part of it. If the reliction area mentioned above can only be functionally used in connection with the real estate, the owner of the real estate is obliged to claim the reliction area or part of it in response to the demand of the owner of the reliction area or, if the reliction area is jointly owned, of the joint-owners.

(2) The provisions of subsection 1 on a jointly owned reliction area also apply to the type of insignificant separate reliction area which can only be functionally used in connection with the real estate bordering on it.

SECTION 61

(1) If the real estate borders on a joint property unit which is not a jointly owned forest, a jointly owned reliction area, a jointly owned water area or a jointly owned rapid and which considerably hinders the use of the real estate or which can only be functionally used in connection with a real estate, the owner of the real estate has the right to claim the said area.

If the area referred to above can only be functionally used in connection with a real estate, the owner of the real estate is obliged to claim the area of this type in response to the demand of the joint-owners of the area.

Section 61a (1188/1996)

(1) If the real estate includes a detached piece of land within the boundaries of another village, consisting mainly of farmland of insignificant value or of a form and location such that the owner of the real estate cannot functionally use it and which hinders the use of the pieces of land bordering on it, the parcel may be claimed into the type of real estate bordering on the parcel whose owner demands the redemption and in connection with which it is functional to use. If such a parcel borders on several real estates it may also be claimed in parts to those real estates

whose owners demand the redemption and in connection with which the part of the parcel is functional to use.

SECTION 62 (322/1999)

(1) In order to form a plot or a building site fitting the town plan the owner of a part of a plot or a building site has the right to claim an area included in a plot or building site belonging to another.

(2) When more than one request is lodged to claim an area of a plot or building site fitting the town plan and belonging to another party, priority lies with the party whose share, including buildings and equipment, has the greatest value. If the shares are of equal value, the party who first demanded the redemption has the right to claim.

Section 62a (322/1999)

(1) The municipality has the right to claim the parts belonging to the plot if the owner of a part of a plot has not lodged a demand concerning the redemption of the rest of the plot in accordance with the subdivision plan within one year from the entry into force of the town plan which has set down a binding subdivision plan or from the entry into force of a separate subdivision plan. If the owner of a part of a plot has, however, commenced his or her claim for redemption before the municipality has or within 60 days of when he or she was notified of the demand of the municipality, the municipality has the right to claim only if his or her demand or that of another owner of a part of a plot does not lead to the plot being owned by only one owner.

Section 62b (322/1999)

(1) When the owner of a part of a plot cannot utilize his or her land in accordance with a binding subdivision plan in a reasonably profitable manner due to the incompatibility of the binding subdivision plan with the prevailing ownership relations, the municipality is obliged to claim the part of the plot within a year from the entry into force of the town plan containing the order concerning a binding subdivision plan or of a separate subdivision plan unless another owner of a part of a plot has used his or her right to claim as referred to in section 62.

(2) The municipality is freed from all obligations to claim if the binding subdivision plan has been changed to correspond to the prevailing ownership relations and the matter concerning the obligation to claim has not yet been finally resolved.

SECTION 63

(1) An area claimed under sections 60-62 is transferred into the real estate owned by the redeemer.

Section 64 (322/1999)

(1) If the location of the land can be corrected or a plot or a building site fitting the town plan can be formed by an exchange of land, the exchange of land shall be executed instead of the redemption of the area referred to in sections 60-62. Such an exchange of land may be executed without the consent of the owners even though the conditions referred to in section 52(2) do not exist. Furthermore, a condition of redemption is that it does not cause harm to the clarity of the Real Estate System, hinder formation of real estates fitting the town plan nor cause any considerable harm to any interested party in the case referred to in sections 60 and 61.

Section 65

(1) An area exchanged by land exchange or transferred to another real estate under section 63 is freed from liability for the mortgages concerning the conveying real estate and for other equivalent encumbrances for which the conveying real estate is liable. If there is an easement or a lease or other special right concerning the area exchanged by land exchange or transferred into another real estate, the provisions of sections 86 and 87 apply in the cadastral procedure, as appropriate, to the remaining in force, expiration, redemption or other organisation of such right and to the compensation due to it. The rights for which the receiving property unit is responsible extend to also concern the transferred area.

(2) A registered special right may be ordered to concern the exchanged or transferred area only with the consent of the holder of the right. The level of priority of such a right is dependent on when the notice of the land surveyor concerning the change of object reaches the land registration authorities.

Section 66

(1) The provisions of sections 56-65 on real estate also apply, as appropriate, to a jointly owned forest or other jointly owned area, to an unseparated parcel which is formed into a real estate in connection with a land exchange, or to a procedure as referred to in sections 60-62.

CHAPTER 9 - LAND CONSOLIDATION

SECTION 67

(1) Land consolidation may be executed if the ensuing benefits exceed the costs and hindrance incurred and if the land consolidation allows: 1) improvement of property division and furtherance of the use of real estates; 2) considerable improvement in road and drainage conditions of the area; or 3) furtherance of the use of an area acquired for purposes referred to in the Act on the

Development Fund of Agriculture and Forestry (657/1966). (333/1999)

Paragraph 3 amended by Act 333/1999 enters into force at a time to be provided for by Government decree. The earlier formulation reads: 3) furtherance of the use of an area acquired for the purposes referred to in the Act on

Rural Industries (1295/90).

(2) If land consolidation is deemed likely to cause unreasonable hindrance to the owners of the real estates taking into consideration the local conditions, economic situation of the owners or other such factors, it may be left unexecuted even if the conditions provided in subsection 1 may exist.

(3) If the joint-owners unanimously agree, the land consolidation may be executed although the conditions referred to in subsection 1 do not exist if the benefit from the division is greater than the costs caused by it.

Section 68

(1) A land consolidation may be applied for by the owner or co-owner of a real estate unit.

(2) If land consolidation is able to remove or decrease the considerable harm caused to the users of real estates by the realization of a public road, railroad, power line, airport or other such project, the land consolidation may also be applied for by the party intending to carry out the project. The land survey office may confer a cadastral procedure order without an application for a land consolidation as referred to above and for a land consolidation which would further the conveyance of land for an additional area or if the conditions in the region can be considerably improved in other ways.

Section 69

(1) The land consolidation area must form a functional entity. An area other than agricultural and forestry land covered by the town plan may not be included in land consolidation without special reason. (322/1999)

(2) A real estate entirely in other use than agriculture and forestry may be included in land consolidation without the owner's consent only if it is essential for realising land consolidation objectives. If necessary, only a part of the area of the real estate may be included in the land consolidation.

SECTION 70

(1) The executors shall draft a report on the conditions and extent of the land consolidation and a general report on the principles to be followed in the land consolidation and the measures to be executed. When drafting the reports, the municipality concerned shall be heard as far as possible.

(2) The interested parties shall be heard concerning the report referred to in subsection 1 above, after which the executors shall decide whether the land consolidation is to be executed or not. If a decision is made to execute the land consolidation, a decision on the area of the land consolidation shall be made at the same time. A land consolidation may be extended to also concern an area other than that intended in the cadastral procedure order.

Section 71

(1) A final decision concerning the execution and area of a land consolidation may be later changed due to considerable changes in circumstances or other relevant reasons.

(2) During the cadastral procedure, minor changes may be made in the area of the land consolidation.

SECTION 72

(1) Roads necessary for the realisation of the purpose of the land division are laid in connection with land consolidation.

(2) The water supply and sewerage equipment needed by the participating property units may also be built in connection with a land consolidation. Plans for the construction of the aforementioned equipment shall be drafted or commissioned by the appropriate regional environment centre.

SECTION 73

(1) All necessary drainage work shall be undertaken and any irrigation equipment to be used jointly built as required.

(2) Executing the drainage work and construction of irrigation equipment may also concern such pieces of land outside the land consolidation area whose owners give their consent to it. Implementation of the relevant measures requires the consent of the competent agricultural authority and the conditions for implementation apply as laid down in water legislation.

(3) If construction of a ditch in the area of a real estate which is not part of the land consolidation is required in order to carry out drainage, an easement may be established for ditch construction purposes for the benefit of the real estate receiving the drainage without the consent of the owner of the encumbered property.

Section 74

(1) Arable land may be cleared in connection with a land consolidation if it is deemed necessary for improving production parcel division or the location of the fields, and afforestation may be carried out on arable land whose use as arable land is no longer functional. The arable area of any joint-owner may not, however, be decreased without his or her consent.

SECTION 75 (96/2000)

(1) If the drainage concerns only the land consolidation area or construction of the ditch as referred to in section 73(3), the executors shall decide on the execution of the ditching unless a permit referred to in Chapter 6(2) of the Water Act is required from the environmental permit authority. The same also applies to a decision on drainage when the owners of real estates not belonging to the land consolidation consent to joint the drainage. In other cases the matter is decided in accordance with the provisions on joint drainage set down in the Water Act.

Section 76

(1) Realisation of the projects referred to in sections 72-74 may commence once the executors' decision concerning them has gained legal force. If possible, the projects must be completed during the cadastral procedure.

Section 77

(1) Each joint-owner shall receive pieces of land in accordance with his or her usufruct in such a way that the grading value of the pieces of land he or she has conveyed for division and the grading value of the pieces of land he or she has received correspond to each other (basis of division).

(2) The joint-owner may be given a maximum of 10 per cent less or 20 per cent more pieces of land than he or she is due through division if it is important in order to achieve a functional land location and causes no considerable harm to any joint-owner. A joint-owner may be given more than 20 per cent over his or her share of the pieces of land with the joint-owners' consent.

(3) Compensation shall be paid for the difference if the number of pieces of land a joint-owner receives is less than that belonging to him or her according to the basis of division. The

compensation is paid by those joint-owners who have received more pieces of land than the amount due to them according to the basis of division.

(4) Notwithstanding the provisions of subsections 1-3, a land consolidation may be executed in such a way that the total value of the pieces of land, growing stock, buildings, fixed equipment and structures, shares of joint property units and special benefits of the real estate

to be formed for each joint-owner corresponds to the share of the equivalent value of the entire land consolidation area belonging to the joint-owner according to the basis of division. The land consolidation shall be executed in the manner referred to in this subsection if all joint-owners present are in agreement on it and if executing land consolidation in this way is necessary to achieve a functional result. (273/1998)

Section 78

(1) If a real estate cannot be essentially improved by land consolidation it may not be changed more than is necessary for the improvement of other real estates. A real estate may not be changed in such a way that its suitability for its previous use or for such other use for which the real estate would have been functionally suited is considerably deteriorated, without the consent of the owner.

(2) Pieces of land which are in special use or otherwise especially valuable or whose future use and value cannot be estimated in a sufficiently reliable manner may not be exchanged without the consent of the owner, unless it is necessary to achieve a functional land location. Furthermore, pieces of land in forestry use may not be exchanged without the consent of the owner in such a way that the quantity of the growing stock of felling age changes considerably.

(3) An area assigned for public use in a master plan or a town plan with legal consequence shall be located, as far as possible, in a real estate owned by the municipality, the State, or the parish or other local community for whose needs the area has been assigned. (322/1999)

Section 79

(1) If the joint-owner owns only an area of insignificant value in the land consolidation area which he or she cannot functionally use and which cannot be favourably improved by land consolidation and which cannot be formed into a functional unit of use even through land consolidation, the area may be claimed for full compensation and given to the other joint-owners.

Section 80

(1) A homestead may be moved in the process of land consolidation if the benefits ensued from moving outweigh the costs. Moving a homestead without the consent of the owner of the real estate requires that the removal is highly important to achieving a functional land location and that moving causes no significant damage or detriment to the owner of the real estate.

SECTION 81

(1) If the owner of the location of a building changes, the building shall be ordered to be claimed by the new owner or sold or ordered to be moved by the owner of the building depending on which procedure causes the least loss to the building or is for other reasons deemed the most practical option.

(2) When a building is ordered to be claimed or approved for sale, the part who conveys the building receives compensation for it according to the value which the building had when it was in his / her possession. The redemption price of the building is determined according to the value which the building has as a part of the unit of use of the redeemer. If the redemption price or the sale price is smaller than the compensation to be paid to the owner of the building, building loss damages are incurred, which are compensated to the party conveying the building.

(3) When a building is ordered to be moved by its owner, the owner receives compensation for moving up to the value of the building in its original place in the possession of its owner,

including the costs of demolishing the building and transporting the demolished material, deducted by the use value of the demolished material.

SECTION 82

(1) In addition to the provisions of section 81 on the building, a joint-owner is paid compensation for the costs and losses of moving a homestead incurred through: 1) proper repair of the area of the old and the new homestead; 2) moving the garden and garden plants or acquiring equivalent assets; 3) building a road to the new homestead; 4) making a well or acquiring an equivalent asset and moving water and sewerage pipes, power and telephone lines and other necessary lines, equipment and structures

which the joint-owner had, or acquiring equivalent assets; 5) moving movable property; 6) temporary hindrance of economic activity caused by moving; and 7) other measures comparable to those above.

SECTION 83

(1) The provisions of section 81 concerning a building remaining on the land of another party apply, as appropriate, to the structures, equipment, cabling, vegetation and other such immobile property whose redemption and selling causes less significant loss of property than moving the property as referred to in section 82.

SECTION 84

(1) If it is necessary to build new buildings or equipment prior to the entry into force of a land consolidation plan, the executors shall take all necessary decisions concerning the construction and location of the buildings. In such a case, a location plan of the pieces of land shall be drafted, if necessary.

(2) If a building or equipment in the case referred to in subsection 1 is located on the land of another party, the necessary pieces of land are given for the use of the owner of the building or equipment against a piece of land in exchange or against an annual compensation.

(3) The implementation of the measure referred to in subsection 1 may begin after the decision concerning it has gained legal force.

Section 85

(1) For the joint-owners who agree on it, a jointly owned forest referred to in the Act on Jointly Owned Forests (37/91) may be formed out of the pieces of land to be given to them that are suitable for forestry following, as appropriate, the provisions of Chapter 10.

Section 86

(1) An area leased as referred to in Chapters 2, 3 and 5 of the Act on Tenancy which has permanent buildings or valuable structures or equipment shall, as far as possible, be given to the landlord, unless this considerably hinders the execution of the division. Any other leasehold referred to in the Act on Tenancy shall be amended to pertain to the new pieces of land of the landlord, unless the change causes considerable hindrance to the tenant.

(2) If the position of the tenant cannot be organised in accordance with subsection 1, an agreement must be reached, as far as possible, on the tenancy concerning the area between the new owner of the lease area and the tenant. If an agreement is not reached, the old lease may be ordered to stay in force as binding the new owner of the area, unless this causes him or her considerable hindrance. In any other case the lease shall be ordered to expire.

(3) The above provisions on leasehold are also applicable to all other special rights.

(4) If the owner of the building which has been entirely or partly leased changes due to the division, the new owner has the right to give notice to end the lease within three months from the gaining of legal force of the land consolidation plan.

SECTION 87

(1) The tenant or the holder of the interest referred to in section 83(3) or a joint-owner to whom damage or hindrance is caused by the organisation or expiration of a right referred to in section 83 shall be paid compensation for the said damage or hindrance.

(2) If the owner of the real estate accrues benefit through the organisation or expiration of a right, he or she shall take part in the compensation to be paid to the right holder according to the amount of the benefit he or she has received. Otherwise the provisions of section 93 apply to the payment of the compensation as referred to in subsection 1.

Section 88

(1) In the land consolidation, a land consolidation plan shall be drafted showing the following: 1) the roads to be laid and drainage work to be carried out and the equipment for water supply, sewerage and irrigation to be built, including all appropriate plans; 2) the real estates to be formed for the part-owners, joint property units and joint property unit shares, special benefits, easements and rights of way; 3) the locations of the homesteads to be moved and the orders on the redemption of

buildings and other organisation; 4) the jointly owned forests to be formed; 5) the scheduling for taking into possession of the pieces of land and other regulations

concerning taking into possession; 6) regulations on the organisation of the position of the holder of the leasehold and the holder of other special rights; and 7) plans concerning other measures to be carried out in the land consolidation.

(2) Based on the land consolidation plan, a preliminary proposal concerning the compensations shall be presented if this does not considerably delay the presentation of the land consolidation plan.

Section 89

(1) The land consolidation plan and its grounds shall be explained to the interested parties at the meeting and an opportunity to acquaint themselves with the plan and to raise objections to it shall be provided. A preliminary proposal for compensations shall also be presented in conjunction with the above stage of the meeting, if such a proposal has been made.

(2) After all objections have been addressed, the executors shall come to an agreement concerning the ratification of the land consolidation plan.

Section 90

(1) The land consolidation shall be carried out in accordance with the land consolidation plan. The network of roads, drainage, water supply, irrigation and sewerage may be supplemented to a minor extent and other minor revisions of the land consolidation plan may be made.

SECTION 91

(1) When the land consolidation plan has gained legal force, the formed real estates shall be entered into the Real Estate Register, unless it is more expedient to enter them into the Real Estate Register subsequent to the closing of the cadastral procedure.

Section 92

(1) If the total value of the property to be divided does not divide between the joint-owners in accordance with the land consolidation plan, compensation shall be paid for the difference. Furthermore, compensations shall be paid for losses caused by other measures executed in connection with the division.

SECTION 93

(1) The expenses of the projects referred to in sections 72-74 above, the loss of building referred to in section 81(2), the compensation for moving referred to in section 81(3) and the loss of property referred to in section 83 as well as the compensations and expenses referred to in sections 82 and 84 and section 87(2) are divided between the interested parties to be paid according to the benefit they have obtained from the procedure. If such benefit cannot be estimated, the expenses and compensations are divided according to other relevant grounds.

SECTION 94

(1) In the cadastral survey meeting, the majority of the joint-owners present may elect one or more representatives to take part in the pre-assessment of the matters to be handled in the cadastral procedure.

(2) The representatives shall be heard when drafting the report referred to in section 70 when discussing the principles to be followed in drafting the land consolidation plan and the measures to be carried out and in all other important matters concerning the execution of the cadastral procedure, as needed.

Section 95

(1) The provisions concerning a real estate apply to an unseparated parcel which has been received prior to making the decision on the land consolidation and which is located in the land consolidation area.

(2) The unseparated parcel referred to in subsection 1 shall be formed into a real estate in connection with the land consolidation if the conditions for its subdivision exist. The provisions on subdivision apply to the formation of real estate.

(3) In addition to the provisions on joint partitioning, in a partitioning executed in connection with land consolidation the share to be separated from the real estate may be amalgamated with the real estate owned by the joint-owner and belonging to the land consolidation. The provisions on the conditions for amalgamating real estates apply to the conditions of such an amalgamation. In land consolidation, real estates involved in the consolidation may also be amalgamated if the preconditions for amalgamation exist. (1188/1996)

CHAPTER 10 - FORMATION OF JOINTLY OWNED FOREST

SECTION 96

(1) If the owners of the real estates are in agreement on the issue, a jointly owned forest such as referred to in the Act on Jointly Owned Forest may be formed out of such pieces of land that are to be used for forestry purposes which form a functional entity. With the consent of the owners, pieces of land may also be included into the jointly owned forest whose use for purposes other than forestry is not important and whose annexation to the jointly owned forest is necessary for achieving a functional property division.

SECTION 97

(1) The assessment of the pieces of land to be taken into the jointly owned forest shall be executed in the manner referred to in section 197(2). Each real estate shall have a share of

the jointly owned forest (interest in a jointly owned forest unit) which corresponds to the share of the grading value of the pieces of land conveyed by the real estate out of the total grading value of all of the pieces of land of the jointly owned forest.

(2) Compensation shall be paid for the difference if the value of the growing stock conveyed to the jointly owned forest by the joint-owner departs from the value of the growing stock of the interest in a jointly owned forest unit he or she has received. When estimating the value of the growing stock, the growing stock subject to felling rights or other rights entitling harvesting of the growing stock shall not be taken into consideration.

(3) Compensation for the difference shall be paid if the value of the piece of land to be taken into the jointly owned forest, when used for a purpose other than forestry, departs from the forestry value of the pieces of land corresponding to the interest in a jointly owned forest unit received by the joint-owner.

Section 97a (1188/1996)

(1) Notwithstanding the provisions of section 97, a jointly owned forest may be formed based on an agreement between the interested real estate owners in such a way that the interest in a jointly owned forest unit pertaining to each participating real estate corresponds to the value of

the area conveyed by the real estate when compared with the total value of the jointly owned forest.

(2) If in an agreement concerning the amalgamation of jointly owned forests the groups of joint-owners agree on the sizes of the shares of the real estates and their calculation basis, the formation of the jointly owned forest shall be executed in accordance with the agreement, unless the agreement is in violation of the rights of any individual(s). (111/2003)

SECTION 98

(1) A jointly owned forest shall be formed in a land consolidation or a cadastral procedure executed for that specific purpose. The procedure may be applied for by the party who is ready to convey land for the formation of a jointly owned forest.

(2) A jointly owned forest may be formed in connection with the partitioning of an area of a real estate or a part of an area of a real estate if all joint-owners of the real estate to be partitioned are in agreement concerning its formation, or when the owner of the real estate concerned requests it. (111/2003)

(3) If the joint-owners of a real estate agree on a division of a real estate owned in specified shares according to a division agreement in such a way that a jointly owned forest is formed out of the area of the real estate or out of a part of it, the measures necessary for it shall be carried out in the cadastral procedure to which the provisions for partitioning apply. The same applies when, at the request of the owner of the real estate, the area of the real estate or a part of the area of the real estate owned by him or her is formed through partitioning into two or more real estates which have a share in the jointly owned forest to be formed. (111/2003)

Section 99

(1) New pieces of land may be connected to an existing jointly owned forest by giving the party conveying the pieces of land a corresponding share of the jointly owned forest, if the owner of the pieces of land and the group of joint-owners of the jointly owned forest agree on it. The conditions and procedure of the annexation of land fall under the provisions concerning the formation of a jointly owned forest.

(2) If the interested parties are in agreement concerning the sizes of the shares of the real estates or on their calculation basis with regard to formation of a jointly owned forest or annexation

to an existing jointly owned forest, the procedure shall be executed in accordance with the agreement, unless doing so is in violation of the rights of any individual(s). (111/2003)

Section 100

(1) The expenses incurred due to the cadastral procedure as referred to in this Chapter shall be paid from State funds.

(2) When a jointly owned forest is formed by partitioning as referred to in section 98(2) or in a subdivision as referred to in section 98(3), the cadastral procedure fee incurred by the cadastral procedure is paid from State funds as far as it concerns the formation of a jointly owned forest. (111/2003)

CHAPTER 11 - PROPERTY DEFINITION

SECTION 101

(1) A property definition is executed in order to settle a dispute or handle any ambiguity concerning the dimensions of a real estate or other register unit or property division. The property definition clarifies and resolves the following: 1) any ambiguity concerning the place of the boundary and the boundary marker

(demarcation);

2) any ambiguity concerning which register unit an area belongs to;

3) any ambiguity concerning the easement and the location of the easement;

4) the real estate's share of a joint property unit or joint special benefit and the size of

the share as well as the special benefit belonging to the real estate;

5) the participating real estates of a joint property unit or a joint special benefit and the

sizes of the shares belonging to them; 6) the content of an unclear, lost or damaged cadastral document; 7) any ambiguity caused by conflicting cadastral documents or cadastral maps; and 8) any other ambiguity concerning the property division.

(2) An area left or separated in a cadastral procedure as a public or joint property unit under legislation in force before 1 January 1917 for a broader purpose than that intended by the participating real estates, or a part of such an area which has not later on been formed into a real estate or a joint property unit and which is intended for use as an army training field or as a church, chapel, cemetery, parish school, poorhouse, crown storehouse, parish storehouse, hospital establishment or other such public purpose shall be formed into a real estate or joint property unit, and the owner of the area shall be clarified and resolved by property definition.

Section 102

(1) If the property definition reveals that an error as referred to in section 278 has occurred, the real estate registration authority shall assign the matter to be handled by the central administration of the National Land Survey of Finland after the cadastral procedure has gained legal force.

SECTION 103

(1) Property definition is executed based on an application of the owner or part-owner of the register unit or of another person whose interest the property definition directly concerns.

(2) A property definition necessary for the drafting and implementing of the plan is executed based on an application of the municipality. A demarcation for building, moving or repairing a boundary marker shall also be performed based on the application of the authority, community or other person due to whose measures the demarcation has become

necessary. A demarcation is executed without application in connection with another cadastral procedure if it is necessary for the execution of the cadastral procedure.

Subsection 3 has been repealed by Act 1188/1996.

Section 104

(1) A boundary which earlier has been defined with legal force shall continue to be established to its former position. If the boundary has been defined differently in different cadastral procedures, the position of the boundary shall be defined in accordance with the last resolution with legal force.

(2) If the boundary has not been defined with legal force, the conditions and grounds concerning the position of the boundary shall be clarified in a cadastral procedure and the boundary position shall be resolved based on them and other available reports on the matter.

(3) If the position of the boundary cannot be defined in a completely reliable manner such as in a case as referred to in subsections 1 or 2 and if the owners of the real estates on both sides of the boundary who are present agree on a position of the boundary which is not in conflict with the available report on the boundary position, the boundary shall be established to the position agreed on by the interested parties.

Section 105

(1) If a boundary of a water area located in the water of a village governed by water law has not been defined earlier, it shall be defined in compliance with the provisions of the relevant act containing regulations concerning water boundaries and the division of water areas.

Section 106

(1) When demarcation is executed in water areas between villages, detached lands shall be exchanged and the boundary straightened, if it is expedient to do so.

Section 107 (1188/1996)

(1) When executing the demarcation of a boundary which has not been marked with boundary markers or coordinates, the boundary may be straightened in such a way that areas of insignificant value or surface areas are exchanged between register units or transferred from one register unit to another, if a suitable corresponding area is not found. Compensation is payable for the difference of the values of the area to be exchanged or for the area to be transferred.

Section 108

(1) If a boundary marker is at risk of being destroyed or if it causes hindrance, it may be moved to another place without changing the position of the boundary.

(2) If the boundary marker is dilapidated or otherwise defective and there is no ambiguity or quarrel concerning the correct position of the boundary, the boundary marker may be repaired without defining the position of the boundary.

(3) A new boundary marker may be erected without changing the location of the boundary if it is necessary for indicating the position of the boundary in the terrain.

(4) The measures referred to in subsections 1-3 above are executed as demarcation.

Section 109

(1) The provisions of this Chapter on the position of the boundary and a boundary marker of a register unit apply, as appropriate, to the position of the boundary and the boundary marker of an easement area and any other boundary indicating a property division.

Section 110

(1) The owner of the area referred to in section 101(2) is the party for whom the area has been left or separated as public area or jointly owned area based on a report obtained from the cadastral document or other documents and who has begun to use the area according to its original purpose. If another party who has gained possession of the area has begun to use the area for the original or equivalent purpose, the owner is the party who tends to the task.

(2) In cases other than that referred to in subsection 1, the owner of the area is the one who governs the area as owner. If no party governs the area as owner and the area has not been separated or left to be a joint property unit of the real estates, the municipality owns the area.

(3) The provisions on an area laid down in this section also apply to a part of an area.

Section 111

(1) An area as referred to in section 101(2) is formed into a real estate or connected to an existing real estate in compliance with the provisions of section 41. If the area is a joint property unit its boundaries are defined, if they are unclear, along with the real estates whose joint property unit the area constitutes as well as the sizes of the shares.

Section 112

(1) When granting the title to the party who, in accordance with the property definition as referred to in section 101(2), constitutes the owner of the real estate or the area connected to the real estate formed in a cadastral procedure, an excerpt from the report drafted in the cadastral procedure shall be considered adequate documentation of his or her acquisition.

CHAPTER 12 - URBAN LAND REPLOTTING

Section 113 322/1999)

(1) Urban land replotting may be executed if it can further the formation into real estate of areas assigned for different uses in the town plan or the balancing of the clearly unbalanced division of building right in an area in which the said plan has been ratified for the first time. A further condition for the execution of the replotting is that it is necessary due to imminent construction in the area. Urban land replotting may only be executed if the town plan concerned includes a plan provision according to which urban land replotting may be executed in order to implement the plan.

Section 114

(1) Urban land replotting may be applied for by the municipality or the owner of the area located in an area to be planned. The application must be presented before the town plan for the area has gained legal force. (322/1999)

(2) The order for the execution of replotting may be given after the plan proposal has been made available for public inspection.

Section 115

(1) Urban land replotting is executed in the area which is covered by the plan as referred to in section 113 (replotting area). For a special reason, a part of the area of the plan may constitute the replotting area.

(2)

An area owned by the municipality may be included in the replotting area only if the municipality gives its consent to it or if the area concerned is insignificant, or if including the area in the replotting area is necessary in order to organise a block area.

Section 116

(1)

Before a decision on the execution of the replotting is made, the executors must draft a report on the conditions of the replotting and the replotting area.

(2)

The executors shall decide on the execution of the replotting and the replotting area. Before taking the decision, the interested parties and the municipality shall be provided an opportunity to acquaint them with the report referred to in subsection 1 and to present their opinions concerning the commencement of the replotting and the area concerned.

Section 117

(1) The pieces of land of a real estate or of an unseparated parcel conveyed or retained which is in the replotting area and which consists of only one plot or building site fitting the town plan may not be replotted or claimed without a special reason. (322/1999)

(2) In the decision concerning the execution of the replotting, the real estates and other areas whose pieces of land are not replotted or claimed under subsection 1 are to be mentioned separately. The limitations laid down in section 177 do not apply to these real estates and areas.

SECTION 118 (322/1999)

(1) In the urban land replotting, the public areas referred to in section 83 of the Land Use and Building Act which in the town plan are intended for the purposes of the municipality shall be separated first and in priority to other areas, as far as they are not already owned by the municipality.

Section 119

(1) In urban land replotting, the basis of division is the value of the areas owned by the joint-owner in the replotting area to which they belonged prior to drafting the plan.

(2) The joint-owner is given a share of the areas belonging to the replotting area in accordance with the basis of division excluding the areas referred to in section 118. In this case the areas are estimated according to the value they possess subsequent to the confirmation of the plan. As far as an area cannot be given in accordance with the basis of division, compensation shall be paid for the difference.

SECTION 120

(1) The areas are divided between the joint-owners in such a way that each joint-owner primarily receives his or her share from the areas he or she owns and the division facilitates the drafting of a subdivision plan or the formation of plots or building sites fitting the plan. If there is a binding subdivision plan in the area, the area may not be divided without special reason in such a way that the boundary of the area to be given to the joint-owner departs from the subdivision plan. (322/1999)

(2) The joint-owner shall be given an area that departs from the basis of division as far as is necessary in order to divide the areas in a manner referred to in subsection 1. The joint-owner is not obliged to receive an area that is more than 30 per cent over the value of the area due to him or her in accordance with the basis of division.

Section 121

(1) An area suitable for a plot or building site shall be given to a joint-owner whose share is so insignificant with respect to the basis of division that it does not correspond to any plot or building site fitting the plan if the joint-owner so demands, and if no such joint-owner who has made a similar demand and whose share is greater than the share of the previously mentioned joint-owner's share is left without an equivalent area.

SECTION 122 (322/1999)

(1) If the area to be organised cannot be divided by the measures referred to in sections 120(2) and 121 in a manner referred to in section 120(1), parts may be given from an area suitable as a plot or a building site in accordance with the town plan to several joint-owners owning an insignificant share if none of these desires to claim the entire area. If several joint-owners demand to claim the area, the joint-owner whose share is the largest in accordance with the basis of division has priority.

(2) If none of the joint-owners referred to in subsection 1 have made a demand for redemption, the municipality may claim the entire area.

(3) In a cadastral procedure, the municipality, municipal federation or State may claim the public area or plot of a public building as referred to in section 96 of the Land Use and Building Act assigned for its needs, as long as the area is not separated for the municipality under section 118 of this Act.

Section 123

(1) The number of street areas which the municipality is entitled to receive without compensation in accordance with the Land Use and Building Act is ordered in compliance with the provisions of the said Act. When making the calculation the entire replotting area is considered comparable to an area belonging to one landowner and the areas owned by the municipality are left out of the calculation. (322/1999)

(2)

For the areas referred to in section 118, excluding the areas owned by the municipality or areas to be transferred to the possession of the municipality without compensation as referred to in subsection 1 of this Act, the parties to the replotting are entitled to compensation by the municipality to be divided between the parties in accordance with the basis of division. For the determination of the compensation, the areas are estimated according to the value they possessed before making the decision to draft a plan, adding the increase in value which has occurred subsequent to the said moment due to general increases in price level or to other reasons not related to the planning for which the replotting is carried out.

SECTION 124

(1) If the owner of the location of a building changes in the replotting, the building shall be ordered to be claimed by the new owner of the area.

(2) If the building is not suitable for the purpose laid out in accordance with the plan or if a building referred to in subsection 1 poorly suits the use requirements of the new owner, the building shall be estimated to have the value which it has, taking into consideration the purpose of the area in accordance with the plan and the realistic possibilities to use the building.

(3) If the value estimated in compliance with subsection 2 is inferior to the value that the building had without the influence of the plan or the change of owner, the difference is building loss, for which the interested parties are accountable in compliance with section 130(2).

Section 125

(1) The provisions of section 124 apply, as appropriate, to a structure, equipment, cabling, vegetation, garden and other such items classified as immovable property.

Section 126

(1) The provisions of sections 86 and 87 apply to organising the position of a leaseholder and holder of other special rights concerning the replotting area.

Section 127

(1) In urban land replotting a replotting plan is drafted showing: 1) the areas to be separated for the municipality under section 118; 2) the areas to be given to the shareholders and the areas to be claimed from the

shareholders; 3) the areas to be claimed for the municipality, municipal federation or State under section 122(2) and (3); 4) the easements, shares in joint property units and benefits of the real estates to be formed; 5) the provisions regarding the redemption of the buildings; 6) the provisions regarding organising the position of the leaseholder and holder of

other special right; 7) the time of taking into possession of the areas and other provisions regarding the

taking into possession; 8) the compensations to be paid due to the replotting; and 9) other measures comparable to those above;

Section 128

(1) The replotting plan and the grounds for the plan shall be explained to the interested parties during the meeting proceedings and an opportunity shall be provided for the interested parties to acquaint themselves with the plan and to raise any objections or make any claims concerning it. When all objections have been addressed, the replotting plan shall be confirmed.

Section 129

(1) When the replotting plan has been confirmed, the areas received by each shareholder and other interested parties are formed into either a single or several real estates. (322/1999)

(2) A joint-property unit contained within a replotting area may be transferred to a real estate to be formed in compliance with the provisions for redemption of an area referred to in sections 60 and 61. If the transfer is not executed, the area received by the shareholders remains a jointly owned unit of real estates or is formed into a real estate based on the request of the shareholders.

Subsection 3 is repealed by Act 322/1999.

SECTION 130

(1) The expenses incurred through urban land replotting are divided between the shareholders and the municipality in proportion to the values of the areas they have received in the replotting. The expenses are subsequently divided between the shareholders in proportion to the benefit they have each obtained from the replotting.

(2) The loss of property referred to in sections 124(3) and 125 and the compensations to be paid to the holder of leasehold and of other special right is divided between the shareholders in accordance with the basis referred to in subsection 1 as far as the measure upon which basis the compensation is paid is not beneficial to the owner of the real estate. However, the municipality is not obliged to take part in the payment of the said losses and compensations.

CHAPTER 13 - JOINT PROPERTY UNITS AND SPECIAL BENEFITS

Transferral of a share in a joint property unit and formation into a real estate unit

Section 131

(1) A share conveyed from a real estate into a joint property unit or a specified share of such a share is transferred into the real estate of the recipient of the conveyance or is formed into a real estate, if the transferral is not possible. Similarly, a share in a joint property unit may be transferred into another real estate owned by the real estate owner based on his or her

application. The above-mentioned measures are executed in a cadastral procedure to which the provisions for subdivision apply. (9.4.1998/273)

(2) In the cadastral procedure referred to in subsection 1, a share is considered an unseparated parcel. The transferral of a share may also be executed even in cases in which the real estate from which the share is separated is located in a municipality other than that of the receiver property unit if the share transferral is deemed expedient.

Formation of a joint property unit and joining of an area to a joint property unit

SECTION 132

(1) Based on an agreement of the interested parties, an area containing private pieces of land of one or several real estates may be formed into a joint property unit of the real estates if it is deemed necessary for the respective real estates. Based on an agreement of the owners, an area received by several real estate owners through conveyance as the joint possession thereof may be formed into a joint property unit of the real estates they own. (273/1998)

(2) A joint property unit may not, however, be formed for the purpose of a jointly owned forest, road or main drainage canal or other conduit of water.

(3) A joint property unit may not be formed in an area covered by a town plan. (322/1999)

SECTION 133 (688/2000)

(1) An area for which the joint-owners of a joint property unit have received possession is joined into a joint property unit belonging to the joint-owners.

(2) An area belonging to a real estate may be joined to a joint property unit by giving the real estate a share of the joint property unit corresponding to the area if the owner of the real estate and the joint-owners of the area are in agreement on it.

(3) Joint property units whose joint-owners have agreed on the joining of the joint property units belonging to them are joined together by forming a new joint property unit out of them.

SECTION 134 (688/2000)

(1) An area shall be separated to become a joint property unit and an area as referred to in section 133(1) joined to an existing joint property unit in a cadastral procedure to which the provisions for subdivision apply or in connection with another cadastral procedure.

(2) An area shall be joined to a joint property unit and the joint property units joined together in cases referred to in section 133(2) and (3) in a cadastral procedure to be executed for such purpose. In order to determine the respective shares, the area to be joined and the joint property units are estimated in a cadastral procedure and the share of each real estate in the formed joint property unit determined at a level that corresponds in value to the area which previously belonged to the real estate or to the share of a joint property unit which previously belonged to the real estate.

(3) The joint property unit to be formed is to be principally of the same type, either a land area or water area. Further conditions for joining of the area into a joint property unit are that there are no

mortgages on the real estate from which the area is taken and that the area to be joined is released from liability for the mortgages of the said real estate. A condition for release is that the holder of a lien gives his or her consent to it. The release may take place without the consent of the holder of the lien if the real estate from which the area is taken is clearly adequate to be liable for the mortgages pertaining to it subsequent to the annexation.

Section 135

(1) In a partitioning, the water area of a real estate is separated to become a joint property of the real estates if no special reason for its division exists.

Section 136

(1) If it is deemed necessary in order to achieve a functional division and no considerable harm is caused by it to any joint-owner, the following may be separated as joint property without the consent of the interested parties in connection with partitioning and land consolidation: 1) an area necessary for private car storage or for a boat harbour or dock; 2) an area necessary for drawing water or for damming; 3) an area necessary for quarrying rock, gravel, sand, clay, turf, or other soil; and 4) a land area necessary for the use of a joint water area or fishing rights which

constitute a joint special benefit.

(2) An area may also be separated to become joint property in connection with land consolidation in other special cases.

(3) A joint property unit may not, however, be formed if the need for which the area is to be formed can be equally well satisfied through establishment of an easement.

Division of a joint property unit

SECTION 137

(1) A joint owner of a joint property unit other than a rapid or a jointly owned forest referred to in the Act on Jointly Owned Forests is entitled to have his or her share separated by division if the separation can take place without causing any significant harm to any joint-owner.

(2) Further conditions for division of a jointly owned water area are that the separation of a share is necessary for special use purposes or that other significant reasons for separation exist.

(3) If a share in a jointly owned land area cannot be separated and the share is not necessary for the use of the real estate of the joint-owner, the other joint-owners are obliged to claim the share when he or she so demands. When the share has been claimed, the joint property unit belongs to the remaining participating real estates in proportion to their earlier shares, unless the joint-owners agree otherwise. The joint-owners who have claimed the share shall pay compensation to the joint-owner demanding the claim for his or her loss.

SECTION 138

(1) If a functional land location cannot be achieved by dividing the joint property unit alone and by executing land exchanges, pieces of land bordering the joint property unit may be included in the division to the extent that is necessary to achieve a functional land location. A precondition for

inclusion of these pieces of land in the division is that no significant harm is caused to any individual(s) as a result.

Section 139

(1) The share of each real estate in the joint property unit is the basis of division in dividing a joint property unit. The size of the share is determined in accordance with the basis of division or other decision regarding the size of the share used in the cadastral procedure in which the area has been left or separated to become joint property. If the area has been left or become joint property without having been handled in a cadastral procedure, the sizes of the shares of the formed real estates are those provided in the legislation in force at the time of the cadastral procedure. In as far as the size has been later agreed on, ordered or otherwise provided for in the law, the share is determined in accordance with such agreement, decision or provision.

(2) An amount equivalent to the usufruct of the pieces of land included in the division is given to the real estate from which pieces of land have been taken for the division of a joint property unit under section 138.

Section 140

(1) In the division of a water area, an area of rapids belonging to the water area shall be left as joint property. If the water power of the rapids is of less value than its use for fishing or other use, or if the rapids may be given to someone without causing harm to any of the joint-owners, the rapids area may be included in the division in connection with the rest of the water area.

(2) If the right to the water power of the rapids has been legally separated before 1 March 1903 through means other than division, the rapids area is included in the division exclusive of its water power.

(3) In the division of a water area, a special fishing site may be formed into a joint property unit if it is necessary for the realization of the division. Another water area may be formed as a joint property of the participating real estates based on an agreement of the interested parties present.

Section 141

(1) If the jointly owned land area to be divided is located in such a way that the area or a part of the area can only be functionally used in connection with the pieces of land belonging privately to real estates, or if the land area to be divided is of insignificant value, the jointly owned area or a part of it may be claimed and joined as regional parts to those real estates on whose pieces of land the joint property unit borders as far as a satisfactory land location is not achieved by measures referred to in section 138. In special cases, some of a joint property unit may be ordered to be claimed by a participating real estate which does not border on the joint property unit. The provisions above for real estate apply also to jointly owned forest.

(2) A joint property unit or part of it referred to in subsection 1 which is located in an area covered by a town plan and which the municipality would be entitled to claim without special permit under the Land Use and Building Act may be ordered to be claimed by the municipality in a division. (322/1999)

(3) When a joint property unit is joined to a real estate or a jointly owned forest under subsection 1 or claimed by the municipality under subsection 2, the joint-owner of a joint property unit is

entitled to compensation determined in accordance with the same basis as the share of his or her real estate in the joint property unit.

SECTION 142

(1) The executors shall decide on the conditions and the extent of the division of a joint property unit. They shall also decide in conjunction with these proceedings to what extent the division is to be executed as a division as referred to in section 137(1) and to what extent to apply the redemption procedure referred to in section 141 and which shares are to be ordered to be claimed under section 137(3).

Section 143

(1) In the division of a joint property unit a partitioning plan is drafted presenting: 1) the joining of the divided pieces of land to the real estates of the joint-owners or formation of them into separate real estates;

2) the giving of pieces of land to real estates in cases referred to in section 139(2);

3) the leaving or forming of areas as joint property;

4) the claiming of areas and joining of them to real estates or to a jointly owned forest, or formation of them into a separate real estate;

5) the claiming of the share referred to in section 137(3) and its division between the real estates;

6) the easements to be established;

7) the organisation of the position of a holder of a right as referred to in section 145 or

expiration of rights; 8) the compensations to be paid due to the division; and 9) any other necessary measures comparable with those above;

Section 144

(1) The partitioning plan and its grounds shall be explained to the interested parties during the meeting and an opportunity shall be provided for the interested parties to acquaint themselves with the partitioning plan and to raise any objections to it. Once all objections have been handled, the executors shall decide on the confirmation of the partitioning plan.

(2) If the partitioning plan has gained legal force, the entries due to it may be made in the Real Estate Register before the closing of the cadastral procedure.

SECTION 145

(1) If the area to be divided is subject to leasehold or other special right, the provisions of sections 86 and 87 apply to the organising of the position of the holder of the right.

Section 146

(1) The area received by the real estate is joined to the participating real estate or an area corresponding to the separated share is formed for a special reason into a separate real estate. The same applies to an area which is claimed by the municipality under section 141(2).

Section 147

(1) An area or share of an area which in a division of a joint property unit is transferred from one real estate to another, or is formed into a separate real estate, is released from the liens encumbering it. The liens encumbering the receiving real estate also concern the area or share transferred to the real estate after the entry into force of the cadastral procedure.

Special benefits

SECTION 148

(1) If a special benefit such as the right to water power, fishing or quarrying concerning a specific area located in the area to be divided belongs to several real estates jointly, such a benefit remains valid in the division. The benefit may, however, be cancelled in compliance

with section 149. If the special benefit belongs only to the real estates involved in the division, it may be included in the division if there is a special reason for doing so.

(2) The area which is the object of the benefit may be separated according to the division to become a joint property of the real estates entitled to the benefit if it is expedient to do so.

(3) A special benefit directed at the area to be divided and belonging privately to a real estate remains valid. The benefit may, however, be cancelled in compliance with the provisions of section 149 or included in the division if the benefit belongs to a real estate involved in the division and if there is special cause to include the benefit in the division.

SECTION 149

(1) A joint special benefit or a private special benefit concerning the area of the real estate or of another register unit may be cancelled on the basis of the demand of the owner of the encumbered register unit, if the benefit due to a change in circumstances has become insignificant in value to the real estates entitled to it or if the easement due to the use of the benefit has become unreasonably great in proportion to the benefit obtained from it. The cancellation is executed in a separate cadastral procedure or in connection with another cadastral procedure.

(2) The owner of the encumbered register unit shall pay compensation for the loss due to the cancellation of the benefit.

Miscellaneous provisions

SECTION 150

(1) The share of a jointly owned land area or of a joint special benefit belonging to a real estate to be partitioned or a special benefit belonging to it privately shall be given to one of the real estates formed in the partitioning if the division of the share or benefit between several real estates formed in the partitioning is not functional from the point of view of the use of the real estates, or if

the interested parties do not agree on the division. The share of the real estate to be partitioned of a jointly owned water area shall be divided between the real estates in accordance with the basis of division followed in the cadastral procedure, unless the interested parties agree otherwise.

(2) If the interested parties have so agreed, a share of the original property unit of the joint property unit or of a joint special benefit or a private special benefit of the original property unit shall be given to the subdivided real estate unit or the property unit formed out of the receiver property unit and the transferred unseparated parcel. Unless the interested parties have agreed otherwise, the share of the subdivided property unit or of the real estate formed out of the receiver property unit and the unseparated parcel transferred to it shall be ordered in proportion to the surface area of the subdivided property unit or the transferred unseparated parcel and the residual property unit or, for special reason, according to other reasonable grounds. (1188/1996)

Section 150a (322/1999)

(1) A public area does not have a share in joint property units or special benefits.

Section 151

(1) A share in a joint special benefit can be transferred into another real estate in compliance with the provisions for transferring a share of a joint property unit.

(2) If the entire area of a real estate which has a share in a joint property unit or in a joint special benefit or a private special benefit is formed into a public area, a redemption unit, a

road or an annexed area, or is joined to a jointly owned forest, the share or benefit belonging to the real estate forms a remaining real estate.

Section 152

(1) In a cadastral procedure it must always be noted in which joint property units or joint special benefits the formed real estates have shares and the size of the share belonging to each real estate must be stated. If the amount of the original property unit of the real estate to be formed in a cadastral procedure has not been validly solved, the share of the original property unit's share of a joint property unit or special benefit that each real estate to be formed possesses must be noted in the cadastral procedure. The special benefits belonging privately to the formed real estates must also be noted in the cadastral procedure.

Section 153

(1) The provisions of this Chapter apply to a jointly owned forest and a share in a jointly owned forest only if it is separately provided for. The provisions of section 152 apply, as appropriate, to a share in a jointly owned forest.

CHAPTER 14 - EASEMENTS

Section 154

(1) To benefit a real estate, a right as a permanent easement may be established in the area of another register unit: 1) to take and conduct household water or to place and use the equipment and structures connected to it;

2) to conduct water for the drainage of the land;

3) to place and use the equipment and structures connected with sewage handling;

4) to place and use the equipment and structures connected with telephone, electricity, gas, heating and other such cables and wiring;

5) to use an area necessary for keeping private cars or as a boat harbour, dock, swimming place, timber storage bay, loading area or fishing area;

6) to quarry rock, gravel, sand, clay, turf, or other equivalent soil;

7) to establish and use structures necessary for civil defence;

8) to establish and use a common heating plant or a waste collection site for the real estate; and 9) to create an area necessary for transportation purposes in an area covered by town plan. (322/1999)

(2) If the establishment of the right referred to in subsection 1 is not considered functional as a permanent easement due to an expected change in the circumstances or for other special reason, the said right may be established as a fixed-term easement. The cadastral procedure shall determine the date until which the fixed-term easement is in force. If necessary, the cadastral procedure may also determine the event which determines the expiry of the fixed-term easement before the end of the fixed term.

(3) Separate provisions shall be issued for a building easement.

Section 154a (322/1999)

(1) To benefit a real estate in a shore plan area, a right to the use of a commonhold referred to in section 75 of the Land Use and Building Act shall be established in the area of another register unit as an easement for those real estates for whose use the area is intended in the plan. The same applies to the areas referred to in section 91(2) of the Land Use and Building Act.

Section 155 (322/1999)

(1) The easement referred to in section 154(1)(1-4), (7) and (9) and the easement referred to in point 5 of the said subsection for the use of an area necessary for keeping cars may also be established for the municipality in an area covered by town plan.

SECTION 156

(1) An easement may be established if the owners of the encumbered real estate and the dominant real estate or, when the easement may be established for the municipality, the municipality and the real estate owner agree on it and the easement is necessary for the real estate or municipality and does not cause considerable harm to the encumbered register unit or to the dominant tenement holding an earlier easement on the area. However, if the establishment

of an easement is necessary for partitioning, division of a joint property unit, mandatory land exchange, area transferral, land consolidation or urban land replotting in a functional manner, the easement referred to in section 154(1)(1-6) and (9) may be established without the consent of the interested parties in the area subject to the cadastral procedure.

(2)

In an area covered by a town plan, an easement referred to in section 154(1)(1-3) and (9) and the easement referred to in point 5 necessary for keeping cars may be established without the consent of the owner of the encumbered register unit if the easement is important to the dominant real estate or municipality and no considerable harm is caused by it to the encumbered register unit or to the dominant tenement holding an earlier easement on the area. (322/1999)

(3)

In the cadastral procedure, each real estate and parcel shall be provided access to a street, building plan road, public road or such private road for which a private road maintenance association has been founded by establishing an easement referred to in section 154(1)(9) or by establishing a permanent or fixed-term right of way referred to in the Act on Private Roads (358/1962) or other right necessary for access to a road. The provisions of the Act on Private Roads apply to the conditions of establishing such a right. If the owner of the interested real estate so requests, the cadastral procedure shall decide on giving right of way also to the private road referred to above. (273/1998)

Section 157

(1) The establishment of an easement may not hinder the realisation of a town plan. In other respects the easement shall also be established in such a way that its purpose is achieved as economically as possible and that the easement or the use of it do not cause unnecessary harm to the environment and no greater damage or harm than is necessary is caused to any person. (322/1999)

(2) An easement may not be established if the use of it is forbidden on the basis of other legislation. If the use of the easement requires permission from the authorities laid down in other legislation, the establishment of an easement does not replace such permission. The use of an easement referred to in section 154(1) does not require the consent of the owner referred to in Chapter 9(4)(3).

Section 158

(1) The cadastral procedure shall determine the area to which the established easement is to be directed, as well as the necessary conditions and limitations of the use of the easement.

(2) If the use of the easement or right as referred to in section 156(3) requires the construction of a road or building, structure or equipment, or other repair work of the easement area, and the easement or right does not refer to a road formed by joint-owners through the right of a private road maintenance association or belonging jointly to the joint-owners of a private road maintenance association, the cadastral procedure shall give necessary orders regarding the participation of the owners of the dominating real estates and the owner of the encumbered area concerning reparatory expenses if any of the interested parties so demands or if it is otherwise deemed necessary. If the interested parties do not agree on the division of reparatory expenses,

the basis of division shall be the benefit obtained by each real estate. The benefit obtained by an easement for drainage purposes is determined in compliance with Chapter 6 of the Water Act. In this case, a joint irrigation unit, as referred to in the Water Act, may also be established. The provisions of this subsection concerning reparatory expenses also apply to the maintenance expenses of the easement area. The provisions of the Water Act for maintenance of a ditch apply to the maintenance of an easement established for drainage. (273/1998)

(3) If the easement has been established for the municipality, the provisions of subsection 2 for the owner of the dominant tenement apply to the municipality.

Section 159

(1) A cadastral procedure in which real estates are formed, areas are exchanged or joined to a real estate shall determine the real estate to which the benefits of the earlier established easements or rights, as referred to in section 153(3), shall remain in force.

(2) If the given easement or right is a requirement for a number of real estates formed in the cadastral procedure, it may be ordered to remain in force to the benefit of these as well, if the conditions for the establishment of an easement referred to in sections 156 and 157 prevail.

(3) Any easement pertaining to the cadastral procedure area which is deemed unnecessary may be annulled in connection with the cadastral procedure.

Section 160 (322/1999)

(1) An easement established in a cadastral procedure may be moved to another place in the area of the encumbered register unit or new regulations regarding the limitation of the use of the easement may be given or changes may be made to the earlier regulations regarding the use of the easement if the interested parties are in agreement on it and the measure does not hinder the realization of the town plan. Such a measure may even be taken without the agreement of the interested parties if a hindrance caused by the easement due to a change of circumstances can be removed or alleviated and the measure does not cause considerable harm to the dominant real estates.

Section 161

(1) An easement established in a cadastral procedure may be cancelled if the circumstances have changed in such a way that the easement can no longer be established in compliance with sections 156 and 157 and the easement is not necessary to the dominant real estate or the municipality. A necessary easement may be annulled if unreasonable hindrance caused by the easement cannot be removed through the measures referred to in section 160 and if, instead of the cancelled easement, an equivalent easement may be established in another place in compliance with the conditions referred to in sections 156 and 157.

(2) If an unreasonable hindrance caused by the easement cannot be removed through the measures referred to in subsection 1 and if an increase in encumbrance of the easement is caused by the change of use of the easement, those dominant tenements whose use has caused the increase in encumbrance shall compensate the owner of the encumbered register unit for the additional hindrance.

Section 162

(1) The owner and possessor of an encumbered register unit is entitled to receive compensation for the losses caused by the establishment of the easement from the party to whose benefit the easement is established. In a subdivision, the owner of the residual property unit is entitled to compensation concerning an easement or right established to the benefit of the subdivided real estate unit that is necessary for access to a road as referred to in section 156(3) only on special grounds. If the encumbrance is noticeably increased due to an order referred to in section 159(2), the owner of the encumbered register unit is entitled to receive compensation for the additional hindrance from the dominant tenements referred to in the said subsection.

SECTION 163

(1) When a permanent right referred to in section 156(3) is established in a division between all participating real estates, the share of the grading value of the pieces of land needed for the right may be counted as the share of each joint-owner in accordance with the basis of division if it is deemed expedient, taking into consideration the benefit obtained from the establishment of the right by the joint-owners. In this case, no compensation is payable regarding the conveyance of an area for the establishment of a right.

Section 164

(1) If the easement is deleted or transferred or its use is limited or the regulations regarding its use are changed, the dominant tenement is entitled to compensation for the losses caused by the measure from the party who benefits from the measure. The compensation is reduced in proportion to the benefit obtained from the measure by the recipient of the compensation. If there are several liable parties, they shall each participate in the payment of the compensation in proportion to the benefit they have obtained.

Section 165 (322/1999)

(1) The establishment, transferral or annulment of an easement as referred to in this Chapter or all other matters regarding an easement or right shall be handled in an easement survey or in connection with another cadastral procedure.

(2) A matter regarding a right referred to in the Act on Private Roads as referred to in section 156(3) may be handled in an easement survey in an area covered by a town plan only if the matter regards the transferral, changing or annulment of such a right. In an area other than that referred to above, a right referred to in the Act on Private Roads as referred to in section 156(3) may be handled in an easement survey only if at the same time a cadastral procedure regarding an easement referred to in section 154(1) is concerned.

Section 166

(1) An easement survey may be applied for by the owner of a register unit. A municipality may apply for an easement survey if an easement established or to be established to the benefit of the municipality is concerned. Annulment, transferral or other changing of an easement concerning a joint property unit may also be applied for by a joint-owner of a joint property unit.

Section 167

(1) The execution expenses of the easement survey shall be paid by the applicant. If the cadastral procedure also benefits another interested party, he or she shall participate in the

expenses in proportion to the benefit obtained by him or her from the measure or based on some other reasonable grounds.

(2) The provisions of subsection 1 for the payment of the execution expenses of an easement survey also apply, as appropriate, when the matter concerning the easement is handled in connection with another cadastral procedure.

CHAPTER 15 - CADASTRAL SURVEY PROCEDURE PUBLICATION

SECTION 168

(1) All interested parties are notified of the beginning of the procedure by means of a letter of summons.

(2) If the cadastral procedure concerns a real estate or unseparated parcel owned jointly by many parties, the letter of summons shall be delivered separately to all joint-owners. If the cadastral procedure concerns a joint property unit and the cadastral procedure does not concern its division or a property definition referred to in section 101(1)(2), (4) or (5) or an equivalent measure, the letter of summons shall be delivered to the group of organized joint-owners in compliance with section 26 of the Act on Joint Property and to the unorganized group of joint-owners in compliance with the service of summons procedure or by providing service of the letter of summons to at least one of the joint-owners and providing notification of the letter of summons in at least one newspaper distributed in the region. If the cadastral procedure concerns an area to which several real estates have an easement or a right as referred to in the Act on Private Roads and the matter does not concern annulment, transferral or changing of such a right, it is adequate that the letter of summons be delivered to one of the holders of such a right. The letter shall, however, be delivered to a private road maintenance association if the cadastral procedure application shows or it is otherwise known that the cadastral procedure concerns the road of a private road maintenance association. (688/2000)

(3) If the cadastral procedure is based on an agreement signed between the joint-owners of a death estate, the letter of summons is delivered to the joint-owners of the estate. As far as another cadastral procedure is concerned, the letter of summons to the death estate may be delivered to that joint-owner of the death estate who tends to the administration of the estate. If the estate is administered jointly by several joint-owners of the estate, the letter of summons may be delivered to one of them. The letter of summons may also be delivered to that joint-owner of the estate who tends to the real estate belonging to the death estate which is the object of the cadastral procedure or to another party who tends to the property of the estate or to the party who otherwise is entitled to represent the death estate and use the right to be heard on behalf of the death estate. (273/1998)

(4) Even in the case that the municipality is not an interested party in the cadastral procedure, the interested municipality is sent a letter of summons concerning any cadastral procedure which is executed in an area requiring planning, a shoreline area as referred to in section 72 of the Land Use and Building Act, in an area covered by a master plan or a town plan with legal consequence or in an area in which a building ban is in force for the drafting of a town plan. (322/1999)

Section 169

(1) If the letter of summons cannot be sent to one of the interested parties because he or she or his or her address cannot be identified without difficulty, a notice of the beginning of the cadastral procedure shall be given by publishing the summons in one or two newspapers generally

circulated in the region. Similarly, the summons shall be published in a newspaper when there is ambiguity concerning the identity of the interested parties in the cadastral procedure.

(2) Notice of the beginning of the cadastral procedure is considered to have been given when a letter of summons has been entered into the post to be delivered at least 10 days before the initial meeting or otherwise delivered to the interested parties, or has been handed over to the recipient against written evidence at least seven days before the initial meeting, or if the summons has been published in a newspaper at least 10 days before the initial meeting.

Section 170

(1) If notification of commencement of the cadastral procedure has been published in the manner referred to in sections 168 and 169, the absence of an interested party does not prevent the execution of the cadastral procedure.

(2) The cadastral procedure may be executed without published notification in the manner referred to in sections 168 and 169 if all interested parties consent to it.

(3) If during the cadastral procedure it becomes evident that some interested parties have not been informed of the beginning of the cadastral procedure, another meeting shall be held as part of the cadastral procedure at which the interested parties concerned are informed of the beginning of the cadastral procedure. The cadastral procedure may, however, be completed without another meeting if the interested party who had not been informed of the beginning of the cadastral procedure is present at the cadastral proceedings and does not demand a postponement of the proceedings or if he or she has notified in writing before the ending of the cadastral procedure that he or she does not consider another meeting to be necessary. The provisions of this subsection concerning the interested party also apply to the municipality when a cadastral procedure referred to in section 168(3) is concerned.

SECTION 171

(1) Notification of another meeting in a cadastral procedure shall be made in the cadastral survey meeting or in a manner which is in compliance with the provisions on the beginning of the cadastral procedure. The interested parties present at the meeting may, however, agree on another means of notifying of another meeting which the land surveyor considers adequate.

Meetings and other cadastral survey procedures

SECTION 172

(1) In order to handle and resolve matters raised in the cadastral procedure, one or more meetings shall be held, as needed, unless otherwise provided in section 178(2).

Section 173

(1) The cadastral procedure is considered to have begun when the land surveyor has begun the first meeting. Technical tasks connected with the cadastral procedure may be performed before the beginning of the cadastral procedure.

Section 174

(1) The executors shall ensure that all matters concerning the cadastral procedure are handled during the procedure.

Section 175

(1) The matters handled during the cadastral procedure shall be settled by decision of the executors. Matters concerning technical tasks are, however, settled by the land surveyor alone.

(2) The provisions of subsection 1 do not apply to matters on which the interested parties have the right to agree and on which an agreement has been made.

(3)

If the executors are not unanimous on a decision, the matter shall be decided by a vote to which the provisions on a vote in a multimember court of the Code of Judicial Procedure apply.

Section 176

(1) Any agreement regarding a matter to be decided in a cadastral procedure which is made during the cadastral survey meeting shall be entered into the minutes. If the interested parties agree on a matter during the cadastral procedure but in a manner other than in the cadastral survey meeting, the agreement shall be made in writing. Such an agreement is valid even though a person to whom the agreement concerns has not signed it if he or she declares in a cadastral survey meeting after the making of the agreement that he or she accepts the agreement.

(2) Any agreement between the interested parties regarding the cadastral survey procedure shall be made in the cadastral survey meeting and entered into the minutes.

SECTION 177

(1) The maintenance of an area that constitutes an object in the cadastral procedure and whose ownership may change during the cadastral procedure may not be neglected. In the period between public notification of the beginning of the cadastral procedure and the taking of possession of the pieces of land in such an area, the execution of felling of growing stock or the removal of soil for sale or for transportation, the building of new buildings or the renovation of existing buildings or other such measures that change the value or purpose of the property may only be undertaken within the limits set by the executors or with special permission given by them. The limitations shall be set in such a way that they do not needlessly hinder the implementation of measures that are insignificant to the execution of the cadastral procedure. Permission to carry out the measure shall be granted if the measure does not considerably hinder the execution of the cadastral procedure or endanger the realization of the purpose of the cadastral procedure.

(2) If all of the joint-owners of a real estate to be partitioned have agreed on the sale or transportation of timber or soil, subsection 1 does not apply to this part.

(3) In cadastral procedures to which the provisions of subsection 1 apply, the land surveyor shall explain the said regulations and the limitations due to them. The executors shall give the necessary regulations concerning the limitations within which the measure may be carried out without special permission. The limitations set by the executors and their decision on the permission shall be followed regardless of appeal.

SECTION 178

(1) If an applicant cancels his or her application before the beginning of the cadastral procedure has been published, the cadastral procedure order shall be cancelled. The same applies if the applicant cancels his or her application in the period between the publishing of notification of the cadastral procedure and its commencement and if the information concerning their cancellation reaches all interested parties before the initial meeting.

(2) If the applicant of the cadastral procedure renounces the application after the beginning of the cadastral procedure or after the technical tasks required by the cadastral procedure have been performed, the matter shall be handled in the cadastral survey meeting. The cadastral

procedure lapses if none of the interested parties present at the meeting and eligible to apply for a cadastral procedure demand its execution. The land surveyor may, however, decide on the lapsing of the cadastral procedure without calling a meeting if all interested parties give their consent and the holding of the meeting is not necessary due to handling of compensations or cadastral procedure fees.

(3)

> If commencement of partitioning has occurred in accordance with section 22(2) and the land surveyor notes that the execution of the partitioning is unnecessary because the unseparated parcel and real estate from which the unseparated parcel has been conveyed are in the possession of the same person and he or she has the title to the real estate, or if there is another similar reason for not executing the partitioning, the cadastral procedure lapses unless the owner of the unseparated parcel demands the execution of the partitioning. Otherwise, the provisions of subsection 2 apply to the lapsing. (273/1998)

Section 179

(1) If after the beginning of the cadastral procedure it appears that the cadastral procedure cannot be executed at all, the cadastral procedure shall be dismissed. Regardless of the dismissal of the cadastral procedure, a separate task or measure belonging to the cadastral procedure may be completed if the said task or measure is incomplete and the interested party requests its completion.

(2) If subsequent to the commencement of the cadastral procedure an inadequacy in the conditions for execution of the cadastral procedure which may be remedied is revealed, the cadastral procedure shall be interrupted if any of the interested parties demands it or if interruption is otherwise deemed expedient.

SECTION 180

(1) The responsibility of the land surveyor is to supply the assisting personnel required in the execution of the cadastral procedure and the necessary equipment and tools for marking the boundaries and for other work in the field.

(2) The land surveyor may assign a task to an interested party. The interested party is entitled to receive compensation for expenses incurred due to the task and for the working time spent on implementing it. The compensation is paid to the interested party in accordance with section

208(1) or, if deemed more appropriate or necessary, the payments between the interested parties regarding compensation shall be determined in the cadastral procedure.

Section 181

(1) If the type and extent of the cadastral procedure requires it, one or more agents shall be appointed. No person may be appointed an agent without his or her consent.

(2) The duty of the agent is to assist the land surveyor in the carrying out of the responsibilities referred to in section 180(1) and to inform the interested parties of the notices of the executors, to see to the collection and forwarding of compensations and to carry out other similar tasks and given by the land surveyor.

(3) The agent is entitled to receive commission for his or her duties, whose grounds shall be determined in the cadastral procedure.

SECTION 182

(1) For purposes of executing the cadastral procedure, the executors and their assistants are entitled full access to the area of the cadastral procedure and to the buildings of the interested parties, to open mapping lines and to mark the area. Any possible damage or harm shall be avoided when doing so. Trees and vegetation in the yard, garden or other equivalent area may not be damaged or felled without the consent of the owner or the

possessor. Similarly, an interested party is entitled to move within the area of the cadastral procedure and to have access to a building owned by another interested party at a time set in the cadastral survey meeting, if it is deemed necessary in order to supervise his or her interests in the cadastral procedure. The measures referred to above may also be carried out outside the area of the cadastral procedure, if deemed necessary.

(2) If the measures referred to in subsection 1 cause considerable damage or harm to the property of an interested party during the cadastral procedure, compensation shall be paid upon demand. Compensation shall also be paid for any damage or harm caused to the property of another person.

Section 183

(1) If an agreement governed by private law exists regarding the area that the cadastral procedure concerns or its use prior to the commencement of the cadastral procedure, the cadastral procedure shall as far as possible be performed so that the agreement can be adhered to, unless the result of the cadastral procedure becomes inappropriate or adherence to the agreement offends the right of another interested party.

SECTION 184

(1) If before the beginning of the cadastral procedure a dispute is pending in a court of law whose settlement may influence the result of the cadastral procedure, the cadastral procedure may not be completed before the dispute is settled. If such a dispute arises after the beginning of the cadastral procedure, it shall be settled during the cadastral procedure.

Section 185

(1) All new register unit boundaries shall be defined precisely and marked permanently in the terrain. The position of the boundary may, however, be left unmarked in the terrain in an area covered by a town plan, with the exception of shore plan areas as referred to in Chapter 10 of the Land Use and Building Act and for special reasons elsewhere if demarcation is not necessary for the clarity of property division and the owner of the real estate to be formed does not demand demarcation. Furthermore, clear natural boundaries may be left unmarked. If a water boundary cannot be appropriately marked with boundary markers it shall be marked on a map only. (322/1999)

(2) The provisions of subsection 1 on boundary marking apply to an existing boundary of a register unit ordered in connection with a property definition or another cadastral procedure.

(3) The boundary of an easement area shall be ordered and marked in the terrain in compliance with the provisions of subsections 1 and 2 on the boundary of a register unit, unless marking the area in the terrain is clearly unnecessary.

Section 186

(1) If necessary, the moment of taking into possession of the pieces of land shall be ordered and orders shall be given concerning the harvesting of crop and growing stock and transportation of property in the area to be replaced. The provisions of subsection 1 above apply, as appropriate, to an area for which an easement or other usufruct has been established or a right which had been encumbering it has been repealed.

(2)

If the matter in question does not concern land consolidation or urban land replotting, the interested parties are entitled to agree on the matters referred to in subsection 1. Transferral and changing of property may not be begun before the property has been sorted for assessment.

Section 187

(1) Minutes shall be kept of the cadastral procedure. The demands of the interested parties and the content of other statements, agreements, decisions of the executors and their grounds and other matters pertinent to the cadastral procedure shall be entered into the minutes if they are not included in the other documents of the cadastral procedure. The land surveyor shall sign the minutes and other documents drafted in the cadastral procedure.

Section 188

(1) A map shall be made of the area that the cadastral procedure concerns, unless doing so is unnecessary due to the type of cadastral procedure.

Section 189

(1) The decisions and agreements made in the cadastral procedure shall be presented to the interested parties present as the cadastral procedure progresses.

SECTION 190

(1) When all matters belonging to the cadastral procedure have been handled, the land surveyor shall complete the cadastral procedure and inform the interested parties present of the right of appeal and of the appellate procedure. Similarly, the right of appeal and the appellate procedure shall be notified when a cadastral procedure makes a decision which can be appealed against during the cadastral proceedings.

(2) Upon request, an interested party shall be given instructions for appeal immediately after the closing of the cadastral procedure or when the decision referred to in subsection 1 has been made.

Section 191

(1) The minutes and other documents regarding the cadastral procedure shall be made available to the interested parties within 14 days of the closing date of the cadastral procedure if an interested party so requests in the cadastral procedure or within the time limit from the request referred to above, if the request is presented after the closing of the cadastral procedure. If a decision as referred to in section 190(1) has been made in the cadastral procedure, the minutes and other documents concerning a decision which can be appealed against shall be made available to the interested parties within 14 days from the giving of the decision.

Registration of a cadastral procedure

SECTION 192

(1)

When the cadastral procedure has gained legal force under section 284, entries concerning the cadastral procedure are made in the Real Estate Register. If all interested parties have informed their acceptance of the cadastral procedure, the entries in the Real Estate Register may be made before the expiration of the appeal period.

(2)

Before making the entries it shall be verified that the information to be entered based on the cadastral procedure fulfils the requirements for clarity and reliability of the Real Estate System and the provisions of the Real Estate Register Act.

(3)

If entries in the Real Estate Register cannot be made concerning the cadastral procedure because the information to be entered into the register does not fulfil the requirements referred to in subsection 2, the cadastral procedure shall be corrected.

(4)

A real estate or another register unit as well as the rights established for them in the cadastral procedure arise or expire when an entry of the cadastral procedure is made into the Real Estate Register, unless otherwise provided separately.

Section 193

(1) The provisions of section 192(2) and (3) apply, as appropriate, to the making of entries in the Real Estate Register during a cadastral procedure concerning partitioning, land consolidation or division of a joint property unit.

Section 194

(1) If a demarcation or a land exchange executed in connection with another cadastral procedure gains legal force during the cadastral procedure, it may be entered into the Real Estate Register immediately after gaining legal force.

Assessment and other valuation

SECTION 195

(1) If it is deemed necessary to define the relative values of the pieces of land for the execution of the cadastral procedure, an assessment of the pieces of land shall be executed.

(2) The different types of land shall be sorted for assessment purposes according to the purpose of the cadastral procedure and an assessed unit value given to each piece of land which indicates the value of the piece of land in proportion to the values of the other pieces of land.

Section 196

(1) The assessed unit value is determined based on the market value or income value or sustainable productivity. The purpose and the possibilities of use of the piece of land, its type and location as well as other factors influencing the value of the piece of land are taken into consideration in determining the assessed unit value.

(2) If pieces of land are assessed according to different grounds in the same cadastral procedure, the pieces of land assessed according to different grounds shall be compared with each other according to market value or income value.

SECTION 197

(1) If the use value of a piece of agricultural land is to be assessed on the basis of arable area or other such piece of land in agricultural use, the assessed unit value shall be determined based on sustainable productivity.

(2) If the use of a piece of land in forestry is considered to be the assessment basis of a piece of land, the assessed unit value is determined based on sustainable productivity in such a way that the average growing stock corresponding to the type of forest in the region is included in the assessed unit value of the piece of land.

(3) If the use of a water area for fishing is considered to be the assessment basis of a water area, the assessed unit value is determined based on sustainable productivity.

Section 198

(1) If the pieces of land to be assessed have a general special value when used for building, quarrying of soil, recreation or other such special use, the assessed unit value for the piece of land shall be determined based on the market value or income value.

(2) If only a small part of the pieces of land to be assessed have special value and it is significant compared with the value of the pieces of land when used for agricultural or forestry or fishing, the pieces of land shall be assessed based on the use referred to in section 197, unless the interested parties agree otherwise. When the assessed unit value of the piece of land has been determined without considering the special value of the piece of

land, the difference between the special value and the value used in the assessment shall be compensated with money.

Compensations

SECTION 199

(1) Before ending the cadastral procedure, the final accounts of the compensations to be paid between the interested parties shall be made.

Section 200

(1) Unless otherwise provided in sections 81 and 124, the property which is claimed in a cadastral procedure or for which compensation is otherwise paid is assessed based on the market value (market value method). If the market value does not correspond to the full loss of the conveyor, the property to be compensated for is assessed based on the income value (income value method) or the expenses invested in the property (expenses value method).

(2) When valuating the compensation to be paid for damage or harm, all economic losses are taken into consideration.

(3) The redemption price and compensation is determined based on the price level counted from the time when the decision is given and based on the condition of the property at the moment of taking into possession.

Section 201

(1) Unless otherwise provided in this Act, the compensations shall be examined and decided on even though compensation has not been demanded.

(2) The interested parties present to whom the compensation in settlement applies may agree on the amount and other matters concerning the compensation. The agreement may not violate the right of any party.

Section 202

(1) The party who benefits from the measure on which the determination of the compensation is based shall answer for the compensation as a debtor. If there are several beneficiaries and no specific provisions for the division of the compensation are laid down in this Act, the compensation is divided to be paid by the beneficiaries in proportion to the benefit they have obtained by the measure or based on other reasonable grounds.

Section 203

(1) The compensation shall be paid within three months of the closing date of the cadastral procedure. On special grounds, the executors may decide on a longer payment period not exceeding three years.

(2) The compensations to be paid based on a land consolidation may be ordered to be paid before the ending of the cadastral procedure, if it is deemed important to one or some of the joint-owners and reasonable from the point of view of the debtor.

(3) If the payment period of the compensation has been ordered to be longer than three months from the closing date of the cadastral procedure or from the starting date of the payment period determined on the basis of subsection 2, an annual interest of six per cent shall be paid on the compensation, calculated from the date when three months have lapsed from the beginning of the payment period. If the compensation is not paid within the time limit, an annual interest in accordance with the interest rate referred to in section 4(3) of the Interest Act shall be paid on the unpaid compensation. (1188/1996)

(4) If the amount of the compensation is decreased after it has been paid, the excess amount with the interest paid on it shall be returned to the payer and an annual interest of six per cent on the capital to be returned shall be paid counting from the payment date of the entire compensation.

Section 204

(1) The real estate for which the payment has been ordered to be paid constitutes collateral for the unpaid compensation and the interest to be paid on it in compliance with the provisions of Chapter 20 of the Land Code. The land surveyor shall notify the registration authorities concerning the lien referred to above.

(2) The executors may order restrictions on the use and sale of the growing stock of the real estate even for the period after the taking into possession of the piece of land if it is deemed necessary to ensure payment of the compensation for the real estate.

Section 205

(1) The compensation to the real estate belongs to the real estate.

(2) If sizeable compensation has been ordered to be paid by the owner of a real estate due to the transferral of an area or a share, land exchange, departing from partitioning, redemption of land or a building or other such measure and the value of the real estate has been decreased to such an extent due to the aforementioned measure that the right of a holder of a lien concerning the real estate is compromised, the compensation with interest due to be paid to the owner shall be ordered to be deposited with the State Provincial Office. The holder of a lien has the same right to the deposited compensation as he or she has to the real estate. If the owner of the real estate cannot prove that all holders of a lien have given their permission to withdraw the compensation, the State Provincial Office shall divide the assets in compliance with the provisions of the Recovery Act for dividing a sale price of immovable property.

Section 206

(1) If the group of joint-owners of a joint property unit has organized itself in the manner provided for in the Joint Property Act, the compensation concerning a joint property unit shall be paid to the group of joint-owners.

(2) If the group of joint-owners has not organized itself, the compensation to be paid to the joint-owners shall be divided between the joint-owners, or if the compensation is insignificant compared to the expenses of sorting out the shareholding proportions of the joint-property unit, the compensation shall be deposited with the State Provincial Office. If the deposited compensation is not withdrawn within 14 days, the State Provincial Office shall deposit the sum of the compensation in a bank on an account to be opened for this purpose.

(3) The deposited compensation shall be paid to the group of joint-owners after the group of joint-owners has organized itself or decided in its meeting on the withdrawal and use of the compensation and has appointed an agent to carry out the task. Until the compensation has been paid to the group of joint-owners, the State Provincial Office shall pay the share of the amount of compensation belonging to a joint-owner of an unorganized group of joint-owners if the joint-owner presents a reliable account of the size of his or her share.

CHAPTER 16 - CADASTRAL PROCEDURE FEES

Section 207

(1) The cadastral procedure fee includes the cadastral procedure cost and cadastral survey fee.

(2) The cadastral procedure costs are: 1) costs and fees incurred due to implementation of the duties referred to in section180; 2) compensations referred to in section 182(2); 3) commissions and compensations to be paid to the trustees, executors and experts; and

4) other costs and compensations due to the execution of the cadastral procedure which are not part of the cadastral survey fee or which do not constitute legal costs or other fees.

(3) Further provisions are issued regarding the cadastral survey fee.

SECTION 208

(1) The executors shall decide on the payment of cadastral procedure costs and, unless otherwise provided for in section 180, they shall be paid in advance from State funds or, if the land surveyor is a cadastral surveyor, from the funds of the municipality as they accrue.

(2) The cadastral procedure costs paid in advance from State or municipal funds shall be collected back to the State or municipality in connection with the collection of the cadastral survey fee in compliance with the provisions on the collection of the cadastral survey fee.

Section 209

(1) The cadastral procedure costs are divided between the interested parties to be paid according to the benefit they have obtained from the cadastral procedure, unless otherwise provided in this Act or unless the interested parties agree otherwise on the division.

(2) The cadastral procedure costs of a cadastral procedure concerning the formation of a public area are paid by the municipality. (322/1999)

Section 210

(1) When a cadastral procedure order is cancelled or the cadastral procedure lapses, the applicant shall pay the cadastral procedure costs.

(2) If the cadastral procedure is dismissed, the applicant shall pay the cadastral procedure costs. On special and reasonable grounds, an interested party other than the applicant may also be ordered to contribute to the cadastral procedure costs.

Section 211

(1) If the cadastral procedure has been applied for without due grounds, the applicant shall pay the cadastral procedure costs. In this case the applicant shall also pay to another interested party the necessary legal fees caused by the cadastral procedure either entirely or in part, if this is deemed reasonable.

(2) If the interested party has deliberately caused clearly unjustified cadastral procedure costs, he of she alone shall pay them. In this case the interested party shall also pay any extra legal fees he or she has deliberately caused to another interested party.

SECTION 212

(1) The cadastral procedure costs of a land consolidation which has been ordered without application shall be paid exclusively out of State funds.

(2) The cadastral procedure costs for a property definition and other cadastral procedures which allow removal of a defect from the Real Estate Register or the property division, or enable correction of an error in the Real Estate System or in other ways further the reliability and clarity of the Real Estate System shall be paid in accordance with further provisions to be given by Government decree from State funds if the keeper of the Real Estate Register is the land survey office, or from municipal funds if the keeper of the Real Estate Register is a municipal authority, either entirely or in part, as far as the execution of the cadastral procedure has been demanded by public interest. This matter shall be decided on by the executors. However, cadastral procedure costs incurred due to the cadastral procedure referred to in section 283 shall be paid entirely from State or municipal funds. (322/1999)

(3) The cadastral procedure costs for a cadastral procedure as referred to in section 103(2) shall be paid by the instigator of the cadastral procedure.

Section 213

(1) In a cadastral procedure for which the cadastral survey fee is paid in part or entirely from State or municipal funds, the equivalent cadastral procedure costs are also paid from State or municipal funds.

(2) In a cadastral procedure for which no cadastral survey fee is collected, the cadastral procedure costs are paid conclusively from State funds or, if the land surveyor is the cadastral surveyor, from municipal funds. If the cadastral survey fee is collected at a reduced price in a case other than that referred to in section 5 of the Act on Cadastral Survey Fees (558/1995), the cadastral procedure costs paid from State or municipal funds are left uncollected from the interested parties in the same proportion. (1188/1996)

CHAPTER 17 – AMALGAMATION OF REAL ESTATES

Section 214

(1) Real estates may be amalgamated if: 1) the real estates belong to the same owner or owners in such a way that the share of each joint-owner in each real estate is equal and the party requesting the amalgamation has a title to the real estates to be amalgamated when the acquisition concerning the real estate must be registered by law; (273/1998) 2) the real estates are owned with the same rights; 3) the real estates are located in the same municipality; 4) the real estates are of the same type; 5) the real estates belong to or have been intended to belong to the same unit of use; 6) the amalgamation does not cause impractical land location and nor compromise the clarity of the Real Estate System; 7) the real estate to be amalgamated has not been foreclosed and does not belong to a bankrupt estate and none of the real estates are subject to precautionary measures; and

8) no mortgages are held on the real estates, or only joint mortgages of the same amount and priority concerning the real estates are held, or in addition to these, mortgages held of an inferior priority to the joint mortgages only pertain to one of the real estates.

(2) If there are different mortgages concerning the real estates to be amalgamated, the amalgamation may be executed notwithstanding the provisions of subsection 1(8), if: 1) the value of the real estate to be amalgamated considering all the special rights concerning it clearly exceeds the amount of all registered mortgages of the real estates to be amalgamated; or

2) there is an agreement between the holders of a lien and the holders of registered special rights regarding the priority of the registered mortgages and other registrations of the real estates to be amalgamated concerning the real estate to be formed through amalgamation.

(3) The provisions of subsection 1(8) also apply to registered special rights concerning the real estates to be amalgamated. Before deciding on the matter referred to in subsection 2(1), all the holders of a lien shall be reserved a possibility to express their opinion on the matter.

Section 215

(1) The provisions of section 214(1)(4) do not prevent the amalgamation of another real estate to a plot.

(2) A real estate of another type may be amalgamated with a public area, redemption and expropriation unit, State forest land or conservation area, if there are no mortgages on it and it has no share in a jointly owned forest. A real estate to be amalgamated to a public area may not have a share in any other joint property unit nor a right to a special benefit.

(1188/1996)

Section 216

(1) The amalgamation of real estates is executed by the keeper of the Real Estate Register based on the application of the owner of the real estates to be amalgamated.

(2) The keeper of the Real Estate Register may execute the amalgamation of real estates even without an application, if the owner gives his or her consent to it.

Section 217

(1) The real estate to be formed by amalgamation is entered into the Real Estate Register when the decision on the amalgamation has gained legal force. The real estate is considered to have been formed when the real estate has been entered into the Real Estate Register.

(2) Notwithstanding the provisions of subsection 1, the real estate to be formed by amalgamation may be entered into the Real Estate Register before the expiration of the appeal period if the decision concerning the amalgamation has been given according to an application under section 214(1) or under the said legal provision and under an agreement referred to in section 214(2)(2), or if all of the interested parties have informed their acceptance of the decision. (273/1998)

(3) The keeper of the Real Estate Register shall inform without delay the legal registration authority about the decision concerning amalgamation. All changes due to the amalgamation shall be made in Register of Titles and Mortgages after the real estate formed by amalgamation has been entered into the Real Estate Register.

Section 218

(1) After the amalgamation, the registered mortgages and other registrations of the real estates to be amalgamated are directed at the real estate formed by amalgamation but are not, however, directed at an unseparated parcel conveyed by the real estate to be amalgamated to which no mortgage or registration concerning the real estate to be amalgamated was directed before the amalgamation. In the case referred to in section 214(2)(1) above, the mortgages and other registrations are directed at the real estate to be amalgamated with the same priority and in the case referred to in paragraph 2, in the priority laid down in an agreement. (273/1998)

(2) The amalgamation does not affect leasehold or any other special right directed at the real estate to be amalgamated.

(3) The mutual easements of the real estates to be amalgamated expire.

Chapter 18 has been repealed by Act 322/1999.

CHAPTER 19 - APPEAL SECTION 231

(1) A decision given in the cadastral procedure may be appealed to the Land Court by an interested party, unless the appeal is prohibited by law.

(2) In addition to the provisions of subsection 1, the municipality may appeal to the Land Court a decision on a cadastral procedure executed in an area referred to in section 163(3) which concerns matters referred to in sections 32, 33, 34, 35, 36 or 53.

SECTION 232

(1) An appeal can be made during the cadastral procedure concerning: 1) the right to be an interested party in a cadastral procedure; 2) the rejection of an objection on the grounds of prejudice; 3) the limitations concerning the carrying out of measures or use of areas referred to in section 177;

4) the interruption of a cadastral procedure;

5) the conditions of a land consolidation or the extent of the land consolidation;

6) the projects referred to in sections 72-74 or matters referred to in section 84;

7) a land consolidation plan where a separate appeal has not been allowed on a matter included in the plan;

8) the conditions for the execution and urban land replotting and the extent of the replotting area;

9) a decision referred to in section 142 concerning the division of a joint property area;

10) a rejection of a demand for the dismissal of a partitioning, as well as a division plan in the case referred to in section 52(2);

10a) a decision on whether a partitioning is to be executed as a joint partitioning in compliance with section 48, unless the decision is based on an agreement of the joint-owners; (273/1998)

11) a division plan of a joint property area when part of the division is executed in the manner referred to in section 137(1);

12) the payment of compensation in the case referred to in section 203(2); or

13) a decision on whether partitioning is to be executed in compliance with section 50(1)

or (2), unless the decision is based on an agreement of the interested parties.

(1188/1996)

(2) During the cadastral procedure a decision concerning a demarcation or land exchange executed in connection with partitioning, division of a joint property area, land consolidation or urban land replotting, or the rejection of a demand concerning their execution may be appealed separately, if the land surveyor considers allowing the appeal during the cadastral procedure to be expedient. The same applies to decisions concerning the division plan of a partitioning when the partitioning is executed in compliance with section 50(2) and a decision given in a dispute referred to in section 184. (273/1998)

(3) When a decision of the executors under subsections 1 or 2 has been appealed, no such measure may be taken in the cadastral procedure which may be influenced by the decision to be given on the appeal. Based on the land surveyor's proposal, the Land Court may, however, decide before giving the decision on the appeal that the cadastral procedure may be continued, including such measures.

(4) If a decision given in the cadastral procedure need not be appealed during the cadastral procedure in compliance with the provisions of this section, the completed cadastral procedure shall be appealed.

Section 233

(1) Written instructions for appeal are given for a cadastral procedure and a decision which may be appealed separately under section 232.

(2) The instructions for appeal shall state the Land Court to which an appeal is to be lodged as well as the appeal period and the expiration of the appeal period. Furthermore, the regulations concerning the lodging of an appeal as well as the content and appendices of the petition of appeal shall be explained.

(3) If the instructions for appeal are erroneous and the error is not clearly detectable, the appeal has been made correctly if the interested party has followed either the instructions for appeal or the provisions on the matter.

SECTION 234

(1) The deadline for submitting the appeal is 30 days from the date when the cadastral procedure was completed or the decision referred to in section 232 was given.

(2) The appeal documents are submitted to the land survey office of the National Land Survey of Finland. The appeal documents concerning a cadastral procedure based on the cadastral procedure order of the keeper of the Real Estate Register of the municipality are, however, submitted to the keeper of the Real Estate Register of the municipality.

Section 235

(1) If an interested party cannot lodge the appeal within the deadline due to a legal impediment or other acceptable reason, the Land Court may set a new deadline for lodging the appeal based on a petition.

(2) The new deadline is petitioned for by written application addressed to the Land Court and submitted within the expiration of the appeal period in accordance with section 234(2) to the land survey office or to the keeper of the Real Estate Register of the municipality to which a report of the grounds of the application are appended. The provisions for the documents of appeal apply to this case, as appropriate. (273/1998)

Section 236

(1) The documents of appeal addressed to the relevant Land Court shall state: (1180/.2000) 1) the cadastral procedure or decision that the appeal refers to; 2) which points of the cadastral procedure or decision given in it are being appealed; 3) what changes are demanded to be made; 4) the grounds on which the appeal is made; 5) the evidence intended to be shown and what is intended to be proven by them; (1180/.2000) 6) the demand concerning the compensation of legal fees if the appellant considers it reasonable; and (1180/.2000) 7) a possible request with grounds to have the matter settled without executing a main hearing. (1180/2000)

(2) The documents of appeal are appended with the documents to which the appeal refers to and which are not included in the documents of the cadastral procedure or decision subject to the appeal.

Section 237

(1)

The documents of appeal shall state the name and contact information of the appellant and his or her legal representative, agent or assistant and the postal address to which summons, requests and notices concerning the matter may be sent. The contact information of a witness or another person to be heard shall also be stated in an appropriate manner. (1180/2000)

(2) The documents of appeal shall be signed by the appellant or if he or she has not drafted them him or herself, by the person who has drafted them. The profession and domicile of the person who has drafted the documents shall be given in the documents of appeal.

Section 238

(1) A judgment or decision of the Land Court concerning a matter referred to in this Act may be appealed to the Supreme Court if the Supreme Court grants permission to appeal under Chapter 30(3) of the Code of Judicial Procedure.

(2) A judgment or decision of the Land Court is enforced in accordance with the provisions for the enforcement of a legally final judgment. A pending cadastral procedure may be continued even though a permission to appeal has been applied for concerning the judgment or decision under subsection 1. The Supreme Court may, however, decide before the final decision in the matter that the judgment or decision may not be enforced for the time being or that the enforcement that has already begun may not be continued.

Section 239 (1180/2000)

(1) The documents of appeal, including the application for permission and the appeal, are to be delivered together with the judgment or decision of the Land Court submitted under section 234(2) to the land survey office or to the keeper of the Real Estate Register of the municipality not later than the sixtieth day after the decision of the Land Court has been pronounced or given. If several parties are appealing against the decision of the Land Court, only one copy of the decision of the Land Court must be appended to the documents of appeal.

Section 240

(1) If an interested party who intends to appeal against the judgment or decision of the Land Court presents a legal impediment or other weighty reason within the appeal period due to which he or she cannot submit the appeal within the prescribed time, the Land Court shall set another deadline for it based on a petition. The decision on postponement of the deadline shall be appended to the documents of appeal.

SECTION 241

(1) The land survey office shall send the documents of appeal submitted to it to the Supreme Court after the deadline provided for the appeal. At the same time, the cadastral documents shall be sent to the Supreme Court for inspection. If the appeal has clearly been submitted too late, the documents of appeal shall be sent without the cadastral documents.

(2) The Supreme Court may request the land surveyor to submit to the Supreme Court his or her written statement concerning the matter in hand if the Supreme Court considers it necessary.

(3) Unless otherwise provided in this Act or in another Act with provisions on the Supreme Court, the provisions of Chapter 30 of the Code of Judicial Procedure concerning an appeal of a matter which the Supreme Court handles as the second instance apply to the appeal, as appropriate.

CHAPTER 20 - LAND COURT

Section 241a (1180/2000)

(1) The District Courts of Hämeenlinna, Kuopio, Mikkeli, Oulu, Rovaniemi, Turku, Vaasa and Vantaa function as Land Courts in the composition provided for in this Act. Further provisions on the judicial district of the courts are given by Government decree.

Section 242

(1)

The Land Court decides on the appeals to be processed as set down in the law and appeals for nullification in similar matters.

(2)

Jurisdiction lies with the Land Court in whose judicial district the area concerned in the matter is located. If the area belongs to the judicial district of two or more Land Courts or if the matter concerns a boundary which at the same time constitutes the boundary between the judicial districts of two or more Land Courts, the matter shall be decided by the Land Court in whose judicial district the place of administration of the authority whose cadastral procedure or decision is being appealed is located.

Subsection 3 has been repealed by Act 1180/2000.

Section 243 (1180/2000)

(1) The Chairman of the Land Court shall be a legally trained member of the District Court, and the other members shall include the Land Court Surveyor and two lay members of the court. If a lay member is prevented from attending after the beginning of the main hearing, a quorum of the Land Court is constituted with one lay member. The Land Court may also include another legally trained member of the court if it is considered justified due to the extent of the case or other special grounds. The Land Court may include an additional Land Court Surveyor on the same grounds.

(2) Only the Chairman constitutes a quorum in the Land Court: 1) when the matter concerns a measure referred to in sections 232(3), 235 or 254-258 or other measure intended for the preparation of proceedings, or a matter referred to in sections 7(2), 240 or 264(1) or (3) or 275(2); 2) when the Land Court is hearing an appeal against a decision of the executors in which a challenge on the grounds of prejudice of an executor has been dismissed or if the appeal concerns a decision on amalgamation of real estates or a decision under the Real Estate Register Act given by the keeper of the Real Estate Register or a decision on rectification referred to in section 277(2); and

3) when a matter is decided under section 259(3) without holding the main hearing on the basis of written trial documents.

(3) When necessary, the Land Court Surveyor shall take part in the preparation of the matters referred to in subsection 2.

Sections 244-246 have been repealed by Act 1180/2000.

Section 247 has been repealed by Act 212/2000.

Sections 248-253 have been repealed by Act 1180/2000.

CHAPTER 21 - HEARING THE MATTER IN THE LAND COURT

Section 254

(1) If the appeal is defective, the Land Court shall request the appellant to correct the defect by a given deadline if the correction is necessary in order to continue the legal proceedings. At the same time the appellant shall be notified of the manner in which the documents of appeal are defective and informed that the appeal may be left unprocessed if the appellant does not comply with the request.

(2) On special grounds, a renewed opportunity to correct the defect may be reserved for an interested party whose appeal is defective even after the correction.

SECTION 255

(1) The Land Court shall dismiss the appeal immediately if: 1) the appellant fails to comply with the request put to him or her, as referred to in section 254; 2) the documents of appeal are still defective to the extent that they are not fit as

grounds for legal proceedings even after being corrected; 3) the appeal does not belong to cases to be processed in the Land Court; 4) the appeal has been made too late; or 5) other grounds for legal proceedings are missing.

(2) A decision on the dismissal of an appeal shall be served on the land survey office, the cadastral surveyor or the private road maintenance association and in the matter of appeal, if the cadastral procedure is pending, also on the land surveyor to be presented at the cadastral survey meeting to the other interested parties on whom the decision is considered to have been served at that moment. (1180/2000)

(3) If a separate appeal has been made lodged the decision of the executors on a challenge on the grounds of prejudice, the Land Court shall decide the matter without delay and the decision shall be served on the interested parties in compliance with the provisions of subsection 2.

Section 256 (1180/2000)

(1) If the appeal has not been dismissed under section 255, the Land Court shall request the interested party of a cadastral procedure whose right the appeal concerns to present a reply to the appeal, unless it is clearly considered unnecessary from the point of view of making the decision or of holding the main hearing; at the same time, if necessary, the Land Court shall rule the matters which the reply must especially address.

(2) In connection with the request, the documents of appeal and the documents connected to it shall be served.

(3) If the interested parties referred to in subsection 1 are joint-owners of a real estate or joint-owners of a joint property unit, for their part the provisions of section 260(2) apply to the request.

(4) In the reply the interested party shall state: 1) the matter which the given reply concerns; 2) whether he or she admits the appeal or opposes it; 3) his or her understanding of the grounds of the demands of the appellant and matters which he or she desires to refer to; 4) the evidence intended to be displayed and what is intended to be demonstrated by them; 5) a claim concerning the compensation of legal expenses if he or she considers it reasonable; and 6) a possible request or consent with grounds to settle the matter without holding the main hearing.

(5) The reply is requested to be given in writing to the Land Court by the deadline given by it or orally in a hearing under penalty of possible investigation into the matter even if no reply is given. The provisions of sections 235, 236(2) as well as 237 and 254 on appeal and documents of appeal also apply, as appropriate, to a written reply.

(6) The reply and the appended documents shall be served on the appellant and on such other interested party whom the reply concerns.

Section 257

(1) If the Land Court considers it necessary for processing the case, it may request the interested party to submit a written statement to the Land Court by a given deadline. In this case, the Land Court shall give an order on the matter upon which the interested party is called to make a statement. The statement shall be served on the interested party whose right the statement concerns.

(2) If it furthers the preparation of the matter, the Land Court may decide that the interested parties or some of them are called to be heard in the preparation.

Section 258

(1) Before the main hearing, the Land Court may request the land surveyor to submit to the Land Court a written statement on the matter at hand by a given deadline if the Land Court considers it expedient in order to further the proceedings. The statement shall also be served on the interested party to be called to the main hearing.

SECTION 259

(1) When the preparation has been completed, the matter shall be assigned to the main hearing.

(2) The main hearing is held in the municipality where the area concerning the appealed cadastral procedure is located. The Land Court may also convene in a neighbouring municipality or in the municipality where the office of the Land Court is, unless this causes unreasonable expenses or harm to the interested parties.

(3) The main hearing need not be held at all and the matter may be settled based on written trial documents, if the matter is such that coming to a decision on it does not require a hearing and the interested parties whose right the appeal concerns give their consent to deciding the matter without holding the main hearing. (1180/2000)

Section 260 (1180/2000)

(1) The appellant and the party having made claims, or the interested party present in the cadastral procedure whose right the appeal concerns in compliance with the provisions of Chapter 11 of the Code of Judicial Procedure, as appropriate, shall be invited to the hearing of the Land Court. Other interested parties in the cadastral procedure whose right the appeal concerns or who have requested notification shall be notified of the main hearing by letter. If the notification of the main hearing by letter to such other interested parties who have not requested notification causes considerable difficulties due to lack of addresses, or if it is deemed unnecessary considering the number of interested parties and the matter at hand, notification of the main hearing shall, nevertheless, be published by announcing it in a newspaper distributed in the region of the cadastral procedure not later than 14 days prior to commencement of the session.

(2) If the appeal concerns a real estate owned jointly by several parties or an unseparated parcel and the matter does not concern the division of the real estate, it shall suffice that one of the owners is notified of the session. A joint-owner who has requested it shall, however, always be notified of the session. If the appeal concerns a joint property unit and the matter does not concern its division or supplementation of its division, a notice of the session shall be given to the group of joint-owners in compliance with section 26 of the Act on Joint Property.

(3) The publishing of notification of the session of the Land Court provided for in this section is considered to have been duly performed if the aforementioned letter has been left to the post for delivery or otherwise delivered to the interested party 14 days prior to commencement of the session.

(4) The Land Court may send a request for a reply and other requests and summons referred to in this Chapter to the interested party by post using the address last given in a cadastral procedure or notified to the court of law by the interested party.

Section 260a (1180/2000)

(1) The appellant shall be summoned to the main hearing under penalty of having the appeal dismissed in his or her absence.

(2) The opponent of the appellant shall be summoned to court under penalty of a fine, if processing of the matter requires his or her attendance.

(3) The opponent of an appellant whose hearing is not considered necessary shall be summoned to the main hearing under penalty of having the matter settled regardless of his or her absence.

(4) The interested party or his or her legal representative may be obliged to attend the main hearing in person under penalty of a fine, if hearing him or her is considered necessary for clarifying the matter.

Section 261

(1) If the appellant does not appear at the session of the Land Court, the appeal shall be dismissed. The absence of another interested party does not prevent the matter from being settled.

(2) If the interested party or his or her legal representative fails to appear at the main hearing to which he or she has been summoned under penalty of a fine, the provisions of Chapter 26(20)(2) and section 21 of the Code of Judicial Procedure shall apply, as appropriate. (1180/2000)

Section 262

(1) The main hearing is an oral hearing. The interested party is not permitted to read or give the Land Court a written statement or otherwise present the case in writing.

(2) The interested party may, however, read his or her claim and direct references to legal practice, legal literature and to such documents containing much technical and numeric information which are difficult to understand when presented merely orally from a written document. Furthermore, he or she may use written notes to refresh his or her memory. For clarifying technical and other similar questions, references may be made to written trial documents by briefly explaining their content as far as the references are concerned.

(3) At the main hearing, in the following order: (1180/2000) 1) the Chairman or Land Court Surveyor shall briefly explain the matter at hand;

(1180/2000)

2) the appellant shall report to the court which points of the decisions given in the cadastral procedure are appealed and what changes are demanded to be made to them; (1180/2000)

3) the other interested parties shall express their understanding of the appeal; 4) the interested parties on both sides shall argue their position in more detail and shall

state their opinions concerning the arguments of the other interested parties: 5) evidence shall be accepted; and 6) the interested parties shall give their closing statements.

(4) The order provided for in subsection 3 above may, however, be departed from where necessary. (1180/2000)

Section 263 has been repealed by Act 1180/2000.

SECTION 264

(1) On its own initiative, the Land Court may acquire or request the interested parties to acquire a report deemed essential to furthering the conclusion of the matter.

(2) The Land Court may summon the land surveyor to be heard in the matter, as and when necessary.

Section 265

(1) If the Land Court finds that the cadastral procedure regarding the appeal must be interrupted or that an interrupted cadastral procedure may continue regardless of the processing of the appeal, the court shall give a decision and serve it on the land surveyor. (1188/1996)

(2)

The order concerning the interruption or continuation of a cadastral procedure shall enter into force immediately and shall be observed until other orders are issued.

(3)

When a decision has been appealed regarding a measure or other fact which pertains to the grounds for compensation or to the amount of the compensation or otherwise pertains to the payment of the compensation, the Land Court may prohibit the execution of the decision concerning the payment of compensation, or order it to be interrupted until the appeal has been settled. (1188/1996)

Section 266

(1) The Land Court shall arrange an on-site inspection if it is deemed necessary in order to clarify the matter.

Subsection 2 has been repealed by Act 1180/2000.

Section 267

(1) When coming to a decision on the matter in the Land Court, first the Land Court Surveyor, followed by the lay members of the court and finally the Land Court Judge, shall express their views on the matter.

(2) If the views diverge, the provisions of Chapter 23 of the Code of Judicial Procedure on voting in litigation shall apply to the determination of the outcome of the vote.

Section 268 (1180/2000)

(1) Only those trial materials which have been presented or introduced in the main hearing or inspection may be taken into consideration in the decision. If the matter is decided without holding a main hearing, the matter shall be decided based on written trial materials. When an archive investigation has been carried out or the Land Court has, under section 264(1), otherwise acquired a report on its own initiative, the said materials shall form part of the written trial materials referred to in this subsection. In order for the investigation report to be taken into consideration when giving the decision, it shall be presented to the interested parties at the main hearing or, if the matter is decided without a main hearing, the interested parties shall be given an opportunity to give their statement.

(2) If the matter is decided based on written trial materials and the opponent of the appellant has not exercised his or her right to be heard in the Land Court, or if the matter is decided in a main hearing in spite of the absence of the opponent of the appellant, the trial material previously presented by him or her in the matter shall, however, be taken into consideration when deciding on the matter.

Section 269 has been repealed by Act 1180/2000.

Section 270

(1) Unless otherwise provided in this law or other law which contains provisions concerning the Land Court or in a decree issued pursuant to them, the provisions in force concerning ordinary courts apply, as appropriate, to the Land Court and the trial in it and to the judgment or decision of the Land Court.

CHAPTER 22 - CORRECTION OF AN ERROR DETECTED IN THE CADASTRAL PROCEDURE AND EXTRAORDINARY APPEAL

(273/1998)

Section 271

(1) If it appears after the ending of the cadastral procedure and before the cadastral procedure has been entered into the Real Estate Register that the decision given in the cadastral procedure is clearly based on an erroneous or defective report or an incorrect application of the law, the erroneous decision may be invalidated and the matter decided again (correction of a factual error).

SECTION 272

(1) If it appears after the ending of the cadastral procedure and before the cadastral procedure has been entered into the Real Estate Register that an error in measurement, calculation, writing or notation has occurred, it shall be corrected (correcting an error in writing)

(2) If the error in writing is such that correcting it alone may lead to an unreasonable outcome for one of the interested parties, the error may not, however, be corrected, unless other changes due to the correction of the error are made at the same time.

Section 273

(1) The land surveyor shall decide on whether to process the correction on his or her own initiative or on the demand of the interested party or because the cadastral procedure has been returned for correction in compliance with section 192(3).

(2) The land surveyor's decision on whether to process a correction may not be appealed.

Section 274

(1) An error in writing as referred to in section 272(1) above shall be corrected by the land surveyor.

(2) The interested party whose right is affected by the decision to correct shall be reserved an opportunity to be heard before giving the decision.

Section 275

(1) Correction of a factual error or an error in writing as referred to in section 272(2) shall be handled in the cadastral survey meeting where parts of the cadastral procedure shall be taken up again as deemed necessary in order to correct the error.

(2) The cadastral procedure may be taken up again provided that the interested parties whose right the correction affects give their consent to it or the Land Court orders it based on the proposal of the land surveyor. The cadastral procedure may, however, be taken up again without the consent of the interested parties for purposes of correcting an error which prevents the cadastral procedure from being registered.

Section 276

(1) If the cadastral procedure has been appealed, the taking up of the correction shall be notified to the Land Court to whom the decision in the matter is to be sent.

(2) A note of the correction shall be entered into the cadastral documents and the information sent to the interested parties whenever this is deemed necessary.

SECTION 277

(1) If an error in measurement, calculation, writing or notation has occurred in the cadastral procedure entered into the Real Estate Register, or an error in marking the boundary in the terrain for which the said error is not insignificant and which affects the right of the interested party, the error may be corrected in a property definition procedure if the correction does not cause unreasonable harm to the interested party. The cadastral procedure order may be given even without an application. Correction of an error as referred to in this subsection may be carried out if the cadastral procedure concerning it has been applied for within five years of the registration of the cadastral procedure.

(2) If the documents of a cadastral procedure entered into the Real Estate Register contain an error as referred to in subsection 1 which is insignificant or does not affect the right of any interested party, the keeper of the Real Estate Register may correct the error after having heard the owners of the real estates concerned, when necessary.

SECTION 278

(1) If the matter regards an error other than that referred to in section 277, the provisions of Chapter 31 of the Code of Judicial Procedure for extraordinary appeal in litigation apply to amending a decision given in a cadastral procedure which has gained legal force.

(2) The central administration of the National Land Survey of Finland is entitled to make a proposal to the Supreme Court or the Supreme Administrative Court concerning a cancellation due to an error of a cadastral procedure entered into the Real Estate Register or a decision with legal force, to which a correction is required due to the clarity or reliability of the Real Estate System or other public interest. Before making the proposal, those interested parties whose right is affected by the correction of the error shall be reserved an opportunity to be heard.

Section 279

(1) If the correction or rectification of an error made in the cadastral procedure by changing the cadastral procedure is deemed likely to incur such expenses or harm that would obviously render them unreasonable when compared with the benefit obtained by the change, the interested party who has obtained the benefit from the error may be obligated to compensate the economic benefit obtained in money to the party suffering the loss.

(2) The matter concerning the compensation referred to in subsection 1 above shall be decided in the same cadastral procedure as the correction or rectification of the error.

SECTION 280

(1) When handling the rectification of an error referred to in this Chapter, the interested parties constitute those holders of a right whose right is concerned in the matter.

Section 280a 273/1998)

(1) If before ending the cadastral procedure a factual error or error in writing appears after a decision referred to in section 232(1) and (2) has been given, the correction of the error may be taken up notwithstanding that decision, in compliance with the provisions of this Chapter for the correction of an error which has appeared in a completed cadastral procedure.

CHAPTER 23 - MISCELLANEOUS PROVISIONS

Chapter 281

(1) A matter which under section 101 is decided in the cadastral procedure may not be taken up in a general court of first instance.

SECTION 282

(1) If joint drainage is executed in connection with the cadastral procedure, the provisions of the Water Act on the foundation of a joint irrigation unit in ditching proceedings apply to the foundation of the joint irrigation unit in connection with a cadastral procedure.

Section 282a has been repealed by Act 322/1999.

SECTION 283 (322/1999)

(1) The order to execute the cadastral procedure referred to in section 212(2) may be given by the keeper of the Real Estate Register without an application.

SECTION 284

(1) The cadastral procedure is legally valid when the appeal period concerning the cadastral procedure has expired or if the cadastral procedure has been appealed, when the appeal has been finally decided by a decision of a court of law.

SECTION 285

(1) When appealing a decision of the land survey office referred to in this Act, the provisions of the Act on Application of Administrative Law (586/1996) apply, unless otherwise provided. (273/1998)

(2) Any appeals against the decision of the keeper of the Real Estate Register concerning amalgamation of real estates and rectification of an error as referred to in subsection 277(2) shall be appealed to the Land Court. The deadline for appeal is 30 days after the publishing of the decision. Otherwise the provisions on appealing a completed cadastral procedure apply to the appeal. (322/1999)

(3) The decision of the land survey office or the keeper of the Real Estate Register of the municipality which has denied the giving of a cadastral procedure order is appealed to the central administration of the National Land Survey of Finland.

Section 285a (322/1999)

(1) In a matter concerning an amalgamation of real estates, an interested party constitutes the applicant and any other person whose right is directly concerned in the matter. The holder of a

lien is an interested party when a release from mortgage is performed without the consent of the holder of a lien.

Section 286

(1) The provisions of Chapter 15 of the Code on Judicial Procedure apply to the agent of an interested party used in a matter referred to in this Act.

SECTION 287

(1) For the execution of the cadastral procedure, the land surveyor is entitled to receive executive assistance from a competent authority.

(2) If it is deemed necessary for the clarification of the matter and the interested parties request it, the executors may request witnesses or experts to be heard under oath in a general court of first instance at which the hearing can most conveniently be carried out.

Section 287a (273/1998)

(1) Any party who deliberately or through negligence violates the provisions of section 177(1) or the provisions, restrictions or conditions of permission issued under section 177(1) and

(3) shall be sentenced to a fine for a cadastral procedure crime or to prison for a maximum period of two months.

(2) The provisions of Chapter 2(16) of the penal code apply to the forfeiture to the State of the proceeds of the crime referred to in subsection 1. The forfeiture may be waived or limited to apply only to a part of the proceeds of the crime if the punishable act which constitutes the condition for the forfeiture is a minor one or if the circumstances are otherwise mitigating or if sentencing of the forfeiture would be otherwise unreasonable.

(3) The land surveyor shall notify the prosecutor of the purpose of raising charges after having noted the act referred to in subsection 1. The notice may be left undone if the act is considered a minor one considering the circumstances.

SECTION 288

(1) The compensation to be paid with interest may be distrained on the request of the executor or the interested party on the basis of a copy or an excerpt of the cadastral document in compliance with the provisions of the Execution Act on the execution of a legally valid judgment. (816/1996)

(2) If an interested party is prevented from taking into possession an area or other property that has come to him or her or from harvesting or from receiving something else to which he or she has a right based on a legally valid decision given in the cadastral procedure, the distraint officer shall give executive assistance at the request of the interested party. As grounds for the request, a certificate of the land surveyor or an officially certified excerpt of the cadastral document and a report of when the decision on taking into possession has gained legal force shall be presented.

Section 288a (322/1999)

(1) The release from liability for a mortgage referred to in section 28(1) above is executed at the request of the owner of the subdivided real estate unit or plot. Release from a mortgage referred to in the cases referred to in sections 28(2) and 134(2) shall be executed without the request of the owner.

(2) The provisions of Chapter 18(6)(2) and (3) on the consent of the owners of real estates that remain the objects of a mortgage and of the holders of a lien and of special rights directed to these real estates apply to the release of mortgages in the cases referred to in section 28(1) and (2) or section 134(2).

Section 289

(1) If a real estate has been released from liability for a mortgage under this Act without the consent of the owner of the real estate or the holder of a lien and if the release causes damage to the owner of the real estate or the holder of a lien, the damage shall be compensated for by the State or, when the decision has been given by an authority of the municipality, by the relevant municipality. The above provisions for the mortgage and the holder of a lien apply to a registered pension entitlement and the holder of a pension entitlement in cases referred to in sections 28(2) and 134(2). (273/1998)

(2)

The provisions of subsection 1 above also apply to a decision on the payment of compensation to the owner of a real estate as referred to in section 205(2) and to a decision concerning amalgamation of real estates under section 214(2).

Section 290

(1) The provisions of this Act on a mortgage also apply to other liens entered into the Register of Titles and Mortgages.

(2) The provisions of this Act on a mortgage registered to the real estate and for a holder of a lien directed to the real estate also apply, as appropriate, to a mortgage registered to a specified share and an unseparated parcel of a real estate and to the holder of a lien directed to one of these. (1188/1996)

Section 290a (273/1998)

(1) If it has been noted in a cadastral procedure that after the cadastral procedure the registered leasehold or other special right is directed to another real estate or register unit than the one it has been registered to, the legal register authority shall be notified of the matter.

(2) If a joint-owner has requested the amalgamation of shares or real estates in a joint partitioning or land consolidation, the land surveyor shall notify the legal registration authority of the matter without delay. Changes in the Register of Titles and Mortgages due to the amalgamation shall be made after the real estate concerning the amalgamation has been entered into the Real Estate Register.

Section 291

(1) Further provisions on the implementation of this Act are given by Government decree.

(2) For the execution of the cadastral procedures and duties referred to in this Act, the central administration of the National Land Survey of Finland shall provide the necessary forms for the documents and regulations for the boundary markers to be used, for the markings to be made on the map and for the accuracy of the measurements to be made in the cadastral procedure.

CHAPTER 24 - PROVISIONS FOR THE ENTRY INTO FORCE AND TRANSITION

Section 292

(1) This Act enters into force 1 January 1997.

(2) This Act repeals the following acts with possible subsequent amendments: 1) Act on Division (604/51) of 14 December 1951, 2) Act on Division of a Planning Area (101/60) of 20 February 1960, 3) Act on Amalgamation of Real Estate Units (403/51) of 29 June 1951 and 4) Act on Land Organisation (54/75) of 31 January 1975.

(3) Measures necessary for the implementation of this Act may be undertaken before the Act's entry into force.

Section 293 has been repealed by Act 322/1999.

Section 293a (1188/1996)

(1) If a private reliction area belonging to another real estate existing at a real estate formed before the entry into force of this Act and which has been formed out of a private water area before the entry into force of this Act, the provisions of section 60 on the redemption of a reliction area apply to the redemption of such a reliction area even in the case that the real estate at the reliction area has been formed after the appearance of the reliction area.

Section 294

(1) This Act shall also be applied to those matters to be solved in cadastral procedures which have been started before the entry into force of this Act and which are taken up after the entry into force of this Act.

(2) When appealing the decision of executors to the Land Court and the decision of the Land Court to the Supreme Court, the right of appeal and the appellate procedure are determined according to the law under which the decision subject to appeal has been made in the cadastral procedure.

Section 295

(1) The provisions in force at the moment of entry into force of this Act apply in a land consolidation area where land consolidation has not been executed before the entry into force of this Act.

Section 296

(1) A matter submitted to the land survey office, building board or legal registration authority which under this Act is to be submitted to another authority and which has not been decided before the entry into force of this Act shall be reassigned to the authority referred to in this Act.

Section 297

(1) When an act or decree refers to a point in legislation which has been replaced by a provision of this Act, the latter shall apply.

(2) The provisions laid down in the legislation on cadastral procedures under the Act on Division and the Act on Division of a Planning Area apply to the equivalent cadastral procedure under this Act after the entry into force of this Act.

ENTRY INTO FORCE AND APPLICATION OF AMENDMENTS:

816/1996:

(1) This Act enters into force on 1 January 1997.

1106/1996:

(1) This Act enters into force on 1 January 1997. **1188/1996:**

(1) This Act enters into force on 1 January 1997.

168/1998:

(1) This Act enters into force on 1 May 1998.

273/1998:

(1) This Act enters into force on 1 May 1998.

(2) This Act applies, as appropriate, also to cadastral procedures which have become pending before the entry into force of this Act as far as those matters are concerned which are taken up after the entry into force of this Act.

322/1999:

(1) This Act enters into force on 1 January 2000.

(2) If the surveying of a plot or of a public area has become pending during the validity of the legislation in force at the moment of entry into force of this Act and has been completed before the entry into force of this Act, the provisions valid at the moment of entry into force of this Act and the regulations pursuant to them apply to them.

333/1999:

(1) This Act will enter into force on a date to be defined by decree.

96/2000:

(1) Separate provisions shall be issued regarding the entry into force of this Act. (Act 96/2000 entered into force in compliance with Act 113/2000 on 1 March 2000.)

212/2000:

(1) This Act enters into force on 1 March 2000.

688/2000:

(1) This Act enters into force on 1 January 2001.

1180/2000:

(1) This Act enters into force on 1 March 2001.

(2) The procedural provisions of this Act apply to matters in which the decision subject to appeal is given in a cadastral procedure after the entry into force of this Act. The matter is, however, always processed in the composition referred to in this Act, unless the main hearing of the matter has already begun upon the entry into force of this Act.

(3) If the main hearing of the matter has begun in the Land Court before the entry into force of this Act, the term of the lay members of the Land Court who have participated in the process shall continue until the matter has been decided.

(4) Matters pending in the Land Court upon the entry into force of this Act shall be processed in a District Court that handles issues of the Land Court, in whose judicial district in Land Court issues the office of the appropriate Land Court or its section is located, excluding section 1 of the Land Court of Southern Finland whose Land Court issues are assigned to the District Court of Vantaa.

(5) Upon the entry into force of this Act the President of the Republic appoints the Land Court judges and the Land Court Surveyors in office of the Land Courts to the offices of Circuit Judge (judge responsible for land law matters) and the Land Court Surveyor to be established in the appropriate District Courts without announcing the vacancies. The Circuit Judge of a District Court who has been appointed to the office of Land Court Judge is also entitled to use the name of his or her former office as a title in his or her office as Circuit Judge.

(6) Upon the entry into force of this Act the other personnel of the Land Courts is transferred to the equivalent offices to be established in the relevant District Courts. The Ministry of Justice decides on the transferring of the offices and placement of the personnel in the relevant District Courts.

111/2003:

(1) This Act enters into force on 1 March 2003.

LAND USE AND BUILDING ACT

(132/1999, amendment 222/2003 included)

In accordance with the decision of Parliament the following is enacted:

CHAPTER 1 GENERAL PROVISIONS

Section 1 *General objective of the Act*

The objective of this Act is to ensure that the use of land and water areas and building activities on them create preconditions for a favourable living environment and promote ecologically, economically, socially and culturally sustainable development.

The Act also aims to ensure that everyone has the right to participate in the preparation process, and that planning is high quality and interactive, that expertise is comprehensive and that there is open provision of information on matters being processed.

Section 2 *Scope of application*

The provisions of this Act shall be observed in the planning, building development and use of land and water areas, unless otherwise prescribed.

More detailed provisions and regulations concerning the planning, building development and use of land-areas may be issued by decree, ministerial decision or in a local authority's building ordinance, as prescribed below.

In addition, essential requirements concerning buildings and other construction works referred to in Council Directive 89/106/EEC of 21 December 1988 on the approximation of laws, regulations and administrative provisions of the Member States relating to construction products and requirements based on the said directive concerning construction products are prescribed and issued by this act and under it.

Section 3 *Impact on other planning and decision-making*

Land use objectives and plans in accordance with this Act must be taken into account, as separately prescribed, when planning and deciding on use of the environment on the basis of other legislation.

Section 4 *System of land use planning*

Land use in municipalities is organized and steered by local master plans and local detailed plans. The local master plan indicates the general principles of land use in the municipality. The local detailed plan indicates how land-areas within a municipality are used and built.

Local authorities may draw up a joint master plan.

Regional land use plans contain a general plan for land use for the entire region or for a specific sub-area therein.

The Council of State may adopt national objectives concerning land use and regional structure.

Section 5 *Objectives in land use planning*

The objective in land use planning is to promote the following through interactive planning and sufficient assessment of impact:

The content requirements for the various plans concerning the objectives laid down in paragraph 1 above are prescribed separately below in this Act for each type of plan.

Section 6 *Interaction and publication of planning information*

Plans must be prepared in interaction with such persons and bodies on whose circumstances or benefits the plan may have substantial impact, as prescribed below in this Act.

The authority preparing plans must publicize planning information so that those concerned are able to follow and influence the planning process.

Section 7 *Planning review*

At least once each year, local authorities must draw up a review of all planning matters that are or will in the near future become pending in the local authority or the regional council and which are not of minor importance (*planning review*). The review briefly explains planning matters and the stage of processing reached as well as any such decisions and other actions which have an immediate influence on the basic premises, objectives, content and implementation of plans.

Planning reviews must be publicized in a manner appropriate for their purpose.

Section 8 *Development negotiations*

At least once each year, the local authority and the regional environment centre shall conduct development negotiations on issues concerning the planning of land use and land development within the local authority's territory, important planning matters that are or will in the near future become pending, and issues pertaining to cooperation between the local authority and the regional environment centre.

Section 9 *Impact assessment in connection with planning*

Plans must be founded on sufficient studies and reports. When a plan is drawn up, the environmental impact of implementing the plan, including socio-economic, social, cultural and other impacts, must be assessed to the necessary extent. Such an assessment must cover the entire area where the plan may be expected to have material impact.

Section 10 *Planners' qualifications*

Persons drawing up a plan must be qualified for the task. Qualifications will be prescribed in more detail by decree.

Section 11 *Land use agreements*

Section 11 has been repealed (222/2003).

Section 12 *Objectives of building guidance*

The objective of building guidance is to promote:

Section 13 *The Finnish Building Code*

The competent ministry will issue technical and corresponding general regulations and instructions supplementing this Act, which are published in the Finnish Building Code. In addition, the ministry is in charge of harmonizing regulations concerning buildings issued by government authorities. Furthermore, regulations that concern building but are issued under other legislation may also be included in the Building Code.

The regulations in the Building Code are binding. Instructions are not binding, however, and approaches other than those suggested in them may be applied if they meet the requirements set for building.

The regulations in the Building Code concern the construction of new buildings. Unless otherwise specifically prescribed by the regulations, they are applicable to renovation and alteration work only in so far as the type and extent of the measure and a possible change in use of the building or part thereof require.

Section 14 *Building ordinance*

A local authority must have a building ordinance. The building ordinance may contain different regulations for different areas of the local authority.

The building ordinance issues regulations that are based on local conditions and that are necessary for organized and appropriate building, taking cultural, ecological and scenic values into account, and for creating and maintaining a good living environment. The building ordinance regulations shall not be unreasonable in relation to landowners or other titleholders.

The building ordinance regulations may concern construction sites, the size and location of buildings, a building's suitability for its surroundings, the method of construction, planting, fences and other constructions, management of the built environment, organization of water supply and drainage, definition of areas requiring planning, and other corresponding matters of local importance pertaining to building.

The building ordinance regulations are not applied in matters where a legally binding local master plan, local detailed plan or the Finnish Building Code provides otherwise.

Section 15 *Approving a building ordinance*

The building ordinance is approved by the local council. The provisions of section 62 on interaction and of section 65 on making land use plan proposals available to the public shall be observed, where applicable, when drawing up the building ordinance. More detailed provisions concerning the drawing up of building ordinances will be issued by decree.

Section 16 *Areas requiring planning*

An area requiring planning is an area the use of which involves needs that require special measures, such as road, water main or sewer construction or arranging other areas.

Provisions concerning areas requiring planning also apply to construction where the environmental impact is so substantial as to require more comprehensive consideration than the normal permit procedure.

In a legally binding local master plan or building ordinance, local authorities may also designate areas where, due to their location, community development requiring planning may be expected, or where land use planning is warranted by particular environmental values or hazards, as areas requiring planning. An order in a local master plan or a building ordinance designating an area as requiring planning may be in force for a maximum of ten years at a time.

The special preconditions concerning building permits in areas requiring planning as referred to in this section are laid down in section 137.

The need for planning in shore areas is prescribed in section 72.

CHAPTER 2 AUTHORITIES

Section 17 *Functions of the competent ministry*

The functions of the competent ministry include the general development and guidance of land use planning and building activities. The competent ministry promotes, steers and monitors regional planning.

The functions of the competent ministry also include the obligations to take action laid down for Member States in the Construction Products Directive.

In this Act, the competent ministry refers to the Ministry of the Environment, unless otherwise prescribed by decree.

Section 18 *Functions of the regional environment centre*

The regional environment centre promotes and steers the organization of land use planning and building activity within the areas covered by a local authority.

The regional environment centre must especially exercise control to ensure that national land use objectives, other goals pertaining to land use and building, and provisions concerning the management of planning matters and building activities are taken into account in planning, building and other land use, as provided in this Act. In addition, the regional environment centre performs the functions entrusted to it in section 4 of the Act on the Environmental Administration (55/1995).

Section 19 *Functions of the regional council*

It is the regional council's function to carry out regional planning.

Section 20 *Functions of the local authority*

The local authority shall take charge of land use planning and building guidance and control within its territory. The local authority must have sufficient resources and expertise available for these functions.

If the local authority's population is greater than 6,000, it must have *a planner* who is qualified to manage the local authority's planning functions. Local authorities may also share a planner, or a local authority may, under an agreement, assign the duties to a planner employed by another local authority or a joint municipal board.

If special cause exists, the competent ministry may grant a local authority a fixed-term exemption from the functions referred to in paragraph 2.

Section 21 *Local building control authority*

Statutory functions regarding building control are the charge of a committee or some other multimember body, excluding the municipal board, appointed by the local authority.

The local authority must have *a building inspector* for the purpose of building guidance and control. Local authorities may share a building inspector, if this is appropriate in terms of carrying out the functions. Also, the local authority may, under an agreement, delegate building control functions to an officeholder in another local authority.

The qualifications required of a building inspector will be prescribed in more detail by decree.

The provisions of the Local Government Act (365/1995) are applied to delegation of the powers of a building control authority. However, decisions in matters concerning administrative enforcement or claim for rectification may not be delegated to an officeholder.

CHAPTER 3 NATIONAL LAND USE OBJECTIVES

Section 22 *National land use objectives*

National land use objectives are decided upon by the Council of State.

National land use objectives may concern matters which have:

When national land use objectives are issued, the general objectives of this Act and the objectives for land use planning laid down in section 5 must be taken into account.

Section 23 *Drafting of objectives*

The competent ministry is in charge of drafting national land use objectives, in collaboration with the other ministries, regional councils and other authorities and parties whom the matter concerns. Drafting of objectives shall be based on interaction between the various parties.

Section 24 *Implementing objectives and taking them into account*

Government authorities must take national land use objectives into account, promote their implementation and assess the impact of their actions on local structure and land use.

In regional and other land use planning, national land use objectives must be taken into account in a way that promotes their implementation.

CHAPTER 4 REGIONAL PLANNING

Section 25 *Purpose of regional planning*

Regional planning includes the regional scheme, the regional plan which steers other land use planning, and the regional development programme. Provisions concerning the regional development programme are laid down separately.

National objectives are taken into account in regional planning by adapting them to regional and local land use objectives.

The regional scheme indicates the regional development goals.

The regional plan sets out the principles of land use and community structure, and designates areas as necessary for regional development. Areas are designated as reserved only to the extent and accuracy required by national or regional land use goals or by harmonizing the use of land in more than one municipality.

Section 26 *Regional council*

Drawing up a regional plan and other regional planning is the charge of the joint municipal board (*regional council*), of which the area's local authorities must be members.

Provisions concerning division into regions will be laid down separately.

Section 27 *Drawing up a regional plan*

The regional council must see to it that a regional plan is drawn up as needed and that it is kept up-to-date and developed.

The regional plan may also be drawn up in stages or by sub-area. When the plan is drawn up by sub-area, a body must be appointed under the regional council to steer the drafting, with members proposed by the relevant local authorities.

Section 28 *Required content of the regional plan*

National land use objectives must be taken into account in drawing up regional plans, as provided above. Special needs deriving from regional conditions must also be taken into account in drawing up the plan. The plan must be harmonized as far as possible with the regional plans of other areas adjacent to the land-area it covers.

Nature conservation programmes and decisions referred to in sections 7 and 77, and designation decisions concerning landscape conservation areas referred to in section 32 of the Nature Conservation Act (1096/1996) must be used as a guideline in drawing up the plan.

In planning, special attention shall be paid to the following:

In addition, when drawing up a plan, attention must be paid to the economy of land use and to avoiding unreasonable harm to landowners or other titleholders. When a plan is drawn up, the party responsible for implementing the plan and the measures it requires must be indicated.

The matters referred to above in this section must be settled and taken into account to the extent that the purpose of the regional plan as a general plan requires.

Section 29 *Presentation of the regional plan*

The regional plan is presented on a map. The plan includes a key to the symbols used and written regulations.

The regional plan includes a report which provides the information required for assessing the goals and options of the plan and their impacts, and the justification for the approaches adopted, as provided in more detail by decree.

Section 30 *Regulations issued in a regional plan*

Regulations required in planning or developing the area covered by the regional plan may be given in the plan, taking into account its purpose and the demands set for its content (*regional plan regulations*).

When an area requires protection due to its landscape, natural values, built environment, cultural and historical values or special environmental values, the necessary regulations for this purpose may be given in the regional plan (*protection regulations*).

Section 31 *Approving and ratifying the regional plan*

The regional plan is approved by the regional council's highest decision-making body. Following approval, the regional plan is submitted to the competent ministry for ratification.

The competent ministry must obtain opinions regarding the regional plan from such other ministries as the matter concerns.

If the plan does not meet the content requirements prescribed for it in section 28, or if the decision is otherwise unlawful, the competent ministry shall not ratify the plan or will ratify it only in part. Otherwise, the plan shall be ratified.

If the various ministries' opinions are essentially divergent, the competent ministry must refer the matter to a Council of State plenary session for a decision.

If a regional plan has not been submitted for ratification within one year of its approval, the decision to approve the plan shall be considered void.

Corrective adjustments and, with the regional council's approval, minor amendments may be made to the regional plan in connection with ratification. Those whose interests or rights are directly affected must be heard regarding amendments.

Section 32 *The regional plan's legal consequences for other planning and authorities' activities*

The regional plan shall be used as a guideline in drawing up and amending local master plans and local detailed plans, and when any other measures are taken to organize land use.

When planning measures concerning land use and deciding on their implementation, authorities shall take the regional plan into account, seek to promote implementation of the plan and ensure that taking the measures does not hinder the plan's implementation.

The regional plan is not valid in areas where a legally binding local master plan or local detailed plan is in force, except concerning amendment as referred to in paragraph 1.

Section 33 *Building restriction*

A building restriction is in force in areas designated by the regional plan as recreation or protection areas or areas for transportation or technical service networks. The area covered by building restrictions may be increased or decreased by a special order in the plan.

Where a building restriction is in force, a building permit may not be granted if it hinders implementation of the regional plan. The permit shall be granted, however, if its denial on the basis of the regional plan would cause substantial harm to the applicant, and the local authority or, when the area should be considered reserved for its needs, some other public entity does not expropriate the area or does not provide reasonable compensation for the said harm (*conditional building restriction*). Changes in ownership that have taken place after approval of the regional plan are not taken into consideration when assessing harm, unless the changes have been made for the purpose of implementing the said plan. Similarly, when the land reservation in a regional plan corresponds in the main to a regional plan reservation as defined in the Building Act (370/1958), changes in ownership that have taken place after approval of the regional plan referred to in the Act of 1958 are not taken into consideration.

If necessary in order to ensure the organization of land use, the regional council may prohibit the use of land covered by a building restriction based on a plan proposal or approved plan, for construction in conflict with the proposal or plan (*building restriction*). The restriction does not concern the construction of an outbuilding belonging to an existing dwelling, nor construction required by agriculture or forestry. The restriction is in force until the regional plan has been ratified, though not longer than two years. If a special reason exists, the competent ministry may extend this period by a maximum of two years.

Section 34 *Expropriation of land*

Provisions concerning expropriation for the purpose of implementing a regional plan are laid down in section 99.

CHAPTER 5 LOCAL MASTER PLAN

Section 35 *Purpose of the local master plan*

The purpose of the local master plan is to provide general guidance regarding the community structure and land use of a municipality or a part thereof, and to integrate functions. A local master plan may also be drawn up to guide land use and building in a specified area.

The local master plan presents the principles of targeted development and indicates the areas required as a foundation for detailed planning, other planning and building, and other land use.

The local master plan may also be drawn up in stages or by sub-area.

Section 36 *Need to draw up a local master plan*

The local authority must see to the necessary drawing up of a local master plan and to keeping it up-to-date.

Section 37 *Approving the local master plan*

The local master plan is approved by the local council.

Section 38 *Prohibitions during the drafting of the local master plan*

When the drafting or amendment of a local master plan has been initiated, the local authority may impose a building prohibition in the area and a restriction on action referred to in section 128.

The maximum term of building prohibitions and restrictions on action is five years. While planning remains incomplete, the local authority may extend the term by a maximum of five years and the regional environment centre, under application from the local authority and for a specific reason, for a further maximum of five years.

A building prohibition and restriction on action referred to in paragraph 1 imposed by the local authority also apply to areas covered by an approved local master plan or an approved amendment thereof, until the approval decision has taken legal effect.

Section 39 *Required content of the local master plan*

When the local master plan is drafted, the regional plan must be taken into account as provided above.

The following must be taken into account when a local master plan is drafted:

The issues referred to above in paragraph 2 must be resolved and taken into account to the extent required by the steering goal and degree of detail of the local master plan.

The local master plan shall not cause unreasonable harm to landowners or other titleholders.

Section 40 *Presentation of the local master plan*

The local master plan is presented on a map. The plan includes a key to the symbols used and written regulations.

The local master plan includes a report which provides the information required for assessing the goals and options of the plan and their impacts, and justification for the approaches adopted, as provided in more detail by decree.

Section 41 *Regulations issued in a local master plan*

Regulations required in planning or developing the area of the local master plan may be issued in it, taking the plan's purpose and the demands set for its content into account (*local master plan regulations*). Regulations issued in a local master plan may, among other things, concern special guidance on land use and building in a specific area and the prevention or limitation of harmful environmental impacts.

When an area or building requires protection due to its landscape, natural values, built environment, cultural and historical values or other special environmental values, the necessary regulations for this purpose may be issued in the local master plan (*protection regulations*).

Section 42 *The local master plan's legal consequences for other planning and authorities' activities*

The local master plan shall be used as a guideline in drawing up and amending local detailed plans, and when any other measures are taken to organize land use.

When planning measures concerning land use and deciding on their implementation, authorities shall ensure that taking the measures will not hinder the plan's implementation.

The local master plan replaces any previously approved local master plan for the same area, unless otherwise stipulated in the plan. The local master plan is not valid in areas where a local detailed plan is in force, except concerning amendment of the detailed plan as referred to in paragraph 1.

Section 43 *Restrictions on building and actions*

A building permit may not be granted if it hinders implementation of the local master plan. The permit shall be granted if, however, its denial on the basis of the local master plan would cause substantial harm to the applicant, and the local authority or, when the area should be considered reserved for its needs, some other public entity does not expropriate the area or does not provide reasonable compensation for the said harm (*conditional building restriction*). Changes in ownership that have taken place after approval of the local master plan are not taken into consideration when assessing harm, unless the changes have been made for the purpose of implementing the said plan.

It may be stipulated in the local master plan that building which hinders the implementation of the local master plan is not allowed in the plan area or part thereof (*building restriction*). In such cases, the provisions of paragraph 1 are not applied. It may also be stipulated in the local master plan that action altering the landscape may not be taken without the permit referred to in section 128 (*restriction on action*).

A special order may be included in the local master plan, prohibiting for a maximum period of five years the use of land designated for building for any construction other than that serving the needs of agriculture or corresponding means of livelihood (*fixed-term building restriction*).

Provisions concerning expropriation and compensation obligations due to restrictions laid down in this section are prescribed in sections 101 and 140.

Section 44 *Using the local master plans as grounds for a building permit*

Use of the local master plan as grounds for a building permit in the case of shore areas is prescribed in section 72 and in the case of areas requiring planning in section 137.

Section 45 *Local master plan with no legal consequences*

The local master plan may also be drawn up and approved so that it lacks the legal consequences referred to in this Act with regard to its entire area or a part thereof. However, the provisions of section 99, paragraph 3, concerning expropriation apply to such local master plans.

CHAPTER 6 JOINT MUNICIPAL MASTER PLAN

Section 46 *Joint municipal master plan*

For the purposes of general guidance of land use and harmonization of activities, local authorities may cooperate in drawing up the local master plan (*joint master plan*).

Section 47

Drawing up, approving and ratifying the joint master plan

The local authorities may delegate the drawing up and approval of the joint master plan to the regional council, some other suitable joint municipal board or some other joint body of the local authorities.

What is provided in this Act regarding local authorities applies to the body referred to above in paragraph 1.

A joint master plan that has legal consequences is submitted to the competent ministry for ratification. The provisions of section 31 on ratification of the regional plan apply to ratification of the joint master plan.

Section 48 *The regional plan and the joint master plan*

The regional plan functions as a guideline for drawing up and amending the joint master plan, as provided in section 32.

If there is a justifiable reason, the content of the joint master plan may deviate from the provisions of paragraph 1. In such a case, however, care must be taken to ensure that the joint master plan conforms with the whole of the regional plan, while the provisions of section 28 regarding the required content of the regional plan shall be taken into account where applicable.

Section 49 *Application of provisions pertaining to local master plans*

Unless otherwise provided above in this chapter, what is laid down in law pertaining to local master plans applies to joint master plans.

CHAPTER 7 LOCAL DETAILED PLAN

Section 50 *Purpose of the local detailed plan*

The local detailed plan is drawn up for the purpose of detailed organization of land use, building and development, with the aim of designating areas necessary for different purposes and of steering building and other land use, as required by local conditions, townscape and landscape, good building practice, promoting the use of existing building stock and other steering goals of the plan.

Section 51 *Need to draw up a local detailed plan*

The local detailed plan must be drawn up and kept up-to-date as required by development of the municipality or by the need to steer land use.

Section 52 *Approval of the local detailed plan*

The local detailed plan is approved by the local council. When the plan does not have significant impact, the local council's authority may be delegated in the standing orders to the municipal board or to a committee.

Section 53 *Prohibitions during drafting of the local detailed plan*

The local authority may impose a building prohibition in an area concerning which a local detailed plan is being drafted or amended. Alteration of the landscape in areas where building is prohibited is subject to permit as laid down in section 128 (*restriction on action*).

A building prohibition is in force for a maximum period of two years. While the plan remains incomplete, the local authority may extend the term by a maximum of two years at a time. However, a building prohibition imposed by the local authority for the purpose of extending the area of the plan may not exceed eight years in duration.

A building prohibition is also in force in areas covered by an approved local master plan or an approved amendment thereof, until the approval decision has taken legal effect.

Section 54 *Required content of the local detailed plan*

When the local detailed plan is drafted, the regional plan and the legally binding local master plan must be taken into account as provided above.

The local detailed plan shall be drawn up so as to create the preconditions for a healthy, safe and pleasant living environment, locally available services and the organization of traffic. The built and the natural environment must be preserved and their special values must not be destroyed. There must be sufficient parks or other areas suitable for local recreation in the area covered by the plan or in its vicinity.

The local detailed plan must not substantially weaken the quality of anyone's living environment in a manner that is not justified by the plan's purpose. Moreover, the local detailed plan may not impose restrictions on or cause unreasonable harm to landowners or other titleholders that could be avoided without disregarding the objectives or requirements of the plan.

If a local detailed plan is drawn up for an area which is not covered by a legally binding local master plan, the provisions concerning the required content of local master plans must, where applicable, also be taken into account in drawing up the local detailed plan.

Section 55 *Presentation of the local detailed plan*

The local detailed plan shall be presented on a map indicating the following:

The local detailed plan also includes a key to the symbols used and written regulations.

The local detailed plan shall include a report which provides the information required for assessing the aims and alternatives of the plan and their impact, and the justification of decisions taken, as provided in more detail by decree.

Section 56 *Local detailed plan for underground facilities*

When detailed planning of land use is necessary only for the building of underground facilities or for their other use, the local detailed plan may also be drawn up in stages so that it covers only areas underground. The provisions of this and other acts concerning the use of land without a local detailed plan apply to areas where the local detailed plan concerns only underground facilities.

Section 57 *Regulations issued in the local detailed plan*

Regulations required because of the local detailed plan's purpose and the demands set for its content in building or otherwise using the area covered by it may be issued in the said plan (*regulations in a local detailed plan*). Regulations issued in a local detailed plan may, among other things, concern the prevention or limitation of harmful environmental impacts, and the type and size of a retail shop, if necessary to ensure the availability of retail services.

When an area or building requires protection due to its landscape, natural values, built environment, cultural and historical values or other special environmental values, the necessary regulations for this purpose may be issued in the local detailed plan (*protection regulations*). The protection regulations must treat landowners reasonably.

Notwithstanding the provisions of paragraph 2, regulations required to protect an object referred to in section 2 of the Act on the Protection of Buildings (60/1985) may be included in the local detailed plan. In such cases, the provisions of section 11 and section 12, paragraphs 2 and 3, of the said Act concerning the right to compensation will be applied. However, the local authority will be the party liable to pay compensation. Compensation paid by the local authority may be subsidized from government funds within the limits of the State budget. What is provided above concerning the local authority's liability to pay compensation does not apply to buildings owned by public bodies.

Section 58 *Legal consequences of the local detailed plan*

Buildings may not be built in violation of the local detailed plan (*building restriction*). The local detailed plan shall be taken into account with regard to other measures altering the environment, as provided below.

Functions which hinder the use designated for other areas in the local detailed plan may not be located in the plan area. Moreover, functions which are in conflict with regulations issued in the local detailed plan concerning the prevention or restriction of harmful or disturbing environmental impacts may not be located in the local detailed plan area.

A large retail unit may not be located outside the area designated in the regional plan or the local master plan for central functions, unless the area is specifically designated for such a purpose in the local detailed plan. A large retail unit is defined in section 114.

When the timing of the local detailed plan's implementation so requires, the construction of a new building may be prohibited in the plan for a maximum of three years. When special cause exists, the local authority may extend the prohibition for a maximum period of three years at a time.

Section 59 *Compensation payable for drawing up a local detailed plan*

When the local detailed plan or an amendment to it is mainly required by private interests and drawn up on the initiative of the landowner or other titleholder, the local authority is entitled to charge the costs incurred in drawing up and processing the plan to the landowner or titleholder concerned.

Section 60 *Assessment of whether the local detailed plan is up-to-date*

The local authority must monitor local detailed plans to ensure that they are kept up-to-date and, when necessary, take action to revise outdated plans.

A building permit may not be granted for the construction of a new building which has substantial impact on land use or the surrounding landscape in an area where the local detailed plan has been in force for more than 13 years and remains to a significant extent unimplemented, before the local authority has assessed whether the plan is up-to-date. Assessment is not required, however, if no more than five years have passed since the previous assessment. The assessment of the local detailed plan may be conducted so as to cover an area which forms a functional entity in terms of the assessment. A local authority's decision that the local detailed plan is up-to-date may not be appealed.

When special cause exists, the 13-year period referred to above in paragraph 2 may be extended or reduced in the local detailed plan. The period may not, however, be less than five years, or more than 20 years.

Periods when a building prohibition as provided in section 53, paragraph 1, for the purpose of amending the local detailed plan, or a prohibition as referred to in section 58, paragraph 4, are in force in the area concerned are not included when computing the 13-year period referred to in paragraph 2 above.

More detailed provisions concerning assessment of whether the local detailed plan is up-to-date will be issued by decree.

Section 61 *Implications of the above assessment*

If the assessment indicates that the local detailed plan is outdated, a building permit may not be granted before the plan has been amended. A building prohibition for the purpose of amending a local detailed plan as referred to in section 53, paragraph 1, comes into force as of the local authority's decision that the plan is outdated.

CHAPTER 8 PLANNING PROCEDURE AND INTERACTION

Section 62 *Interaction in drawing up a plan*

Planning procedures must be organized and the principles, objectives and goals and possible alternatives of planning publicized so that the landowners in the area and those on whose living, working or other conditions the plan may have a substantial impact, and the authorities and corporations whose sphere of activity the planning involves (*interested party*), have the opportunity to participate in preparing the plan, estimate its impact and state their opinion on it, in writing or orally.

Section 63 *Participation and assessment scheme*

When a plan is being drawn up, a scheme covering participation and interaction procedures and assessment of the plan's impact must be drawn up in good time, as required by the purpose and the significance of the plan.

The initiation of the planning process must be publicized so that interested parties have the opportunity to obtain information on the principles of the planning and of the participation and assessment procedure. Such publicity must be arranged in a manner appropriate to the purpose and significance of the plan. The publicity may also take place in connection with the publication of a planning review.

Section 64 *Negotiation on the participation and assessment scheme*

The local authority may negotiate with the regional environment centre on the adequacy and implementation of the participation and assessment scheme.

Before the plan proposal is made available to the public, interested parties have the opportunity to propose negotiations to the regional environment centre on the adequacy of the participation and assessment scheme. If the scheme is clearly inadequate, the regional environment centre shall, without delay, arrange negotiations with the local authority to examine what additions are required.

The interested party making the proposal and, as necessary, authorities and organizations whose sphere of activities the matter concerns, shall be invited to attend the negotiations.

Section 65 *Presenting the plan proposal in public*

The plan proposal shall be presented in public. The presentation of the proposal must be publicized in an appropriate manner in view of the purpose and significance of the plan. Members of the municipality and interested parties shall be provided with an opportunity to express their opinion on the matter (*objection*).

The local authority's reasoned opinion on the objection shall be made known to objectors who have so requested in writing and, at the same time, provided their address.

With regard to regional plans, what is provided in this section concerning local authorities applies to regional councils.

More detailed provisions concerning presentation of the plan proposal in public will be issued by decree.

Section 66 *Negotiations between authorities*

When the regional plan is being drafted there shall be contact with the competent ministry and the regional environment centre. Negotiations shall be set up between the competent ministry, the regional environment centre and the regional council to clarify how national objectives and other key goals pertain to drawing up of the plan.

Other plans which concern national or important regional land use objectives, or which are otherwise important in terms of land use, natural values, cultural environment or government authorities' implementing obligations shall be prepared in contact with the regional environment centre. Negotiations shall be set up between the regional environment council and the local authority to clarify how national objectives, and regional and other key goals pertain to drawing up such a plan.

The authorities whose sphere of activity the matter may concern shall be invited to the negotiations referred to in paragraphs 1 and 2 above.

Section 67 *Publicizing approval of a plan*

The decision to approve a plan must be sent immediately to those members of the municipality and objectors who so requested, and at the same time provided their address, while the plan was available to the public. If a letter stating such a request has several signatories, only the first signatory need be notified of approval of the plan. The first signatory is responsible for making the information known to the other signatories.

CHAPTER 9 NATIONAL URBAN PARKS

Section 68 *National urban park*

A national urban park may be established to protect and maintain the beauty of the cultural or natural landscape, historical characteristics or related values concerning the townscaping, social, recreational or other special values of an area in an urban environment.

Areas designated in a plan referred to in this Act as parks, recreation or conservation areas, or areas of outstanding landscape value, or marked out for some other use appropriate for the purpose of national urban parks, may be designated to form a part of a national urban park.

Areas designated as parks shall primarily be owned by the State, local authority or other public body. Other areas may be so designated with the owner's consent.

Section 69 *Establishing a national urban park*

The decision to establish a national urban park is made by the competent ministry. The park may be established at the local authority's request or if the local authority recommends its establishment.

Section 70 *Regulations concerning the park*

With the consent of the local authority, regulations needed to protect the essential values of a national urban park area may be entered in the decision establishing the park. Other regulations needed for the maintenance and usage of the area are issued in a maintenance and usage scheme drawn up by the local authority in cooperation with the regional environment centre.

The maintenance and usage scheme must be prepared in interaction with the parties on whose circumstances the matter may have substantial impact.

The maintenance and usage scheme is approved by the competent ministry.

Regulations concerning the national urban park must be taken into account in planning the areas of the park and in other planning and decision-making affecting the area.

Section 71 *Closing a national urban park or amending the park's regulations*

A national urban park may be closed or its boundaries changed if the value of the area has decreased essentially or if required for implementation of a project or scheme with great significance to public interest.

The provisions of section 69 on establishing the park and the provisions of section 70 on regulations concerning the park apply to closing of the park or to amendment of the regulations, as appropriate.

CHAPTER 10 SPECIAL PROVISIONS CONCERNING SHORE AREAS

Section 72 *Need for planning in shore areas*

Buildings may not be constructed in shore zones in the shore area of the sea or of a body of water without a local detailed plan or a legally binding local master plan which contains special provisions concerning use of the local master plan or a part thereof as the basis for granting a building permit.

The provisions of paragraph 1 also apply to shore areas where planning of building and other use to arrange for holiday homes which are mainly shore-based is necessary because of anticipated building development in the area.

The provisions of paragraphs 1 and 2 do not apply to the following:

After having heard the regional environment centre, a local authority may designate areas in the building ordinance where the restriction laid down in paragraph 1 is not in force because no building activity is anticipated in the area due to its location and the area has no special natural or landscape values or is not needed for recreational use. The maximum term of such a building-ordinance regulation is six years at a time, though not continuing if the conditions from which the regulation derives change and the preconditions for the regulation no longer exist.

Section 23 provides for granting of exceptions to the restriction referred to in paragraphs 1 and 2.

The provisions of paragraph 1 do not apply to the construction of a sauna building connected to a residential building or farm that existed before January 1, 1997. If an application for an exception to the restriction referred to in paragraph 1 concerns an area the ownership of which has been transferred to the applicant before May 10, 1996, and work on drawing up a plan for the area has not been initiated in reasonable time because of reasons independent of the landowner, the exception may not be refused unless significant cause exists, provided that the building is for the applicant's personal use, the local authority is in favour of the application, and construction does not endanger natural or landscape values. The provisions of this paragraph do not, however, apply to areas where planning is necessary as referred to in paragraph 2.

Section 73 *Special requirements regarding local master plans and local detailed plans which concern holiday homes in shore areas*

When a local master plan or a local detailed plan (*detailed shore plan*) is drawn up for the principal purpose of arranging for holiday homes in a shore area, care must be taken to ensure that, in addition to what is otherwise provided concerning local master plans and local detailed plans:

What is provided concerning the local detailed plan is otherwise in force regarding detailed shore plans. The provisions of section 60 on assessment of whether the local detailed plan is up-to-date, apply to detailed shore plans, however.

Section 74 *Landowner's right to draw up the detailed shore plan*

Landowners may take charge of drawing up a proposal for the detailed shore plan of the shore areas they own. Before the process begins, the local authority must be contacted and provided with a participation and assessment scheme as referred to in section 63.

The area of a detailed shore plan drawn up by the landowner must form a functional whole.

The provisions of chapter 8 otherwise apply to the processing of a local detailed plan proposal drawn up by a landowner. A local detailed plan proposal drawn up by a landowner shall be processed by the local authority without undue delay.

Section 75 *Areas of joint-use and public areas*

In the detailed shore plan, areas may be designated for the internal use of the plan area (*joint-use areas*). Joint-use areas are formed by partition as referred to in the Partition Act (554/1995). Implementation and maintenance of such areas rest with the properties for the use of which the areas have been designated in the detailed shore plan.

Areas may also be designated for public use in the detailed shore plan (*public areas*). In a local detailed plan of this kind, implementation of the public areas may be assigned to the owner of the property by special order, unless this must be considered unreasonable in view of the minor benefit the property owner will gain from the plan.

Section 76 *Cost of drawing up a local master plan for shore areas*

When a local master plan is drawn up for shore areas for the principal purpose of arranging for holiday homes, no more than half of the costs of drawing up the plan can be charged to the landowners in relation to the benefit they gain from the plan. The local authority approves the basis for the charge, which is collected by plan area, and the manner and date of payment.

Section 77 *Negotiations between authorities*

The provisions of section 66, paragraph 2, on maintaining contact and the obligation to negotiate always apply to drawing up a local master plan for a shore area for the principal purpose of arranging for holiday homes, and to drawing up a shore plan.

CHAPTER 11 PLOT DIVISION

Section 78 *Plot division*

In the local detailed plan, an area within a building block is divided into plots if necessary to arrange for land use (*plot division*). The plot division may be binding or may act as a guideline. When the central location of the area, the building density of the block or the explicitness of the land administration system so require, the plot division shall be made binding. The division is indicated on the map of the local detailed plan and prescribed as binding in the local detailed plan.

A building block can comprise a single plot or it can be divided into several plots. Plot division can also be carried out for part of the block only, unless this prevents or hinders practicable plot division in other parts of the block. Division can also be made binding on part of the plan area or block.

If so ordered in the local detailed plan, or if necessary to draw up or amend a binding plot division, a separate plot division can be drawn up for the building block or part thereof; such division is always binding.

Plot division shall be appropriate for its purpose and it must take circumstances of land ownership into account, where feasible.

Provisions concerning plot division do not apply in the area of an underground local detailed plan.

Section 79 *Drawing up a separate plot division*

The local detailed plan is used as a guideline in drawing up a separate plot division. A map shall be drawn of the separate division.

The separate plot division shall be drawn up and approved by the local authority. In preparing a separate division, the owners and titleholders of the properties located within or adjacent to the area to be divided, and the owners and titleholders of properties lying opposite, when the decision may have a material impact on the building or other use of the opposite property, shall be heard. More detailed provisions will be issued by decree concerning hearing and plot divisions carried out otherwise.

The person drawing up the separate plot division must possess the qualifications required for the task. More detailed provisions concerning the said qualifications will be issued by decree.

Section 80 *Amending or annulling a plot division*

The provisions concerning the drawing up of a separate plot division also apply to the amendment and annulment of plot divisions. A plot division conforming to the local detailed plan and intended as a guideline can be made a binding division by applying the corresponding provisions.

A binding plot division can be amended when this is viewed as promoting the appropriate organization of a block or part thereof, when:

The Partition Act contains provisions on the making of minor adjustments.

The owner of a plot or part thereof can propose plot division amendment to the local authority.

Section 81 *Legal consequences of a plot division*

A building may not be constructed in contravention of a binding plot division.

A building permit may not be granted:

Moreover, a building permit may not be granted unless the permit applicant controls the entire building site, or if it would hinder the use of other parts of the block for the purpose indicated in the plan.

Section 82 *Costs incurred from drawing up a plot division*

If the drawing up or amendment of a plot division is mainly required by private interest and if it has been applied for by the landowner or other titleholder, the local authority is entitled to charge the costs incurred from drawing up or amending the plot division to said owner or titleholder.

CHAPTER 12 STREETS AND OTHER PUBLIC AREAS

Section 83 *Public area, street area and traffic area*

In this Act, 'public area' means an area designated in the local detailed plan as a street area, market place, traffic area, recreational area or some other corresponding area, intended for implementation by the local authority, State or other public body.

A 'street area' comprises the street area so designated in the local detailed plan, including its underground, surface and above-ground service conduits, equipment and structures, unless otherwise indicated in the plan.

'Traffic areas' comprise the areas designated in the local detailed plan for public roads, railways, waterways, harbours and airports.

The traffic areas of public roads may be designated for first and second class main roads, regional roads, and roads connecting and continuing them, that mainly serve other than local traffic. If local conditions so warrant, a separate traffic area can be designated for a non-motorized traffic way that forms a part of a public road.

Section 84 *Street management*

Street management comprises the planning, building, maintenance, and cleaning and clearing of streets and other measure required to integrate the street area and the service conduits, equipment and structures both above and below it.

The local authority is in charge of organizing street management. The street-management duties of properties are prescribed in the Act on the maintenance, cleaning and clearing of public areas (669/1978). The local authority may delegate its street-management duties completely or in part to others.

Section 85 *Street construction*

Streets are constructed according to a plan approved by the local authority. Streets must be planned and constructed so that they conform to their surroundings based on the local detailed plan and meet the requirements of function, safety and pleasantness. Correspondingly, the provisions of section 62 shall be observed when drawing up the plan.

More detailed provisions concerning the plan will be issued by decree.

Section 86 *Commencement of a street-management duty and the street-management decision*

The street-management duty commences when the traffic need of the realized land use based on the local detailed plan so requires, and the costs incurred by the local authority in building the street are not considered unreasonable considering the traffic need the street construction answers.

With the consent of the landowner, the local authority may commence street management before the local detailed plan has gained legal force. When processing a complaint concerning the local detailed plan, the appeal authority can prohibit the commencement of street management before the plan matter is resolved.

The duties referred to in the Act on the maintenance, cleaning and clearing of public areas commence when the street or part thereof satisfies the needs of realized land use based on the local detailed plan and the local authority has made the related decision (*street-management decision*). The street is considered to have been handed over for public use as of the same date.

The local authority can decide to discontinue street management when the realized land use no longer requires it.

Section 87 *Notification of a street-management decision*

The owners and titleholders of properties in the street or part thereof must be notified of a street-management decision and the commencement of the street-management duty based thereon, as provided in section 95 of the Local Government Act.

Section 88 *Plot access and access road*

The owners or titleholders of properties are in charge of building plot access at their own cost from the edge of an existing roadway or a street to the property.

If building activity takes place on a property before the street serving the property is built, the owner or titleholder shall provide a passable access road to the plot.

The local authority is required to allow a street area available to it to be used free of charge for the purpose of building an access road.

Section 89 *Moving service conduits, equipment and structures*

If a service conduit, piece of equipment or a structure located in a public area hinder the implementation of the local detailed plan or street management, or are not suitable for the landscape or townscape, the owner or titleholder of the service conduit, piece of equipment or structure is obliged to move it to a location approved by the local authority.

The local authority or the party in charge of implementation of public areas is responsible for the costs of moving, unless it is reasonable to expect the owner or titleholder of the service conduit, piece of equipment or structure to bear the cost in full or in part, or unless otherwise has been agreed regarding the distribution of the said costs.

Section 90 *Implementation of other public areas*

When land use based on the local detailed plan so requires, the local authority must implement public areas designated for its use other than street areas for the implementation of which it is responsible, unless postponing implementation is justified because of the local authority's financial standing.

Public areas must be planned and implemented so that they are suitable for their surroundings, based on the local detailed plan.

Implementation of a public area comprises its construction or renovation and maintenance as required by the land use based on the local detailed plan.

When the special significance of a public area so requires, the local authority shall draw up a plan for implementation of the area, observing the provisions of section 85 on street planning as appropriate.

Section 91 *Assigning the responsibility for implementation to the landowner or titleholder*

If the local detailed plan is mainly drawn up for private benefit to serve a holiday or travel or corresponding project, an order can be included in the plan whereby the responsibility for implementing the plan with regard to a street or some other public area is delegated fully or in part to the landowner or titleholder. If the landowner or titleholder does not implement the plan in the manner required by the order, the local authority has secondary responsibility for implementation. In such a case, the local authority is entitled to charge the costs to the negligent party.

With regard to public areas other than streets, the responsibility for implementing a local detailed plan may also be delegated to landowners or titleholders jointly by an order included in the plan in cases other than those referred to in paragraph 1, when the area is intended to serve only the needs arising within the plan area. The provisions of section 75, paragraph 1, on areas of joint use are observed with regard to such areas. When special cause exists, the local detailed plan may also designate an area of joint use to serve other common needs within the plan area.

CHAPTER 12A COMPENSATION OF COSTS INCURRED BY LOCAL AUTHORITIES FROM COMMUNITY BUILDING (222/2003)

Section 91 a *Landowners' duty to share in the costs of community building*

A landowner in an area for which a local detailed plan is to be drawn up who stands to gain substantial benefit from the plan is obliged to share in the costs incurred by the local authority from community building as laid down below. Agreement should be reached with the landowner on sharing in the costs.

Landowners shall be treated equally with regard to fulfilling the obligation referred to in subsection 1 above.

Section 104 contains provisions on compensation to be paid for street areas and section 105 on compensation for a street area which the landowner is ordered to pay.

Section 91 b *Land use agreements*

A local authority may enter into agreements on planning and implementing plans (*land use agreement*). However, land use agreements cannot be binding on the content of plans.

A land use agreement that is binding on the parties to the agreement can be made only after the draft plan or proposal has been publicized. This does not apply to agreements to initiate planning.

Notwithstanding the provisions of this chapter on development compensation, land use agreements may be used to agree more comprehensively on the mutual rights and obligations of the parties to the agreement.

A land use agreement shall be publicized in conjunction with drawing up the plan. The intention to agree on land use must be publicized in the participation and assessment scheme. If the intention to agree on land use becomes known only after the participation and assessment scheme has been drawn up, it must be publicized in conjunction with the drawing up of the plan in a manner that best serves the purpose of informing interested parties.

Section 91 c *Development compensation*

When agreement is not reached with landowners concerning their sharing in the costs of community building, the local authority may collect from the landowners a share of the estimated costs of community building that contribute to the development of the plan area relative to the increase in plot value brought about by the building rights, increase in building rights or change of permissible use based on the local detailed plan (*development compensation*).

Increase in plot value is assessed by applying, as appropriate, the provisions on grounds for compensation in the Act on Expropriation of Immovable Property and Special Rights (603/1977), hereinafter the Expropriation Act.

The value of street areas transferred without compensation under section 104 and the street area compensation collected from landowners under section 105 are deducted from the development compensation.

When the building rights assigned by the local detailed plan concern only housing and the amount of building rights or increase in building rights does not exceed 500 m2 in gross floor area, the landowner concerned cannot be required to pay development compensation. Other landowners may be required to pay development compensation if the local detailed plan brings substantial benefit as referred to in section 91 a. Local authorities may establish a higher minimum to apply in their municipality or in a particular plan area.

Section 91 d *Costs incurred by the local authority from community building*

The costs referred to above of community building that serves a plan area may include the acquisition, planning and construction costs of streets, parks and other public areas both in the plan area and outside it that substantially serve the plan area, and the costs incurred from acquiring land to build public buildings that substantially serve the plan area, relative to the benefit they bring to the plan area. Costs incurred by local authorities from soil improvement and from necessary noise abatement in the plan area and the costs incurred from planning that have not been collected under section 59 may also be taken into account.

The costs referred to above shall include both the estimated costs of implementing the plan and the costs incurred by the local authority from measures taken in advance to implement the plan. Costs must be reasonable regarding the character of the area and the circumstances in it.

When the costs of measures have been taken into account in development compensation the local authority must endeavour to carry out these measures within 10 years after the decision to collect the compensation has become legally valid.

Section 91 e

Development compensation in areas where the local authority has built community infrastructure

If a local detailed plan or an amendment to a local detailed plan is drawn up for an area where the measures referred to in section 91 d have already been implemented to a significant degree and the benefit from the plan is particularly substantial, the development compensation may be assessed by estimating the costs of realizing the community infrastructure referred to in section 91 d that would significantly improve the plan area at the time of approving the plan.

Compensation paid on the basis of an earlier plan by agreement or under section 91 c, 104, 105 or 112 by plot owners on the community building costs referred to in section 91 d will be deducted in the assessment of development compensation.

Section 91 f *Maximum of development compensation*

Development compensation may not exceed 60 per cent of the increase in the value of a plot that meets the requirements of the local detailed plan, and is due to the plan. The local councils may decide to apply lower maximum development compensation within the municipality or the area that is to be planned.

Section 91 g *Assessment of development compensation and interest payable on the compensation*

The decision to assess the development compensation is made by the local authority. The decision must be made without delay when the local detailed plan has been approved. The decision must give the grounds for imposing the compensation.

Development compensation may be assessed only if a binding plot division is laid out in the local detailed plan. The development compensation is assessed separately for each plot in the plan. When an entire block that is owned by a single party has a sole intended use, no plot division need be laid out in the local detailed plan. In such cases the development compensation may be assessed on the entire block.

Annual interest of 2 per cent is payable on the development compensation beginning from two years after the local detailed plan has entered into force and the decision to assess development compensation has become legal. No interest is payable for a period when a building prohibition under section 53(1), or section 58(4), is in force on the plot.

Section 91 h *Requesting opinions and consulting landowners*

Before development compensation is assessed, an opinion on the assessment proposal must be obtained from the District Survey Office, and the landowners concerned must be informed of the proposal as laid down in section 95 of the Local Government Act. Landowners are entitled to file complaints on proposals. Complaints must be filed with the local authority within 30 days of receiving knowledge of the proposal.

The opinion referred to above in subsection 1 must be requested and the consultation, also referred to above in subsection 1, must be carried out before the local detailed plan is approved.

In the assessment of development compensation, the opinion of the District Survey Office may be deviated from only for a special reason with regard to the increase in property value.

Section 91 i *Liability to pay development compensation and time of imposing the compensation*

The party that owns the land in question at the time development compensation is assessed or a party that has gratuitously acquired the land from the previous party is liable to pay the development compensation.

The local authority must impose the development compensation without delay as soon as construction is allowed to begin on the property on the basis of a legally valid building permit based on the local detailed plan. If an area which is part of a planned plot has been assigned in return for a compensation before said time, the development compensation must be imposed without delay when the assignment has taken place.

Section 91 j *Imposing of development compensation, maturity and penalty interest*

For the purpose of collecting development compensation, local authorities must provide the party liable to pay the compensation with a payment slip that indicates the assessed development compensation on the plot and the interest calculated on it.

If only a nominal share of the building rights or increase in building rights assigned in the local detailed plan is used in connection with a building permit, only a proportion of the assessed development compensation on the plot corresponding to the amount built under the building permit will be collected.

Development compensation must be paid within three months after it has been imposed. An overdue development compensation may be distrained without a separate court order or decision as laid down in the Act on the Recovery of Taxes and Fees by Recovery Proceedings (367/1961). When a building permit concerns a plot on which a reminder to build has been issued, the compensation must he paid within a year after it has been imposed.

If development compensation is not paid within the prescribed term of payment, interest in accordance with section 4(1), of the Interest Act (633/1982) will be collected on the delay period.

Section 91 k *Special payment arrangements*

Local authorities may agree with landowners that the payment of the development compensation may be made partially or in full in the form of land or other assets.

At the request of the landowner, the development compensation may be imposed even before the plot concerned can be developed on the basis of a legally valid building permit.

Section 91 l *Allocating development compensation before its imposition*

When development compensation has not been assessed for each plot, it must be allocated to each plot in relation to the surface area of the plots before it may be imposed.

When development compensation has been assessed for an entire block under section 91 g (2), it must also be allocated before it is imposed to a part of the plan plot or block that has been assigned in return for compensation. In such cases, allocation is carried out by the landowner in accordance with the grounds laid down in section 91 c.

Section 91 m *Decision not to collect development compensation*

When a local authority amends the local detailed plan or plot division so that grounds for development compensation are effectively removed, the local authority must make a decision not to collect development compensation without delay.

Section 91 n *Exemption from or postponement of payment of development compensation*

When payment of development compensation would be unreasonable due to a material change in the grounds for assessing it, local authorities may grant a full or partial exemption from or a postponement of the payment of the development compensation.

Section 91 o *Adjustment of development compensation in conjunction with imposition*

When changes to plot division or some other equivalent cause bring about minor changes in the grounds for development compensation, the compensation must be adjusted in accordance with the altered circumstances.

Section 91 p *Registering development compensation*

Local authorities must keep a register of development compensation.

When a local authority has ordered the collection of development compensation, it must without delay inform the district court in whose district the property concerned is located of the fact for entry in the register of land ownership and mortgages. The local authority must include with the notification made to the district court a list of properties and the development compensation that pertain to each of them. The district court shall also be notified without delay of allocation by plot and reallocation of development compensation for entry in the register of land ownership and mortgages.

The registry authority must be notified of development compensation that has been paid for entry in the register of land ownership and mortgages.

CHAPTER 13 ASSIGNING AND EXPROPRIATING LAND

Section 92 *The local authority's right to the area of a private road*

When, in a local master plan area, a private road as referred to in section 1 of the Act on private roads (358/62), hereinafter Private Road Act, or a road reserved by the landowner as a road area in connection with community building, is located in an area designated in the plan as a traffic way, the local authority is entitled, without compensation, to repair the road area and its drains, place service conduits in it and assign it for general traffic.

Section 93 *Transfer of the road area of a public road to the local authority*

When the local detailed plan comes into force, the road area of a public road included in the plan area is transferred to the local authority's ownership without compensation.

Section 94 *Transfer of a street area to the local authority*

When a local detailed plan is approved for an area for the first time, the local authority gains possession of any street area not previously in its possession by means of a partition under the Partition Act.

Compensation for street areas is prescribed in section 104. Section 95

Taking possession of a street area

The local authority gains possession of an area referred to in section 94 when construction commences or it is needed for some other use and partition to separate the area has been initiated, or when the local authority has paid compensation for the area as referred to in 104.

If a building with greater than minor value, or a valuable structure or piece of equipment is located in the area referred to in paragraph 1, or the area is necessary for their use, the local authority may not take possession of the land before agreement is reached on compensation or an expropriation procedure has been initiated.

Once the expropriation procedure has been initiated, the local authority may take possession of land which will become part of a street area when the local detailed plan is amended.

Section 96 *Expropriation right of local authorities and other public bodies in local detailed plan areas*

Within local detailed plan areas, the local authority may, without a specific permit, expropriate such public areas and such plots of public building based on the local detailed plan which the plan designates to a municipal agency or for other needs of the local authority. Correspondingly, the State and a joint municipal board are entitled to expropriate plots of public buildings and public areas based on the local detailed plan which the plan designates to agencies of the State or the joint municipal board or for their other needs.

The provisions of paragraph 1 shall also be observed when right of use is restricted in the local detailed plan in an area which the plan designates for the needs of the local authority, the joint municipal board or the State for the purpose of underground construction.

Section 97 *Expropriation based on a reminder to build*

After the local detailed plan has been in force for at least two years, the local authority can issue an owner or titleholder of a plot based on a binding plot division with a reminder to build if less than half of the gross floor area permitted for the plot has been used or, considering the purpose, location and mode of construction of the buildings on the plot and other factors, if a plot covered by a local detailed plan has not been developed in keeping with the plan.

The owner or titleholder of a plot covered by the local detailed plan and intended for the construction of a residential building with no more than two dwellings may not be issued with a reminder, however, if a residential building already exists on the plot and is being used. Moreover, a reminder to build may not be issued when a building prohibition referred to in section

53, or section 58, paragraph 4, is in force. If such a building prohibition takes effect for the plot after a reminder to build has been issued, the reminder becomes void.

If a plot covered by a local detailed plan has not been built on in the manner referred to in paragraph 1 within three years after the party in question has been informed of the reminder to build, the local authority is entitled to expropriate the said plot without special permission. Enforcement of the expropriation shall be applied for within one year of the end of the period reserved for building.

The provisions of this section concerning the plot and its owner or titleholder also apply to areas designated in the local detailed plan as construction sites, and to the owners and titleholders of such areas.

The local authority shall keep a public record of reminders to build it has issued. Reminders also apply to any new owners or titleholders to whom a property is transferred after a reminder to build has been entered in the register. The local authority must immediately notify the office of the district court of the issuance, reversal or lapse of a reminder to build and of fulfilment of the obligation, so that an entry can be a made in the Mortgage Register.

Section 98 *Right to expropriate the building or right of another party*

The local authority is entitled to expropriate a building or installation belonging to another located on municipal land, or a usufruct, easement or other such right concerning said land belonging to another party under the same conditions and in the same order as it is entitled to expropriate them in connection with the expropriation of land belonging to another.

If a building or installation belonging to another, or usufruct, easement, or other such right prevents the owner of a plot based on the local detailed plan from developing the plot within reasonable time and mainly according to the plan, and the plot has not been so developed, the owner of the plot concerned is entitled to expropriate it in the order prescribed in the Partition Act for the expropriation of part of a plot, provided that expropriation is considered important for implementation of the local detailed plan. The owner of the plot is not, however, entitled to expropriate if the building or installation forming the obstacle was constructed or the corresponding rights arose after the plan being implemented was approved, or if, under the Partition Act, the expropriation right rests with a party other than the owner of the plot according to the local detailed plan.

Section 99 *Expropriation of land on the basis of an expropriation permit*

When the general need so demands, the competent ministry may permit the local authority to expropriate an area needed for community construction and related arrangements, or for other planned development by the municipality.

The competent ministry may grant an authority implementing a plan a permit to expropriate an area included in a regional plan, or to restrict the relevant right of use, if this is required to implement the regional plan in order to meet the common needs of the State, region or joint municipal board, or the common needs of the municipality's population.

In addition, the competent ministry may grant the local authority a permit to expropriate an area designated in the local master plan as a traffic way, or for housing development or related community construction, and which is required to develop the community according to the local authority's plan, and an area intended for an agency of the local authority or joint municipal board, or for other needs. An area expropriated for housing development or related community construction may also include recreation or conservation areas.

Section 100 *Expropriation facilitating implementation of a plan*

The competent ministry may grant the local authority a permit to expropriate a building block or other area included in the local detailed plan, if its expropriation is justified for the purpose of implementing the plan, and the public need so requires.

Section 101 *Duty to expropriate or pay compensation*

When the local detailed plan or, under a regulation referred to in section 43, paragraph 2, the local master plan, designates land for a purpose other than private construction and the landowner cannot therefore use the area in a manner generating reasonable return, the local authority or, if the area is intended or designated in the plan for State needs, the State is required to expropriate the area or pay compensation for the harm. What benefit the landowner derives from the local master plan or detailed shore plan is taken into consideration in assessing reasonable gain. The obligation to expropriate or pay compensation does not apply to areas of joint use referred to in section 75, areas referred to in section 91, road areas of public roads referred to in section 93 or street areas referred to in section 94. The expropriation and compensation duty referred to in this paragraph may apply to an area designated for agriculture and forestry only if special restrictions on use of the area have been imposed in the plan.

When it is necessary to purchase only part of a continuous area belonging to the owner and included in the local master plan or the local detailed plan under paragraph 1, the local authority or the State is entitled to expropriate the area in its entirety.

Section 102 *Restriction on the duty to expropriate or pay compensation*

The duty of the local authority or the State to expropriate or pay compensation as laid down in section 101 takes effect only after the landowner's application for an exemption to the restriction has been denied and the decision has gained legal force.

The local authority and the State are released from their duty to expropriate or pay compensation when, due to an amendment of the local master plan or the local detailed plan, the area can be used for private purposes in a manner generating reasonable return and the matter concerning the duty to expropriate or pay compensation has not been resolved or gained legal force.

When resolving a matter concerning the obligation to expropriate or compensate, no changes in ownership or property division that have taken place after the local master plan or the local detailed plan has been approved are taken into account, unless they have been made in order to implement the plan.

Section 103 *Expropriation procedure and determining compensation*

Unless otherwise provided elsewhere in this Act, the Act on Expropriation of Immovable Property and Special Rights (603/1977), hereinafter the Expropriation Act, shall be observed when an expropriation is implemented under this Act, or when the compensation deriving from a transfer or restriction on land use as referred to in this Act is determined.

CHAPTER 14 COMPENSATION RESULTING FROM IMPLEMENTATION OF THE LOCAL MASTER PLAN OR LOCAL DETAILED PLAN

Section 104 *Compensation to be paid for street areas*

The local authority is required to pay compensation to the landowner for a street area transferred to it under section 94 in so far as the surface-area of the area concerned exceeds 20 per cent of the total land owned by said landowner in the local detailed plan area in question, or is larger than the building volume permitted for the land remaining in his ownership in the plan area concerned. Land designated in the local detailed plan as agricultural or forestry areas or water areas is not taken into consideration in determining the obligation to pay compensation.

The size of the transferable area referred to in paragraph 1 above is calculated according to the first local detailed plan.

In cases other than those referred to in paragraph 1, the local authority is required to pay compensation for the street area to the landowner, determined according to the provisions of the Expropriation Act on the grounds for compensation, excluding section 36 of the Act. Notwithstanding the provisions of paragraph 1, the local authority is obliged to pay the landowner compensation for the street area if, taking into account the total impact of the transfer and the plan on said landowner, transferral without compensation is, exceptionally, manifestly unreasonable.

Notwithstanding the provisions of paragraph 1, the landowner is not entitled to compensation on a private road referred to in section 1 of the Private Roads Act if the road has been designated a street area in the local detailed plan.

If an area handed over by a landowner for use as a street area is returned to the plot in question by an amendment of the plan, the local authority may not collect compensation from the landowner for the corresponding area of land it received without compensation under subsection 1, provided that the plot is still owned by the same party and that the principal intended use of the plot has not been changed by amendment of the plan. (222/2003)

Section 105 *Compensation for a street area which the landowner is ordered to pay*

If the landowner does not have to transfer a street area without receiving compensation as referred to in section 104, or has to transfer a significantly smaller area, the local authority may set reasonable compensation to be paid by the landowner (*compensation for a street area*).

When the partition of a public area has been initiated in accordance with the Partition Act, the local authority is entitled to collect the compensation for a street area within three years of the local detailed plan coming into force. The party owning the property at the time the local detailed plan comes into force is responsible for paying the compensation.

Section 106 *Compensation resulting from the implementation of a local detailed plan*

If implementation of a local detailed plan causes the landowner special harm or losses, the local authority or, if the area is intended or designated for State needs, the State is obliged to pay compensation for such losses, provided they are not considered to be insignificant.

Section 107 *Lapsing of rights concerning road and street areas*

When the road area of a public road or a street area as referred to in section 94 is transferred to the ownership of a local authority, any rights concerning the said areas lapse. If the property to which the area belonged was subject to a claim when the area was transferred to the local authority and the owner of the area is paid compensation, the holder of the claim has the same right to the compensation as to the property.

Section 108 *Compensation for a building and other compensations and compensation for special loss*

The local authority shall pay compensation to the landowner for all buildings, trees, plants and equipment in an area transferred to it.

When the landowner is caused special loss because no compensation was paid on the transfer of the area to the local authority and the loss must be considered unreasonable in view of the circumstances, the local authority shall pay compensation for the loss. The same applies when the lapse of rights concerning an area causes the holder of the rights loss.

Compensation for the loss of a building site or gravel pit is paid as provided in the Expropriation Act.

Section 109 *Provisions concerning compensation*

An agreement made on the implementation of a local master plan or a local detailed plan and on related compensation is also binding on subsequent owners of the property.

If no agreement is reached on the compensation referred to in paragraph 1, the matter is resolved in accordance with the Expropriation Act.

CHAPTER 15 SPECIAL DEVELOPMENT AREAS

Section 110 *Special development areas*

The local authority may designate one or more specified areas of the municipality as special development areas for a maximum fixed period of 10 years.

Built areas where special development or implementation measures are necessary for renewal, conservation, improvement of the living environment or change of use, or to attain other goals concerning a common need, may be designated as special development areas.

Unbuilt areas can also be designated as special development areas when their development is necessary due to housing or business policies, and special development or implementation measures are required because of fragmented ownership or partition, or for some other corresponding reason.

Section 111 *Designation decision*

The decision to designate a special development area may be made in connection with a decision to draw up or amend the local master plan or the local detailed plan, or in a legally binding local master plan or in the local detailed plan. When the special development of the area does not require a plan to be drawn up or amended, the decision concerning a special development area can also be made separately.

When a special development area is decided on otherwise than in a plan, the provisions of section 62 on interaction shall be observed, as appropriate, in preparing the decision.

The decision or the plan must indicate what special arrangements as referred to in section 112 shall be made in the area, and the grounds for making them.

A decision to designate a special development area does not override the requirements prescribed in this Act on the drawing up of a plan or on its content.

Section 112 *Special arrangements in special development areas*

Notwithstanding the provisions of this Act and of other legislation, decisions may be taken to make the following special arrangements in a special development area:

CHAPTER 16 DEFINITIONS CONCERNING BUILDING ACTIVITIES

Section 113 *A building*

A 'building' is a construction, structure or installation which is fixed or intended to remain in one place, and which is intended for living, working, storage or some other use, and which, because of its attributes, requires supervision by the authorities for reasons of safety, health, the landscape, comfort and pleasantness, the environment or other reasons related to the objectives of this Act.

However, lightweight structures of minor size or smallish installations shall not be considered buildings unless they have special impact on land use or the environment.

Section 114 *Large retail units*

In this Act, 'large retail units' refers to retail shops larger than 2,000 m2 in gross floor area.

The provisions of paragraph 1 do not, however, apply to trading in special goods that require a great deal of space.

Section 115 *Gross floor area*

When applied to a plot or building site, 'gross floor area' means the total gross floor area of the buildings for which permission is granted.

The floors or storeys of a building are located completely or mainly above ground level, the basement storey completely or mainly below ground level and the attic or loft, if any, mainly above the level of the intersection of the elevation and the roof and above the highest floor level. The local detailed plan may allow the building of more than one basement storey and the premises required for the principal intended use of the building to be located either below ground level or at attic or loft level.

The gross floor area of a building includes the floor areas of each storey measured to the outer face of the exterior walls, and the area of the basement storey, attic or loft in which premises for the building's principal intended use are located or in which such premises could be located on the basis of position, access, size, available light and other attributes. If the thickness of the external wall exceeds 250 mm, the gross floor area of the building may exceed the permitted gross floor area by the floor area caused by the excess thickness of the wall.

CHAPTER 17 GENERAL PRECONDITIONS FOR BUILDING ACTIVITIES

Section 116 *Requirements concerning the building site*

In local detailed plan areas, the suitability of a building site is resolved in the local detailed plan.

Outside the areas covered by a local detailed plan, building sites must be appropriate for the purpose, fit for construction and sufficiently large, at least 2,000 m2. When the appropriateness and fitness for purpose of a building site are considered, care must be taken to ensure that there is no danger from flood, earth or rock fall, or landslide. Also, it must be possible to locate buildings at a sufficient distance from the boundaries of the property, public roads and a neighbour's land.

Outside the areas covered by a local detailed plan, the distance of a building from land owned or held by another and from a building on such land will be prescribed by decree.

Section 117 *Requirements concerning construction*

A building must fit into the built environment and landscape, and must fulfil the requirements of beauty and proportion.

A building must meet the essential requirements for structural strength and stability, fire safety, hygiene, health and environment, safety in use, noise abatement, and energy economy and insulation, as set by its intended use (*essential technical requirements*).

A building must conform with its purpose and be capable of being repaired, maintained and altered, and, in so far as its use requires, also be suitable for people whose capacity to move or function is limited.

In repair work and alteration, the attributes and special features of the building and its suitability for the intended use must be taken into account. Alterations may not endanger the safety of the building's users or weaken their health conditions.

In addition, construction must in any case comply with good building practice.

Section 118 *Protecting architecture and townscape*

Care shall be taken to ensure that buildings or townscape of historic or architectural value are not marred when construction work, repairs or alterations are carried out on buildings, or when a building or part thereof is demolished.

Section 119 *Duty to take care in building activities*

A party engaging in a building project shall ensure that the building is designed and constructed in accordance with building provisions and regulations and the permit granted. The party shall have the necessary competence to implement the project, as required by its difficulty, and access to qualified personnel.

Section 120 *Designing a building*

A design shall be prepared for construction that meets the requirements of this Act and provisions and regulations issued under it, and the requirements of good building practice.

A qualified person shall be in charge of the design in its entirety and of its quality, ensuring that the building design and any special designs form a complete entity which meets the requirements set for it (*principal designer*).

The person in charge of each special design shall ensure that the design meets the requirements set for it. When a special design is prepared by more than one designer, one of them must be appointed as the designer responsible for the special field concerned in its entirety.

Section 121 *Start-up meeting*

What is required of parties undertaking a building project in order to meet their duty to take care can be established in more detail in the building permit or in a start-up meeting for the construction work, arranged when necessary before the work is begun. At the same time, the parties undertaking a building project may be required to report on measures taken to ensure the quality of construction.

More detailed provisions on the start-up meeting and the quality assurance report will be issued by decree.

Section 122 *Construction management*

In any construction work requiring a permit or other approval from the authorities, there must be a person who is responsible for carrying out the work and for the quality of the work, who directs the construction work and ensures that work is carried out according to the building provisions and regulations, the permit granted and good building practice (*site manager*). Specialist foremen shall be used in construction work when needed, as prescribed by decree.

The site manager and the specialist foremen will be approved by the local building authority. Construction work may not be begun or continued without an approved site manager. The approval must be revoked if so warranted by negligence or other such reasons.

Section 123 *The demands of duties and the qualifications of persons working on a building project*

The person drawing up a building or special design, the site manager in charge of the construction work and specialist foremen must have the training and expertise required by the type of building project concerned and the demands of the duties involved.

The qualifications required in designing are judged according to the intended use of the building and the spaces within it, the structural loads and fire loads, the design, calculation and dimensioning methods, environmental requirements and in addition to the above any unconventional aspects of the design approach. The qualifications required in managing construction work are judged according to the construction conditions and any special methods used in carrying out the work.

Design and management duties can be classified in requirement classes in order to specify the minimum qualifications. The minimum qualifications shall be prescribed by decree, and more detailed regulations and guidelines will be issued in the Finnish Building Code.

Section 124 *Supervision of building activities by the authorities*

It rests with the local building supervision authority, based on the public interest, to supervise building and ensure that the provisions of this Act, and provisions and regulations issued under it, are observed in building activities.

The extent and type of supervision shall depend on the difficulty of each building project, the expertise and professional skill of the permit applicants and the persons in charge of project design and construction, and other issues relevant in terms of supervision.

It also rests with the local building supervision authority to take charge of general steering of building and related advisory services needed in the municipality.

Chapter 18 Permits required for building activities and other action

Section 125 *Building permit*

A building permit is required for the construction of a building.

A building permit is also required for repair and alteration work which is comparable to building construction, and for extending a building or increasing its gross floor area.

A building permit is required for repair and alteration work to a building other than that referred to above, if it is obvious that the work may affect the safety or health conditions of those using the building.

A building permit is required to substantially alter the intended use of a building or part thereof. When the need for the permit is considered, the impact the alteration will have on implementation of a land use plan and on other land use, and on the attributes required of the building are taken into account. Alteration of intended use requiring a permit includes altering a holiday home so that it is fit for permanent residence. Unless the area is specifically designated for this purpose in the local detailed plan, the building of a large retail unit shall be considered to have the aforementioned impact on land use.

When a building is intended to remain in the same location for a limited time, a time limit may be included in the building permit.

Section 126 *Action permit*

Instead of a building permit, an action permit may be applied for in the case of structures and installations such as masts, containers and smokestacks, when deciding the permit issue does not in every respect require the steering otherwise necessary in building.

In addition, an action permit is required to install or locate a structure or installation that is not considered a building, if the action has an impact on nature, townscape or landscape or on the use of surrounding land areas. An action permit is also required for measures altering the appearance of a building when a building permit is not required, and for rearrangement of dwellings in a residential building.

No permit is required for actions based on a street plan as referred to in this Act or on an approved road plan as referred to in the Act on Public Roads (243/1954).

More detailed provisions concerning actions referred to in paragraph 2 above will be issued by decree.

Section 127 *Permit to demolish a building*

In an area covered by a local detailed plan or where a building prohibition for the purpose of drawing up a local detailed plan, as referred to in section 53, is in force, a building or part thereof may not be demolished without a permit. A permit is also needed if so required in the local master plan.

No permit is required if a currently valid building permit, a street plan based on this Act or an approved road plan based on the Act on Public Roads requires the demolition of the building. Neither is a permit required for the demolition of an outbuilding or any other corresponding minor building, unless the building can be considered to be historically important or architecturally valuable, or to be a part of such an entity.

Unless the demolition requires a permit, the local building supervision authority shall be notified in writing of the demolition of a building or part thereof 30 days before the demolition work begins (*demolition notification*). During the said period, the building supervision authority may, if justified cause exists, demand that a permit be applied for.

Section 128 *Permit for landscape work*

Earth works, tree-felling or corresponding action altering the landscape may not be carried out without a permit (*restriction on action*) in areas:

No permit is required to carry out work that is necessary in order to implement a local detailed plan or a local master plan, or that is in accordance with a building or action permit that has been granted, or to take action that has only minor impact.

Neither is a permit required for action based on a road plan as referred to in the Act on Public Roads.

Provisions concerning the landscape-work permit do not apply to extraction of land resources that requires the permit referred to in the Extractable Land Resources Act (555/1981).

Section 129 *Use of the notification procedure*

A local authority may stipulate in the building ordinance that building or other activities with minor importance and impact may be commenced without a building or action permit once the party concerned has notified the local building supervision authority of the matter.
When required by public interest or protection of neighbours' rights, the local building supervision authority must require the party to apply for a building or action permit, instead of making a notification. Building or other activity may begin if the local building supervision authority does not, within 14 days of receiving the notification, require an application for a permit for the project concerned to be made.
More detailed provisions on the notification procedure will be issued by decree.

CHAPTER 19 PERMIT PROCEDURE AND CONSIDERATION OF A PERMIT

Section 130 *Principles of the permit procedure*

The local building supervision authority approves building permits, action permits, demolition permits and landscape-work permits. Decisions concerning the landscape-work permit may be delegated to another authority, as determined by the local authority.

The provisions of this chapter concerning the building permit procedure also apply to action, demolition and landscape-work permit procedures, as appropriate.

More detailed provisions concerning permit procedure will be issued by decree.

Section 131 *Building permit application*

Building permits shall be applied for in writing. Applications shall include proof that the applicant is the titleholder of the building site, and the master drawings signed by the designer. If necessary, the applicant may be required to provide additional information needed to decide on the application.

More detailed provisions concerning applications for a permit and the building designs required will be issued by decree.

Section 132 *Environmental impact assessment*

When the environmental impact assessment report referred to in the Act on Environmental Impact Assessment Procedure (468/1994) is required for building or other action subject to permit or official approval under this Act, the report must be enclosed with the permit application or notification as prescribed in this Act.

Section 133 *Hearing and opinions*

Neighbours shall be notified when an application for a building permit is submitted, unless notification is clearly not necessary with regard to the neighbours' interest, due to the smallness or location of the project, or to the contents of the plan. 'Neighbour' refers to owners and other titleholders of adjacent or opposite properties. The fact that the application has been submitted shall at the same time be publicized on the building site by suitable means.

When needed, a review shall be conducted on the building site in order to assess how the building fits in with the surroundings and the impact of construction, and in order to hear the neighbours. The applicant and the titleholders of the neighbouring properties shall be notified of the time and date of the review.

When a building permit is applied for in an area important to nature conservation as referred to in the Nature Conservation Act and prescribed in more detail by decree, or in an area that has been reserved for recreation or conservation purposes in the regional plan, an opinion on the application must be obtained from the regional environment centre.

More detailed provisions on notification of the permit application, publicity and making an objection will be issued by decree.

Section 134 *Processing a building permit application*

The master drawings to be followed in construction are approved in connection with grant of the building permit.

Permit matters may also be processed so that the general preconditions for building are assessed on the basis of a report, other than that referred to in section 131, paragraph 1, on the building's location, intended use, use of the permitted building volume and the environmental impact. Appropriate drawings concerning each stage of construction shall, however, be submitted for approval before the work concerned is begun.

Regulations on preparing special designs and submitting them to the local building supervision authority may be included in the building permit.

Regulations on drawing up instructions for use and maintenance of the building shall be included in the building permit, as provided in more detail by decree.

When the permit referred to in the Act on the Environmental Permit Procedure (731/1991) is required for activities referred to as building, deciding the building-permit question may be postponed until the environmental permit question has been settled, provided that this is justified in view of the potential uses of the building and the environmental impact of the intended activities.

Section 135 *Preconditions for a building permit in local detailed plan areas*

In areas covered by a local detailed plan, a building permit is granted under the following conditions:

When determining a permit question concerning renovation and alteration work referred to in section 125, paragraphs 3 and 4, above, the provisions pertaining to the preconditions for a building permit are applied, as appropriate.

Section 136 *preconditions for a building permit outside local detailed plan areas*

In areas not covered by a local detailed plan, a building permit is granted under the following conditions:

In areas not covered by a local detailed plan the provisions of section 135, paragraph 2, also apply to construction.

Section 137 *Special preconditions for granting a building permit in areas where planning is required*

In addition to what is otherwise laid down on the preconditions for a building permit, a building permit is granted in an area requiring planning referred to in section 16 that is not covered by a local detailed plan, provided that construction:

Notwithstanding the provisions of paragraph 1, an outbuilding may be built in connection with an existing dwelling or farm.

When a legally binding local master plan is in force in a village area or other rural area where there is only a minor need to build, the local master plan shall be considered to have determined whether a building supplementing existing habitation and necessary for a residential building containing no more than two dwellings or for the purposes of agriculture meets the special preconditions for a building permit laid down in paragraph 1.

Moreover, in other areas requiring planning, building activities shall not lead to construction of major significance or cause substantially harmful environmental or other impact.

Whether the preconditions referred to in paragraph 1 are met is resolved by an authority appointed by the local authority in connection with the building permit procedure or in a separate procedure.

When a building permit is considered for an area requiring planning, or otherwise resolving a matter pertaining to the need for planning is resolved otherwise, the provisions of section 173 on deviation procedures shall be observed with regard to hearing interested parties and authorities. The local authority must inform the regional environment centre of the permit decisions as referred to herein.

Section 138 *Preconditions for an action permit*

When a matter concerning an action permit is resolved, the provisions on the preconditions for building permits shall be observed only in so far as is necessary to assess the impact of the action on land use and the environment.

When an action is based on an expropriation permit granted under the Expropriation Act, care must be taken to ensure that implementation of the purpose of the expropriation permit is not unnecessarily hindered.

Section 139 *Preconditions for a demolition permit*

A demolition permit is granted on condition that the demolition will not destroy values pertaining to the heritage, beauty or other aspects of the built environment or hinder the implementation of land use planning.

The permit application must explain how the demolition work will be organized and the capacity to handle resulting building waste and to reuse any usable building components.

Section 140 *Preconditions for a landscape-work permit*

A landscape-work permit must be granted in areas where a local detailed plan or a local master plan is in force, provided that the action concerned will not hinder use of the area for the purpose designated in the plan, or mar either townscape or landscape.

In areas where the local authority has imposed a building prohibition for the purpose of drawing up or amending the local detailed plan, or where a restriction on action has been imposed for the purpose of drawing up the local master plan, a permit may be granted unless the action substantially hinders the drawing up of the plan or spoils the townscape or landscape.

When a permit for excavating or quarrying is denied under a special regulation in the local master plan or in an area covered by a local detailed plan when no decision has been made to amend the plan, the provisions of section 8 of the Extractable Land Resources Act apply concerning the duty to expropriate. When a permit is denied for other actions in the said areas and the landowner is therefore unable to use his land in a manner generating reasonable return, he is entitled to compensation for the losses sustained by him from the local authority or from the State, if the area has been intended or designated for State needs.

Section 141 *Permit regulations*

Whatever regulations are necessary may be included in the permit decision. Regulations may concern, among other things, how construction work is carried out or action taken, and the limitation of any harm that may be caused by them.

Section 142 *Notification of a permit decision*

A permit decision shall be issued after the permit issue has been made public; interested parties are deemed to have knowledge of the decision when it has been issued.

Permit decisions are delivered to the applicant. The decision or a copy thereof is also sent to the authorities provided by decree, and for those who have so requested in an objection or separately otherwise.

When a single objection or request has several signatories, the decision only has to be sent to the first signatory. The first signatory is required to provide the other signatories with the information.

Section 143 *Validity and extension of a permit*

The permit expires if construction work is not begun within three years or completed within five years. Permits or approvals issued by an authority for other action expire if the action has not been taken within three years. These periods begin when the permit or approval become legally valid.

The local building supervision authority may extend the validity of a permit or approval for a maximum period of two years, provided that the legal conditions required for building and other action are still met. These periods may be extended by a maximum of three years at a time in order to complete the work.

Section 144 *Right to commence*

Before a decision on a building, action or landscape-work permit, or a decision referred to in section 161, 162 or 163 on location, alteration or removal concerning equipment has become legally valid, the permit authority can grant a permit to carry out construction work or take other action completely or in part (*right to commence*).

The applicant shall provide acceptable sureties as security against any harm, losses or costs caused by revoking the decision or amending the permit. The appeal authority may, however, prohibit enforcement of the decision.

The duty to provide sureties does not apply to the State, local authorities or joint municipal boards.

Section 145 *Permit and supervision fee*

The permit applicant or party taking action is required to pay a fee to the local authority for inspection and supervision measures and other official duties, in accordance with a tariff approved by the local authority. Collection of the fee in advance may be ordered. If the measure is not completed or is completed only in part, the fee shall be returned on application in so far as it is groundless.

If inspection or supervision measures result from unauthorized construction, or construction that contravenes permits, or from neglect of duties by the permit applicant or the party responsible for the action, the fee may be increased on the basis of the costs incurred by the local authority through the measures taken.

Interest shall be paid on overdue fees, as provided in the Interest Act (633/1982).

Section 146 *Construction for defence purposes*

In areas where the State is the titleholder, buildings, structures and equipment directly connected with defence purposes may be constructed without a permit as referred to in this Act. Provisions on building supervision by the authorities do not apply to construction for defence purposes.

Section 147 *Construction statistics*

When applying for a permit for construction or renovation or alteration work or demolition of a building, the applicant must enclose with the application all information that the local authority is required to submit to the population register system under the Population Register Act (507/1993).

Section 148 *Type approval*

On application, the competent ministry may approve for a fixed period the use of a structure or an element of construction, or an implement, product or piece of equipment closely connected to a building for use in construction (*type approval*). In connection with the approval, regulations concerning construction may be deviated from.

An inspection body approved by the ministry shall supervise the quality of type-approved products continuously. Type approval must be revoked if this is considered appropriate because of problems in the manufacture of the product or in quality control.

The type-approval procedure will be laid down by decree.

CHAPTER 20 CARRYING OUT CONSTRUCTION WORK

Section 149 *Carrying out and supervising construction work*

Construction work shall be carried out so that it meets the requirements of the provisions and regulations issued in and under this Act as well as the requirements of good building practice.

Supervision of construction work by the authorities begins when work subject to a permit is commenced, and ends with a final inspection. Supervision takes place at the stages of work and on the scale decided by the authorities, and focuses on aspects that are significant to achieving a satisfactory end-result.

Before construction work is commenced, the local building supervision authority shall be notified thereof (*commencement notification*). More detailed provisions on commencing construction work will be issued by decree.

Section 150 *Inspection by authorities*

The setting out of the location and level of a building, checking them after completion of the foundation work, and the inspections to be made during the course of the work are specified in the permit concerning construction.

If an inspection or check warrants admonition, any action that is required to remove and remedy the defect or error and the period within which it has to be taken must be specified in written instructions. The party concerned is entitled to place such instructions before the local building supervision authority for consideration by means of a claim for rectification.

In order to guarantee that construction work has been carried out properly and to verify inspections an inspection record is kept at the building site. Checks, inspections by the authorities and inspections of work specified as being carried out by private parties are entered in the record.

Provisions on checks and inspections needed to supervise construction work will be issued by decree.

Section 151 *Supervision by the developer and other private inspections*

On application, the local building supervision authority may allow the supervision of construction, excluding that of a residential building, to be assigned to the developer in accordance with an approved supervision plan (*developer supervision*). When approving a supervision plan, the building supervision authority decides where supervision by the authorities is not required.

The developer shall ensure that the supervision plan is observed, and notify the building supervision authority in good time in writing of any need to deviate from the plan. The decision concerning builder supervision may be revoked if it is found that such supervision is not warranted.

The building supervision authority may allow the inspection made to verify that construction work conforms to the building design to be carried out by the person who has drawn up the building design or report, or some other person with sufficient professional skills in the employ of the party engaging in the building project (*expert inspection*). That an inspection has been carried out must be confirmed by an entry in the records.

While processing a permit application, or during the course of construction work, the building supervision authority may, if necessary to assess a building project, require that the applicant provide an expert opinion on whether the planned approach or the construction work meets the demands prescribed for it under this Act (*external inspection*). The party engaging in the building project is responsible for the costs incurred.

Consent for developer supervision or expert inspection does not reduce the building supervision authority's power to intervene when construction is in contravention of permits or deviates from the provisions or regulations.

More detailed provisions concerning developer supervision and other inspection carried out while work is in progress will be issued by decree.

Section 152 *Properties of construction products*

The properties of construction products intended for use as permanent elements in a building shall be such that the building, when properly designed and constructed, meets the essential requirements set for construction during its economic service life if maintained normally.

Construction products that have been appropriately labelled with the CE marking and provide the required performance are deemed to meet the technical requirements of the product's designated use.

A construction product with type approval is considered to meet the requirements set for it in so far as the matter has been resolved in the approval process.

Separate provisions apply to proving that products meet the requirements and to related assessment and approval institutions, as referred to in the Construction Products Directive.

Section 153 *Commissioning a building*

A building or part thereof shall not be commissioned before it has been finally inspected and approved for use. Any inspections based on other legislation that have substantial impact on the building's safe use shall be conducted before the final inspection.

When applying for a final inspection, the building's instructions for use and maintenance, if such have been required, must be sufficiently complete and ready to be handed over to the owner of the building.

When the activity intended to take place in a building requires a permit as referred to in the Environmental Permit Procedures Act, the building may not be approved for commissioning before said permit has gained legal force.

Section 154 *Organizing the demolition of a building*

The demolition of a building or part thereof must be organized so as to make it possible to recycle usable parts of the building and process any building waste.

CHAPTER 21 ARRANGEMENTS CONCERNING CONSTRUCTION

Section 155 *Play areas and areas for the enjoyment of residents*

Adequate outdoor areas must be provided in connection with residential buildings for play areas and areas for the enjoyment of residents. They must be separated safely from areas reserved for traffic. When estimating the adequacy of the areas, the corresponding areas available in the vicinity and the joint arrangements of properties may also be taken into account.

A deviation from the duty to provide play areas and areas for the enjoyment of residents may be allowed with regard to minor additional construction and to renovation and alteration work on a building, if this is justifiable on the basis of the size of the property, the terrain or some other reason.

Section 156 *Providing parking space*

The number of parking spaces stipulated in the local detailed plan and the building permit for a property must be provided in connection with the construction work.

When the local detailed plan so stipulates, the local authority may designate the required parking space a reasonable distance away and assign it to a property. In such a case, a fee corresponding in value to the exemption from the duty to provide parking space shall be collected from the property owner, according to a tariff approved by the local authority.

The duty to provide parking space does not apply to minor additional construction or to renovation and alteration work on a building. When changing the intended use of a building or part thereof, the ensuing need for parking space must, however, be taken into account.

Section 157 *Waste management*

The premises and structures required for the waste management of a property must already be provided during construction. Waste management must be organized so that no harm is caused to health or the environment.

Section 158 *Building easement*

An easement may be established on another property for the purposes of a plot or a property used as a building site, giving a permanent right to use a building or structure or to take corresponding action (*building easement*). Establishing an easement requires the interested parties to agree in writing.

A building easement may be established if it promotes appropriate development or use of a property, is needed by the easement holder and does not cause substantial harm to the encumbered property. An easement required by the local detailed plan may be established unless this is manifestly unnecessary or unreasonable for the encumbered property due to a change in circumstances that has taken place since the plan has entered into force.

If establishing the easement as a permanent right is not appropriate, a fixed-term building easement which is in force until the specified date or event may be established for a special cause.

Decisions concerning the establishment, amendment or removal of a building easement are made by the local building supervision authority. Provisions on easement types and the registration of easements will be laid down by decree.

Section 159 *Easement required by the local detailed plan*

A building easement required by the local detailed plan can be established even if the interested parties do not agree thereon:

The easement referred to in this section can also be established for the purposes of the local authority or for an installation in its control.

Easements other than building easements required by local detailed plans are laid down in the Partition Act.

Section 160 *Organization of easements*

A building easement may be amended or removed if the interested parties so agree and appropriate construction, or proper use or maintenance of the property or implementation of the local detailed plan is not hindered.

A building easement may be amended or removed without the easement holder's consent if:

If agreement is not reached regarding compensation payable on amendment or removal of a building easement, the matter shall be resolved as laid down in the Expropriation Act.

Section 161 *Locating community infrastructure equipment*

Property owners and titleholders are obliged to allow the location of service conduits serving the community or the property in the area they own or hold the title to, unless the location can be organized satisfactorily by some other means and at reasonable cost. The same applies to minor equipment, structures and installations related to service conduits. Service conduits or other equipment may not be built so that planning of the area or implementation of a plan is hindered. Unless agreement has been reached with the property owner or titleholder on the location, the decision concerning it is made by the local building supervision authority. Causing undue harm to the property shall be avoided when the location is decided on.

The agreement on the location of equipment referred to in paragraph 1 is also binding on new owners and titleholders of the property.

The owner or titleholder of a property is entitled to be paid compensation for harm and damage caused by the location of service conduits or other equipment. Unless agreement is made on compensation, the matter shall be resolved as laid down in the Expropriation Act.

The provisions of paragraph 1 may be applied to the location of a water main or sewer belonging to a public water and sewage works even when the required right would also be justifiable under the provisions of the Water Act (264/1961).

The provisions of the section on property owners and titleholders also apply to the owners and titleholders of common areas.

Section 162 *Altering and removing community infrastructure equipment*

The local building supervision authority may decide to alter the location of a service conduit or piece of equipment referred to in section 161, observing section 160 of the Partition Act as appropriate. With regard to service conduits and equipment serving the community, the provisions of the said section of the Partition Act on entitled properties apply to the local authority or the party maintaining the service conduits or equipment.

The local building supervision authority may also decide on the removal of a service conduit or piece of equipment in the case of a change in circumstances, observing the provisions of section 161, paragraph 1, of the Partition Act, as appropriate; it shall, however, observe the provisions of section 161 of this Act rather than sections 156 and 157 of the Partition Act.

Provisions on moving a service conduit, piece of equipment or structure located in a common area are laid down in section 89.

Section 163 *Location of minor equipment*

The provisions of sections 161 and 162, where appropriate, also apply to the duty of the owner or titleholder of a property, public area or building to allow fastenings for lighting, traffic or telecommunications lines, traffic signs, traffic control devices and signals and minor street-structure elements to be fixed to or located on the property, area or building.

Section 164 *Joint arrangements between properties*

If implementation of the local detailed plan requires joint arrangements between several properties, the local building supervision authority may, on the initiative of one owner of a property and after having heard the other owners or titleholders of the property, stipulate, in connection with building or otherwise, joint use of the area of a block area or part thereof or of premises forming part of the property.

Decisions concerning joint arrangements must include an arrangement scheme. The scheme lays down the use of the area or premises, its repair and maintenance, and the basis for sharing the costs of the arrangement and their payment.

A regulation concerning joint arrangements may be issued when the arrangement would always promote the use of several properties and would not cause unreasonable harm to any property. If no agreement is reached by the interested parties on the costs of the arrangement, the matter will be resolved in accordance with the Expropriation Act.

Provisions concerning registration of rights established by a decision concerning joint arrangements will be laid down by decree.

Section 165

Altering the natural course of water

If the natural level of the property used as a building site is altered or if other action is taken which alters the natural course of water on the property, it is the duty of the property owner or titleholder to ensure that the action does not cause substantial harm to neighbours. If owners or titleholders of a property neglect their duties, the local building supervision authority shall, on application, stipulate how the harm shall be remedied or eliminated.

The provisions of paragraph 1 also apply to the owners of streets, street areas and other public areas.

CHAPTER 22 CARE OF THE BUILT ENVIRONMENT

Section 166 *Maintenance of buildings*

Buildings and their surroundings must be kept in a condition that meets standards of health, safety and fitness for use at all times and does not cause environmental harm or damage the beauty of the environment.

Moreover, in the use and maintenance of buildings protected by a land use plan or under the Building Conservation Act, the purpose of building conservation must also be taken into account.

If the duty to keep a building in proper repair is neglected, the local building supervision authority may order that the building be repaired or its surroundings cleared and cleaned. If the building poses an imminent danger to safety, its demolition must be ordered or its use must be prohibited.

Before issuing a repair order, the local building supervision authority may order the building's owner to present an inspection report on the building's condition, in order to assess what repairs are clearly necessary for reasons of health and safety.

Section 167 *Maintenance of the environment*

The built environment must be used as prescribed in the building permit and kept in good condition.

An authority appointed for the purpose by the local authority shall ensure that traffic ways, streets, market places and squares, and parks and areas intended for the enjoyment of residents meet the standards of a satisfactory townscape and of pleasantness and comfort. Routes provided for non-motorized traffic must be kept safe and free of obstacles.

If organization of the area of a block has not been stipulated in the local detailed plan or building permit and said organization is a substantial impediment to the organization of land use, the local building supervision authority may stipulate on reorganization of the use and repair of the block area (*organization of a block area*). Such regulations may be issued on condition that the organization is not clearly unreasonable to property owners.

A plot or building site may not be used in a manner which reduces the areas designated in its building permit for planting or as play areas or areas for the enjoyment of residents or other areas that affect pleasantness and comfort. Accessways indicated in the building permit for emergency vehicles or maintenance use must be kept in a suitable condition for motor vehicles.

Section 168 *Lightweight structures and smallish installations*

Lightweight structures and smallish installations must meet reasonable requirements for health, safety and outward appearance. Structures and installations must suit their surroundings and must not impede traffic.

The local building supervision authority may order that a structure or installation that is in violation of this section be demolished or altered to meet the requirements of this Act.

Section 169 *Outside storage*

Outside storage must be organized so that landscape visible from a road or other public thoroughfare or area is not damaged or the surrounding habitation disturbed.

In areas covered by a local detailed plan, spaces may not be used for storage that causes disturbance or degrades the surroundings or for long-term or extensive outside storage of goods, unless otherwise provided in the local detailed plan.

Section 170 *Incomplete construction work or abandoned buildings*

When construction work or other action has been started but not completed before a permit or approval by the authorities expires, the local building supervision authority shall order the party concerned to complete the work within a fixed period or take other action necessary for reasons of health or safety, or because of harm or disturbance caused to the surroundings.

When a building has been destroyed partially or completely, construction work has been discontinued or the building is no longer used, the building site and its surroundings must be put into a condition that does not compromise safety or degrade the environment. The building must also be protected against weather and potential vandalism.

CHAPTER 23 DEVIATION

Section 171 *Authority to deviate*

When special cause exists, the local authority may grant a right to deviate from the provisions, regulations, prohibitions and other restrictions issued in or under this Act concerning building and other action.

The local authority may not, however, grant a right to deviate:

In cases referred to in paragraph 2, right to deviate may be granted by the regional environment centre.

A right to deviate as defined in this section may not be granted concerning provisions on the landscape-work permit or the special conditions laid down in section 137 of a building permit in areas requiring planning.

Section 172 *Conditions of deviation*

Deviation shall not:

A right to deviate may not be granted if it leads to building with substantial impact or if it has other substantially harmful environmental or other impact.

Section 173 *Deviation procedure*

Before a matter concerning deviation as laid down in section 171 is resolved, neighbours and others on whose life, work and other circumstances the project may have significant impact shall be given the opportunity to make a written objection. The local authority shall notify neighbours and other aforementioned parties of applications at the applicant's expense. More detailed provisions concerning hearing will be issued by decree.

Before a matter concerning deviation is resolved, the opinion of the regional environment centre, some other State authority or of the regional council must be obtained, if necessary, when the deviation has substantial bearing on their sphere of authority. When deviation has substantial bearing on land use in a neighbouring municipality, its opinion must also be obtained.

However, an opinion shall always be requested from the regional environment centre when deviation concerns:

The authorities referred to in paragraph 2 above must provide their opinion within two months.

Before deciding on a deviation as referred to in section 171, paragraph 3, the regional environment centre shall request an opinion from the local authority concerned. The provisions of paragraphs 1 and 2 apply, as appropriate, to hearing interested parties and requesting other opinions.

Section 174 *Deviation decision and its notification*

Deviation decisions shall be justified as laid down in the Administrative Procedures Act (598/1982). Any necessary regulations and conditions may be included in the decision.

The applicant shall be provided with the decision immediately. In addition, the decision or a copy thereof is sent to the authorities prescribed by decree, to those who have entered an objection in the matter, and to those who have separately requested it. When a single objection has been made by several objectors, the decision or a copy of it need only be sent to the first signatory of the objection. The first signatory is responsible for informing the other signatories.

The local authority shall send the deviation decision referred to in section 171 to the regional environment centre for information.

The provisions of section 145 on permit and supervision fees apply to a deviation decision made by the local authority.

Section 175 *Minor deviation in connection with a building permit*

Under the conditions and restrictions referred to in sections 171 and 172, the local building supervision authority may grant a building permit in the case of minor deviation from provisions, regulations, prohibitions and other restrictions concerning building.

In addition, minor deviation from the technical and corresponding requirements of a building requires that the deviation does not set aside the essential requirements of building.

Section 176 *Temporary buildings*

Under the conditions and restrictions referred to in sections 172, the local building supervision authority may grant a building permit for the construction of a temporary building to remain in place for a maximum period of five years. A building is deemed to be temporary if, taking into account its structure, value and intended use, it must be considered to be intended to remain in place for the said maximum period.

When examining a permit application for the construction of a temporary building, the building's purpose and standards of strength, health, traffic, fire safety and suitability for the environment shall be taken into account.

The provisions of section 173 shall be applied, as appropriate, to permit procedures concerning temporary buildings.

CHAPTER 24 COERCIVE MEANS AND CONSEQUENCES

Section 177 *Order for the enforcement of planning duties*

If the local authority does not draw up a building ordinance, the necessary local master plans or local detailed plans, or keep them up-to-date, and it is evident that it impedes the attainment of goals set in legislation for land use planning and for the steering of building, the competent ministry may issue an order that a decision concerning it shall be made within a specified period.

Negotiations shall be conducted with the local authority before the order referred to in paragraph 1 is issued. The local authority must also be requested to provide an opinion.

If the order referred to in paragraph 1 is not observed, the ministry may impose a conditional fine requiring the local authority to observe the order.

What is provided above in this section concerning local authorities correspondingly applies to regional councils that do not draw up necessary regional plans or keep them up-to-date.

When the ministry has issued the order referred to in paragraph 1 on drawing up or amending a local detailed plan or a local master plan, a building prohibition and a restriction on action as referred to in section 128 are in force in the area referred to in the order.

Section 178 *Order for the purpose of attaining a national land use objective*

If, in the interest of the public good, it is vital that conditions are created for particular use of an area in order to attain a national land use objective, and no solution is provided in the regional plan or the local master plan or the local detailed plan, the competent ministry may issue the regional council or the local authority with pertinent orders concerning planning of the area.

Negotiations shall be conducted with the regional council, the local authority and other parties affected by the matter before the order referred to in paragraph 1 is issued. Opinions shall also be requested from said bodies and parties.

Section 179 *Order to fulfil a street management duty*

If a street or part thereof is not constructed so that it is in the condition required by the land use referred to in the legally binding local detailed plan within a reasonable time from when the street management duty begins, and this may be harmful to health or safety or cause some other special harm to the organization of land use or traffic, the regional environment centre may impose a conditional fine to obligate the local authority to fulfil its duty.

Section 180 *Suspension of construction work*

If construction work is commenced or other action is taken or carried out contrary to the provisions or regulations issued in and under this Act, or contrary to a permit or approval granted by an authority, the building inspector or another local authority official supervising building is entitled to issue a written order to suspend the work.

The local building supervision authority shall be immediately notified of the suspension of construction work. The building supervision authority will decide whether the suspension shall remain in force. Irrespective of appeal, the decision shall be observed unless the appeal authority orders otherwise.

Section 181 *Market surveillance*

The competent ministry and an authority authorized by it shall function as the market surveillance authority referred to in the Construction Product Directive.

If there are grounds to suspect that the CE marking has been used on a construction product which does not meet the relevant preconditions, the market surveillance authority may prohibit the supply of the product or its use for building until the preconditions for using the marking are met.

If it is indicated by an examination of the matter that the CE marking continues to be used unjustifiably on a construction product, the market surveillance authority may prohibit sales of the product and its other supply in connection with business activities. The importer or manufacturer of the construction product may also be required to take action to remove the product from the market or to make it comply with the requirements.

The importer or manufacturer of the construction product is responsible for the costs incurred by the State from examinations that prove warranted. Such costs may be collected in accordance with the Act on collecting taxes and fees by distraint (367/1961).

The local building supervision authority shall monitor the use of construction products and notify the competent ministry of any incorrect use of the CE marking.

Section 182 *Conditional fines and threat of action*

If a party takes action against the provisions or regulations issued in and under this Act, or is negligent in carrying out duties based on them, the local building supervision authority and the competent ministry, as the market surveillance authority, may issue a decision requiring the recalcitrant party to rectify the misdeed or negligence within a specified period.

A prohibition or order issued by the authorities may be reinforced by a conditional fine or a threat that the action not taken will be taken at the expense of the negligent party.

Otherwise, the provisions of the Conditional Fines Act (1113/1990) apply to matters pertaining to conditional fines and threats of action.

Section 183 *Right to inspect*

For the purpose of carrying out its supervisory duties prescribed in this Act, the local building supervision authority has right of access to building sites and is entitled to carry out inspections and investigations on the site.

When there are grounds for suspecting that provisions, regulations or prohibitions concerning construction or the maintenance of buildings have been contravened, the building supervision authority is also entitled to enter buildings or rooms. The owner or titleholder of the buildings or rooms shall be notified about an inspection at least 24 hours before it is carried out.

In a shop or warehouse or on the premises of the importer or manufacturer, the market surveillance authority has right of access to construction products, documents related to their manufacture, other documents and all other material needed to assess the product. The authority is also entitled to carry out inspections and investigations related to market surveillance.

Section 184 *Executive assistance*

It is the duty of the police to provide the local building supervision authority and the construction product market surveillance authority with executive assistance in supervising provisions and regulations issued in and under this Act.

Section 185 *Penalties*

A party that commences construction without a permit or notification as required in this Act, or takes other action in contravention of this Act or provisions and regulations issued under it, or is otherwise negligent in carrying out duties prescribed or stipulated for him therein concerning construction or management of the environment, shall be sentenced to a fine for committing a *building violation*.

The penalty for damaging the environment or committing a building violation in contravention of this Act or provisions issued under it or of plan or permit regulations or prohibitions is prescribed in chapter 48, sections 1-4 and section 6 of the Penal Code (39/1889).

The provisions of chapter 2, section 16, of the Penal Code are observed in confiscating the financial benefit gained from violations and crimes referred to above in this section, and any object and other property used to commit them.

Section 186 *Notification of prosecution*

Having observed action or negligence requiring the suspension of construction work or the imposition of a conditional fine or threat of action, the local building supervision authority shall notify the police for the purposes of pre-trial investigation.

The notification need not be made if, taking the circumstances into account, the act or negligence can be deemed to be minor and it is not considered that public interest necessitates prosecution.

CHAPTER 25 APPEAL AND RECTIFICATION ISSUED BY AN AUTHORITY

Section 187 *Request for rectification*

The decision of an official to whom the relevant question has been delegated by the local building supervision authority or some other municipal authority cannot be appealed. A party that is unsatisfied with a decision is entitled to have the question handled by the relevant authority (*request for rectification*). The right to request rectification is determined on the same basis as the interested party's right to appeal.

A request for rectification shall be made in writing to the official concerned within 14 days of the decision. Instructions for requesting rectification shall be appended to the decision. The relevant authority shall begin processing the request without delay.

If building supervision has been delegated by agreement to an official in another local authority, processing of the request for rectification concerning the administrative decision made by the said official is determined according to the municipality where the construction took place or where the action was taken.

Section 188 *Appeal against a decision to approve a land use plan or a building ordinance*

Decisions to approve a local master plan, a local detailed plan or a building ordinance are appealed to an administrative court as laid down in the Local Government Act. However, the rectification procedure laid down in the Local Government Act is not applied in questions concerning approval of a local detailed plan even if decision-making power has been delegated to the municipal board or a committee, as laid down in section 52.

Appeals concerning local detailed plans which must be considered essential to housing development or otherwise socially significant shall be processed urgently.

Decisions to approve a regional plan are appealed to the competent ministry. The appeal is processed in connection with the plan ratification referred to in section 31. The provisions of the Local Government Act otherwise apply to appeal.

The provisions of paragraph 3 also apply to legally binding joint master plans. The provisions of the Local Government Act on the right to appeal of a member of a municipality apply to all members of the relevant municipality.

Interested parties are considered to have been notified of a decision approving a plan or a building ordinance when the decision has been made available to the public as laid down in section 63.

Section 189 *Appeal against a decision on special development areas*

A local authority's decision to establish a special development area, when not made in connection with approval of a land use plan, may be appealed as laid down in the Local Government Act.

Section 189 a *Appeal against a decision to assess development compensation (222/2003)*

Decisions of local authorities to assess development compensation may be appealed as laid down in the Local Government Act. The right to appeal is determined, however, by the provisions in the Administrative Judicial Procedure Act.

The provisions of the Administrative Judicial Procedure Act are otherwise applied to appeals.

With regard to determining the value of a property, the Administrative Court must request the opinion of the District Survey Office, unless this is manifestly unnecessary.

Section 189 b *Appeal against a decision to impose development compensation (222/2003)*

Appeals against a decision of a local authority to impose development compensation are made to the Administrative Court. Appeals against imposition of development compensation may not be made on the legally valid grounds of the compensation.

The provisions of the Administrative Judicial Procedure Act are applied to appeals. Appeals do not, however, postpone the implementation of a decision, unless otherwise decided by the appeals authority.

Section 190 *Appeal against other decisions by the authorities*

Decisions of a municipal authority other than those referred to in section 188 and 189, the regional council decision referred to in section 33, paragraph 3, and decisions made by the regional environment centre under this Act are appealed to an administrative court. The competent administrative court is determined on the basis of section 12 of the Administrative Procedures Act (586/1996). When appealing a decision made by the regional environment centre, the competent administrative court is, however, that within the jurisdiction of which the majority of the area concerned lies.

An authority that has made a decision on the basis of this Act is entitled to appeal the decision of an administrative court if the court has amended the authority's decision or revoked it.

Otherwise, the provisions of the Administrative Procedures Act apply to appeal.

Section 191 *Right of appeal against decisions to approve a land use plan or a building ordinance*

In addition to what is laid down on the right of appeal in section 92 of the Local Government Act, regional environment centres and other authorities, in questions within their sphere of administration, have the right to appeal decisions by which a plan or a building ordinance is approved. Regional councils and local authorities whose area the land use indicated in the plan or the building ordinance affects are also entitled to appeal.

In addition to what is separately provided on appeal, registered local and regional organizations are entitled, when the matter concerns their sphere of activity, to appeal decisions concerning the approval of a plan or building ordinance within the area in which they operate. Nationally active organizations are also entitled to appeal decisions to approve regional plans if they contravene national land use objectives.

Only local authorities are entitled to appeal a decision of the administrative court revoking the local authority's decision to approve a land use plan or a building ordinance. If a detailed shore plan has been drawn up by a landowner, however, the landowner is entitled to appeal the decision of the administrative court. Only the regional council and the local authority have a right to appeal a decision not to ratify a regional plan.

Section 192 *Right of appeal against building and action permit, landscape-work permit and demolition permit decisions*

The following have the right to appeal building and action permit decisions:

The following have the right to appeal landscape and demolition permit decisions:

Section 193 *Right of appeal against deviation decisions and decisions concerning the need for planning*

The following have the right to appeal deviation decisions and decisions referred to in section 137 made by a local authority official regarding the need for planning:

Section 194 *Right of appeal against separate plot division*

The following have the right to appeal the approval of separate plot division;

Section 195 *Rectification reminder issued by the authorities in questions concerning land use plans*

Notwithstanding the provisions of this Act concerning appeal, the regional environment centre may issue a written rectification reminder to a local authority after the authority has approved a local master plan or a local detailed plan if the plan has been drawn up without taking national land use objectives into account or otherwise in contravention of the law, and it is in the interest of the public good that that the question is placed before the local authority for a new decision.

The rectification reminder must be made within the appeal period concerning the plan. The issue of the reminder may not be appealed.

The regional environment centre shall notify the administrative court that it has issued a rectification reminder. Having received the notification, the administrative court shall notify the local authority of any appeals made concerning the decision. Moreover, the administrative court shall also notify the appellants of any rectification reminder that has been issued.

When a rectification reminder has been issued, the municipal council shall decide upon the land use plan. If the council does not make the decision within six months of the reminder, the decision to approve the plan shall be deemed void.

Section 196 *Impact on appeals of a decision made on the basis of a rectification reminder*

If an earlier decision of a local authority had been appealed to the administrative court, the local authority shall notify the administrative court and any appellants in writing that a new decision has been made on the basis of a rectification reminder. Appeals against the earlier decision are considered to concern the new approval decision. When the local authority decides to retain the approval decision, only those who have already filed an appeal are entitled to appeal. The regional environment centre has the right to appeal, however.

If the local authority decides to amend an approved land use plan, the administrative court shall provide all appellants with an opportunity to supplement or amend their appeal. In such cases, all others who are so entitled may appeal the sections of the decision that have been amended.

If the grounds for an appeal made to the administrative court become invalid after the local authority has amended its decision or returned it for reprocessing, the administrative court will determine any claim for reimbursement of costs.

CHAPTER 26 MISCELLANEOUS PROVISIONS

Section 197 *Relation to other legislation*

In addition to the provisions of this Act, those of chapter 10 of the Nature Conservation Act shall be observed when land use plans are approved and ratified. When determining permit questions or making other decisions, the authorities shall also observe provisions issued in and under the Nature Conservation Act.

If an application for a building permit or an action permit has been denied on the basis of a restriction under section 66 of the Nature Conservation Act, and no other reason for denial of the permit exists, the landowner is entitled to be paid compensation by the State for the harm caused if denial of the permit prevents him from using his land in a manner generating reasonable return. When assessing the liability to pay compensation, changes that have taken place in partition or in ownership after August 20, 1998, are not taken into account. Moreover, if the area has been designated for conservation or recreation in a regional or master plan ratified under the Building Act (370/1958) before the said date, any changes in partition or ownership that have taken place after the ratification of the plan are not taken into account.

When a land use plan is drawn up, approved or ratified, the provisions of section 13 of the Antiquities Act (295/1963) shall also be observed, in addition to the provisions of this Act. When determining permit questions or making other decisions, the authorities shall also observe the provisions of the Antiquities Act.

Section 198 *Publishing certain decisions*

The Government Decision referred to in section 22 shall only be made after the matter has been made available to the public.

Decisions of the administrative court and the local authority concerning permit questions, and decisions of the local authority, regional environment centre and administrative court in questions pertaining to deviation as referred to in section 171 shall only be made after the matter has been made available to the public. Decisions of the competent ministry referred to in section 31, paragraph 1, section 33, paragraph 3, section 177, paragraph 1, and section 178, and decisions of the regional environment centre referred to in section 38, paragraph 2, and section 179 shall also only be taken after the matter has been made available to the public.

Interested parties are deemed to have been notified of decisions when they have been made.

Section 199 *Cross-border environmental impact*

If the implementation of an international treaty that is binding on Finland requires cooperation with another state when the environmental impact of implementation of a land use plan based on this Act is assessed, the regional council or the local authority drawing up the plan shall, before it is approved, provide the competent ministry or the regional environment centre with the data required for the notification to be made to the other state as prescribed in the treaty.

The competent ministry is responsible for notification and negotiation duties based on the treaty referred to in paragraph 1.

More detailed provisions on notification and negotiations will be issued by decree.

Section 200 *Entry into force of certain decisions*

Land use plans, building ordinances, plot divisions, building prohibitions and the building restriction referred to in section 33, paragraph 3, shall only come into force when they have been made available to the public as laid down in more detail by decree. The building restriction referred to in section 53, paragraph 3, however, comes into force through a decision to approve the land use plan.

Decisions to approve a local detailed plan, local master plan, regional plan or building ordinance shall be presented publicly in the manner that municipal notices are published in the municipality. The same applies to decisions concerning building prohibitions, restrictions on action and the building restriction referred to in section 33, paragraph 3.

The local authority shall immediately send the decision referred to in paragraph 2 for information to the authorities prescribed in more detail by decree.

Land use plans or summaries of them and building ordinances shall be available to the public at reasonable cost.

Section 201 *Eligibility for implementation of land use plan decisions*

The decision to ratify a regional plan or a joint local master plan may stipulate that the plan will come into force before it takes legal effect. After the appeal period, the municipal board may stipulate that sections of a local master plan or local detailed plan which cannot be deemed subject to appeal will come into force before they take legal effect. The local authority shall immediately notify the appellants and the appeal authority of the decision. The appeal authority may prohibit implementation of the decision.

If the authorities have issued a rectification reminder under section 195 concerning a decision to approve a land use plan, implementation of the plan shall be suspended until the local authority has made a new decision on the matter.

Section 202 *Eligibility for implementation of other decisions*

Decisions concerning the approval of a building ordinance, building restriction, plot division, building prohibition, restriction on action, establishing a special development area or revoking type approval may stipulate that the decision will come into force before it takes legal effect. The appeal authority may prohibit implementation of the decision.

Section 203 *Corrections made to a land use plan or building ordinance in connection with appeal*

The appeal authority may make corrective adjustments to a land use plan or building ordinance.

Section 204 *Amending or repealing a land use plan or building ordinance*

The provisions of this Act on drawing up land use plans and building ordinances apply correspondingly to amending and repealing them.

Section 205 *The authorities' right to receive information*

The competent ministry and the regional environment centres are entitled to receive without charge from local authorities, regional councils and other authorities any information they possess that is needed for monitoring land use and the built environment, and any documents needed for the supervision and other duties of authorities laid down in this Act, as provided in more detail by decree.

Provisions on providing the authorities with certain decisions for information will be issued separately.

Section 206 *More detailed provisions*

More detailed provisions on the implementation of this Act will be issued by decree.

The competent ministry may issue stipulations on the keys to symbols used in land use plans.

The National Land Survey of Finland may issue regulations on the technical means used for surveying and mapping for planning purposes.

CHAPTER 27 ENTRY INTO FORCE AND TRANSITIONAL PROVISIONS

Section 207 *Entry into force*

This Act comes into force on January 1, 2000.

However, in addition to what is laid down in and under the Building Act (370/1958), the following provisions of this Act will apply as of March 1, 1999, to the construction of a retail store defined in section 114, and to drawing up a town plan or a building plan for the area required by such a store:

The provisions of paragraph 2 above apply in determining a permit question concerning a large retail unit and decisions to approve a land use plan that are made on the date referred to in paragraph 2 or thereafter but before entry into force of this Act. The relevant provisions of the Building Act (370/1958) apply to administrative procedures and to appeal.

The provisions of section 197, paragraph 2, apply even before this Act comes into force if a building or action permit based on the Building Act (370/1958) is denied under section 66 of the Nature Conservation Act and no other reason for denial of the permit exists.

Measures required to implement this Act may be taken before it comes into force.

Section 208 *General transitional provisions*

This Act repeals the Building Act (370/1958) issued on August 16, 1958, including any amendments made to it thereafter. When this Act has come into force, references to the Building Act (370/1958) in other legislation and to land use plans prescribed therein shall refer to this Act and the land use plans prescribed in it.

The provisions in force when this Act comes into force apply to matters being processed by administrative authorities or courts when this Act comes into force, unless otherwise indicated in section 207, paragraphs 2 and 3, or provided below.

Section 209 *General transitional provisions concerning land use plans, building regulations and building ordinances*

Land use plans that have been approved under the Building Act (370/1958) before the entry into force of this Act may be ratified under the Building Act (370/1958) and enforced even after this Act comes into force.

Building regulations and instructions issued in the Finnish Building Code before the entry into force of this Act remain in force as building regulations and instructions governing construction of buildings and renovation and alteration work carried out under them as prescribed in this Act.

A building ordinance approved before the entry into force of this Act remains in force or may be enforced as a building ordinance prescribed in this Act.

A local detailed plan, a local master plan or a building ordinance that is being prepared when this Act comes into force may be approved within two years of the entry into force of this Act, provided that, instead of the provisions of chapter 8 of this Act, the corresponding provisions issued in and under the Building Act (370/1958) on planning procedure were applied when the plan was drawn up or those on building ordinances when the building ordinance was drawn up. A local detailed plan or a local master plan that is being prepared when this Act comes into force may also be approved after the aforementioned period, even if a participation and assessment scheme as laid down in section 63 was not drawn up when the plan was being prepared, provided that this is justifiable on grounds of the plan's completeness when this Act comes into force. The provisions of this Act apply to the approval decision and its appeal.

The provisions of paragraph 4 also apply to approval, as a regional plan prescribed in this Act, of a regional plan based on the Building Act (370/1958) that is under preparation, to the approval, as a local detailed plan, of a building plan that is under preparation and to the approval, as a detailed shore plan referred to in chapter 10, of a shore plan that is under preparation.

The provisions of section 60 on the relevance to current circumstances of a local detailed plan apply to town plans and building plans based on the Building Act (370/1958), so that the 13-year period referred to in section 60, paragraph 2, begins when this Act comes into force.

Section 210 *Transitional provision concerning regional plans based on the Building Act (370/1958) that are now in force*

Regional plans effective under the Building Act (370/1958) have the legal consequences laid down for regional plans in the said Act until they are replaced by regional plans based on this Act or repealed. If a regional plan effective under the Building Act (370/1958) is not replaced by a regional plan based on this Act or repealed within 10 years as of the entry into force of this Act, it will remain in force as a regional plan based on this Act.

Notwithstanding the provisions on the legal consequences of regional plans based on the Building Act (370/1958), the local authority may, with the consent of the competent ministry and having heard the regional council, approve a local master plan in deviation from such a regional plan if special cause exists and the land use indicated in the regional plan is deemed to be out of date when the local master plan is drawn up. In such a case, however, care must be taken to ensure that the local master plan conforms with the regional plan based on the Building Act (370/1958) as a complete entity, and that the provisions of section 28 are taken into account, as appropriate.

Section 211 *Transitional provision concerning master plans now in force*

A ratified master plan effective under the Building Act (370/1958) shall remain in force as a legally binding local master plan based on this Act, and an unratified master plan as a non-binding local master plan.

Section 212 *Transitional provision concerning town plans and plot divisions now in force*

A town plan effective under the Building Act (370/1958) shall remain in force as a local detailed plan based on this Act.

A plot division effective under the Building Act shall remain in force as a binding plot division based on this Act.

A town plan effective under the Building Act within the area of which there does not exist an approved plot division shall remain in force as a local detailed plan based on this Act that requires a separate plot division to be drawn up under section 78 of this Act.

A first town plan effective under the Building Act shall remain in force as a first local detailed plan based on this Act which is subject to the principles laid down in section 104 on the transfer of street areas.

Section 213

Transitional provision concerning building plans now in force

A building plan enforced under the Building Act (370/1958) shall remain in force as a local detailed plan based on this Act without a binding plot division.

With regard to the grounds for transfer of a street area, the provisions of the Building Act (370/1958) on building plans apply to local detailed plans as referred to in paragraph 1 in computing the amount of the transfer, rather than section 104 of this Act.

If, due to land use planning, essential changes take place in transportation networks or in land use with regard to a traffic area designated in the local detailed plan, the relevant sections of the traffic areas of the local detailed plan referred to in paragraph 1 shall be revised by amending the plan so that they meet the requirements of section 83, paragraph 4. Otherwise, an amendment of the local detailed plan referred to in paragraph 1 may be approved within 10 years of the entry into force of this Act, notwithstanding, the provisions of section 83, paragraph 4, on designating public road traffic areas.

Section 214 *Transitional provision concerning shore plans now in force*

A shore plan shall remain in force as a detailed shore plan based on this Act to which the provisions on detailed shore plans referred to in chapter 10 of this Act apply.

A shore plan in force when this Act comes into force shall not be considered a first local detailed plan as referred to in section 104. If a local detailed plan other than a detailed shore plan is later drawn up for the area of such a shore plan, the principles for the transfer of street areas laid down in section 104 concerning a first local detailed plan shall apply.

Section 215 *Transitional provisions concerning building prohibitions and prohibitions on action*

A building prohibition and a prohibition on action referred to in section 124a of the Building Act (370/1958) imposed before this Act comes into force shall remain in force or may be enforced for the period they are to remain in force as a building prohibition under this Act or as a restriction on action under section 128.

The maximum periods of extension prescribed for building prohibitions and restrictions on action in section 38, paragraph 2, and section 53, paragraph 2, are calculated as of the entry into force of this Act. A prohibition that has been in force for at least 10 years before this Act comes into force may be extended only once.

Section 216 *Transitional permit provisions*

Permits granted before this Act comes into force on the basis of the Building Act (370/1958) or provisions issued under it shall remain force in accordance with earlier provisions. The provisions of this Act apply in the supervision of these permits and construction based on them, as appropriate.

Section 217 *Transitional provision on gross floor area*

The provisions on gross floor area in force when this Act comes into force apply when the permitted gross floor area in construction based on a land use plan in force or approved when this Act comes into force is calculated.

Section 218 *Transformation of a building plan road into a street*

The area of a building plan road taken over by the local authority under the Building Act (370/1958) becomes the property of the local authority when this Act comes into force. The Partition Act applies to its partitioning. Before the building plan road referred to above is entered as a public area in the Property Register, a survey of the property shall be carried out when needed to establish its boundaries and surface area. The cost of these procedures shall be borne by the local authority.

The area of a building plan road which is managed by the local authority when this Act comes into force remains a building plan road as referred to in earlier legislation until it has been entered in the Property Register as a public area.

The local authority gains possession of the area of a building plan road not in its control when this Act comes into force, in accordance with the provisions on street areas in section 94 of this Act.

The area of a building plan road which the local authority has taken into its control and for which it has paid compensation under the Building Act (370/1958) becomes the property of the authority without compensation. If no agreement has been reached on the compensation for the area of a building plan road, or the question of compensation has not been settled by a court or by expropriation proceedings before this Act comes into force, the compensation question shall be determined by expropriation proceedings under the Expropriation Act.

Section 219 *Transitional provision on the implementation of a public area*

Instead of the provisions of section 90, paragraph 1, of this Act, the provisions in force when this Act comes into force shall apply to the duty to build a market place, park or corresponding public area designated in a land use plan in force when this Act comes into effect.

Street management shall be considered to cover streets and building plan roads transferred to public use under earlier legislation, which remain in public use without separate decision.

Section 220 *Transitional provision on the planner required of a local authority*

Local authorities shall comply with the duty concerning a planner laid down in section 20, paragraph 2, within two years of this Act coming into force.

ACT ON THE RIGHT TO TRANSFER STATE REAL ESTATE ASSETS

(973/2002)

In accordance with the decision of Parliament, the following is enacted:

SECTION 1 – SCOPE OF APPLICATION

(1) This Act provides on the transfer of State real estate assets, the lease of State land assets and the grant of special rights.

(2) This Act applies to State agencies and institutions and the enterprises referred to in the State Enterprise Act (627/1987). This Act also applies to the Office of the President of Finland and to extra-budgetary funds, unless otherwise provided concerning the funds.

(3) This Act does not apply to the Finnish Parliament, its organs, offices or institutions, the Bank of Finland or the Social Insurance Institution (KELA).

SECTION 2 – RELATION OF THE ACT TO OTHER PROVISIONS

If provisions deviating from this Act are laid down elsewhere in the law or under authori-zation elsewhere in the law, they thereby apply in place of this Act.

SECTION 3 – *DEFINITIONS*

For the purposes of this Act:

1) *State real estate assets means*

a) State-owned real estate, other real estate units and land and water areas, and shares in them (*State land property*);

b) State-owned buildings and shares in them on land owned by the State or others;

c) State-owned shares in housing companies and shares in companies the principal pur-pose of which is to own or manage real property; and

d) special rights of the State;

2) *transfer* means sale, exchange or other surrender of right of ownership;

3) *leasing* means land tenure as referred to in the Land Tenancy Act (258/1966); and

4) *special right* means usufruct, easement right, right of severance and other correspond-ing rights.

SECTION 4 – TERMS OF TRANSFER

(1) State real estate assets may be transferred, unless otherwise provided in subsection 2 or 4, if transfer is deemed financially expedient or if special grounds exist and there are no jus-tifiable grounds to keep them in State ownership.

(2) State real estate assets may not be transferred under this Act if:

1) their current value is more than ten million euros; or

2) they are crucial for nature protection, the protection of buildings with substantial his-torical value, or the preservation of immovable antiquities.

(3) However, State real estate assets located abroad may be transferred regardless of value.

(4) Real property in a shore zone may be transferred for use as private recreational dwellings or for recreational building only if special grounds exist.

SECTION 5 – SELLING PRICE OR OTHER CONSIDERATION

Unless special grounds exist to justify a price or consideration lower than the current value, State real estate assets may only be transferred at the current value or considera-tion.

SECTION 6 – TRANSFER DECISIONS

(1) The decision to transfer State real estate assets is made by the Government.

(2) Within their spheres of administration, each ministry may decide on the transfer of State real estate assets the current value of which does not exceed five million euros.

(3) The provisions of subsection 2 also apply to the Office of the President of Finland and unincorporated State enterprises with regard to State real estate assets of which they hold possession.

(4) The Government may delegate the authority of a ministry to an agency or institution un-der that ministry, although not the right to transfer State real estate assets at a price or other consideration lower than the current value.

SECTION 7 – TERMS OF LEASE

(1) State real estate assets may be leased if leasing is financially profitable or appropriate in view of use of the assets. Leasing may not complicate implementation of the protection or preservation referred to in section 4(2).

(2) Land property within a shore zone may be leased for use for private holiday building if the area has been designated for this purpose in an approved or ratified local detailed plan or master plan under the Land Use and Building Act (132/1999), or if the area has been granted an exemption from the provisions and regulations concerning planning require-ments as laid down elsewhere.

(3) Land property as referred to in subsection 2 above may also be leased for building to which planning requirements do not apply, or which is minor considering the circum-stances or in the

case of a lease extension or re-lease of essentially the same area to the same tenant, or if some other corresponding grounds call for leasing.

SECTION 8 – *SIZE OF RENT*

(1) The size of the rent for State-owned land property must be determined on commercial criteria.

(2) If especially important grounds exist, the rent may be lower than that determined on commercial criteria, or a decision may be made not to charge any rent.

SECTION 9 – LEASING DECISIONS

(1) Lease of State-owned land property is subject to Government approval if:

1) the current value of the land property to be leased is in excess of ten million euros; or

2) the current value of the land property is in excess of five million euros and the lease period is longer than 30 years; or

3) leasing has substantial significance in principle.

(2) Otherwise, decisions to lease are subject to approval by the ministry to whose sphere of administration the land property in question belongs, or the unincorporated State enter-prise in possession of the land property in question.

(3) Decisions to lease land property in the possession of the Office of the President of Finland are subject to the Office's approval.

(4) Ministries may delegate their decision-making authority to agencies and institutions under them, although not the right to lease land property for a rent lower than that determined on commercial criteria or not to charge any rent.

SECTION 10 – *SPECIAL RIGHTS*

(1) Special rights may be granted regarding State real estate assets, provided that this does not hinder the use of the property for Government purposes or complicate implementation of the protection or preservation referred to in section 4(2). The body in possession of the State real estate assets in question grants the special right. Agreements on grant of a spe-cial right must be made in writing.

(2) A consideration at current value must be charged on grant of a special right. A gratuitous right to use State real estate assets may be granted only if the right is minor or other spe-cial grounds exist for doing so.

(3) When a special right concerning State real estate assets involves the extraction of surface deposits, including rock, gravel, sand, peat and earth, for other than household use or the grant of right to use State-owned hydro-power, what this Act provides on the terms of transfer of State real estate assets, the consideration to be charged on transfers, and the making of transfer decisions applies to grant of said right.

(4) The provisions laid down in subsection 3 on grant of a special right involving the extrac-tion of surface deposits also applies to other transfers of such deposits.

SECTION 11 – DETERMINING THE DECISION-MAKING AUTHORITY IN CERTAIN CASES

(1) If the same deed of transfer, lease agreement or other agreement is used to transfer or lease several sites, the authority to make decisions is determined based on the total price or value of the agreement.

(2) If a single deed of transfer or lease is subdivided and separate agreements are made for each subdivision with the same party, the authority to make decisions is determined based on the sum of the prices or values of the agreements.

SECTION 12 – OPINIONS TO BE REQUESTED

Before State real estate assets are transferred or leased or special rights involving them are granted, an opinion must be requested from the Ministry of the Environment if the State real estate assets to be transferred or, leased, or concerning which a special right is to be granted, may have considerable significance for the protection of historically valu-able buildings or for nature protection, or from the Ministry of Education if the real estate assets may have considerable significance for the preservation of immovable antiquities.

SECTION 13 – *RECORDS*

(1) The possessor of State real estate assets must keep an itemized record of transfers, leases and special rights concerning the assets.

(2) The record must indicate the assets concerned, the date of agreements and their duration, the type of the right transferred, consideration charged and the parties with whom agree-ments were made. The record must also include identification and contact details on the transferee, tenant or holder of special right.

(3) Personal data may only be used in managing contractual relations and may be transferred for that purpose when State real estate assets are transferred. State authorities are entitled to the records kept by possessors of State real estate assets and to information in them that they need in order to carry out their duties.

(4) Personal data is stored as long as the relevant agreement is in force, after which it is ar-chived as laid down in the Archives Act (831/1994).

SECTION 14 – ISSUING A DECREE

More detailed provisions on the information to be included in the records referred to in section 13 and on any other matters concerning the implementation of this Act may be is-sued by Government decree.

SECTION 15 – ACQUIRING, MANAGING AND RECORDING STATE REAL ESTATE ASSETS

(1) Provisions on acquiring real estate assets for the State, leasing real estate assets to the State for its use, and leasing State real estate assets to outside parties, on their possession, management and use, and on their registration and recording may be laid down by Gov-ernment decree. Provisions on the lease of State land property are, however, laid down in this Act.

(2) This section does not apply to unincorporated State enterprises, with the exception of the registration and recording of State real estate assets.

SECTION 16 – IMPLEMENTING AND TRANSITIONAL PROVISIONS

(1) This Act enters into force on 1 January 2003.

(2) This Act repeals the Act on the Right to Dispose of State Land and Income Producing Rights issued on 31 August 1978 (687/1978), as amended. Decisions concerning delega-tion of decision-making authority made under the repealed Act remains in force for two years after this Act comes into force, unless they are separately repealed.

(3) This Act does not apply to lease agreements and agreements on the grant of special rights that have been made before the Act enters into force. Unless otherwise is provided in the Land Tenancy Act, leases based on said agreements must, nevertheless, be reviewed or other consideration specified to comply with the provisions of this Act as soon as possible under the terms of the agreement in question.

(4) Measures necessary for the implementation of this Act may be under-taken before the Act's entry into force.

(5) Government proposal 102/2002, Finance Committee report 15/2002, Parliamentary reply 146/2002.

PRACTICAL AND LEGAL INFORMATION FOR BUSINESS AND TRADE

FINLAND INVESTMENT AND BUSINESS CLIMATE - STRATEGIC INFORMATION AND CONTACTS FOR STARTING BUSINESS IN FINLAND

Contact
Rodney Hunter
Political/Economic Section Chief
Itainen Puitotie 14, 00140 Helsinki
+358-9-6162-5478
HunterRM@state.gov

Given its geographic location and history, Finland offers a prime location and strong opportunity for American businesses to tap into the entire region's economic growth. The U.S. Embassy in Helsinki, through the Foreign Commercial Services and Political/Economic Sections, is a strong partner with U.S. businesses that wish to connect to this market and seize these opportunities. There are opportunities in Finland for U.S. businesses and investors to enter Arctic, Russian, Nordic, and Baltic Sea markets, places where U.S. growth prospects are great.

The Finnish government takes increased investment seriously, and has recently created "Team Finland" to pull together all the trade and investment promotion agencies in Finland under one umbrella. While this "one-stop shop" is not fully functional yet, it will assist U.S. companies in answering their questions about Finland's markets in one place.

Businesses know that location can be critical and Finland can provide the right location and connections for U.S. businesses to be successful in Finland and beyond. The Embassy has worked to create an affirmative and robust trade and investment agenda that works to attract investment in America and creates new markets for U.S. products and services in Finland and the broader region. Finnish counterparts are very active in the fields of information technology, energy, biotech, clean water, and other topics. With St. Petersburg only three hours by train, Tallinn two hours by ferry, and Stockholm and the Arctic Circle only one hour by flight, Finland can be a good base camp for consolidating regional operations.

1. OPENNESS TO, AND RESTRICTIONS UPON, FOREIGN INVESTMENT

The Finnish government is open to direct foreign investment. There are no general regulatory limitations relating to acquisitions. Legislative control of mergers and acquisitions is mainly governed by domestic and EU competition rules. Certain acquisitions of large Finnish companies may require follow-up clearance from the Ministry of Employment and the Economy in accordance with the Act on the Control of Foreign Acquisitions of Finnish Companies. The stated purpose of the clearance is to protect "essential national interests."

The Act on the Monitoring of Foreign Corporate Acquisitions in Finland entered into force in June 2012. The Act calls for the Ministry of Employment and the Economy to monitor and confirm foreign corporate acquisitions. A "corporate acquisition" is defined as a transaction in which a foreign owner gains control of at least ten percent of the total number of votes accompanying shares in a limited liability company, or, in the case of another type of corporation or business undertaking, gains corresponding, dominant control over the acquired enterprise. The Ministry decides whether an acquisition conflicts with vital national interests. Only corporate acquisitions in the defense and dual-use goods sector are subject, without exception, to advance confirmation by the Ministry. In defense matters, monitoring covers all foreign owners. In the civilian sector, monitoring is targeted at Finnish enterprises considered critical in terms of vital infrastructures necessary for maintaining functions fundamental to society (according to the Security Strategy for Society, Government resolution of 16.12.2010), such as Energy, Communications, or Food supply. In civilian cases, monitoring only applies to foreign owners domiciled outside the EU and European Free Trade Association (EFTA) states. For more information see: http://www.tem.fi/files/33479/Monitoring_of_foreign_corporate_acquisitions_by_the_Ministry_of_Employment_and_the_Economy_041012.pdf

Finland does not preclude foreign investment, but some tax policies may make it unattractive to investors. Finnish tax authorities treat the movement of ownership of shares in a Finnish company into a foreign company as a taxable event. Finland complies with EU directives that require it to allow such transactions based in other EU member states without taxing them.

The Finnish government has recently made significant cuts to the corporate tax rate from 24.5 percent to 20 percent, compared to the EU average of 22.4 percent.

The World Bank's 2014 Doing Business Report, which ranked Finland number 12 in "Ease of Doing Business":

http://www.doingbusiness.org/data/exploreeconomies/~/media/giawb/doing%20business/documents/profiles/country/FIN.pdf?ver=2 . The Research Institute of the Finnish Economy (ETLA), regularly publishes reports that review different sectors in the Finnish economy and factors that may impact investment: http://www.etla.fi/en/?s=finland&cat=11&searchsubmit=Search&orderby=post_date&order=DESC . Finland has not undergone any recent investment policy reviews from the UN Conference on Trade and Development (UNCTAD), the World Trade Organization (WTO), or the Organization for Economic Cooperation and Development (OECD).

Finland does not "positively" discriminate in favor of foreign-owned firms by giving them tax holidays or other subsidies not available to other firms. Instead, Finland relies on "condition-providing policies" that offer all firms, "appropriate conditions and sufficient pools of advanced factors of production, including an educated labor force and well-functioning infrastructure."

Laws/Regulations of FDI

There are some legal requirements for non-European Economic Area (EEA) residents (persons or companies) to conduct business in Finland. A non-EEA resident operating in Finland must obtain a license or a notification when starting a business in "regulated" forms of trade. These trades include:

Vehicles, transport and traffic
Alcohol and tobacco
Food
Animals
Beauty and hair care field
Plants, fertilizers and feeds
Chemicals
Real estate, construction and contracting
Extractable soil resources and soil
Tourism, restaurants and leisure time
Money and assets

Social welfare and health services
Security
Communications
Other lines of business
Temporary provision of services
Businesses not requiring a license

A comprehensive list of regulated trades can be found at Enterprise Finland: http://www.yrityssuomi.fi/luvat

The autonomously-governed Aland Islands are an exception to common Finnish practice. Based on international agreements dating from 1921, property ownership and the right to conduct business are limited to individuals with the right of domicile in the Aland Islands. It does not prevent people from settling in or trading with the Aland Islands. Immigrants who have lived in Aland for five years and have an adequate knowledge of Swedish may apply for domicile status. The Aland Government can grant exemptions from the requirement of right of domicile for those wishing to acquire real property or conduct a business there.

In February 2014, 90 members of the 200-member Finnish Parliament signed an initiative that would require non-EEA citizens and organizations to meet certain requirements, such as residing in Finland for a set amount of time, before being able to purchase or rent property. The initiative remains in the Parliament's Legal Affairs Committee for debate.

In 2006, the United States and Finland signed a protocol amending the 1990 Double Taxation Treaty, which significantly reduced tax-related barriers to trade and investment flows between the countries.

On March 5, 2014, Finland signed a Foreign Account Tax Compliance Act (FATCA). Financial institutions will begin the collection of FATCA information during 2014 and the first reports will be made in 2015. The obligations brought by the FATCA will be entered in Finnish legislation, and the tax administration is preparing detailed guidelines on how the agreement will be applied in Finland. For full text of the agreement, see: http://www.treasury.gov/resource-center/tax-policy/treaties/Documents/FATCA-Agreement-Finland-3-5-2014.pdf

The salary and fringe benefits paid to qualifying foreign key employees, such as employees with special knowledge or competence, are taxed at a flat rate of 35 percent during a maximum of 48 months of assignment in Finland provided that the employee has a special tax card (which must be applied for separately). For detailed tax guidance see the Finnish Tax Administration's website: http://www.vero.fi/en-US/Companies_and_organisations and the Finnish Foundation for Share Promotion's Tax Guide for Investors:
http://www.porssisaatio.fi/en/files/2013/09/vero_opas_2013_eng_final.pdf

Industrial Strategy & Privatization Program

In 2013, the Ministry published the "Industrial Competitiveness Approach: Means to Guarantee Economic Growth in Finland in the 2010s" which highlights the need for increased foreign investment. The report can be found at:
https://www.tem.fi/files/37744/TEMjul_9_2013_web_17102013.pdf

Invest in Finland is a government agency that promotes foreign direct investment (FDI) in Finland. They provide information and consulting services focused on services and promoting research, development, and innovation (R&D&I) in Environmental Technologies, Energy & Mining, Health

Technologies, and Information & Communication. Invest in Finland's website can be found at: http://www.investinfinland.fi/about-us/6

In March 2014, members of the government and the opposition agreed to sell EUR 1.9 billion worth of government-owned assets. In May 2014, the government of Finland announced that it will sell its infrastructure and construction firm charged with planning and constructing traffic routes and industrial environments Destia Ltd (formerly the Finnish Road Administration).

Competition Law

Finland's Competition Act entered into force in November 2011, bringing Finland's competition regime closer to that of the EU. The most important changes relate to merger control, procedural rules, leniency, and damages. The full act can be found at: https://www.kilpailuvirasto.fi/cgi-bin/english.cgi?luku=legislation&sivu=competition-act

The Finnish Competition Authority merged with the Consumer Agency to form the Finnish Competition and Consumer Authority (FCCA) in January 2013. The purpose of the agency is, "to ensure a healthy and functioning market where enterprises and other players act responsibly and in the interest of consumers."

Measure	Year	Rank or value	Website Address
TI Corruption Perceptions index	2013	(3 of 177)	http://cpi.transparency.org/cpi2013/results/
Heritage Foundation's Economic Freedom index	2013	(19 of 178)	http://www.heritage.org/index/ranking
World Bank's Doing Business Report "Ease of Doing Business"	2013	(12 of 189)	http//doingbusiness.org/rankings
Global Innovation Index	2013	(6 of 142)	http://www.globalinnovationindex.org/content.aspx?page=gii-full-report-2013#pdfopener
World Bank GNI per capita	2012	USD 46,490	http://data.worldbank.org/indicator/NY.GNP.PCAP.CD

2. CONVERSION AND TRANSFER POLICIES

Except for those relating to money laundering, there are neither legal obstacles to direct foreign investment in Finnish securities nor exchange controls regarding payments into and out of Finland. Funds from Finland or to Finland are freely transferable. Legal provisions prevent money laundering and the financing of terrorism and banks must identify their customers and report suspected cases of money laundering. Banks and credit institutions must also report single payments or transfers of EUR 15,000 or more. If banks have reason to suspect the origin of the funds, they are required to immediately inform the National Bureau of Investigation.

There are no restrictions on current transfers or repatriation of profits. Residents and non-residents may hold foreign exchange accounts. There is no limit on dividend distributions, as long as they correspond to a company's official earnings records.

In June 2007, Finland implemented an EU regulation on the transport of currency over EU borders. The regulation requires persons carrying more than EUR 10,000 to declare cash upon entering or leaving EU territory, but does not restrict or prohibit the import or export of the currency.

Finland adopted the Euro in January 1999. The Euro replaced the Finnish Markka at the end of a three-year transition period in January 2002.

A Financial Action Task Force (FATF) member, Finland observes most of FATF's 49 standards. According to the FATF's 9th follow-up report in 2013, Finland has made significant progress in addressing the deficiencies identified in the 2007 mutual evaluation report and will be removed from the follow-up process. FATF praised Finland for improvements in its anti-money laundering legal frameworks. See the FATF report at: http://www.fatf-gafi.org/media/fatf/documents/reports/mer/Finland_FUR_2013.pdf

The Bureau of International Narcotics and Law Enforcement's 2013 International Narcotics Control Strategy Report (INCSR) categorizes Finland as "monitored" - http://www.state.gov/j/inl/rls/nrcrpt/2013/database/211176.htm

3. EXPROPRIATION AND COMPENSATION

Private property rights are protected in Finland. Private property is only expropriated for public purposes (eminent domain) in a non-discriminatory manner with reasonable compensation and in accordance with established principles of international law.

4. DISPUTE SETTLEMENT

There is no reported significant investment dispute in Finland in recent years. Finland has a civil law system. European Community (EC) law is directly applicable in Finland and takes precedence over national legislation. Finland has consistently applied its commercial and bankruptcy laws. Secured interests in property are recognized and enforced. The Bankruptcy Act can be found at: http://www.finlex.fi/en/laki/kaannokset/2004/en20040120.pdf

The Market Court was established in 2002 as a special court for rulings in market law, competition, and public procurement cases, and may issue injunctions and penalties against the illegal restriction of competition. It also supervises mergers and acquisitions and may overturn public procurement decisions, adjust the procurement process, and order compensatory payments. The Market Court has jurisdiction in disputes between the Consumer Ombudsman and businesses as to whether goods or services have been marketed in an unfair manner. Since 2013 the Market Court also hears industrial and civil IPR cases.

According to the World Bank's 2014 Doing Business Report, Finland ranks 3rd for ease of "resolving insolvency." The report can be found at: http://www.doingbusiness.org/data/exploreeconomies/finland#resolving-insolvency

Finland ratified the Convention on the Settlement of Investment Disputes between States and Nationals of other States (also known as the ICSID Convention or the Washington Convention) and became a Contracting States to the ICSID Convention in 1969. Finland ratified the New York Convention on the Recognition and Enforcement of Foreign Arbitral Awards in 1962.The impartial Arbitration Institute of the Finland Chamber of Commerce, established in 1911, promotes the settlement of business disputes through arbitration. The Institute appoints arbitrators both to domestic and international arbitration proceedings. For more information see: http://arbitration.fi/en/. Arbitration statistics can be found at: http://arbitration.fi/en/statistics/.

Major revisions to Finnish competition legislation took effect in May 2004. The Act on Competition Restrictions was harmonized with EU competition rules. A new Competition Act entered into force in Finland on November 1, 2011. It brought Finland's competition regime closer to that of the EU's. The most important changes relate to merger control, certain procedural rules, leniency, and damages. For more information see the Competition Act (No 948/2011) : http://www.kilpailuvirasto.fi/cgi-in/english.cgi?luku=legislation&sivu=competition-act

The Finnish Competition Authority merged with the Consumer Agency to form the Finnish Competition and Consumer Authority (FCCA) on January 1, 2013. The purpose of the new agency is to ensure a healthy and functioning market where enterprises and other players act responsibly and in the interest of consumers.

Finland brought the EU Mediation Directive (2008/52/EC) into force by implementing the Act on Mediation in Civil Disputes and Certification of Settlements by Courts (394/2011) in May 2011. Both the directive and the new act aim to facilitate access to alternative dispute resolution, and promote the amicable settlement of disputes by encouraging the use of mediation and by ensuring a balanced relationship between mediation and judicial proceedings. The new act also applies to settlements concluded in other EU member states.

Duration of Dispute Settlement

Arbitration is frequently used to settle business disputes in Finland, which is usually faster than court proceedings. An arbitral award is generally final and non-appealable. The Arbitration Institute's rules (the "FCC Rules") are the rules that are most commonly used. The FCC Rules can be found in English at www.arbitration.fi/en/indextemp.html. If arbitration is conducted according to FCC Rules, the time limit for rendering the arbitral award is one year after the Arbitration Institute has sent the case file to the arbitral tribunal. By request of the arbitral tribunal or the Chairman of the arbitral tribunal, the time limit may be extended by the Arbitration Institute. The median duration of arbitration under the FCC Rules is about nine months.

In 2004 the Arbitration Institute introduced fast track rules. According to the Arbitration Institute's Rules for Expedited Arbitration, the arbitral award shall be rendered within three months after the Institute has sent the file in the case to the arbitrator. This time limit may be extended by the Arbitration Institute by at most three months. The Finnish Arbitration Act (967/1992) explicitly states that foreign nationals can act as arbitrators in Finland.

5. PERFORMANCE REQUIREMENTS AND INVESTMENT INCENTIVES

Notification submitted to the WTO by the EU and WTO disputes involving the EU are valid for and include Finland. However, Finland as an individual country has not notified the WTO of any measures that are inconsistent with Trade Related Investment Measures (TRIM) requirements, nor does Finland maintain any measures that are alleged to violate the WTO's TRIM obligations.

There are no performance requirements or commitments imposed on foreign investment in Finland. However, to conduct business in Finland, some residency requirements must be met in order to ensure that persons liable for the company's acts can be brought to court if necessary.

Amendments to the Finnish Limited Liability Companies Act entered into force in August 2009 to allow the participation of shareholders in the general meetings of listed companies.

The Limited Liability Companies Act of Finland can be found at:
http://www.finlex.fi/fi/laki/kaannokset/2006/en20060624.pdf

Foreign-owned companies are eligible for government incentives on an equal footing with Finnish-owned companies. Support is given in the form of grants, loans, tax benefits, equity participation, guarantees, and employee training.

Business aid to companies is coordinated by 15 Centers for Economic Development, Transport, and the Environment (ELY), which provide advisory, financing, and development services for enterprises; employment-based aid and labor market training; and advice on immigration matters and EU structural projects. For more information see: http://www.ely-keskus.fi/en/web/ely-en/business-and-industry

The state-owned financing company Finnvera offers services to businesses of all sizes and in all sectors, except building developers, forestry, field cultivation, and animal husbandry. Finnvera serves its clients through 15 regional offices Finnvera is also Finland's official Export Credit Agency (ECA). For more information see: http://www.finnvera.fi/eng.

The Finnish Funding Agency for Technology and Innovation (Tekes) provides low-interest loans and grants to innovative projects. Foreign-owned companies with R&D activities in Finland are eligible for funding, although the financed project must contribute to the Finnish economy. For more information see: http://www.tekes.fi/en/programmes-and-services/international-companies/. Support for innovative business ventures can also be obtained from the Foundation for Finnish Inventions. For more information see: www.keksintosaatio.fi

Invest in Finland, a government agency promoting FDI into Finland, assists international companies to find business opportunities in Finland. Finpro is a Finnish trade, internationalization and investment development organization established by Finnish companies in 1919. The operations of Invest in Finland were merged with Finpro and its international network in June 2012. For more information see: http://www.investinfinland.fi/main.php/ and http://www.finpro.fi/web/english-pages/frontpage

There is no "forced localization" policy on foreign investments in Finland, either in terms of forcing investors to use domestic content in goods and technology or local employment. However, the Finnish language often acts as a barrier to employing non-Finnish persons.

In cloud computing services, stored material is located on servers owned by the service provider. In most cases, these servers are located outside Finland and are typically accessed through a browser over an internet connection. Personal data may be transferred across international borders to server locations supporting the service, but the company must fulfill the requirements of the Finnish Personal Data Act (PDA). According to section 22 of the PDA, personal data may be transferred to outside the European Union or the European Economic Area only if the country in question guarantees an adequate level of data protection.

6. RIGHT TO PRIVATE OWNERSHIP AND ESTABLISHMENT

Private ownership is normal in Finland. In most fields of business activity, participation by foreign companies or individuals is unrestricted. When the government privatizes state-owned companies, both private and foreign participation is allowed except in enterprises operating in sectors related to national security.

7. PROTECTION OF PROPERTY RIGHTS

Secured interest in property, both movable and real, is recognized and enforced. The Finnish legal system protects property rights.

The concept of mortgage exists in Finland, and can be applied to both owned and rented real estate. The significance of mortgage banks has remained minor as deposit banks have traditionally handled housing loans in Finland.

The National Land Survey of Finland provides a reliable system for recording secured interests registers all land in Finland. In Finland real property formation, mutation, land consolidation, cadastral mapping, registration of real properties, ownership and legal rights, real property valuation, and taxation are all combined within one basic cadastral system (real estate register). The register is owned and maintained by the National Land Survey. For more information see: http://www.maanmittauslaitos.fi/en/aineistot-ja-palvelut

Finland is ranked 26th according to ease of Registering Property according to the World Bank's 2014 Doing Business Report.

The government of Finland issued a resolution on a program to step up its activities to tackle non-observed economic activity and economic crime in 2012. Implemented in 2012–2015, the program comprises 22 projects steered by a number of ministries and authorities. Finland's grey economy is estimated at 13.0% of GDP (2013), down from 17.6% in 2003.

Intellectual Property

The Finnish legal system protects intellectual property rights, and Finland adheres to numerous international agreements concerning intellectual property rights (IPR). However, Finland is also identified as a potential host of the major BitTorrent aggregator internet site "Torrentz.eu". The USTR 2013 Out-of-Cycle Review on Notorious Markets, released in February 2014, ties both Finland and Canada to the site.

Finland is a member of World International Property Organization (WIPO). In March 2009, the government of Finland published a national IPR strategy, found at: http://www.tem.fi/files/26944/TEM_27_2010_netti.pdf

Finland has been a member of the Paris Convention for the Protection of Industrial Property since 1921; the Berne Convention for the Protection of Literary and Artistic works since 1928; the Rome International Convention for the Protection of Performers, Producers of Phonograms, and Broadcasting Organizations since 1983; and the Hague Agreement Concerning the International Deposit of Industrial Designs (Geneva Act 1999) since May 2011.

Patents

Patent rights are consistent with international standards, and a granted patent applies for 20 years. The period of validity of patents concerning medicinal products and plant protection products can under certain conditions be prolonged by a maximum of five years through a Supplementary Protection Certificate. In 1996, Finland joined the European Patent Convention (EPC) and the European Patent Organization (EPO). Finland Joined WIPO's Patent Law Treaty (PLT) in March 2006.

Given concerns over pharmaceutical patent protections, Finland was placed on the 2009 Watch List in the Office of the U.S. Trade Representative's Special 301 report, and has been included

every year since. The Special 301 report can be found at:
http://www.ustr.gov/sites/default/files/05012013%202013%20Special%20301%20Report.pdf

Copyrights

The Finnish Copyright Act, which also grants protection to authors, performing artists, record producers, broadcasting organizations and catalog producers, sets the period of copyright protection at 70 years from the death of the author. Databases, including catalogues, are protected for 15 years. The Finnish Copyright Act provides for sanctions ranging from fines to imprisonment for up to two years. Search and seizure is authorized in the case of criminal piracy, as is the forfeiture of financial gains. The Copyright Act has covered computer software since 1991. The WIPO Copyright Treaty (WCT) and the WIPO Performances and Phonograms Treaty (WPPT) entered into force in Finland in March 2010.Finland acceded to the Agreement on Trade-Related Aspects of Intellectual Property Rights in 1995.

Finnish copyright legislation was amended in 2005 to meet the demands of the digital environment and the internet. The amendments to the Copyright Act and the amended section 49 of the Criminal Code came into force from the beginning of 2006. This reform implemented the Copyright Directive adopted by the EU in 2001. The amendments also addressed a number of national issues, such as the prohibition of the importation of pirated recordings for personal use.

The Copyright Act was further amended in September 2013.

Information on copyright infringement is provided by the following copyright holder interest organizations: Copyright Society of Performing Artists and Phonogram Producers in Finland (Gramex), Finnish Composers' Copyright Society (Teosto), Copyright Organization for Authors and Publishers (Kopiosto), The Visual Artists Copyright Society (Kuvasto), Finnish Audiovisual Producers' Copyright Society (Tuotos), Finnish Copyright Society Managing the Rights of Literary Copyright Holders (Sanasto), the Copyright Information and Anti-Piracy Center (CIAPC), The Finnish Copyright Society, The Finnish Copyright Institute, the Copyright Information Centre, and the IPR University Centre. The Business Software Alliance (BSA), a worldwide software anti-piracy organization, began operations in Finland in January 1994.

Trademarks

Amendments to the Trademarks Act which entered into force on January 2011 require that a trademark applicant or proprietor not domiciled in Finland have a representative resident in the European Economic Area. Finland signed the Singapore Treaty on the Law of Trademarks in October 2006.

Trade Secrets

In the Finnish legal system, the protection of trade secrets forms part of the general concept of protection against unfair competition. In 1979, Finland implemented the Unfair Business Practices Act which prohibits competitors from, "unjustifiably obtaining or seeking to obtain information regarding a business secret or using or revealing information obtained in such a manner." An English version of the Act is available at:
http://www.finlex.fi/fi/laki/kaannokset/1978/en19781061.pdf

The Penal Code (39/1889) contains provisions regarding industrial espionage (chapter 30, section 4), violation of business secrets (chapter 30, section 5) and misuse of business secrets (chapter 30, section 6). Trade secret protection is also regulated by the Employment Contracts

Act (55/2001), according to which the employee may neither utilize nor divulge to third parties the employer's trade or business secrets during the term of employment.

According to the 2010 International Association for the Protection of Intellectual Property group report, Finnish legal protection of trade secrets is fundamentally sound, although the introduction of common and consistent terminology for relevant legislation would be desirable. The report can be found at: https://www.aippi.org/download/commitees/215/GR215finland.pdf

Semiconductor Chip Layout Design

In 1991, Finland adopted the Act on the Exclusive Right in the Layout-Design (Topography) of an Integrated Circuit. The Act gives exclusive rights in a layout-design to the creator (or to anyone to whom the right of the creator has been transferred) who is a Finnish citizen, a person with a permanent residence in Finland, or place of business in Finland. In cases of industrial infringement of IPR the integrated circuit used by the defendant may be confiscated.

An English translation of the Act, is available at: http://www.finlex.fi/fi/laki/kaannokset/1991/en19910032.pdf. In general, the exclusive rights come to an end 10 years from the end of the calendar year in which the topography was first commercially exploited.

For additional information about treaty obligations and points of contact at local IP offices, please see WIPO's country profiles at http://www.wipo.int/directory/en/

Resources for Rights Holders

Contact at Mission: IP issues are handled by the Political/Economic Section in Helsinki.

Rodney Hunter
Political/Economic Section Chief
+358-9-6162-5478
HunterRM@state.gov

The American Chamber of Commerce in Finland's (AmCham) legal committee offers free legal advice to all AmCham member companies: http://www.amcham.fi/legal-committee/. The AmCham's legal guide can be found at: http://www.amcham.fi/wp-content/uploads/2012/04/Legal_Guide_2011.pdf

8. TRANSPARENCY OF THE REGULATORY SYSTEM

The Securities Market Act (SMA) contains regulations on corporate disclosure procedures and requirements, responsibility for flagging share ownership, insider regulations and offenses, the issuing and marketing of securities, and trading. The law defines and takes into account new instruments, which have become common in financial markets, such as repurchase agreements. Regulations concerning the clearing of securities trades have been incorporated into the law since 1998. Clearing has become subject to licensing, and is supervised by the Financial Supervision Authority, which oversees the financial markets.

A New Securities Market Act took effect in January 2013. The new Act broke the former Securities Market Act into the Securities Market Act, the Act on Trading in Financial Instruments, the Act on the Book-Entry System and Clearing Operations, and the Investment Services Act. These acts constitute the new securities market framework with the already separate existing acts on Book-Entry Accounts and on the Financial Supervisory Authority. The new Securities Market Act's general principles are (i) prohibition of actions against good conduct on the securities markets and of improper business practices, (ii) prohibition to give false or misleading information on the securities market, and (iii) the duty to provide investors with equal access to sufficient information on matters that may have a material effect on the value of the relevant security. For more information see the Financial Supervisory Authority's overview of regulations for listed companies at: http://www.fin-fsa.fi/en/Listed_companies/Regulation/Pages/Default.aspx

In Finland, the Act on the Openness of Public Documents of 1951 established the openness of all records and documents in the possession of officials of the state, municipalities, and registered religious communities. Exceptions to the basic principle could only be made by law, or by an executive order for specific enumerated reasons such as national security. A 1999 revision of the law, the Act on the Openness of Government Activities, extended the principle of openness to corporations that perform legally mandated public duties, such as pension funds and public utilities, and to computer documents. For more information see the Ministry of Justice's page on Openness of Government Activities at:
http://oikeusministerio.fi/en/index/basicprovisions/legislation/actontheopennessofgovernmentactivities.html

The Finnish state administration discussion forum at http://www.otakantaa.fi/fi-FI provides an opportunity for all citizens to comment on planned or on-going projects, legislative reforms, or other current issues being drafted within the public administration.

A new law on Citizens' Initiatives entered into force in March 2012 mandating that any citizen initiative that gets 50,000 signatures be taken up for discussion in Parliament. The organizer of an initiative has six months to collect the necessary statements of support. The law has proven popular, and four initiatives have been presented to Parliament for consideration since the Act's implementation. The most popular initiative, with over 166,000 votes, calls for legalizing same-sex marriage. As of May 2014, no Citizens' Initiatives have yet become law.

9. EFFICIENT CAPITAL MARKETS AND PORTFOLIO INVESTMENT

Finland is open to foreign portfolio investment, and there is an effective regulatory system established. According to the IMF, in February 2014 Finland had USD 1.1 billion worth of official reserve assets, mainly in foreign currency reserves and securities.

Credit is allocated on market terms and is made available to foreign investors in a non-discriminatory manner. The private sector has access to a variety of credit instruments. Legal, regulatory, and accounting systems are transparent and consistent with international norms.

The Helsinki Stock Exchange is part of OMX, referred to as NASDAQ OMX Helsinki (OMXH). NASDAQ OMX Helsinki is part of the NASDAQ OMX Nordic division, together with the stock exchanges in Stockholm, Copenhagen, Iceland, Tallinn, Riga, and Vilnius.

Banking is open to foreign competition. Compared to the international average, the number of banks in Finland is high. The reason for this is the high number of banks in the OP-Pohjola Group, a cooperative of independent, local deposit banks that are engaged in retail banking. In April 2014 there were 187 OP-Pohjola Group banks, 8 commercial banks, 34 local cooperative banks, 29 savings banks, and 15 branches of foreign deposit taking banks. The total assets of the domestic banking groups and branches of foreign banks operating in Finland amounted to EUR 468 billion in 2013. For more info see the Federation of Finnish Financial Services report (in Finnish) at: http://www.fkl.fi/materiaalipankki/julkaisut/Julkaisut/Pankit_Suomessa_2013.pdf

All authorized deposit-taking banks are members of the Deposit Guarantee Fund. If an individual bank becomes insolvent, the Fund will compensate its customers' deposits to a maximum of EUR 100,000 per depositor.

Finland's banking system was the strongest in the EU in terms of its financial position, according to credit rating company Moody's "Banking System Outlook: Baltics" report released in November 2012. Finland's banking system is also ranked as the strongest in the Eurozone, according to a Moody's global comparison of national banking systems. Moody's ranked the financial strength of Finland's banking system as 11th internationally. As of April 2014, Finland maintained a triple-A rating from Moody's, Standard & Poor's, and Fitch. However, Standard & Poor's cut Finland's outlook on its credit rating from "Stable" to "Negative" in April 2014, citing Finland's economic stagnation since 2008. In May 2014, Moody's maintained its top AAA credit rating for Finland with a stable outlook, stating that Finland has many strengths to pull through the economic challenges it is currently facing. Finland, Luxembourg, and Germany are the only Eurozone countries with triple-A credit ratings.

Hostile takeovers have not in the past been part of the Finnish business culture and Finnish law does not distinguish between friendly and hostile takeovers. Finnish legislation does not expressly address takeover defenses. In Finnish law, the legality of takeover defenses is evaluated primarily in light of the leading principles of the Security Markets Act (SMA), the principle of equal treatment of all shareholders, and general principles of company law. If challenged, the legality of the defensive measures is subject to review by the courts.

The Takeover Board issues recommendations that provide direction for mergers and acquisitions. One can contact the panel board for a statement regarding interpretation of the recommendations, good securities markets practices, as well as an individual company's legal issues. For more see: http://cgfinland.fi/en/the-takeover-board/

Finland changed over to the Single Euro Payments Area (SEPA) in January 2008. The system began with credit transfers and cards, and starting from July 2010, International Bank Account Numbers (IBAN) and Bank Identification Code (BIC) data have been compulsory on invoices and credit transfer forms, along with Finnish account numbers. Since November 2010 Finnish banks offering domestic direct debit services have offered SEPA Core Direct Debit to payer customers requiring such services.

10. COMPETITION FROM STATE OWNED ENTERPRISES

State Owned Enterprises (SOEs) in Finland are active in a number of industries, such as Chemicals, Petrochemicals, Plastics & Composites; Energy & Mining; Environmental Technologies; Food Processing & Packaging; Industrial Equipment & Supplies; Marine Technology; Media & Entertainment; Metal Manufacturing & Products; Services; and Travel. The Ownership Steering Act (1368/2007) regulates the administration of state-owned companies. The act can be found at: http://valtionomistus.fi/english/files/2011/12/VALTIONYHTIOeLAKI_en.pdf

In general, State Owned Enterprises are open to competition except where they have a monopoly position, namely in alcohol, retail, and gambling. Alko is an independent limited company fully-owned by the Finnish government and administered and supervised by the Ministry of Social Affairs and Health. Alko has the exclusive right to the retail sale of beverages containing more than 4.7 percent alcohol by volume. Gambling activities are provided by the three operators licensed under the Gambling Act: Fintoto Oy, RAY (Finland's Slot Machine Association), and Veikkaus Oy. In Finland, gambling activities are subject to strict state control and monitoring. Public authority control enables to guarantee players' legal protection, prevent abuse and criminal activity related to gambling, and reduce the negative social and health effects of gambling. The aim is also to prevent illegal gambling activities. Foreign or other domestic operators are not allowed to market or offer their games in Finland.

Passenger rail transportation in Finland is a monopoly operated solely by the state-owned company, Valtion Rautatiet Oy (VR), but freight transport has been open to free competition since 2007. However, freight transportation by rail between Finland and Russia still remains an exclusive right of VR. The new Railway Act (304/2011) enables free competition on passenger transport within Finland. However, competition may be limited by the fact that officials can conclude agreements to only use the railway services provided by a specific company for ten years at a time.

Solidium, a limited liability company fully owned by the government of Finland, invests in companies that are considered to be of national importance. Solidium invests in Finnish listed companies and foreign listed companies with extensive operations in Finland.

As of April 2014, Finland has direct ownership of shares in three listed companies (Finnair, Fortum, and Neste Oil). Finland also owns 32 non-listed companies. A list of state-owned companies can be found here: http://valtionomistus.fi/english/companies/state-majority-owned-companies/

The Ownership Steering Department, under Minister Pekka Haavisto, handles duties relating to state ownership. The department is responsible for state ownership policy, expansion of the ownership base, branch re-organizations, share investments, and coordination of ministries' ownership steering procedures. All government resolutions, statements of the Cabinet Committee on Economic Policy, and recommendations and statements by Ministries are public and available to all market actors. SOEs in Finland adhere to the OECD Guidelines on Corporate Governance for SOEs.

The government, in November 2000, published "Handling of Corporate Governance Issues in State-owned Companies and Associated Companies." These guidelines stress the independence of the state-owned companies' boards and their goal to increase shareholder value. The Finnish government publishes the salaries and remunerations of the management and boards of state-owned and associated companies.

In November 2011, the Government adopted a government resolution outlining the objectives and principles for its state ownership policy, replacing the previous government resolution on ownership steering adopted in 2007. The adopted resolution places greater emphasis on responsibility, openness and long-term goal setting. The resolution calls for responsibility and openness as it regards reporting, remuneration, and the overall transparency of business activities. According to the resolution, non-listed state-owned and state majority-owned companies must, in the future, report their responsibilities in an accurate manner. This will allow comparison between companies. The Finnish government expects companies to ensure that their subcontractors also follow the same principles of responsibility. The resolution also focuses on the composition of companies' boards of directors and emphasizes the need to promote equal opportunities. This includes gender equality.

The government resolution, based on the Government Program, provides guidelines for ownership steering within ministries. It also provides companies, stakeholders and markets with information about the main practices of the Finnish government as an owner. The resolution builds on the continuation of the government's active, market-based ownership policy. The underlying principle is that corporate assets held by the Finnish government constitute an important part of its national wealth.

In August 2012, the Cabinet Committee on Economic Policy adopted a statement on remuneration of management in state-owned companies (the previous statement dated from autumn 2009). Openness and moderation are the statement's fundamental premises. Remuneration must be predictable and transparent, so that everyone involved can assess its efficiency. According to the statement, the threshold for remuneration must be sufficiently challenging to reach and it is particularly important to ensure that remuneration does not lead to excesses jeopardizing the targets set for remuneration schemes.

On December 16, 2013, Minister Haavisto announced that the age limit previously applied to board members of companies in which the state is the major shareholder will be abolished in spring 2014. In companies whose articles of association specify an age limit, the required changes will have to be agreed in an AGM. The current age limits range between 68 to 70. For companies in which the state is a minority shareholder, the new policy will apply to appointments in which the state can have a say.

Finland does not have a sovereign wealth fund.

11. CORPORATE SOCIAL RESPONSIBILITY

Finland is committed to compliance with and the promotion of corporate social responsibility by supporting the implementation of international codes of conduct guiding the operations of multinational enterprises, such as the OECD Guidelines for Multinational Enterprises, the ILO Declaration on Fundamental Principles and Rights at Work, and the tripartite declaration of principles concerning multinational enterprises and social policy by the ILO. Compliance with the guidelines is voluntary for enterprises.

The Committee on Corporate Social Responsibility, operating in connection with the Ministry of Employment and the Economy, monitors the application of the OECD Guidelines for Multinational Enterprises in Finnish multinational corporations. The Government Decree on the Committee on Corporate Social Responsibility can be found at:
http://www.tem.fi/files/23532/Government_Decree_on_the_Committee_on_Social_and_Corporat
e_Responsibility_(.pdf

In Finland, the Securities Market Association established by the Central Chamber of Commerce, the Confederation of Finnish Industries (EK) and NASDAQ OMX Helsinki has developed and updated the Finnish Corporate Governance Code for companies listed on the Helsinki Stock Exchange. The Code can be found at:
http://www.nasdaqomx.com/digitalAssets/71/71589_finnish_cg_code_2010.pdf

The Corporate Responsibility Network (FiBS), established in 2000, is the leading corporate responsibility network in Finland, with around 200 members. The Human Rights Centre (HRC), administratively connected to the Office of the Parliamentary Ombudsman, encourages foreign and local enterprises to follow the most important international norms in the field.

Labor and environmental laws and regulations are not waived in order to attract or retain investments.

The Government of Finland published a new guide on socially responsible public procurement in November 2013, found here: http://www.tem.fi/files/38102/TEM_Opas_Sos.hank_EN_netti.pdf

The Government is committed to promoting CSR through its CSR action plan (see Government Resolution on CSR, https://www.tem.fi/files/35134/Government_Resolution_on_CSR_FINLAND.pdf), in partnership with the public sector, enterprises, NGOs, labor market organizations and other expert organizations.

12. POLITICAL VIOLENCE

There are no instances of political violence.

13. CORRUPTION

Corruption is not perceived as a serious threat and Finland has no dedicated national anti-corruption strategy. The Internal Security Program of 2012 discusses the risks of corruption in public procurement and for Finnish enterprises or their representatives when conducting business abroad.

Corruption in Finland is covered by the Criminal Code and provides for sanctions ranging from fines to imprisonment of up to four years. Both giving and accepting a bribe is considered a criminal act under the Criminal Code. Finland has statutory tax rules concerning non-deductibility of bribes. Finland is a signatory to the OECD Convention on Anti-Bribery. A Transparency International progress report on enforcement of the OECD Convention, released in October 2013, rated Finland's enforcement as "moderate."
http://issuu.com/transparencyinternational/docs/2013_exportingcorruption_oecdprogre

Finland does not have an authority specifically charged with the prevention of corruption. The Ministry of Justice is responsible for the coordination of anti-corruption matters although Finland's anti-corruption contact point for EU purposes is in the Ministry of the Interior. Ministry of Justice in 2002 set up a special anti-corruption network which meets to discuss and exchange information. The National Bureau of Investigation has an officer whose full-time duty is to follow matters related to corruption in Finland. The tax administration has, after recommendations from the Organization for Economic Cooperation and Development (OECD), published guidelines for tax officials stating their obligation to report suspected criminal offences, including foreign bribery. The Ministry of Finance has also published guidelines for government officials on hospitality, benefits, and gifts.

For more, see the Ministry of Justice's "Corruption and the Prevention of Corruption in Finland," found at:
http://www.oikeusministerio.fi/material/attachments/om/tiedotteet/en/2009/6AH99u1tG/Corruption.pdf

Over the past decade, Finland has placed first or second on Transparency International's Corruption Perceptions Index (CPI). In 2013, Transparency International ranked Finland as the third least corrupt country in the world. Transparency International says that Finland still faces some corruption issues related to "old-boys' networks" where a small group of elites, sometimes with political connections, make deals and decisions in a non-transparent manner.

The Act on a Candidate's Election Funding (273/2009) delineates election funding and disclosure rules in parliamentary, presidential, municipal, and European Parliamentary elections. The Act requires presidential candidates, Members of Parliament and Deputy Members to declare their total campaign financing and the financial value of each contribution as well as the name of the donor for donations exceeding EUR 1,500. The National Audit Office of Finland keeps a register containing the information in the election funding disclosures, available at:
http://www.vaalirahoitusvalvonta.fi

Lobbying is not regulated in Finland. There is no requirement for lobbyists to register or for reporting contacts between public officials and lobbyists.

The Convention on Laundering, Search, Seizure and Confiscation of the Proceeds from Crime entered into force in July 1994. Finland ratified the Council of Europe Civil Law Convention on Corruption in October 2001. Finland ratified the Criminal Law Convention on Corruption in October 2002. The UN Convention against Transnational Organized Crime was ratified in February 2003. Finland ratified the UN Convention against Corruption in July 2006. In 2008 and 2011, Finland renewed the reservations in respect to Article 12 (trading in influence) and Article 17 (jurisdiction).

Finland is a member of the European Partners against Corruption (EPAC), which cooperates with national police oversight bodies and anti-corruption authorities of the European Union. Finland has joined the Extractive Industries Transparency Initiative (EITI), which supports improved governance in resource-rich countries through the verification and full publication of company payments and government revenues from oil, gas, and mining.

Finland is a party to the 1957 European Convention on Extradition. Finland has ratified the 1959 European Convention on Mutual Legal Assistance in Criminal Matters and its 1978 Additional Protocol. Finland is a party to the 1996 Convention on Extradition between EU member States as well the 1995 Convention on Simplified Extradition Procedure within the EU.

The United States and Finland have an extradition treaty, signed in June 1976; that entered into force in May 1980. The United States and the EU signed a bilateral extradition and mutual legal assistance treaty (MLAT) in December 2003. The United States and Finland signed a bilateral MLAT in December 2004. Finland ratified the MLAT agreements and approved the necessary implementing bilateral instruments in December 2007.

Resources to Report Corruption

The National Bureau of Investigation is the law enforcement body responsible for the investigation of complex organized and international crimes, including economic crime and corruption. Since 2007, the National Bureau of Investigation has operated an anti-corruption unit whose main function it is to detect economic offences. The corruption-detection unit consists of one officer.

Contact at government agency

Jouni Hirvonen
Detective Chief Inspector specialized in corruption
National Board of Investigation
P.O. Box 285, 01310 Vantaa
+358 295480141
Jouni.hirvonen@poliisi.fi

Contact at "watchdog" organization:
Annukka Timonen (since April 3, 2014)
Chairperson
Transparency Finland
Töölönkatu 3A, 3rd Floor, 00100 Helsinki, Finland
annukka.timonen@transparency.fi

Transparency International's national chapter Transparency Finland was founded in late 2003. More information can be found at: http://www.transparency.fi/

14. BILATERAL INVESTMENT AGREEMENTS

Finland has concluded bilateral investment agreements with the following 66 countries: Albania, Algeria, Argentina, Armenia, Azerbaijan, Belarus, Bosnia-Herzegovina, Bulgaria, Chile, China, Croatia, the Czech Republic, the Dominican Republic, Ecuador, Egypt, El Salvador, Estonia, Ethiopia, Georgia, Guatemala, Hong Kong, Hungary, India, Indonesia, Iran, Jordan, Kazakhstan, Kyrgyzstan, Kuwait, Latvia, Lebanon, Lithuania, Macedonia, Malaysia, Mauritius, Mexico, Moldova, Mongolia, Morocco, Mozambique, Namibia, Nepal, Nigeria, Oman, Panama, Peru, Philippines, Poland, Qatar, Romania, Russia, Slovakia, Slovenia, South Africa, South Korea, Sri Lanka, Tanzania, Thailand, Tunisia, Turkey, Ukraine, United Arab Emirates, Uruguay, Uzbekistan, Vietnam, and Zambia.

Finland does not have a bilateral investment treaty or free trade agreement with the United States. In September 1989, Finland and the United States signed a convention (TIAS 12101) for the avoidance of double taxation and the prevention of fiscal evasion with respect to taxes on income and on capital. The convention entered into force December 30, 1990. The tax convention was amended on May 31, 2006 under a protocol signed in Helsinki. Among other things, the protocol eliminates the source-country withholding tax on many intercompany dividends and on dividends paid to pension funds and eliminates source-country withholding royalties payment regardless of the type of intellectual property. For more see: http://www.treasury.gov/resource-center/tax-policy/treaties/Documents/js4298_attachment_finnishprotocol06.pdf

15. OPIC AND OTHER INVESTMENT INSURANCE PROGRAMS

In January 1996, OPIC and Finnvera (the former Finnish Guarantee Board) signed an agreement to encourage joint U.S.-Finnish private investments in Russia and the Baltic States. For more information see http://www.finnvera.fi/eng/Exports-and-internationalisation/Export-guarantees/Export-Credit-Guarantees/International-co-operation/Co-operation-agreements

Finland has been a member of the Multilateral Investment Guarantee Agency (MIGA) since 1988.

16. LABOR

The Finnish labor force is highly skilled and well-educated. Of the 2.46 million persons employed in 2013, 4.3 percent were employed in the primary sector, 23 percent in industry and construction and 72.7 percent in services. Employment fell slightly in the private sector and rose in the public sector.

Finland has a long tradition of trade unions and has a unionization rate of around 75 percent. Wage formation and labor market institutions are based on legislation and agreements. Working life legislation has been prepared on a tripartite basis by government and social partners. Collective bargaining and collective labor agreements are generally binding in nature. Finland adheres to most ILO conventions; enforcement of worker rights is effective.

Regulation of the labor market - minimum wages, working hours, working conditions, etc. - to a large extent takes place through collective agreements instead of parliamentary legislation. In recent years, labor market partners at the local level have been given more flexibility in enforcing the stipulations of the collective agreements.

There were a total of 108 strikes in 2013, but none posed major threats to investment. The largest strike took place in the postal service Itella when 1,800 workers went on strike. The relevant parties came to an agreement, and delays to the postal service were minimal.

Any trade union and employers' association may make collective agreements. Nearly all collective agreements are branch-specific. The Ministry of Labor and the Economy decides on the universal validity of the agreement. The parties to collective agreements are trade unions and the central organizations of employers' associations. The role of the government has been, when needed, to support the conclusion of collective agreements by making the appropriate economic policy decisions, such as in cases involving taxes. Extensive tripartite cooperation between the government, employers groups, and trade unions characterize the country's labor market system.

The Act on Employment Contracts is the main regulating act applied to employment relationships. It includes the minimum conditions regarding working hours, annual leave, safety conditions, etc.

In April 2014 the European Parliament passed the enforcement directive on the posting of workers. Posted workers are employees who are posted by an employer in one country to work temporarily in another EU member state for the purpose of providing cross-border services. The measure compels employers to abide by the terms of employment of posted workers in practice. Finland has many posted workers in the construction sector, and the directive allows for national enforcement measures such as the tax number system, which is important for efficient tax collection. The terms of employment of posted workers have already been defined in a previous directive, but the new directive adds to the effectiveness of their implementation.

The unemployment rate in April 2014 was 9 percent, against 8.8 percent a year earlier. Youth unemployment (15-24 years old) in April 2014 was 25.6 percent which was 1.2 percent higher compared to a year ago. The unemployed are granted compensation (a labor market subsidy) which, if linked to earnings as has been the case for about 60 percent of the unemployed, guarantees moderate income for a period up to 500 working days. People without jobs after a maximum of 500 days need to demonstrate that they are actively pursuing employment in order to continue receiving the benefit. For more info see The Social Insurance Institution of Finland: http://www.kela.fi/in/internet/english.nsf/NET/081101150015EH?OpenDocument

Finland allows the free movement of EU citizen workers.

Due to the aging population in Finland, all sectors of the economy are estimated to face labor shortages in the future.

17. FOREIGN FREE ZONES/FREE PORTS

Finland has two free warehouse areas, Hanko and Oulu, and four free zones, Hamina Lappeenranta, Turku, and Kemi. The duty-free storage areas, which are usually run by municipal corporations, are available to domestic and foreign-owned companies. Warehousing, assembly and manufacturing are allowed in these areas, with permission from the Board of Customs. The free zone area regulations have been harmonized in the EU by the Community Customs Code.

All shipments from the United States, Canada, China, and Japan containing non-manufactured wood packing materials (NWPM) of coniferous wood, must be treated and marked as such. See the Board of Customs for more information at: http://www.tulli.fi/en/index.jsp

18. FOREIGN DIRECT INVESTMENT AND FOREIGN PORTFOLIO INVESTMENT STATISTICS

TABLE 2: Key Macroeconomic data, U.S. FDI in host country/economy

	Host Country Statistical source*		USG or international statistical source		USG or international Source of Data: BEA; IMF; Eurostat; UNCTAD, Other
Economic Data	Year	Amount	Year	Amount	
Host Country Gross Domestic Product (GDP) (Millions U.S. Dollars)	2012	266,782 (Tilasto-keskus)	2012	247,545	http://www.worldbank.org/en/country
Foreign Direct Investment	Host Country Statistical source*		USG or international statistical source		USG or international Source of data: BEA; IMF; Eurostat; UNCTAD, Other
U.S. FDI in partner country (Millions U.S. Dollars, stock positions)	2012	1,650 (Bank of Finland)	2012	2,013	(BEA) click selections to reach. eau of Economic Analysis ance of Payments and Direct Investment ition Data . Direct Investment Position Abroad on a orical-Cost Basis Country only (all countries) (Millions of Dollars)
Host country's FDI in the United States (Millions U.S. Dollars, stock positions)	2012	13,572 (Bank of Finland)	2012	7,162	(BEA) click selections to reach ance of Payments and Direct Investment ition Data eign Direct Investment Position in the United es on a Historical-Cost Basis Country only (all countries) (Millions of Dollars)
Total inbound stock of FDI as % host GDP (calculate)	0,61%	2012	0.8%	2012	

http://www.tilastokeskus.fi/tup/suoluk/suoluk_kansantalous_en.html

http://www.suomenpankki.fi/en/tilastot/maksutase/pages/tilastot_maksutase_ja_suorat_sijoitukset _maksutase_suorat_sijoitukset_suomeen_kanta_maittain_en.aspx

http://www.suomenpankki.fi/en/tilastot/maksutase/Pages/tilastot_maksutase_ja_suorat_sijoitukset _maksutase_suorat_sijoitukset_suomesta_kanta_maittain_en.aspx

TABLE 3: Sources and Destination of FDI Finland, 2012

Direct Investment from/in Counterpart Economy Data	
From Top Five Sources/To Top Five Destinations (US Dollars, Millions)	
Inward Direct Investment	Outward Direct Investment

Total Inward	85,202	100%	Total Outward	139,945	100%
Sweden	44,439	52%	Sweden	37,322	27%
Netherlands	14,656	17%	Netherlands	28,902	21%
Denmark	5,880	7%	Ireland	14,859	11%
Luxembourg	4,373	5%	Belgium	12,675	9%
Germany	4,177	5%	United States	12,591	9%
"0" reflects amounts rounded to +/- USD 500,000.					

Source: http://cdis.imf.org

TABLE 4: Sources of Portfolio Investment Finland, End of June 2013

Portfolio Investment Assets Top Five Partners (Millions, US Dollars)

Total			Equity Securities			Total Debt Securities		
World	327,105	100%	World	154,906	100%	World	172,199	100%
Sweden	40,995	13%	United States	23,776	15%	Germany	28,072	16%
United States	32,157	10%	Ireland	18,361	12%	Denmark	25,500	15%
Germany	31,759	10%	Sweden	16,042	10%	Sweden	24,954	14%
Denmark	28,736	9%	Cayman Islands	11,581	7%	France	16,176	9%
Ireland	21,269	7%	France	4,203	3%	Netherlands	15,720	9%

Source: http://cpis.imf.org/

No policies exist that govern the export of capital and outward direct investment. Holders of capital, Finnish and foreign, can move funds at will.

IMPORTANT BUSINESS AND LEGAL CONTACTS

Asianajotoimisto Jouko Aaltonen Oy
Mäntytie 4, 00270 Helsinki 09 - 477 5669 09 - 477 5660 www.joukoaaltonen.fi

Advocates
Heikki Aaltonen Puhelin 050 376 7840 Email heikki.aaltonen@joukoaaltonen.fi Osaamisalueet Scope of experience

Asianajotoimisto Kari Aarrevuo Oy
Melkonkatu 28 D, 2. krs, 00210 Helsinki 09 - 278 8571 09 - 278 8572
asianajaja@kariaarrevuo.fi www.kariaarrevuo.fi

Advocates
Kari Aarrevuo Puhelin 0500 449 534 Email asianajaja@kariaarrevuo.fi Osaamisalueet Scope of experience

Asianajotoimisto Aasa-Law Oy
Vuorikatu 6 A 12, 00100 Helsinki 09 - 612 9240 09 - 6129 2460 info@aasa-law.fi
www.aasa-law.fi

Advocates

Simo Ellilä Puhelin 09 - 6129 2420 , 0400 876 559 Email simo.ellila@aasa-law.fi Osaamisalueet Scope of experience
Pasi Pirinen Puhelin 09 - 6129 2450 , 040 708 7825 Email pasi.pirinen@aasa-law.fi Osaamisalueet Scope of experience
Petri Rissanen Puhelin 09 - 6129 2440 , 040 738 1212 Email petri.rissanen@aasa-law.fi Osaamisalueet Scope of experience

Asianajotoimisto Activatus Oy
Mannerheimintie 12 B, 00100 Helsinki 09 - 2516 6216 09 - 612 3171 www.activatus.fi

Advocates
Johan Hjelt Puhelin 0400 315 170 Email johan.hjelt@activatus.fi Osaamisalueet Scope of experience

ADVISE. Asianajotoimisto Olli Pohjakallio Oy

Yrjönkatu 23 A 6, 00100 Helsinki 010 835 3400 010 835 3409 toimisto@advise.fi www.advise.fi

Advocates
Olli Pohjakallio Puhelin 050 554 5120 Email olli.pohjakallio@advise.fi Osaamisalueet Scope of experience

Asianajotoimisto ADVOCARE - Patrick Lindgren Oy
Erottajankatu 11 A 22, 00130 Helsinki 010 666 5680 09 - 685 2244 www.advocare.fi

Advocates
Patrick Lindgren Puhelin 0500 409 818 Email patrick.lindgren@advocare.fi Osaamisalueet Scope of experience

Asianajotoimisto Advoline Oy
Snellmaninkatu 25 A 3, 00170 Helsinki 09 - 4289 0130 020 781 8250 info@advoline.fi www.advoline.fi

Advocates
Tatu Henriksson Puhelin 045 130 0567 Email tatu.henriksson@advoline.fi Osaamisalueet Scope of experience
Susanna Kallaskari Puhelin 045 879 7345 Email susanna.kallaskari@advoline.fi Osaamisalueet Scope of experience
Juha Räihä Puhelin 045 136 3345 Email juha.raiha@advoline.fi Osaamisalueet Scope of experience

Asianajotoimisto Ahola & Sokka Oy
Juhannuspolku 1 E, 02200 Espoo 0400 709 342

Advocates
Ossi Sokka Email ossi.sokka@ahola-sokka.fi Osaamisalueet Scope of experience

Asianajotoimisto AKG Oy
Innopoli I, Tekniikantie 12, 02150 Espoo 020 781 1890 020 781 1899 info@akg.fi www.akg.fi

Advocates

Jarmo Havukunnas Puhelin 050 563 2897 Email jarmo.havukunnas@akg.fi Osaamisalueet Scope of experience
Pasi Kainulainen Puhelin 020 781 1892 , 040 523 4844 Email pasi.kainulainen@akg.fi Osaamisalueet Scope of experience
Leo Koskenvuo Puhelin 020 781 1893 , 050 591 5900 Email leo.koskenvuo@akg.fi Osaamisalueet Scope of experience
Lauri Mäki Puhelin 040 723 0984 Email lauri.maki@akg.fi Osaamisalueet Scope of experience

Asianajotoimisto Alex Oy
- 4241 4508 office@alexlaw.fi www.alexlaw.fi

STARTING BUSINESS IN FINLAND

TYPES OF COMPANIES IN FINLAND

A company who's willing to **start a business in Finland** must first check the types of Finnish companies, in order to choose the one that best suits the type of business it's covering it.

Private Person Carrying on Trade (yksityinen elinkeinonharjoittaja), or a private trader, is an entrepreneur member of EEA who establish a company in Finland. It's responsible for paying the taxes and it's free to withhold profit.

A **Partnership (avoin yhtiö-Ay) in Finland is** composed by at least two members (one of them must be a EEA resident).The profits are divided among the partners according to the number of shares they have (except the case when the partnership agreement dispose something else).There is no originally share capital required.

The **Limited Partnership (kommandiittiyhtiö,-Ky) in Finland,** must have at least 2 partners, one of them must be the general partner and one the silent partner. The general one has the right to contribute to the management's decisions and ask for profit, unlike the limited one. The silent one has no decisional power but doesn't absorb the losses.

The **Limited Company (osakeyhtiö-Oy) in Finland has** the following attributes: the minimum share capital is 2500 euros (cash or property) a person is sufficient to set up the company and the management is provided by the management board. It must be recorded at the Trade Register before the beginning of activity.

A **Public Limited Company (julkinen osakeyhtiö-Oyj) in Finland** is founded after registration in the Trade Register. It must have a share capital of minimum 80000 euros (cash or property). At least one statutory person establishes the company. If the company has the share capital above 80000 euro, the management board must have more than 3 members (more than 50% of them must be EEA residents) and a managing director. An Oyj must also provide semi-annuals reports and can be listed on the Helsinki Stock Exchange.

The basic difference between a Limited and a Public company is that only the Public Limited Company can trade or transfer the shares. They are both governed by the Companies Act (Osakeyhtiölaki, 21.7.2006/624).

A **Branch of a Foreign Company (sivuliike)** it's a society that operates in Finland even though it has it's headquarters in another country. The branch representative must have a Finnish domicile and if it's not an EEA member a special permission must be granted by NBPR.

FORM AN OY (LIMITED LIABILITY COMPANY) IN FINLAND

A **Limited Liability Company in Finland** is also known as osakeyhtiö(Oy), and it's the most usual form a small or medium company can take.

In **Finland setting up an Oy** is covered by the Companies Act, fully reformed in 2006.

There's a minimal share capital of 2,500 euro (cash or property) that has to be deposited into a bank before the company registration.

To **establish an Oy in Finland**, a Memorandum of Association must be developed and signed. This Memorandum includes: the date of the Memorandum, information regarding the Management Board, the auditors, the shareholders, the shares, the price of the shares, the payment term of the shares.

Also next to the Memorandum of Association the entrepreneur must enclose: the name of the company, the domicile and the type of business. These are all included in the Articles of Association.

Within three months after signing the Memorandum, the company must be enrolled at the Trade Register; otherwise the setting up the company expires.

A **Limited Liability Company in Finland** can be formed by one or more legal persons.

All the shareholders have equal rights in the company except the case when the difference it's clearly stipulated in the Memorandum of Association.

An Oy in Finland must have a Board of Directors (according to the Companies Act), elected by the General Meeting of Shareholders.

The Board of Directors must include one or two common members and at least one adjunct. It is responsible for the administration and the suitable disposal of the operations as well as for the proper monitoring of the accountancy and the check of the financial issues of the company.

Also a managing director, named by the Board of Directors must be invested. In the matters which belong to his tasks he has the right to represent the Company. Furthermore, it is the duty of the Managing Director to see if the accountancy and that the financial issues are being handled reliably.

Extended or unusual acts (considering the scope and the kind of the company's transactions) may be taken by the Managing Director only when he's authorized by the Board of Directors.

Also an external audit can be requested by a shareholder, at Ordinary General Meeting or at a General Meeting where the matter is according to the notice to be approached. The special auditor can be an individual or an audit firm.

It is not mandatory for a **Finnish LTD company** to name an internal auditor unless certain conditions are met: the staff is composed by more than three employees, the balance sheet total overcome 100.000 euro; net sales or appropriate gains overcome 200.000 euro.

As a special requirement in setting up an Oy, at least half of the Board of the Directors must be EU residents. Also a Finnish headquarters is requested for a **Limited Liability Company in Finland.**

LIMITED LIABILITY COMPANIES ACT IN FINLAND

The act that governs all the Finnish organization and function of all types of **limited liability companies is the Companies Act**, also known as osakeyhtiölaki (first posted in 1978 and reformed in its entirety in September 2006). It applies to the public and private companies as well.

This act governs all the concerns regarding the Limited Liability Companies in Finland, in matters such as: the company operations and the applications of this, incorporation of a limited liability company, shares, administration and financial statements(the general meeting, management and representation of the company, audit and special audit, equity, financial statements, annual report and group),finance(share issue, increase of the share capital, capital loan),distribution of the company assets, changes in company structure and the dissolution of the company, sanctions and remedies.

Establishment and articles of association of an OY:

The first step in setting up a limited liability company in Finland is the preparation of the Memorandum of Association, signed by the shareholders. This has to be registered at the Trade Register within three months from signing it. Also the articles of association (containing the company name, the headquarters and the type of business) must be included in the registration.

The minimum share capital for a Finnish limited liability company is 2500 euro and 80000 euro if it's a public one.

Leadership and representatives of the Finnish company:

A Finnish limited liability company must have a Board of Directors, responsible for the proper control of the company accounts and finances.

It may also have a Managing Director and a Supervisory Board, if the dimension of it requires it.

The Managing Director must make sure that the accounts of the company are in accordance with the law and that its financial affairs have been arranged in a reliable manner .

The Supervisory Board supervises the administration of the company (the responsibility of the Board of Directors and the Managing Director).

Shares:

Is not compulsory for the shares to have a nominal value, (in certain cases it may have in the future but this should be specified in the articles of association.)

Changes in the company structure and the dissolution of the company:

An Oy can merge in another limited liability company, the assets and liabilities of the merging company are transferred to the buying company (also it may transfer cash, further assets and future enterprises). The shareholders of the merging company receive shares in the acquiring company.

A limited liability company can be changed in a public one if it meets the demands of a public company. In this case it must amend the Articles of Association within a month from the General Meeting decision and register it at the Trade Register, if not, the changing decision fails.

The decision of liquidation can only be taken by the General Meeting, and it's made for paying the company's debts(by changing the needed amount of assets into cash).After this, the surplus is returned to the shareholders or others, as specified in the Articles of Association.

COMPANY REGISTRATION IN FINLAND

The **company registration in Finland** requires only a few straightforward steps. The laws are very encouraging to the investors (as an exemple in the north where local authorities have special interests to attract foreign investments or domestic, some facilities are granted).

The company registration in Finland is governed by the Foundations Act nr. 734 from 1930 and The Finnish Companies Act from 1978 (the last one has been reformed in its entirety on 2006 and it is now modern and comprehensible).

To **register a company in Finland** first of all the entrepreneur must deposit the paid-in share capital in a bank (2500 eur if it's a limited liability company, 80000 eur if it's a Public Liability Company) and pay the registration fee and obtain a receipt. This process usually takes approximately one day.

There are six forms of business ventures: Limited Company (Oy), Public Limited Company (Oyj), Limited Partnership(Ky), Partnership (Ay), Private Person Carrying on Trade, Branch of a Foreign Company (sivuliike).

All the companies must be registered at the National Board of Patents and Registration. The application must include the Memorandum of Association (containing information on the members of the Board of Directors and the auditors of the Company, all the shareholders and the shares they have subscribed, the subscription price of the shares, the term of payment of the shares), the minute of the founding meeting and Board meeting, the receipt certifying that the minimum capital was deposited into a bank account.

A Limited Company must be announced for registration at the Trade Register within three months from the signing of the Memorandum of the Association, or the forming of the company shall expire. The registration is regulated in Trade Register Act (Kaupparekisterilaki, 129/1979)

The process of registration can take from two weeks to eight weeks (according to the type of company). Meanwhile, the company may start trading before registration but with limited liability.

The last step (if the company will hire employees) is to file with a private insurer for a list of employee insurances (eg. pension, accident, medical etc.)

If a company wants to **establish a branch in Finland** must submit a statutory notice concerning its branch to the Trade Register before the branch commences its operations. If the foreign investor setting up the branch is from a country located outside the European Economic area, it will also need a special approval from the Finnish Trade Register for the setup of the branch on the country's territory.

The branch, which is a part of a foreign company, must have a representative, whose domicile must be in Finland. The representative must be named in the special notification.

For an entrepreneur who wants to open a subsidiary in Finland and has his main organization outside the European Economic Area(EEA), the Start-up Notification registered at NBPR must also mention the state whose laws govern it, the place of legal residence and the central government. Also if the foreign trader is from a country outside the EEA is a limited liability company, the notification must also mention the share capital (except the case it's already given in the memorandum of association, the articles of association or in a affiliated document.)

Company formation in Finland is preferred because it offers an industrialized economic environment, extremely competitive in manufacturing, engineering, telecommunications and electronics industries. Finland also excels in high-tech exports such as mobile phones.

Finland is well-known as one of the world's leading wood producers and provider of raw materials for the wood-processing industries (2/3 of the Finland surface is covered with woods)

Also the communication network is highly developed, especially in the waterway transport (90% foreign trade is carried by sea).

DOING BUSINESS IN FINLAND

MARKET OVERVIEW

Finland, a member of the European Union (EU) since 1995, has been on a remarkable journey, redefining itself from a quiet agricultural based economy to a trend setting, global center for technology. Local company Nokia is often cast as the country's flagship illustration of Finland's penchant for technology oriented businesses. Finland has commercial clout far in excess of its modest 5.3 million population. Finland routinely ranks at the very top in international surveys of research and development funding, competitiveness, transparency, literacy, and education.

Helsinki, a modest sized metropolis, was recently designated the Design Capital for 2012, underscoring the global influence of Finnish design and innovation. In Finland, nature reigns supreme and it is no surprise that Helsinki was the site of the first LEED certified building in the Nordics. Finland, along with all its Nordic neighbors, has a focused interest in green build and energy efficient products, services and technologies.

Contrary to popular misconception, Finland is not a part of Scandinavia. It does share with Russia a 900-mile long border, the longest contiguous land border in the EU. Interestingly, some 40 percent of the EU's overland transshipments into Russia go through Finland underscoring Finland's role as a regional business hub complemented by its logistical capabilities. Russia is Finland's largest trading partner and a variety of Finnish companies are successful in Russia, a challenging marketplace. We believe that there are opportunities for certain U.S. exporters to exploit this existing business by providing U.S. goods via the Finnish corridor. Finland is striving to capitalize upon its unique position as the center of a rapidly developing marketplace formed by northwestern Russia, the Scandinavian countries, and the Baltic States, with more than 80 million prospective consumers.

Two-way trade between the U.S. and Finland was about $8.8 billion in 2008, chiefly in the electronics, paper, medical equipment, and telecommunications industries. The U.S. remains an important trading partner for Finland outside of Europe. With Finnish imports of U.S. goods and services in 2008 valued at around $2.7 billion, the United States was Finland's ninth largest supplier after Russia, Germany, Sweden, China, the Netherlands, United Kingdom, France and Italy. In 2008, the U.S. was Finland's fourth largest customer after Russia, Sweden, and Germany, with Finnish exports of goods and services to the United States valued at about $6.1 billion.

Finland is the only Nordic country to replace its national currency, the Finnish mark, with the euro. Finland has a largely homogeneous population. There are about 5,000 Americans resident in Finland and some 50,000 visit the country each year. Per capita income was about $46,300 in 2008.

MARKET CHALLENGES

Finland's import climate is open and receptive to U.S. products and investments. While the domestic market is small, Finland can effectively serve as a base for business operations in the Nordic, Baltic, and/or Western Russian markets. There is one specific trade barrier that starkly contrasts with an otherwise remarkable transparent and predictable business environment. In 2008, the Finnish government approved a pharmaceutical reference pricing system. The new law casts products protected by process patents to the reference pricing restrictions applicable to generic products and deprives pharmaceutical process patent holders in Finland appropriate compensation for the value of the intellectual property they created in the original products.

MARKET ENTRY STRATEGY

Finnish businesspeople and consumers are sophisticated and conscious of quality and value. Prices in Finland, as well as throughout the Nordics, are high. Flexibility in consumer behavior and in Finland's distribution channels allows for a variety of market entry strategies. Representatives and distributors are common methods employed for initial market entry.

TRAVEL TO FINLAND

US STATE DEPARTMENT SUGGESTIONS

COUNTRY DESCRIPTION: Finland is a highly developed democracy with a modern economy. It is a member of the European Union. Tourist facilities are widely available.

ENTRY REQUIREMENTS: A passport is required. A visa is not required for tourist or business stays up to 90 days. For additional information concerning entry requirements, travelers may contact the Embassy of Finland at 3301 Massachusetts Avenue, N.W., Washington, D.C. 20048, tel. (202) 298-5800, or the Finnish Consulate General in Los Angeles or New York. Additional information is available via the Internet at http://www.finland.org.

CRIME INFORMATION: Although the crime rate in Finland is low compared to the U.S. and most European countries, it has increased approximately 15 percent since 1998. However, Finland remains relatively safe. Americans visiting Finland are seldom victims of crime, but visitors should not be complacent regarding personal safety or the protection of valuables. The same precautions employed in the U.S. should be followed in Finland. Finnish police services are excellent; however, some police officers speak little English. The telephone number for police and other emergency services throughout Finland is 112. All forms of public transportation are considered safe. Street crimes such as muggings and pickpocketing remain relatively uncommon, but they do occur. The loss or theft of a U.S. passport should be reported immediately to the local police (112) and the U.S. Embassy (171-931 ext. 271). U.S. citizens may refer to the Department of State's pamphlet *A Safe Trip Abroad* for ways to promote a more trouble-free journey. The pamphlet is available from the Superintendent of Documents, U.S. Government Printing Office, Washington, D.C. 20402, via the Internet at http://www.access.gpo.gov/su_docs, or via the Bureau of Consular Affairs home page at http://travel.state.gov.

MEDICAL FACILITIES: Medical facilities are widely available for emergency services. The public hospital system and many private hospitals honor foreign credit cards. Serious medical problems requiring hospitalization and/or medical evacuation to the United States can cost thousands of dollars or more.

MEDICAL INSURANCE: U.S. medical insurance is not always valid outside the United States. U.S. Medicare and Medicaid programs do not provide payment for medical services outside the United States. Uninsured travelers who require medical care overseas may face extreme difficulties. Please check with your own insurance company to confirm whether your policy applies overseas, including provision for medical evacuation. Please ascertain whether payment will be made to the overseas hospital or doctor or whether you will be reimbursed later for expenses that you incur. Some insurance policies also include coverage for psychiatric treatment and for disposition of remains in the event of death. Useful information on medical emergencies abroad, including overseas insurance programs, is provided in the Department of State's Bureau of Consular Affairs brochure, *Medical Information for Americans Traveling Abroad*, which is available via its home page.

OTHER HEALTH INFORMATION: Information on vaccinations and other health precautions may be obtained from the Centers for Disease Control and Prevention's hotline for international travelers at 1-877-FYI-TRIP (1-877-394-8747), via CDC's autofax service at 1-888-CDC-FAXX (1-888-232-3299), or via CDC's Internet site at http://www.cdc.gov.

TRAFFIC SAFETY AND ROAD CONDITIONS: While in a foreign country, U.S. citizens may encounter road conditions that differ significantly from those in the United States. The information below concerning Finland is provided for general reference only, and may not be totally accurate in a particular location or circumstance.
Safety of Public Transportation: Excellent
Urban Road Condition/Maintenance: Excellent
Rural Road Condition/Maintenance: Excellent
Availability of Roadside Assistance: Excellent

Finland has an extensive network of highways throughout the country, as well as excellent public transportation services. Travelers should be aware that drunk driving laws are strict, and acceptable blood alcohol levels are much lower in Finland than in the United States. Police strictly enforce all traffic laws and institute random roadside breathalyzer tests. Those drivers who register a .05 or above alcohol content are subject to immediate arrest. Driving regulations and traffic signs differ significantly from those in the United States. Visitors should be familiar with both prior to operating a vehicle in Finland. Driving in Finland during the winter months can be hazardous. Icy road conditions are common. Vehicles are required to be winterized and have studded snow tires, and engine heaters are strongly recommended. When driving at night, drivers must be alert to moose wandering onto major roadways. There have been incidents of moose being struck by vehicles, causing severe damage to the vehicle and even death to the occupants. For specific information concerning Finnish driver's permits, vehicle inspection, road tax and mandatory insurance, please contact the Finland National Tourist Organization offices in New York via the Internet at http://www.mek.fi. The e-mail address is med@mek.fi.

AVIATION SAFETY OVERSIGHT: The U.S. Federal Aviation Administration (FAA) has assessed the Government of Finland's Civil Aviation Authority as Category 1 -- in compliance with international aviation safety standards for oversight of Finland's air carrier operations. For further information, travelers may contact the Department of Transportation within the U.S. at tel. 1-800-322-7873, or visit the FAA Internet home page at http://www.faa.gov/avr/iasa/. The U.S. Department of Defense (DOD) separately assesses some foreign air carriers for suitability as official providers of air services. For information regarding the DOD policy on specific carriers, travelers may contact the DOD at tel. (618) 229-4801.

CUSTOMS REGULATIONS: Finland's customs authorities encourage the use of an ATA (Admission Temporaire/Temporary Admission) Carnet for the temporary admission of professional equipment, commercial samples, and/or goods for exhibitions and fair purposes. ATA Carnet Headquarters, located at the U.S. Council for International Business, 1212 Avenue of the Americas, New York, NY 10036, issues and guarantees the ATA Carnet in the United States. For additional information, please call 212-354-4480, send an e-mail to atacarnet@uscib.org, or visit http://www.uscib.org for details.

CRIMINAL PENALTIES: While in a foreign country, a U.S. citizen is subject to that country's laws and regulations, which sometimes differ significantly from those in the United States and may not afford the protections available to the individual under U.S. law. Penalties for breaking the law can be more severe than in the United States for similar offenses. Persons violating Finland's laws, even unknowingly, may be expelled, arrested or imprisoned. Penalties for possession, use, or trafficking in illegal drugs in Finland are strict and convicted offenders can expect jail sentences and heavy fines.

CHILDREN'S ISSUES: For information on international adoption of children and international parental child abduction, please refer to our Internet site at http://travel.state.gov/children's_issues.html or telephone (202) 736-7000.

REGISTRATION AND EMBASSY LOCATION: U.S. citizens are encouraged to register and obtain updated information on travel and security in Finland at the Consular Section of the U.S. Embassy in Helsinki. It is located at Itainen Puistotie 14B; tel: 358-9-171931 or after hours: 358-9-605414; fax: 358-9-652057; e-mail address: consular@usembassy.fi; home page: http://www.usembassy.fi.

BUSINESS TRAVEL

BUSINESS CUSTOMS

Finland is a modern, commercially mature country that enjoys close relations with its Nordic neighbors. Social and business protocol is similar to that in the United States and requires no special mentions of taboos. It is worth noting that relationships are important within the social and business world as Finns prefer to deal with people they know and trust.

VISA REQUIREMENTS AND BUSINESS MOBILITY GENERALLY

With the exception of Nordic (Sweden, Norway, Denmark, Iceland) citizens, citizens of EU countries (except Greece), and citizens of Switzerland, San Marino and Liechtenstein, foreigners entering Finland must have a valid passport. A tourist or business visa is not required for stays of up to three months. For non-EU citizens a visa is needed for stays exceeding 90 days. Visa applications should be submitted to a Finnish diplomatic mission before entry into Finland.

A foreigner needs a residence permit in order to stay in Finland for a longer period of time. However, residence permits are also needed for short stays of less than three months if the purpose of the stay is to work in Finland. Residence permits require either a valid passport or a travel document. Foreigners must have work permits if they intend to work in Finland. Exceptions are citizens of the Nordic countries or citizens of EU/EEA countries. EU-citizens outside the Nordic countries need to apply for an EEA-card from the local police for stays exceeding 90 days. An EEA-card is a combined work and residence permit.

HOLIDAYS

The national holidays are: New Year's Day (January 1); Epiphany (January 6); Good Friday (April 13); Easter (April 15-16); May Day (May 1); Ascension Day (May 24); Mid-Summer (June 23); All Saints' Day (November 3); Independence Day (December 6); Christmas (December 25-26).

Workweek

The average Finnish workweek is 40 hours per week, with annual leave of 25 days, 12.5 free days, and 9 paid holidays. Part-time employment averages to 17.8 hours per week.

BUSINESS INFRASTRUCTURE

- Transportation and communications - see section Economic Trends and Outlook - Infrastructure

LANGUAGE

The two official languages in Finland are Finnish and Swedish. About 92.5 percent of the population speak Finnish and 5.6 percent speak Swedish. Both languages are compulsory at school. English is widely spoken in Finland, especially among younger people and in major cities.

EDUCATION

Finland invests more in education that the EU countries on average. All children aged 7-15 – even handicapped – attend school in Finland. Comprehensive school is a nine-year compulsory general schooling for all children aged 7-16. The municipalities pay teachers' salaries, books, health care, and school meals. After completing comprehensive school, students may attend high schools for three years or receive vocational education. High school prepares students for university studies. Tuition at universities is minimal. Helsinki has international, English, German, Russian, French, and Jewish schools in which classes are taught partly in foreign languages and partly in Finnish. The International, English, German and Jewish schools are private and charge tuition. University level education is mainly in Finnish, with exception of English language BBA and MBA programs in certain universities and polytechnics.

MEDICAL SERVICES

Medical facilities are widely available. The public hospital system will not honor foreign credit cards and/or U.S. insurance coverage. However, private hospitals and clinics that accept major credit cards are widely available. Travelers have found that, in some cases, a letter from their carrier describing supplemental medical insurance with specific overseas coverage has proved useful. A foreigner is usually covered by the Finnish social security after moving to Finland, with health care as one of the benefits. Services are provided within each municipality. The quality of public health care is equivalent to care given by private doctors. In addition, the employers subsidize occupational health care.

HOUSING

Most people in Finland own their own housing. The cost to rent an apartment varies depending on the size, age, condition and location. Rents are generally quite high, especially within the Helsinki area, and most places come unfurnished.

FOOD

Despite prices converging with other EU levels, Finland's price structure regarding food and household needs is the lowest of the Nordic countries and only slightly above the OECD average. Finnish food is consistent to produce that is in season, which provides an array of berries, mushrooms, seafood etc. Potatoes are a main staple and accompany most evening dishes. Temporary Entry of Goods - see section Trade Regulations, Customs, and Standards

CONTACT INFORMATION

The Commercial Service staff in Helsinki provides several services for U.S. companies interested in doing business in Finland or using Finland as a gateway to Russia and the Baltic countries, especially Estonia. Please contact us at the following address to set up an appointment prior to your visit to Finland:

Commercial Service Helsinki
American Embassy
It. Puistotie 14 B
FIN-00140 Helsinki, Finland
Tel: (358-9) 171 931
Fax: (358-9) 635 332
E-mail: Helsinki.Office.Box@mail.doc.gov

SUPPLEMENTS

CUSTOMS DISTRICTS

Northern District Tornio
Kajaani
Karigasniemi
Kilpisjärvi
Kivilompolo
Kuusamo
Muonio
Neiden / Näätämö
Oulu
Polmak
Raahe
Raja-Jooseppi
Rovaniemi
Salla
Utsjoki
Vartius
Western District
Turku
Kaskinen
Kokkola
Jyväskylä
Pietarsaari
Pori
Tampere
Rauma
Vaasa
Eastern District

Lappeenranta
Hamina
Imatra
Kotka
Kouvola
Kuopio
Niirala
Nuijamaa
Parikkala
Vaalimaa
Vainikkala
Åland District Customs Laboratory Southern District Mariehamn Helsinki
41. Espoo
Eckerö 3. Hanko
Långnäs 4. Hämeenlinna
Lahti
Loviisa
Vantaa

National Board of Customs, Statistics Unit
P.O.Box 512, 00101 Helsinki, Finland
Erottajankatu 15-17 A, 00130 Helsinki
Statistics service Tel. +358 20 690 603 Fax +358 20 492 1860 Email: statistics@tulli.fi
www.tulli.fi

CONTACTS FOR ESTABLISHING BUSINESS

ESTATE AGENTS

Helsingin Liiketeollinen Kiinteistönvälitys Oy, www.liiketeollinen.fi
Mikonkatu 13 G 186, 00100 Helsinki
Tel. +358 9 684 0680, Fax +358 9 6840 6840

Catella Property Consultants Ltd, www.catella.fi
Aleksanterinkatu 15 B, 00100 Helsinki
Tel. +358 10 522 0100, Fax +358 10 522 0218

Suomen SKV-Yrityspalvelu Oy,www.skv.fi/yrityspalvelu/
Panuntie 4, 00610 Helsinki
Tel. +358 9 8629 1230, Fax +358 9 8629 1250

The Finnish Real Estates Agents' Association, www.asuntoverkko.com
Malminkaari 5, 00700 Helsinki
Tel. +358 9 530 8500, Fax +358 9 5308 5050

The Finnish Association of Building Owners and Construction Clients, www.rakli.fi
Annankatu 24, 00100 Helsinki
Tel. +358 9 4767 5711, Fax +358 9 4767 5700
Representatives of Foreign Auditing Firms

BDO
www.bdo.fi

BDO Finland Oy
Vattuniemenranta 2, 00210 Helsinki
Tel. +358 207 432 920
Fax +358 9 4780 8210

PricewaterhouseCoopers
www.pwcglobal.com SVH
PriceWaterhouseCoopers Oy
Itämerentori 2, P.O.Box 1015, 00101 Helsinki
Tel. +358 9 228 00
Fax +358 9 174 102

Deloitte Touche Tohmatsu International
www.deloitte.com
Deloitte & Touche Oy
Munkkiniemen puistotie 25, P.O.Box 94, 00331 Helsinki
Tel. +358 20 755 500
Fax +358 20 755 507

Ernst & Young International
www.ey.com
Ernst & Young Oy
Elielinaukio 5 B, 00100 Helsinki
Tel. +358 9 172 771
Fax +358 9 1727 7700

Grant Thornton International
www.revico.fi
Revico Grant Thornton Oy
Paciuksenkatu 27, P.O.Box 18, 00271 Helsinki
Tel. +358 9 512 3330
Fax +358 9 458 0250

KPMG International
www.kpmg.fi
KPMG: Investment in Finland KPMG Wideri Oy Ab
Mannerheimintie 20 B, P.O.Box 1037, 00101 Helsinki
Tel. +358 9 693 931
Fax +358 9 6939 3399

Midsnell Group International
www.mgimidsnell.com
Tilintarkastustoimisto Kalervo Ariluoma Oy
Keskustie 4, 01900 Nurmijärvi or Mannerheimintie 16 A 3, 00100 Helsinki
Tel. +358 9 250 9595
Fax +358 9 250 9715

RECRUITMENT CONSULTANTS

Amrop Hever Finland,
Yrjönkatu 16 A, 00120 Helsinki
tel. +358 9 622 9360, fax +358 9 6229 3619, www.amrop.fi

Boyden Finland,
Mikonkatu 17 A, 00100 Helsinki
tel. +358 9 622 6860, fax +358 9 6226 8666, www.boyden.fi

Heidrick & Struggles,
Kasarmikatu 46-48 B, 00130 Helsinki
tel. +358 9 2511 250, fax +358 9 2511 2511, www.heidrick.com
Horton International Finland,
Annankatu 25, 5th floor, 00100 Helsinki
tel. +358 9 6829 110, fax +358 9 6829 1115, www.horton.fi

HRD Group,
Yrjönkatu 27 A, 00100 Helsinki
tel. +358 9 4763 770, fax +358 9 4780 3333, http://www.hrd-group.fi/eng_index.php

IBI Executive Search,
Karvaamokuja 6, 00380 Helsinki
tel. +358 9 506 1899, fax +358 9 556 787, www.ibi.fi
IMS Oy International Management Search
Urho Kekkosen katu 5 C
00100 Helsinki
tel +358 (0) 9 694 00 44, fax +358 (0) 9 694 55 44, http://www.imssearch.fi

Intersearch Finland,
Iso Roobertinkatu 1 A 5, 00120 Helsinki
tel. +358 9 612 9090, fax +358 9 612 1390, www.intersearch.fi

JL Consultants,
Laulukuja 4, 00420 Helsinki
tel. +358 9 348 3200, fax +358 9 3483 2323, www.jaakkolehto.fi

J. Friisberg & Partners,
Keilasatama 3, 02150 Espoo
tel. +358 9 612 9910, fax +358 9 621 5521, www.friisberg.com (IIC-partners)

Korn/Ferry International Oy,
Eteläesplanadi 24 A, 00100 Helsinki

tel. +358 9 612 2560, fax +358 9 6122 5656, www.kornferry.com

Mercuri Urval,
Mannerheimintie 15 A, 00260 Helsinki
tel. +358 9 476 1700, fax +358 9 476 17777, www.mercuriurval.com

MPS Management Consulting,
Metsänneidonkuja 8, SPEKTRI TRIO, P.O.Box 44, 02131 Espoo
tel. +358 9 430 000, fax +358 9 43 000 301, www.mps.fi

Open Management Oy,
Aleksanterinkatu 17 (WTC), 00100 Helsinki
tel. +358 9 6969 4090, fax +358 9 6969 4099, www.openmanagement.fi

Personnel,
Hitsaajankatu 6,00810 Helsinki
tel. +358 9 7591455, fax +358 9 784627, www.pib.fi

Psyko,
Annankatu 42 C, 00100 Helsinki
tel. +358 9 613141, fax +358 9 6131 4200, www.psyko.fi

S & S Consulting Oy,
Melkonkatu 28 D, 00210 Helsinki
tel. +358 9 686 0570, fax 6860 5769, www.ssconsulting.fi

Selektio Consulting Oy, Accord Group,
Aleksanterinkatu 17 (WTC), 00100 Helsinki
tel. +358 9 6969 2989, fax +358 9 6969 2988, www.accordgroup.net

TEMP-TEAM Finland Oy, Juhler Group,
Fredrikinkatu 47, 00100 Helsinki
tel. +358 207 414 850, fax +358 207 414 851, www.juhlergroup.com
Contacts

THE FINNISH BAR ASSOCIATION

Simonkatu 12 B 20, 4th floor
FI-00100 Helsinki, Finland
Tel. +358 9 6866 120
Fax +358 9 6866 1299
info@barassociation.fi
email: firstname.lastname@barassociation.fi

Bus ID 0202096-1

President
Advocate, LL.M. with court training
Kari Lautjärvi
firstname.lastname@hannessnellman.fi

Vice President
Advocate, LL.M. with court training
Riitta Leppiniemi
firstname.lastname@susiluoto.com

Administration and Development
Secretary General Markku Ylönen

Advocate LawDisciplinary matters
LL.M. with court training Martti Ojala
LL.M. with court training Minna Melender

US AND COUNTRY CONTACTS

U.S. Embassy Trade Personnel

Commercial Service of the United States
It. Puistotie 14 B
FIN-00140 Helsinki, Finland
or
PSC 78, Box H
APO AE 09723
Tel: (358-9) 171 931
Fax: (358-9) 635 332
E-mail: Helsinki.Office.Box@mail.doc.gov
Mr. Thomas Kelsey, Senior Commercial Officer (Stockholm)
Mr. Harri Makinen, Commercial Section Chief
Ms. Tarja Kunnas, Commercial Specialist
Ms. Mia Maki, Commercial Specialist
Ms. Heidi Day, Commercial Assistant

Economic Section
It. Puistotie 14 B
FIN-000140 Helsinki, Finland
Tel: (358-9) 171 931
Fax: (358-9) 174 681
Ms. Ingrid Kollist, Economic Section Chief

Ms. Beatrice Soila, Economic Officer
Ms. Riikka Aho, Economic Assistant

Defense Attache Office
It. Puistotie 14 B
FIN-00140 Helsinki, Finland
Tel: (358-9) 171 931
Fax: (358-9) 171 396
Colonel James R. Luntzel, Defense & Air Attache/Chief, Security Assistance Office
Colonel John M. O'Sullivan, Jr., Army Attache/SAO Officer
Commander Roy N. Peterson, Naval Attache/SAO Officer

Foreign Agricultural Service
Dag Hammarskjolds Vag 31
S-115 89 Stockholm, Sweden
Tel: (46-8) 783 5390
Fax: (46-8) 662 8495
E-mail: agstockholm@fas.usda.gov
Mr. Robert C. Tetro, Agricultural Counselor (for Sweden, Finland, Norway, Estonia and Latvia)
Ms. Asa Lexmon, Agricultural Specialist
Ms. Inger Gozalbez, Agricultural Marketing Specialist
Ms. Bettina Dahlbacka, Agricultural Marketing Assistant
Ms. Ann-Charlotte Bjorkegren, Administrative Assistant

Chambers of Commerce

Mr. Kari Jalas
Managing Director
Central Chamber of Commerce
P.O. Box 1000 (Aleksanterinkatu 17, WTC Helsinki)
FIN-00101 Helsinki, Finland
Tel: (358-9) 696 969
Fax: (358-9) 650 303
Internet: www.keskuskauppakamari.fi
E-mail: keskuskauppakamari@wtc.fi

Mr. Timo Vuori
Secretary General
International Chamber of Commerce (ICC)
Aleksanterinkatu 17, WTC Helsinki
FIN-00100 Helsinki, Finland
Tel: (358-9) 669 459
Fax: (358-9) 6969 6647
Internet: www.iccwbo.fi
E-mail: timo.vuori@wtc.fi

Mr. Heikki J. Perala
Managing Director
Helsinki Chamber of Commerce
Kalevankatu 12
FIN-00100 Helsinki, Finland
Tel: (358-9) 228 601
Fax: (358-9) 2286 0228
Internet: www.helsinki.chamber.fi
E-mail: kauppakamari@helsinki.chamber.fi

Mr. Matti Sundberg
Chairman
Finnish-American Chamber of Commerce
Arkadiankatu 2
FIN-00100 Helsinki, Finland
Tel: (358-9) 4695 539
Fax: (358-9) 695 553
Ms. Sirpa Rissa-Anttilainen
Managing Director
World Trade Center Helsinki
P.O. Box 800 (Aleksanterinkatu 17)
FIN-00100 Helsinki, Finland
Tel: (358-9) 696 911
(358-9) 6969 2021 (trade information)
Fax: (358-9) 6969 2027
Internet: www.wtc.fi
E-mail: noora.salo@wtc.fi

Country Trade Associations

Mr. Guy Wires
Managing Director
Federation of Finnish Commerce and Trade
Mannerheimintie 76 A
FIN-00250 Helsinki, Finland
Tel: (358-9) 531 560
Fax: (358-9) 4315 6302
Internet: www.kaupankl.fi
E-mail: guy.wires@kaupankl.fi

Central organization for 40 branch associations

Ms. Airi Vaaranto
Head of Secretariat
Finnish Foreign Trade Agents' Federation
Elimaenkatu 29
FIN-00510 Helsinki, Finland
Tel: (358-9) 8683 1650
Fax: (358-9) 8683 1651

Internet: www.agenttiliitto.fi
E-mail: fftaf@agenttiliitto.fi

Mr. Sakari Virtanen
Managing Director
Finnish Direct Marketing Association
Lonnrotinkatu 11 A
FIN-00120 Helsinki, Finland
Tel: (358-9) 2287 7400
Fax: (358-9) 6121 039
Internet: www.ssml-fdma.fi
E-mail: sakke@ssml-fdma.fi

Mr. Johannes Koroma
Director General
Confederation of Finnish Industry and Employers
P.O. Box 30 (Etelaranta 10)
FIN-00130 Helsinki, Finland
Tel: (358-9) 686 81
Fax: (358-9) 6868 2316
Internet: www.tt.fi
E-mail: tt@tt.fi

Mr. Harri Malmberg
Director General
Federation of Finnish Metal, Engineering and Electrotechnical Industries (FIMET)
P.O. Box 10 (Etelaranta 10)
FIN-00130 Helsinki, Finland
Tel: (358-9) 192 31
Fax: (358-9) 624 462
Internet: www.met.fi
E-mail: harri.malmberg@met.fi

Mr. Timo Poranen
Managing Director
Finnish Forest Industries' Federation
P.O. Box 336 (Snellmaninkatu 13)
FIN-00170 Helsinki, Finland
Tel: (358-9) 132 61
Fax: (358-9) 1324 445
Internet: www.forestindustries.fi
E-mail: timo.poranen@forestindustries.fi

Mr. Seppo Harkonen
Managing Director
Finpro
P.O. Box 908 (Arkadiankatu 2)
FIN-00100 Helsinki, Finland
Tel: (358-204) 6951
Fax: (358-204) 695 535
Internet: www.finpro.fi
E-mail: info@finpro.fi

Ms. Sirkka Aura
Chief Executive
Invest in Finland Bureau
Aleksanterinkatu 17, WTC Helsinki
FIN-00100 Helsinki, Finland
Tel: (358-9) 6969 125
Fax: (358-9) 6969 2530
Internet: www.investinfinland.fi
E-mail: investinfinland@wtc.fi

Country Government Offices

Dr. Jaana Husu-Kallio
Veterinary Department
Ministry of Agriculture and Forestry
Kluuvikatu 4 A, 6th fl.
FIN-00100 Helsinki, Finland
Tel: (358-9) 1603 385
Fax: (358-9) 1603 338
Internet: www.mmm.fi
E-mail: jaana.husu-kallio@mmm.fi

Ms. Elina Lehto
Director
Employment and Economic Development Center
P.O. Box 15 (Maistraatinportti 2)
FIN-00240 Helsinki, Finland
Tel: (358-9) 2534 2401
Fax: (358-9) 2534 2410
Internet: www.te-keskus.fi
E-mail: elina.lehto@te-keskus.fi

Dr. Osmo Maki-Petays
Head of Meat Hygiene Unit
National Veterinary and Food Research Institute
P.O. Box 368 (Hameentie 57)
FIN-00230 Helsinki, Finland
Tel: (358-9) 3931 899
Fax: (358-9) 3931 811
Internet: www.mmm.fi/hallinnonala/eela
E-mail: osmo.maki-petays@mmm.fi

Mr. Veikko Koskela
Senior Customs Inspector
The Board of Customs
P.O. Box 512 (Erottajankatu 2)
FIN-00120 Helsinki, Finland
Tel: (358-9) 6141

Fax: (358-9) 6142 256
Internet: www.tulli.fi
E-mail: veikko.koskela@tulli.fi

Mr. Timo Relander
Director General
Statistics Finland
Tyopajankatu 13
00033 Tilastokeskus (Helsinki)
Tel: (358-9) 173 41
Fax: (358-9) 1734 2279
Internet: www.stat.fi
E-mail:
kirjasto.tilastokeskus@tilastokeskus.fi

Mr. Heikki Partanen
Chief Inspector
Office of Data Protection Ombudsman
P.O. Box 315 (Albertinkatu 25 A, 3rd fl.)
FIN-00180 Helsinki, Finland
Tel: (358-9) 182 51
Fax: (358-9) 1825 7835
Internet: www.tietosuoja.fi
E-mail: tietosuoja@om.vn.fi

Mr. Jyrki Alanko
Manager, Information Services
Finnish Standardization Association (SFS)
Maistraatinportti 2 A, 3rd fl.
FIN-00240 Helsinki, Finland
Tel: (358-9) 1499 331
Fax: (358-9) 1464 925
Internet: www.sfs.fi
E-mail: info@sfs.fi or jyrki.alanko@sfs.fi

Mr. Tuomo Ilomaki
Managing Director
Finnish Electrotechnical Standard
Association (SESKO)
P.O. Box 134 (Sarkiniementie 3)
FIN-00210 Helsinki, Finland
Tel: (358-9) 696 391
Fax: (358-9) 677 059
Internet: www.sesko.fi
E-mail: myynti@sesko.fi or sales@sfs.fi

Mr. Martti Enajarvi
Director General
National Board of Patents and Registration
Arkadiankatu 6 A
FIN-00100 Helsinki, Finland
Tel: (358-9) 6939 500
Fax: (358-9) 6939 5328
Internet: www.prh.fi
E-mail: martti.enajarvi@prh.fi

Ms. Eeva Kelloniemi
Engineer – Product Safety
National Consumer Administration
P.O. Box 5 (Haapaniemenkatu 4)
FIN-00530 Helsinki, Finland
Tel: (358-9) 772 61
Fax: (358-9) 7726 7557
Internet: www.kuluttajavirasto.fi
E-mail: posti@kuluttajavirasto.fi

Country Market Research Firms

Mr. Ari Heino
Managing Director
Research International RI Finland
(member of Research Int. Group Ltd.)
Lapinlahdenkatu 3 A
FIN-00180 Helsinki, Finland
Tel: (358-9) 6859 930
Fax: (358-9) 6859 9333
Internet: www.research-int.com

Mr. Jyri Seppa
Managing Director
A.C. Nielsen Finland Oy (specialized in retail trade)
Tietajantie 14
FIN-02130 Espoo, Finland
Tel: (358-9) 430 030
Fax: (358-9) 463 628
Internet: www.acnielsen.fi
E-mail: acn@acnielsen.fi

Ms. Tiina Myllykangas-Suonto
Publicist
Agricultural Economics Research Institute
P.O. Box 3
FIN-00411 Helsinki, Finland
Tel: (358-9) 504 471
Fax: (358-9) 563 1164
Internet: www.mttl.fi
E-mail: tiina.myllykangas-suonto@mttl.fi

COUNTRY COMMERCIAL BANKS

Mr. Pertti Voutilainen
President
Merita Pankki Oyj (Merita Bank Plc.)
Aleksanterinkatu 30
FIN-00020 Merita (Helsinki), Finland

Tel: (358-9) 1651
Fax: (358-9) 1654 2838
Internet: www.merita.fi

Mr. Mikael Silvennoinen
Managing Director
Okopankkien Keskuspankki Oyj (Okobank)
Teollisuuskatu 1 b
FIN-00510 Helsinki, Finland
Tel: (358-9) 4041
Fax: (358-9) 4043 703
Internet: www.osuuspankki.fi

Mr. Pentti Hakkarainen
President
Leonia Pankki Oyj (Leonia Bank Plc.)
Etelaesplanadi 8
FIN-00007 Leonia (Helsinki), Finland
Tel: (358-204) 2511
Fax: (358-204) 252 608
Internet: www.leonia.fi

Mr. Stephen L. Dwyre
Managing Director
Citibank International Plc.
Finland Branch
Aleksanterinkatu 48 A
FIN-00100 Helsinki, Finland
Tel: (358-9) 348 871
Fax: (358-9) 3488 7388
Internet: www.citicorp.com

Washington-Based USG Country Contacts

Ms. Leaksmy Norin
International Trade Specialist
U.S. Department of Commerce
Office of European Union and Regional Affairs
Washington, D.C. 20230
Tel: (202) 482-4414
Fax: (202) 482-2897
E-mail: leaksmy_norin@ita.doc.gov

Mr. Andrew Burst
Area Officer – Eastern Europe & Eurasia
Foreign Agricultural Service
U.S. Department of Agriculture
Washington, D.C. 20250
Tel: (202) 690-4053
Fax: (202) 690-2909
E-mail: BurstA@fas.usda.gov

U.S. Department of Agriculture
Foreign Agricultural Service
Trade Assistance and Promotion Office
Tel: (202) 720-7420
Fax: (202) 690-4374
Internet: www.fas.usda.gov/agexport/tapohome.html
E-mail: TAPO@fas.usda.gov

TIC Trade Information Center in Washington
Tel: 1-800-USA-TRADE
Internet: infoserv2.ita.doc.gov/tic.nsf
E-mail: TIC@ita.doc.gov

U.S. Department of State
Office of the Coordinator for Business Affairs
2201 C Street NW
Washington, D.C. 20520-7512
Tel: (202) 647-1625
Fax: (202) 647-3953
Internet: www.state.gov/www/about_state/business/index.html
E-mail: cbaweb@state.gov

Oveseas Private Investment Corporation (OPIC)
1100 New York Avenue, NW, 12th fl.
Washington, D.C. 20527
Tel: (202) 336-8799
Fax: (202) 408-9859
Internet: www.opic.gov
E-mail: info@opic.gov

GOVERNMENT OF FINLAND

Ministry of Trade and Industry
Aleksanterinkatu 4
00170 Helsinki
Tel: +358-9-160 3666

Ministry of Foreign Affairs
Laivastokatu 22
PL 176
00161 Helsinki
Tel: +358-9-135151

Competition Office
PL 332
00531 Helsinki
Tel: +358-9-731 41

Immigration Office
Siltasaarenkatu 12 A
PL 92
00531 Helsinki
Tel: +358-9-476 5500

Financial Supervision Authority
PL 159
Kluuvikatu 5
00101 Helsinki
Tel: +358-9-18 351

EMBASSIES AND CONSULATES

Embassy of Finland
3301 Massachusetts Avenue, NW
Washington, DC 20048
USA
Tel: +202-298 5800

Office of the Counselor
for Science and Technology
Embassy of Finland
3301 Massachusetts Avenue, NW
Washington, DC 20048
USA
Tel: +202-298 5837

Consulate of Finland
1900 Avenue of the Stars
Suite 1025
Los Angeles, CA 90067
Tel: +310-203 9903

Consulate of Finland
15 Long Common Road
Riverside
Chicago, IL 60546
Tel: +708-442 0635

Consulate of Finland
Pinewold Circle
Houston, TX 77056
Tel: +552-1722

FINANCIAL INSTITUTIONS

BANKS

Bank of Finland
Snellmanin aukio
00170 Helsinki
Tel: +358-9-1831

Citibank International plc, Finland Branch
Aleksanterinkatu 48
00100 Helsinki
Tel: +358-9-348 871

Crédit Agricole Indosuez
Keskuskatu 7
00100 Helsinki
Tel: +358-9-69 6991

Den Danske Bank
Aleksanterinkatu 44
00100 Helsinki
Tel: +358-9-7514 5000

Handelsbanken
Eteläranta 8
00130 Helsinki
Tel: +358-9-166 771

Leonia
Unioninkatu 22
00007 Helsinki
Tel: +358-9-42 511

Merita Bank (MeritaNordbanken)
Aleksanterinkatu 30
00100 Helsinki
Tel: +358-9-1651

Okopankki Oy
Arkadiankatu 23
00100 Helsinki
Tel: +358-9-12901
Skandinaviska Enskilda Banken
Unioninkatu 30
00100 Helsinki
Tel: +358-9-6162 8900

BANKING ORGANIZATIONS

Central Union of Cooperative Banks
Arkadiankatu 23
00100 Helsinki
Tel: +358-9-4041

Finnish Bankers' Assn.
Kansakoulukatu 1 A
00100 Helsinki
Tel: +358-9-694 8422

Finnish Savings Banks Assn.
Pohjoisesplanadi 35 A
00100 Helsinki

Tel: +358-9-13341

OTHER FINANCIAL ORGANIZATIONS

Helsinki Exchanges (HEX)
Fabianinkatu 14
00100 Helsinki
Tel: +358-9-616 671

COMMERCIAL INSTITUTIONS

Chambers of Commerce
Central Chamber of Commerce
Aleksanterinkatu 17
PL 1000
00101 Helsinki
Tel: +358-9-696 969
Helsinki Chamber of Commerce
Kalevankatu 12
00100 Helsinki
Tel: +358-9-228 601

The Finnish section of the
International Chamber of Commerce
Aleksanterinkatu 17
PL 1000
00101 Helsinki
Tel: +358-9-696 969
Espoo Chamber of Commerce
Ahlbergin kartano
Sokerilinnantie 7
02600 Espoo
Tel: +358-9-512 3220
Turku Chamber of Commerce
Puolalankatu 1
20100 Turku
Tel: +358-2-274 3400

Tampere Chamber of Commerce
Kehräsaari
33200 Tampere
Tel: +358-3-2141 444
Lahti Chamber of Commerce
Rauhankatu 10
15110 Lahti
Tel: +358-3-871 2500

THE FINNISH-AMERICAN CHAMBER OF COMMERCE

http:// www.finlandtrade.com/

Finland Office
Arkadiankatu 2
00100 Helsinki
Tel: +358-9-69 651

Midwest Office
710 Remmington Road
Schaumburg, IL 60173
Tel: +847-885 3200

New York Office
866 United Nations Plaza
Suite 249
New York, NY 10017
Tel: +212-821 0255

Northwest Office
11045 S.E.
28th Place
Bellevue, WA 98004
Tel: +425-451 3983

Southeast Office
2310 Peachford Road
Atlanta, GA 30338
Tel: +470-457 8795

Southwest Office
1300 Post Oak Boulevard
Suite 1990
Houston, TX 77056
Tel: +713-627 9700

West Coast Office
1900 Avenue of the Stars
Suite 1060
Los Angeles, CA 90067
Tel: +310-203 9903

CONFEDERATION OF FINNISH INDUSTRIES

Eteläranta 10
00100 Helsinki
Tel: +358-9-68 681

FINNISH ASSN. OF CONSULTING FIRMS

Pohjantie 12
02100 Espoo
Tel: +358-9-460 122
Finnish Fair Corp.

HELSINKI EXHIBITION & CONGRESS CENTER

P.O. Box 21

00521 Helsinki Tel: +358-9-15091 Finnish Foreign Trade Association	Arkadiankatu 2 PL 908 00101 Helsinki Tel: +358-9-46 951

MAJOR NEWSPAPERS:

Helsingin Sanomat Aamulehti
P.O. Box 975 Pieni Roobertinkatu 11 A
FIN-00101 Helsinki, Finland FIN-00120 Helsinki, Finland
Tel: 358-9-1221, Fax: 358-9-605 709 Tel: 358-9-853 9560, Fax: 358-9-853 9579

BUSINESS MAGAZINES/JOURNALS:

Kauppalehti (Business daily) Taloussanomat (Business daily)
P.O.Box 189 P.O. Box 1230
FIN-00101 Helsinki, Finland FIN-00101 Helsinki, Finland
Tel: 358-9-507 81, Fax: 358-9-660 383 Tel: 358-9-1221, Fax: 358-9-122 4119

Talouselama (Business weekly)
P.O.Box 920
FIN-00101 Helsinki, Finland
Tel: 358-9-148 801, Fax: 358-9-685 6650

E-Commerce Websites: www.soneraplaza.net, www.elisa.com, www.saunalahti.fi, sirkus.com

TRADE PROMOTION

The main fair centers in Finland are located in the cities of Helsinki, Jyvaskyla, Turku, Tampere and Lahti. In 1999, they had approximately 1.5 million visitors. For further information, please contact:

The Finnish Fair Corporation Jyvaskyla Fair Ltd.
P.O. Box 21 P.O. Box 127
FIN-00521 Helsinki, Finland FIN-40101 Jyvaskyla, Finland
Tel: 358-9-150 91 Tel:358-14-334 0000
Fax: 358-9-142 358 Fax: 358-14-610 272

Turku Fair Center Ltd. Lahti Fair Ltd.
P.O. Box 57 P.O. Box 106
FIN-20201 Turku, Finland FIN-15141 Lahti, Finland
Tel: 358-2-337 111 Tel: 358-3-525 820
Fax: 358-2-2401 440 Fax: 358-3-525 8225

Tampere Trade Fairs Ltd.
33201 Tampere, Finland
Tel: 358-3-2516 111
Fax: 358-3-2123 888

GLOSSARY

Council for Mutual Economic Assistance (CMEA, CEMA, or Comecon).

Members in 1988 included Bulgaria, Cuba, Czechoslovakia, the German Democratic Republic (East Germany), Hungary, Mongolia, Poland, Romania, the Soviet Union, and Vietnam. Its purpose is to further economic cooperation among members.

Council of Europe

Founded in 1949 to foster parliamentary democracy, social and economic progress, and unity among its member states. Membership is limited to those European countries that respect the rule of law and the fundamental human rights and freedoms of all those living within their boundaries. As of 1988, its membership consisted of twenty-one West European countries.

European Community (EC--also commonly called the Community).

The EC comprises three communities: the European Coal and Steel Community (ECSC), the European Economic Community (EEC, also known as the Common Market), and the European Atomic Energy Community (Euratom). Each community is a legally distinct body, but since 1967 all the members have shared common governing institutions. The EC forms more than a framework for free trade and economic cooperation: the signatories to the treaties governing the communities have agreed in principle to integrate their economies and ultimately to form a political union. Belgium, France, Italy, Luxembourg, the Netherlands, and the Federal Republic of Germany (West Germany) are charter members of the EC. Britain, Denmark, and Ireland joined on January 1, 1973; Greece became a member on January 1, 1981; and Portugal and Spain entered on January 1, 1986.

European Economic Community

See European Community.

European Free Trade Association (EFTA)

Founded in 1961, EFTA aims at supporting free trade among its members and increasing the liberalization of trade on a global basis, but particularly within Western Europe. In 1988 the organization's member states were Austria, Finland, Iceland, Norway, Sweden, and Switzerland.

Finnish mark (Fmk)

Also called Finnmark. Consists of 100 *pennia* (singular: *penni*). In terms of the United States dollar, the average annual exchange rate was Fmk3.22 in 1965, Fmk3.86 in 1975, Fmk3.85 in 1980, Fmk5.30 in 1982, Fmk6.54 in 1984, Fmk5.42 in 1995, Fmk4.79 in 1986, Fmk3.95 in 1987, and Fmk4.17 in 1988.

General Agreement on Tariffs and Trade (GATT)

An international organization established in 1948 and headquartered in Geneva that serves as a forum for international trade negotiations. GATT members pledge to further multilateral trade by reducing import tariffs, quotas, and preferential trade agreements, and they promise to extend to each other any favorable trading terms offered in subsequent agreements with third parties.

gross domestic product (GDP)

The total value of goods and services produced by the domestic economy during a given period, usually one year. Obtained by adding the value contributed by each sector of the economy in the form of profits, compensation to employees, and depreciation (consumption of capital). Most GDP usage in this book was based on GDP at factor cost. Real GDP is the value of GDP when inflation has been taken into account.

gross national product (GNP)

Obtained by adding GDP (*q.v.*) and the income received from abroad by residents, less payments remitted abroad to nonresidents. GNP valued at market prices was used in this book. Real GNP is the value of GNP when inflation has been taken into account.

International Monetary Fund (IMF)

Established along with the World Bank (*q.v.*) in 1945, the IMF is a specialized agency, affiliated with the United Nations, that takes responsibility for stabilizing international exchange rates and payments. The main business of the IMF is the provision of loans to its members when they experience balance-of-payment difficulties. These loans often carry conditions that require substantial internal economic adjustments by the recipients.

Organisation for Economic Co- operation and Development (OECD)

Established in 1961 to replace the Organisation for European Economic Co-operation, the OECD is an international organization composed of the industrialized market economy countries (twenty-four full members as of 1988). It seeks to promote economic and social welfare in member countries as well as in developing countries by providing a forum in which to formulate and to coordinate policies.

World Bank

Informal name used to designate a group of three affiliated international institutions: the International Bank for Reconstruction and Development (IBRD), the International Development

Association (IDA), and the International Finance Corporation (IFC). The IBRD, established in 1945, has the primary purpose of providing loans to developing countries for productive projects. THe IDA, a legally separate loan fund administered by staff of the IBRD, was set up in 1960 to furnish credits to the poorest developing counties on much easier terms than those of conventional IBRD loans. The IFC, founded in 1956, supplements the activities of the IBRD through loans and assistance designed specifically to encourage the growth of productive private enterprises in less developed countries. The president and certain senior officers of the IBRD hold the same positions in the IFC. The three institutions are owned by the governments of the countries that subscribe their capital. To participate in the World Bank group, member states must first belong to the IMF (*q.v.*).

BASIC TITLES ON FINLAND

IMPORTANT!

All publications are updated annually!

Please contact IBP, Inc. at ibpusa3@gmail.com for the latest ISBNs and additional information

TITLE
Finland A "Spy" Guide - Strategic Information and Developments
Finland A Spy" Guide"
Finland Air Force Handbook
Finland Air Force Handbook
Finland Army Weapon Systems Handbook
Finland Army Weapon Systems Handbook
Finland Army Weapon Systems Handbook
Finland Army, National Security and Defense Policy Handbook
Finland Army, National Security and Defense Policy Handbook
Finland Aviation and Aerospace Industry Handbook
Finland Aviation and Aerospace Industry Handbook
Finland Banking & Financial Market Handbook
Finland Banking & Financial Market Handbook
Finland Business and Investment Opportunities Yearbook
Finland Business and Investment Opportunities Yearbook
Finland Business and Investment Opportunities Yearbook Volume 1 Strategic Information and Opportunities
Finland Business and Investment Opportunities Yearbook Volume 2 Leading Export-Import, Business, Investment Opportunities and Projects
Finland Business Intelligence Report - Practical Information, Opportunities, Contacts
Finland Business Intelligence Report - Practical Information, Opportunities, Contacts
Finland Business Law Handbook - Strategic Information and Basic Laws
Finland Business Law Handbook - Strategic Information and Basic Laws
Finland Business Law Handbook - Strategic Information and Basic Laws
Finland Business Law Handbook - Strategic Information and Basic Laws
Finland Business Law Handbook Volume 2 Investment and Trade Laws Volume 2 Investment and Trade Laws
Finland Clothing & Textile Industry Handbook
Finland Clothing & Textile Industry Handbook
Finland Company Laws and Regulations Handbook
Finland Constitution and Citizenship Laws Handbook - Strategic Information and Basic Laws
Finland Country Study Guide - Strategic Information and Developments

TITLE
Finland Country Study Guide - Strategic Information and Developments
Finland Country Study Guide - Strategic Information and Developments Volume 1 Strategic Information and Developments
Finland Customs, Trade Regulations and Procedures Handbook
Finland Customs, Trade Regulations and Procedures Handbook
Finland Diplomatic Handbook - Strategic Information and Developments
Finland Diplomatic Handbook - Strategic Information and Developments
Finland Ecology & Nature Protection Handbook
Finland Ecology & Nature Protection Handbook
Finland Ecology & Nature Protection Laws and Regulation Handbook
Finland Economic & Development Strategy Handbook
Finland Economic & Development Strategy Handbook
Finland Education System and Policy Handbook
Finland Energy Policy, Laws and Regulation Handbook
Finland Export-Import Trade and Business Directory
Finland Export-Import Trade and Business Directory
Finland Fishing Industry Business Intelligence Report - Practical Information, Opportunities, Contacts
Finland Fishing Industry Business Intelligence Report - Practical Information, Opportunities, Contacts
Finland Foreign Policy and Government Guide
Finland Foreign Policy and Government Guide
Finland Gold Mining Industry Business Opportunities Handbook
Finland Gold Mining Industry Business Opportunities Handbook
Finland Government and Business Contacts Handbook
Finland Government and Business Contacts Handbook
Finland Healthcare Sector Organization, Management and Payment Systems Handbook - Strategic Information, Programs and Regulations
Finland Immigration Laws and Regulations Handbook - Strategic Information and Basic Laws
Finland Industrial and Business Directory
Finland Industrial and Business Directory
Finland Insolvency (Bankruptcy) Laws and Regulations Handbook - Strategic Information and Basic Laws
Finland Intelligence & Security Activities & Operations Handbook
Finland Intelligence & Security Activities & Operations Handbook
Finland Intelligence, Security Activities & Operations Handbook
Finland Intelligence, Security Activities & Operations Handbook
Finland Internet and E-Commerce Investment and Business Guide - Strategic and Practical Information: Regulations and Opportunities
Finland Internet and E-Commerce Investment and Business Guide - Strategic and Practical Information: Regulations and Opportunities
Finland Investment and Business Guide - Strategic and Practical Information
Finland Investment and Business Guide - Strategic and Practical Information
Finland Investment and Business Guide - Strategic and Practical Information
Finland Investment and Business Guide - Strategic and Practical Information

TITLE
Finland Investment and Business Guide Volume 2 Business, Investment Opportunities and Incentives
Finland Investment and Trade Laws and Regulations Handbook
Finland Justice System and National Police Handbook
Finland Justice System and National Police Handbook
Finland Labor Laws and Regulations Handbook - Strategic Information and Basic Laws
Finland Land Ownership and Agriculture Laws Handbook
Finland Medical & Pharmaceutical Industry Handbook
Finland Medical & Pharmaceutical Industry Handbook
Finland Mineral & Mining Sector Investment and Business Guide - Strategic and Practical Information
Finland Mineral & Mining Sector Investment and Business Guide - Strategic and Practical Information
Finland Mining Industry Business Intelligence Report - Practical Information, Opportunities, Contacts
Finland Mining Industry Business Intelligence Report - Practical Information, Opportunities, Contacts
Finland Mining Laws and Regulations Handbook
Finland Recent Economic and Political Developments Yearbook
Finland Recent Economic and Political Developments Yearbook
Finland Recent Economic and Political Developments Yearbook
Finland Research & Development Policy Handbook
Finland Research & Development Policy Handbook
Finland Research & Development Policy Handbook
Finland Space Agency and Programs Handbook
Finland Space Agency and Programs Handbook
Finland Starting Business (Incorporating) in Finland Guide
Finland Starting Business (Incorporating) in....Guide
Finland Tax Guide
Finland Tax Guide
Finland Taxation Laws and Regulations Handbook
Finland Telecom Laws and Regulations Handbook
Finland Telecommunication Industry Business Opportunities Handbook
Finland Telecommunication Industry Business Opportunities Handbook
Finland Transportation Policy and Regulations Handbook
Finland: How to Invest, Start and Run Profitable Business in Finland Guide - Practical Information, Opportunities, Contacts

BASIC LAWS AND REGULATIONS AFFECTING BUSINESS[1]

COUTRY	LAW TITLE
Finland	Act Amending the Child Welfare Act 2006
Finland	Act of the Medical Use of Human Organs and Tissues
Finland	Act on Assisted Fertility Treatments
Finland	Act on Background Checks
Finland	Act on Book-Entry Accounts(17.5.1991/827)
Finland	Act on checking the criminal backround of persons working with children
Finland	Act on Collective Marks
Finland	Act on Commercial Banks and other Limited Credit Institutions (28.12.2001/1501)
Finland	Act on Communications Administration 29.6.2001/625
Finland	Act on Compensation for Environmental Damage 1994
Finland	Act on Competition Restrictions (480/1992), incl. amendment (318/2004)
Finland	Act on Conciliation in Criminal and Certain Civil Cases
Finland	Act on Conciliation in Criminal and Certain Civil Cases (2005)
Finland	Act on Confirmation of General Applicability of Collective Agreements (2001)
Finland	Act on Confirmation of General Applicability of Collective Agreements (2001)
Finland	Act on Co-operation within Finnish and Community-wide Groups of Undertakings 2007
Finland	Act on Co-operation within Undertakings
Finland	Act on Cooperation within Undertakings (1978, amended 2005)
Finland	Act on Cooperative Banks and other Cooperative Credit Institutions (28.12.2001/1504)
Finland	Act on Credit Institutions
Finland	Act on Disclosure of Election Financing (2000)
Finland	Act on District Prosecutors
Finland	Act on Electronic Services and Communication in the Public Sector
Finland	Act on Electronic Signatures
Finland	Act on Environmental Permit Authorities 2000
Finland	Act on European Schooling Helsinki 2007
Finland	Act on Extradition on the Basis of an Offence Between Finland and Other Member States of the European Union 2003
Finland	Act on Food Hygiene of Foodstuffs of Animal Origin
Finland	Act on Foreign Credit and Financial Institutions in Finland (30.12.1993/1608)
Finland	Act on Foreign Investment Firms' Right to Provide Investment Services in Finland (26.7.1996/580)
Finland	Act on Health Care Professionals
Finland	Act on Implementation of the Legislation on Environmental Protection
Finland	Act on International Legal Assistance in Criminal Matters
Finland	Act on Inventions of Importance to the Defense of the Country
Finland	Act on Involvement of Employees in European Companies (2004)
Finland	Act on Job Alternation Leave
Finland	Act on Jointly Owned Forests

[1] For ordering texts of specific laws in English, French or other languages, please contact Global Investment Center USA at ibpusa3@gmail.com

Finland	Act on Labour Council and Derogation Permits concerning Labour Protection (2004)
Finland	Act on Licenses for Roadworthiness Test of Vehicles
Finland	Act on Measures to Restrict Tobacco Smoking 1976
Finland	Act on Mediation in Labour Disputes (1962, amended 1993)
Finland	Act on Military Crisis Management 2006
Finland	Act on Mortgage Credit Banks
Finland	Act on Mortgage Societies (8.12.1978/936)
Finland	Act on National Aid for Agriculture and Horticulture 2002
Finland	Act on Occupational Safety and Health Enforcement and Cooperation on Occupational Safety and Health at Workplaces (2006)
Finland	Act on Openness of Government Activities (1999 as amended 2002)
Finland	Act on Plant Variety Rights (789/1992; amendments up to 651/2000)
Finland	Act on Preventing and Clearing Money Laundering
Finland	Act on Preventing and Investigating Money Laundering and Personal Data (30.1.1998/68)
Finland	Act on Public Contracts 2007
Finland	Act on Public Prosecutors
Finland	Act on Registered Partnerships 2001
Finland	Act on Registering of Ship's Crew 2006
Finland	Act on Registration Services of Vehicles
Finland	Act on Social Assistance 1998
Finland	Act on Social Enterprises
Finland	Act On State Indemnity For Art Exhibitions (30 May 1986/411)
Finland	Act on Television and Radio Operations 9.10.1998/744
Finland	Act on the Autonomy of Aland
Finland	Act on the Book-Entry System (17.5.1991/826)
Finland	Act On The Classification Of Audiovisual Programs
Finland	Act on the Conformity of Certain Technical Devices to Relevant Requirements 2004
Finland	Act on the Contractor's Obligations and Liability when Work is Contracted Out 2006
Finland	Act on the Exclusive Right in the Layout-Design (Topography) of an Integrated Circuit
Finland	Act on the Exercise of Freedom of Expression in Mass Media 13.6.2003/460
Finland	Act on the Financial Supervision Authority (27.6.2003/587)
Finland	Act on the Finnish Board of Film Classification
Finland	Act on the Finnish Red Cross
Finland	Act on the Government Guarantee Fund (30.4.1992/379)
Finland	Act on the Ice Classes of Ships and Icebreaker Assistance 2005
Finland	Act on the Integration of Immigrants and Reception of Asylum Seekers (1999)
Finland	Act on the Labor Court (1974, amended 2006)
Finland	Act on the Land Information System and Related Information Service 2002
Finland	Act on the Market Court 2001
Finland	Act on the Openness of Government Activities 2003
Finland	Act on the Operations of a Foreign Management Company in Finland
Finland	Act on the Protection of Privacy and Data Security in Telecommunications 22.4.1999/565
Finland	Act on the Protection of Privacy in Electronic Communications
Finland	Act on the Protection of Privacy in Working Life

Finland	Act on the public disclosure and confidentiality of tax information 1999
Finland	Act on the Public Employment Service 2002
Finland	Act on the Right in Employee Inventions
Finland	Act on the Right to Transfer State Real Estate Assets
Finland	Act on the Sami Parliament 1995
Finland	Act on the State Television and Radio Fund 9.10.1998/745
Finland	Act on the Status and Rights of Patients 1992
Finland	Act on the Statutes of Finland
Finland	Act on the Supervision of Financial and Insurance Conglomerates (30.7.2004/699)
Finland	Act on the Supervision of Occupational Safety and Health and Appeal in Occupational Safety and Health Matters (131/1973)
Finland	Act on the Temporary Interruption of the Operations of a Deposit Bank 2001
Finland	Act on Trade in Forest Reproductive Material
Finland	Act on Transport of Dangerous Goods
Finland	Act on Utility Model Rights
Finland	Act on Verification and Notification of Origin of Electricity 2003
Finland	Act on Water Resources Management 2004
Finland	Act on Water Services (119/2001)
Finland	Administrative Judicial Procedure Act 1996
Finland	Administrative Procedure Act 2003
Finland	Adoption Act
Finland	Advocates Act 1958
Finland	Alcohol Act
Finland	Aliens Act (1991, amended 2001)
Finland	Aliens Decree (1994, amended 2000)
Finland	Animal Transport Act 2006
Finland	Animal Welfare Decree
Finland	Annual Holidays Act 2005
Finland	Arbitration Act
Finland	Archives Act
Finland	Archives Act (1994)
Finland	Assembly Act (1999, 2001)
Finland	Associations Act (1989, amended 2002)
Finland	Auditing Act 2007
Finland	Bankruptcy Act
Finland	Basic Education Act
Finland	Code of Inheritance
Finland	Code of Judicial Procedure
Finland	Code of Real Estate 1995
Finland	Coins act 216/1998
Finland	Collective Agreements Act (1946, amended 2001)
Finland	Communicable Diseases Act 1986
Finland	Communications Market Act 1997
Finland	Constitution of Finland 1999
Finland	Consumer Protection Act
Finland	Contracts Act

Finland	Co-operatives Act
Finland	Copyright Act
Finland	Credit Institutions Act (30.12.1993/1607)
Finland	Criminal Procedure Act
Finland	Criminal Records Act
Finland	Decree concerning the Aliens Ombudsman (1991)
Finland	Decree of the Ministry of Social Affairs and Health on the medical use of radiation
Finland	Decree on Marine Equipment
Finland	Decree on the Financing of Sustainable Forestry
Finland	Decree on the Sami Parliament
Finland	Decree on the Transport of Dangerous Goods by Air
Finland	Decree on the Vehicle Registration 1995
Finland	Decree on Utility Model Rights 1991
Finland	Domain Name Act
Finland	Election Act
Finland	Electricity Market Act (386/1995)
Finland	Electricity Market Act (386/1995)
Finland	Emergency Powers Act
Finland	Employment Contracts Act 2001
Finland	Environmental Damage Insurance Act
Finland	Environmental Protection Decree
Finland	Finnish Companies Act 2006
Finland	Firearms Act
Finland	Food Act 23/2006
Finland	Forest Act 1996
Finland	Forest Management Association Act
Finland	Foundations Act (1930 as amended 2001)
Finland	Gene Technology Act
Finland	Government Decision on the Safety of Construction Work
Finland	Government Decree on Auditing
Finland	Government Decree on European Schooling Helsinki 2008
Finland	Government Decree on Joint Procurement in Central Government 2006
Finland	Government Decree on Substances Dangerous and Harmful to the Aquatic Environment 2006
Finland	Government Decree on Television and Radio Operations
Finland	Government Decree on the Assessment of Soil Contamination and Remediation Needs
Finland	Government Decree on the sulphur content of heavy fuel oil, light fuel oil and marine gas 2006
Finland	Government Decree on the Transport and Temporary Storage of Dangerous Goods in a Port Area
Finland	Government Decree on Urban Waste Water Treatment 2006
Finland	Government Decree on Vessel Traffic Service 2005
Finland	Government Decree on Youth Work 2002
Finland	Highways Act
Finland	Housing Companies Act
Finland	Hunting Act 1993

Finland	Insurance Companies Act (28.12.1979/1062)
Finland	Insurance Contracts Act 1994
Finland	Investment Firms Act (26.7.1996/579)
Finland	Land Use and Building Act (132/1999)
Finland	Land Use and Building Decree
Finland	Language Act 2003
Finland	Legal Aid Act
Finland	Library Act 904/1998
Finland	Limited Liability Companies Act 2006
Finland	Local Government Act 1995
Finland	Lotteries Act
Finland	Marriage Act
Finland	Medical Research Act
Finland	Medicines Act
Finland	Mental Health Decree
Finland	Mining Act
Finland	Money Collection Act 2006
Finland	Mortgage Bank Act (23.12.1999/1240)
Finland	Mutual Funds Act (29.1.1999/48)
Finland	Narcotics Act
Finland	Nationality Act 359/2003 (2003)
Finland	Natural Gas Market Act
Finland	Nature Conservation Act (1096/1996)
Finland	Non-Discrimination Act
Finland	Nuclear Energy Act (1987)
Finland	Occupational Safety and Health Act 738/2002
Finland	Parliamentary Ombudsman Act 2002
Finland	Patents act
Finland	Penal Code
Finland	Personal Data Act
Finland	Personal Data Act (1999)
Finland	Police Act (1995, amended 2001)
Finland	Postal Services Act
Finland	Pressure Equipment Act 1999
Finland	Private Security Services Act
Finland	Product Liability Act
Finland	Public Procurement Act
Finland	Radiation Act (592/1991)
Finland	Radiation and Nuclear Safety Authority
Finland	Radio Act 16.11.2001/1015
Finland	Railway Act
Finland	Real Estate Funds Act (19.12.1997/1173)
Finland	Regional Development Act
Finland	Register of Ships Decree
Finland	Registered Designs Decree

Finland	Sale of Goods Act
Finland	Sámi Language Act
Finland	Savings Bank Act (28.12.2001/1502)
Finland	Seamen's Act (1978, amended 2006)
Finland	Securities Markets Act (26.5.1989/495)
Finland	Ship and Port Facility Security Act
Finland	Statistics Finland Act 24.1.1992/48
Finland	Supreme Court Act
Finland	Telecommunications Market Act
Finland	The Act on Plant Breeder's Right (No. 789/1992)
Finland	The Act on the Finnish Competition Authority (711/1988), amended by (482/1992)
Finland	The Market Court Act (1527/2001)
Finland	The Regulation of the Parliamentary Ombudsman (10 January 1920/2, with later amendments)
Finland	Tort Liability Act
Finland	Trademarks Act
Finland	Trademarks Decree 1964
Finland	Travel Agency Act (1080/1994)
Finland	Universities Act 1967
Finland	Value Added Tax Act
Finland	Vehicles Act 1090/2002
Finland	Vehicular and Driver Data Register Act
Finland	Vessel Traffic Service Act
Finland	Waste Decree 1993
Finland	Waste Oil Charge Act (894/1986)
Finland	Waste Tax Act
Finland	Working Hours Act
Finland	Working Hours Act
Finland	Youth Act (72/2006)
Finland	Youth Work Act

TITLE
Belgium Business and Investment Opportunities Yearbook Volume 1 Strategic, Practical Information and Opportunities
Belize Business and Investment Opportunities Yearbook Volume 1 Strategic, Practical Information and Opportunities
Benin Business and Investment Opportunities Yearbook Volume 1 Strategic, Practical Information and Opportunities
Bermuda Business and Investment Opportunities Yearbook Volume 1 Strategic, Practical Information and Opportunities
Bhutan Business and Investment Opportunities Yearbook Volume 1 Strategic, Practical Information and Opportunities
Bolivia Business and Investment Opportunities Yearbook Volume 1 Strategic, Practical Information and Opportunities
Bosnia and Herzegovina Business and Investment Opportunities Yearbook Volume 1 Strategic, Practical Information and Opportunities
Botswana Business and Investment Opportunities Yearbook Volume 1 Strategic, Practical Information and Opportunities
Brazil Business and Investment Opportunities Yearbook Volume 1 Strategic, Practical Information and Opportunities
Brunei Business and Investment Opportunities Yearbook Volume 1 Strategic, Practical Information and Opportunities
Bulgaria Business and Investment Opportunities Yearbook Volume 1 Strategic, Practical Information and Opportunities
Burkina Faso Business and Investment Opportunities Yearbook Volume 1 Strategic, Practical Information and Opportunities
Burundi Business and Investment Opportunities Yearbook Volume 1 Strategic, Practical Information and Opportunities
Cambodia Business and Investment Opportunities Yearbook Volume 1 Strategic, Practical Information and Opportunities
Cameroon Business and Investment Opportunities Yearbook Volume 1 Strategic, Practical Information and Opportunities
Canada Business and Investment Opportunities Yearbook Volume 1 Strategic, Practical Information and Opportunities
Cape Verde Business and Investment Opportunities Yearbook Volume 1 Strategic, Practical Information and Opportunities
Cayman Islands Business and Investment Opportunities Yearbook Volume 1 Strategic, Practical Information and Opportunities
Central African Republic Business and Investment Opportunities Yearbook Volume 1 Strategic, Practical Information and Opportunities
Chad Business and Investment Opportunities Yearbook Volume 1 Strategic, Practical Information and Opportunities
Chile Business and Investment Opportunities Yearbook Volume 1 Strategic, Practical Information and Opportunities
China Business and Investment Opportunities Yearbook Volume 1 Strategic, Practical Information and Opportunities
Colombia Business and Investment Opportunities Yearbook Volume 1 Strategic, Practical Information and Opportunities
Comoros Business and Investment Opportunities Yearbook Volume 1 Strategic, Practical Information and Opportunities
Congo Business and Investment Opportunities Yearbook Volume 1 Strategic, Practical Information and Opportunities
Congo, Democratic Republic Business and Investment Opportunities Yearbook Volume 1 Strategic, Practical Information and Opportunities
Cook Islands Business and Investment Opportunities Yearbook Volume 1 Strategic, Practical Information and Opportunities
Costa Rica Business and Investment Opportunities Yearbook Volume 1 Strategic, Practical Information and Opportunities

TITLE
Cote d'Ivoire Business and Investment Opportunities Yearbook Volume 1 Strategic, Practical Information and Opportunities
Croatia Business and Investment Opportunities Yearbook Volume 1 Strategic, Practical Information and Opportunities
Cuba Business and Investment Opportunities Yearbook Volume 1 Strategic, Practical Information and Opportunities
Cyprus Business and Investment Opportunities Yearbook Volume 1 Strategic, Practical Information and Opportunities
Czech Republic Business and Investment Opportunities Yearbook Volume 1 Strategic, Practical Information and Opportunities
Denmark Business and Investment Opportunities Yearbook Volume 1 Strategic, Practical Information and Opportunities
Djibouti Business and Investment Opportunities Yearbook Volume 1 Strategic, Practical Information and Opportunities
Dominica Business and Investment Opportunities Yearbook Volume 1 Strategic, Practical Information and Opportunities
Dominican Republic Business and Investment Opportunities Yearbook Volume 1 Strategic, Practical Information and Opportunities
Ecuador Business and Investment Opportunities Yearbook Volume 1 Strategic, Practical Information and Opportunities
Egypt Business and Investment Opportunities Yearbook Volume 1 Strategic, Practical Information and Opportunities
El Salvador Business and Investment Opportunities Yearbook Volume 1 Strategic, Practical Information and Opportunities
Equatorial Guinea Business and Investment Opportunities Yearbook Volume 1 Strategic, Practical Information and Opportunities
Eritrea Business and Investment Opportunities Yearbook Volume 1 Strategic, Practical Information and Opportunities
Estonia Business and Investment Opportunities Yearbook Volume 1 Strategic, Practical Information and Opportunities
Ethiopia Business and Investment Opportunities Yearbook Volume 1 Strategic, Practical Information and Opportunities
Falkland Islands Business and Investment Opportunities Yearbook Volume 1 Strategic, Practical Information and Opportunities
Faroes Islands Business and Investment Opportunities Yearbook Volume 1 Strategic, Practical Information and Opportunities
Fiji Business and Investment Opportunities Yearbook Volume 1 Strategic, Practical Information and Opportunities
Finland Business and Investment Opportunities Yearbook Volume 1 Strategic, Practical Information and Opportunities
France Business and Investment Opportunities Yearbook Volume 1 Strategic, Practical Information and Opportunities
Gabon Business and Investment Opportunities Yearbook Volume 1 Strategic, Practical Information and Opportunities
Gambia Business and Investment Opportunities Yearbook Volume 1 Strategic, Practical Information and Opportunities
Georgia Business and Investment Opportunities Yearbook Volume 1 Strategic, Practical Information and Opportunities
Germany Business and Investment Opportunities Yearbook Volume 1 Strategic, Practical Information and Opportunities
Ghana Business and Investment Opportunities Yearbook Volume 1 Strategic, Practical Information and Opportunities
Gibraltar Business and Investment Opportunities Yearbook Volume 1 Strategic, Practical Information and Opportunities
Greece Business and Investment Opportunities Yearbook Volume 1 Strategic, Practical Information and Opportunities

TITLE
Greenland Business and Investment Opportunities Yearbook Volume 1 Strategic, Practical Information and Opportunities
Grenada Business and Investment Opportunities Yearbook Volume 1 Strategic, Practical Information and Opportunities
Guam Business and Investment Opportunities Yearbook Volume 1 Strategic, Practical Information and Opportunities
Guatemala Business and Investment Opportunities Yearbook Volume 1 Strategic, Practical Information and Opportunities
Guernsey Business and Investment Opportunities Yearbook Volume 1 Strategic, Practical Information and Opportunities
Guinea Business and Investment Opportunities Yearbook Volume 1 Strategic, Practical Information and Opportunities
Guinea-Bissau Business and Investment Opportunities Yearbook Volume 1 Strategic, Practical Information and Opportunities
Guyana Business and Investment Opportunities Yearbook Volume 1 Strategic, Practical Information and Opportunities
Haiti Business and Investment Opportunities Yearbook Volume 1 Strategic, Practical Information and Opportunities
Honduras Business and Investment Opportunities Yearbook Volume 1 Strategic, Practical Information and Opportunities
Hungary Business and Investment Opportunities Yearbook Volume 1 Strategic, Practical Information and Opportunities
Iceland Business and Investment Opportunities Yearbook Volume 1 Strategic, Practical Information and Opportunities
India Business and Investment Opportunities Yearbook Volume 1 Strategic, Practical Information and Opportunities
Indonesia Business and Investment Opportunities Yearbook Volume 1 Strategic, Practical Information and Opportunities
Iran Business and Investment Opportunities Yearbook Volume 1 Strategic, Practical Information and Opportunities
Iraq Business and Investment Opportunities Yearbook Volume 1 Strategic, Practical Information and Opportunities
Ireland Business and Investment Opportunities Yearbook Volume 1 Strategic, Practical Information and Opportunities
Israel Business and Investment Opportunities Yearbook Volume 1 Strategic, Practical Information and Opportunities
Italy Business and Investment Opportunities Yearbook Volume 1 Strategic, Practical Information and Opportunities
Jamaica Business and Investment Opportunities Yearbook Volume 1 Strategic, Practical Information and Opportunities
Japan Business and Investment Opportunities Yearbook Volume 1 Strategic, Practical Information and Opportunities
Jersey Business and Investment Opportunities Yearbook Volume 1 Strategic, Practical Information and Opportunities
Jordan Business and Investment Opportunities Yearbook Volume 1 Strategic, Practical Information and Opportunities
Kazakhstan Business and Investment Opportunities Yearbook Volume 1 Strategic, Practical Information and Opportunities
Kenya Business and Investment Opportunities Yearbook Volume 1 Strategic, Practical Information and Opportunities
Kiribati Business and Investment Opportunities Yearbook Volume 1 Strategic, Practical Information and Opportunities
Korea, North Business and Investment Opportunities Yearbook Volume 1 Strategic, Practical Information and Opportunities
Korea, South Business and Investment Opportunities Yearbook Volume 1 Strategic, Practical Information and Opportunities

TITLE
Kosovo Business and Investment Opportunities Yearbook Volume 1 Strategic, Practical Information and Opportunities
Kurdistan Business and Investment Opportunities Yearbook Volume 1 Strategic, Practical Information and Opportunities
Kuwait Business and Investment Opportunities Yearbook Volume 1 Strategic, Practical Information and Opportunities
Kyrgyzstan Business and Investment Opportunities Yearbook Volume 1 Strategic, Practical Information and Opportunities
Laos Business and Investment Opportunities Yearbook Volume 1 Strategic, Practical Information and Opportunities
Latvia Business and Investment Opportunities Yearbook Volume 1 Strategic, Practical Information and Opportunities
Lebanon Business and Investment Opportunities Yearbook Volume 1 Strategic, Practical Information and Opportunities
Lesotho Business and Investment Opportunities Yearbook Volume 1 Strategic, Practical Information and Opportunities
Liberia Business and Investment Opportunities Yearbook Volume 1 Strategic, Practical Information and Opportunities
Libya Business and Investment Opportunities Yearbook Volume 1 Strategic, Practical Information and Opportunities
Liechtenstein Business and Investment Opportunities Yearbook Volume 1 Strategic, Practical Information and Opportunities
Lithuania Business and Investment Opportunities Yearbook Volume 1 Strategic, Practical Information and Opportunities
Luxembourg Business and Investment Opportunities Yearbook Volume 1 Strategic, Practical Information and Opportunities
Macao Business and Investment Opportunities Yearbook Volume 1 Strategic, Practical Information and Opportunities
Macedonia Business and Investment Opportunities Yearbook Volume 1 Strategic, Practical Information and Opportunities
Madagascar Business and Investment Opportunities Yearbook Volume 1 Strategic, Practical Information and Opportunities
Madeira Business and Investment Opportunities Yearbook Volume 1 Strategic, Practical Information and Opportunities
Malawi Business and Investment Opportunities Yearbook Volume 1 Strategic, Practical Information and Opportunities
Malaysia Business and Investment Opportunities Yearbook Volume 1 Strategic, Practical Information and Opportunities
Maldives Business and Investment Opportunities Yearbook Volume 1 Strategic, Practical Information and Opportunities
Mali Business and Investment Opportunities Yearbook Volume 1 Strategic, Practical Information and Opportunities
Malta Business and Investment Opportunities Yearbook Volume 1 Strategic, Practical Information and Opportunities
Man Business and Investment Opportunities Yearbook Volume 1 Strategic, Practical Information and Opportunities
Marshall Islands Business and Investment Opportunities Yearbook Volume 1 Strategic, Practical Information and Opportunities
Mauritania Business and Investment Opportunities Yearbook Volume 1 Strategic, Practical Information and Opportunities
Mauritius Business and Investment Opportunities Yearbook Volume 1 Strategic, Practical Information and Opportunities
Mayotte Business and Investment Opportunities Yearbook Volume 1 Strategic, Practical Information and Opportunities
Mexico Business and Investment Opportunities Yearbook Volume 1 Strategic, Practical Information and Opportunities

TITLE
Micronesia Business and Investment Opportunities Yearbook Volume 1 Strategic, Practical Information and Opportunities
Moldova Business and Investment Opportunities Yearbook Volume 1 Strategic, Practical Information and Opportunities
Monaco Business and Investment Opportunities Yearbook Volume 1 Strategic, Practical Information and Opportunities
Mongolia Business and Investment Opportunities Yearbook Volume 1 Strategic, Practical Information and Opportunities
Montserrat Business and Investment Opportunities Yearbook Volume 1 Strategic, Practical Information and Opportunities
Montenegro Business and Investment Opportunities Yearbook Volume 1 Strategic, Practical Information and Opportunities
Morocco Business and Investment Opportunities Yearbook Volume 1 Strategic, Practical Information and Opportunities
Mozambique Business and Investment Opportunities Yearbook Volume 1 Strategic, Practical Information and Opportunities
Myanmar Business and Investment Opportunities Yearbook Volume 1 Strategic, Practical Information and Opportunities
Nagorno-Karabakh Republic Business and Investment Opportunities Yearbook Volume 1 Strategic, Practical Information and Opportunities
Namibia Business and Investment Opportunities Yearbook Volume 1 Strategic, Practical Information and Opportunities
Nauru Business and Investment Opportunities Yearbook Volume 1 Strategic, Practical Information and Opportunities
Nepal Business and Investment Opportunities Yearbook Volume 1 Strategic, Practical Information and Opportunities
Netherlands Business and Investment Opportunities Yearbook Volume 1 Strategic, Practical Information and Opportunities
New Caledonia Business and Investment Opportunities Yearbook Volume 1 Strategic, Practical Information and Opportunities
New Zealand Business and Investment Opportunities Yearbook Volume 1 Strategic, Practical Information and Opportunities
Nicaragua Business and Investment Opportunities Yearbook Volume 1 Strategic, Practical Information and Opportunities
Niger Business and Investment Opportunities Yearbook Volume 1 Strategic, Practical Information and Opportunities
Nigeria Business and Investment Opportunities Yearbook Volume 1 Strategic, Practical Information and Opportunities
Niue Business and Investment Opportunities Yearbook Volume 1 Strategic, Practical Information and Opportunities
Northern Cyprus (Turkish Republic of Northern Cyprus) Business and Investment Opportunities Yearbook Volume 1 Strategic, Practical Information and Opportunities
Northern Mariana Islands Business and Investment Opportunities Yearbook Volume 1 Strategic, Practical Information and Opportunities
Norway Business and Investment Opportunities Yearbook Volume 1 Strategic, Practical Information and Opportunities
Oman Business and Investment Opportunities Yearbook Volume 1 Strategic, Practical Information and Opportunities
Pakistan Business and Investment Opportunities Yearbook Volume 1 Strategic, Practical Information and Opportunities
Palau Business and Investment Opportunities Yearbook Volume 1 Strategic, Practical Information and Opportunities
Palestine (West Bank & Gaza) Business and Investment Opportunities Yearbook Volume 1 Strategic, Practical Information and Opportunities
Panama Business and Investment Opportunities Yearbook Volume 1 Strategic, Practical Information and Opportunities

TITLE
Papua New Guinea Business and Investment Opportunities Yearbook Volume 1 Strategic, Practical Information and Opportunities
Paraguay Business and Investment Opportunities Yearbook Volume 1 Strategic, Practical Information and Opportunities
Peru Business and Investment Opportunities Yearbook Volume 1 Strategic, Practical Information and Opportunities
Philippines Business and Investment Opportunities Yearbook Volume 1 Strategic, Practical Information and Opportunities
Pitcairn Islands Business and Investment Opportunities Yearbook Volume 1 Strategic, Practical Information and Opportunities
Poland Business and Investment Opportunities Yearbook Volume 1 Strategic, Practical Information and Opportunities
Polynesia French Business and Investment Opportunities Yearbook Volume 1 Strategic, Practical Information and Opportunities
Portugal Business and Investment Opportunities Yearbook Volume 1 Strategic, Practical Information and Opportunities
Qatar Business and Investment Opportunities Yearbook Volume 1 Strategic, Practical Information and Opportunities
Romania Business and Investment Opportunities Yearbook Volume 1 Strategic, Practical Information and Opportunities
Russia Business and Investment Opportunities Yearbook Volume 1 Strategic, Practical Information and Opportunities
Rwanda Business and Investment Opportunities Yearbook Volume 1 Strategic, Practical Information and Opportunities
Sahrawi Arab Democratic Republic Volume 1 Strategic Information and Developments
Saint Kitts and Nevis Business and Investment Opportunities Yearbook Volume 1 Strategic, Practical Information and Opportunities
Saint Lucia Business and Investment Opportunities Yearbook Volume 1 Strategic, Practical Information and Opportunities
Saint Vincent and The Grenadines Business and Investment Opportunities Yearbook Volume 1 Strategic, Practical Information and Opportunities
Samoa (American) A Business and Investment Opportunities Yearbook Volume 1 Strategic, Practical Information and Opportunities
Samoa (Western) Business and Investment Opportunities Yearbook Volume 1 Strategic, Practical Information and Opportunities
San Marino Business and Investment Opportunities Yearbook Volume 1 Strategic, Practical Information and Opportunities
Sao Tome and Principe Business and Investment Opportunities Yearbook Volume 1 Strategic, Practical Information and Opportunities
Saudi Arabia Business and Investment Opportunities Yearbook Volume 1 Strategic, Practical Information and Opportunities
Scotland Business and Investment Opportunities Yearbook Volume 1 Strategic, Practical Information and Opportunities
Senegal Business and Investment Opportunities Yearbook Volume 1 Strategic, Practical Information and Opportunities
Serbia Business and Investment Opportunities Yearbook Volume 1 Strategic, Practical Information and Opportunities
Seychelles Business and Investment Opportunities Yearbook Volume 1 Strategic, Practical Information and Opportunities
Sierra Leone Business and Investment Opportunities Yearbook Volume 1 Strategic, Practical Information and Opportunities
Singapore Business and Investment Opportunities Yearbook Volume 1 Strategic, Practical Information and Opportunities
Slovakia Business and Investment Opportunities Yearbook Volume 1 Strategic, Practical Information and Opportunities

TITLE
Slovenia Business and Investment Opportunities Yearbook Volume 1 Strategic, Practical Information and Opportunities
Solomon Islands Business and Investment Opportunities Yearbook Volume 1 Strategic, Practical Information and Opportunities
Somalia Business and Investment Opportunities Yearbook Volume 1 Strategic, Practical Information and Opportunities
South Africa Business and Investment Opportunities Yearbook Volume 1 Strategic, Practical Information and Opportunities
Spain Business and Investment Opportunities Yearbook Volume 1 Strategic, Practical Information and Opportunities
Sri Lanka Business and Investment Opportunities Yearbook Volume 1 Strategic, Practical Information and Opportunities
St. Helena Business and Investment Opportunities Yearbook Volume 1 Strategic, Practical Information and Opportunities
St. Pierre & Miquelon Business and Investment Opportunities Yearbook Volume 1 Strategic, Practical Information and Opportunities
Sudan (Republic of the Sudan) Business and Investment Opportunities Yearbook Volume 1 Strategic, Practical Information and Opportunities
Sudan South Business and Investment Opportunities Yearbook Volume 1 Strategic, Practical Information and Opportunities
Suriname Business and Investment Opportunities Yearbook Volume 1 Strategic, Practical Information and Opportunities
Swaziland Business and Investment Opportunities Yearbook Volume 1 Strategic, Practical Information and Opportunities
Sweden Business and Investment Opportunities Yearbook Volume 1 Strategic, Practical Information and Opportunities
Switzerland Business and Investment Opportunities Yearbook Volume 1 Strategic, Practical Information and Opportunities
Syria Business and Investment Opportunities Yearbook Volume 1 Strategic, Practical Information and Opportunities
Taiwan Business and Investment Opportunities Yearbook Volume 1 Strategic, Practical Information and Opportunities
Tajikistan Business and Investment Opportunities Yearbook Volume 1 Strategic, Practical Information and Opportunities
Tanzania Business and Investment Opportunities Yearbook Volume 1 Strategic, Practical Information and Opportunities
Thailand Business and Investment Opportunities Yearbook Volume 1 Strategic, Practical Information and Opportunities
Timor Leste (Democratic Republic of Timor-Leste) Business and Investment Opportunities Yearbook Volume 1 Strategic, Practical Information and Opportunities
Togo Business and Investment Opportunities Yearbook Volume 1 Strategic, Practical Information and Opportunities
Tonga Business and Investment Opportunities Yearbook Volume 1 Strategic, Practical Information and Opportunities
Trinidad and Tobago Business and Investment Opportunities Yearbook Volume 1 Strategic, Practical Information and Opportunities
Tunisia Business and Investment Opportunities Yearbook Volume 1 Strategic, Practical Information and Opportunities
Turkey Business and Investment Opportunities Yearbook Volume 1 Strategic, Practical Information and Opportunities
Turkmenistan Business and Investment Opportunities Yearbook Volume 1 Strategic, Practical Information and Opportunities
Turks & Caicos Business and Investment Opportunities Yearbook Volume 1 Strategic, Practical Information and Opportunities
Tuvalu Business and Investment Opportunities Yearbook Volume 1 Strategic, Practical Information and Opportunities

TITLE
Uganda Business and Investment Opportunities Yearbook Volume 1 Strategic, Practical Information and Opportunities
Ukraine Business and Investment Opportunities Yearbook Volume 1 Strategic, Practical Information and Opportunities
United Arab Emirates Business and Investment Opportunities Yearbook Volume 1 Strategic, Practical Information and Opportunities
United Kingdom Business and Investment Opportunities Yearbook Volume 1 Strategic, Practical Information and Opportunities
United States Business and Investment Opportunities Yearbook Volume 1 Strategic, Practical Information and Opportunities
Uruguay Business and Investment Opportunities Yearbook Volume 1 Strategic, Practical Information and Opportunities
Uzbekistan Business and Investment Opportunities Yearbook Volume 1 Strategic, Practical Information and Opportunities
Vanuatu Business and Investment Opportunities Yearbook Volume 1 Strategic, Practical Information and Opportunities
Vatican City (Holy See) Business and Investment Opportunities Yearbook Volume 1 Strategic, Practical Information and Opportunities
Venezuela Business and Investment Opportunities Yearbook Volume 1 Strategic, Practical Information and Opportunities
Vietnam Business and Investment Opportunities Yearbook Volume 1 Strategic, Practical Information and Opportunities
Virgin Islands, British Business and Investment Opportunities Yearbook Volume 1 Strategic, Practical Information and Opportunities
Wake Atoll Business and Investment Opportunities Yearbook Volume 1 Strategic, Practical Information and Opportunities
Wallis & Futuna Business and Investment Opportunities Yearbook Volume 1 Strategic, Practical Information and Opportunities
Western Sahara Business and Investment Opportunities Yearbook Volume 1 Strategic, Practical Information and Opportunities
Yemen Business and Investment Opportunities Yearbook Volume 1 Strategic, Practical Information and Opportunities
Zambia Business and Investment Opportunities Yearbook Volume 1 Strategic, Practical Information and Opportunities
Zimbabwe Business and Investment Opportunities Yearbook Volume 1 Strategic, Practical Information and Opportunities

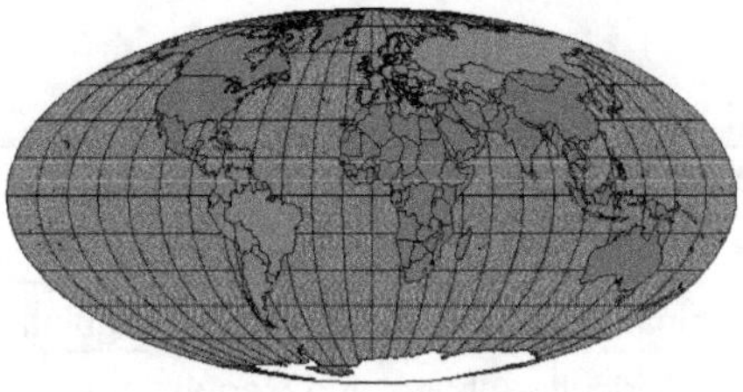

GLOBAL LAND OWNERSHIP AND AGRICULTURE LAWS AND REGULATIONS HANDBOOK LIBRARY

Price: $149.95 Each

1. Albania Land Ownership and Agriculture Laws and Regulations Handbook
2. Algeria Land Ownership and Agriculture Laws and Regulations Handbook
3. Andorra Land Ownership and Agriculture Laws and Regulations Handbook
4. Angola Land Ownership and Agriculture Laws and Regulations Handbook
5. Antigua & Barbuda Land Ownership and Agriculture Laws and Regulations Handbook
6. Antilles (Netherlands) Land Ownership and Agriculture Laws and Regulations Handbook
7. Argentina Land Ownership and Agriculture Laws and Regulations Handbook
8. Armenia Land Ownership and Agriculture Laws and Regulations Handbook
9. Australia Land Ownership and Agriculture Laws and Regulations Handbook
10. Austria Land Ownership and Agriculture Laws and Regulations Handbook
11. Azerbaijan Land Ownership and Agriculture Laws and Regulations Handbook
12. Bahamas Land Ownership and Agriculture Laws and Regulations Handbook
13. Bangladesh Land Ownership and Agriculture Laws and Regulations Handbook
14. Barbados Land Ownership and Agriculture Laws and Regulations Handbook
15. Belarus Land Ownership and Agriculture Laws and Regulations Handbook
16. Belgium Land Ownership and Agriculture Laws and Regulations Handbook
17. Belize Land Ownership and Agriculture Laws and Regulations Handbook
18. Bermuda Land Ownership and Agriculture Laws and Regulations Handbook
19. Bolivia Land Ownership and Agriculture Laws and Regulations Handbook
20. Bosnia and Herzegovina Land Ownership and Agriculture Laws and Regulations Handbook
21. Botswana Land Ownership and Agriculture Laws and Regulations Handbook
22. Brazil Land Ownership and Agriculture Laws and Regulations Handbook
23. Brunei Land Ownership and Agriculture Laws and Regulations Handbook
24. Bulgaria Land Ownership and Agriculture Laws and Regulations Handbook
25. Cambodia Land Ownership and Agriculture Laws and Regulations Handbook
26. Cameroon Land Ownership and Agriculture Laws and Regulations Handbook
27. Canada Land Ownership and Agriculture Laws and Regulations Handbook
28. Cayman Islands Land Ownership and Agriculture Laws and Regulations Handbook
29. Chile Land Ownership and Agriculture Laws and Regulations Handbook
30. China Land Ownership and Agriculture Laws and Regulations Handbook
31. Colombia Land Ownership and Agriculture Laws and Regulations Handbook
32. Comoros Land Ownership and Agriculture Laws and Regulations Handbook
33. Cook Islands Land Ownership and Agriculture Laws and Regulations Handbook
34. Costa Rica Land Ownership and Agriculture Laws and Regulations Handbook
35. Croatia Land Ownership and Agriculture Laws and Regulations Handbook

36.	Cuba Land Ownership and Agriculture Laws and Regulations Handbook
37.	Cyprus Land Ownership and Agriculture Laws and Regulations Handbook
38.	Czech Republic Land Ownership and Agriculture Laws and Regulations Handbook
39.	Denmark Land Ownership and Agriculture Laws and Regulations Handbook
40.	Dominica Land Ownership and Agriculture Laws and Regulations Handbook
41.	Dominican Republic Land Ownership and Agriculture Laws and Regulations Handbook
42.	Dubai Land Ownership and Agriculture Laws and Regulations Handbook
43.	Ecuador Land Ownership and Agriculture Laws and Regulations Handbook
44.	Egypt Land Ownership and Agriculture Laws and Regulations Handbook
45.	El Salvador Land Ownership and Agriculture Laws and Regulations Handbook
46.	Equatorial Guinea Land Ownership and Agriculture Laws and Regulations Handbook
47.	Estonia Land Ownership and Agriculture Laws and Regulations Handbook
48.	Falkland Islands Land Ownership and Agriculture Laws and Regulations Handbook
49.	Fiji Land Ownership and Agriculture Laws and Regulations Handbook
50.	Finland Land Ownership and Agriculture Laws and Regulations Handbook
51.	France Land Ownership and Agriculture Laws and Regulations Handbook
52.	Georgia Land Ownership and Agriculture Laws and Regulations Handbook
53.	Germany Land Ownership and Agriculture Laws and Regulations Handbook
54.	Gibraltar Land Ownership and Agriculture Laws and Regulations Handbook
55.	Greece Land Ownership and Agriculture Laws and Regulations Handbook
56.	Grenada Land Ownership and Agriculture Laws and Regulations Handbook
57.	Guam Investment & Business Guide
58.	Guatemala Land Ownership and Agriculture Laws and Regulations Handbook
59.	Guernsey Land Ownership and Agriculture Laws and Regulations Handbook
60.	Guyana Land Ownership and Agriculture Laws and Regulations Handbook
61.	Haiti Land Ownership and Agriculture Laws and Regulations Handbook
62.	Honduras Land Ownership and Agriculture Laws and Regulations Handbook
63.	Hungary Land Ownership and Agriculture Laws and Regulations Handbook
64.	Iceland Land Ownership and Agriculture Laws and Regulations Handbook
65.	India Land Ownership and Agriculture Laws and Regulations Handbook
66.	Indonesia Land Ownership and Agriculture Laws and Regulations Handbook
67.	Iran Land Ownership and Agriculture Laws and Regulations Handbook
68.	Iraq Land Ownership and Agriculture Laws and Regulations Handbook
69.	Ireland Land Ownership and Agriculture Laws and Regulations Handbook
70.	Israel Land Ownership and Agriculture Laws and Regulations Handbook
71.	Italy Land Ownership and Agriculture Laws and Regulations Handbook
72.	Jamaica Land Ownership and Agriculture Laws and Regulations Handbook
73.	Japan Land Ownership and Agriculture Laws and Regulations Handbook
74.	Jersey Land Ownership and Agriculture Laws and Regulations Handbook
75.	Jordan Land Ownership and Agriculture Laws and Regulations Handbook
76.	Kazakhstan Land Ownership and Agriculture Laws and Regulations Handbook
77.	Kenya Land Ownership and Agriculture Laws and Regulations Handbook
78.	Kiribati Land Ownership and Agriculture Laws and Regulations Handbook

79. Korea, North Land Ownership and Agriculture Laws and Regulations Handbook
80. Korea, South Land Ownership and Agriculture Laws and Regulations Handbook
81. Kuwait Land Ownership and Agriculture Laws and Regulations Handbook
82. Kyrgyzstan Land Ownership and Agriculture Laws and Regulations Handbook
83. Laos Land Ownership and Agriculture Laws and Regulations Handbook
84. Latvia Land Ownership and Agriculture Laws and Regulations Handbook
85. Lebanon Land Ownership and Agriculture Laws and Regulations Handbook
86. Libya Land Ownership and Agriculture Laws and Regulations Handbook
87. Liechtenstein Land Ownership and Agriculture Laws and Regulations Handbook
88. Lithuania Land Ownership and Agriculture Laws and Regulations Handbook
89. Luxemburg Land Ownership and Agriculture Laws and Regulations Handbook
90. Macao Land Ownership and Agriculture Laws and Regulations Handbook
91. Macedonia, Republic Land Ownership and Agriculture Laws and Regulations Handbook
92. Madagascar Land Ownership and Agriculture Laws and Regulations Handbook
93. Malaysia Land Ownership and Agriculture Laws and Regulations Handbook
94. Malta Land Ownership and Agriculture Laws and Regulations Handbook
95. Man Land Ownership and Agriculture Laws and Regulations Handbook
96. Mauritius Land Ownership and Agriculture Laws and Regulations Handbook
97. Mauritius Land Ownership and Agriculture Laws and Regulations Handbook
98. Mexico Land Ownership and Agriculture Laws and Regulations Handbook
99. Micronesia Land Ownership and Agriculture Laws and Regulations Handbook
100. Moldova Land Ownership and Agriculture Laws and Regulations Handbook
101. Monaco Land Ownership and Agriculture Laws and Regulations Handbook
102. Mongolia Land Ownership and Agriculture Laws and Regulations Handbook
103. Morocco Land Ownership and Agriculture Laws and Regulations Handbook
104. Myanmar Land Ownership and Agriculture Laws and Regulations Handbook
105. Namibia Land Ownership and Agriculture Laws and Regulations Handbook
106. Netherlands Land Ownership and Agriculture Laws and Regulations Handbook
107. New Caledonia Land Ownership and Agriculture Laws and Regulations Handbook
108. New Zealand Land Ownership and Agriculture Laws and Regulations Handbook
109. Nicaragua Land Ownership and Agriculture Laws and Regulations Handbook
110. Nigeria Land Ownership and Agriculture Laws and Regulations Handbook
111. Northern Mariana Islands Land Ownership and Agriculture Laws and Regulations Handbook
112. Norway Land Ownership and Agriculture Laws and Regulations Handbook
113. Pakistan Land Ownership and Agriculture Laws and Regulations Handbook
114. Panama Land Ownership and Agriculture Laws and Regulations Handbook
115. Peru Land Ownership and Agriculture Laws and Regulations Handbook
116. Philippines Land Ownership and Agriculture Laws and Regulations Handbook
117. Poland Land Ownership and Agriculture Laws and Regulations Handbook
118. Portugal Land Ownership and Agriculture Laws and Regulations Handbook
119. Romania Land Ownership and Agriculture Laws and Regulations Handbook
120. Russia Land Ownership and Agriculture Laws and Regulations Handbook
121. Samoa (American) Investment & Business Guide

122. Samoa (Western) Land Ownership and Agriculture Laws and Regulations Handbook
123. Saudi Arabia Land Ownership and Agriculture Laws and Regulations Handbook
124. Scotland Land Ownership and Agriculture Laws and Regulations Handbook
125. Singapore Land Ownership and Agriculture Laws and Regulations Handbook
126. Slovakia Land Ownership and Agriculture Laws and Regulations Handbook
127. Slovenia Land Ownership and Agriculture Laws and Regulations Handbook
128. South Africa Land Ownership and Agriculture Laws and Regulations Handbook
129. Spain Land Ownership and Agriculture Laws and Regulations Handbook
130. Sri Lanka Land Ownership and Agriculture Laws and Regulations Handbook
131. St. Helena Land Ownership and Agriculture Laws and Regulations Handbook
132. Sudan Land Ownership and Agriculture Laws and Regulations Handbook
133. Suriname Land Ownership and Agriculture Laws and Regulations Handbook
134. Sweden Land Ownership and Agriculture Laws and Regulations Handbook
135. Switzerland Land Ownership and Agriculture Laws and Regulations Handbook
136. Syria Export Import & Business Directory
137. Taiwan Land Ownership and Agriculture Laws and Regulations Handbook
138. Tajikistan Land Ownership and Agriculture Laws and Regulations Handbook
139. Thailand Land Ownership and Agriculture Laws and Regulations Handbook
140. Tunisia Land Ownership and Agriculture Laws and Regulations Handbook
141. Turkey Land Ownership and Agriculture Laws and Regulations Handbook
142. Turkmenistan Land Ownership and Agriculture Laws and Regulations Handbook
143. Uganda Land Ownership and Agriculture Laws and Regulations Handbook
144. Ukraine Land Ownership and Agriculture Laws and Regulations Handbook
145. United Arab Emirates Land Ownership and Agriculture Laws and Regulations Handbook
146. United Kingdom Land Ownership and Agriculture Laws and Regulations Handbook
147. United States Land Ownership and Agriculture Laws and Regulations Handbook
148. Uruguay Land Ownership and Agriculture Laws and Regulations Handbook
149. US Land Ownership and Agriculture Laws and Regulations Handbook
150. Uzbekistan Land Ownership and Agriculture Laws and Regulations Handbook
151. Venezuela Land Ownership and Agriculture Laws and Regulations Handbook
152. Vietnam Land Ownership and Agriculture Laws and Regulations Handbook
153. Serbia Land Ownership and Agriculture Laws and Regulations Handbook

www.ingramcontent.com/pod-product-compliance
Lightning Source LLC
LaVergne TN
LVHW080030210926
848481LV00011B/3149
* 9 7 8 1 4 3 8 7 5 9 0 1 2 *